1945

Jack and June Williams

THE
American Mercury
READER

THE
American Mercury
READER

A selection of distinguished articles, stories and poems published in THE AMERICAN MERCURY *during the past twenty years*

EDITED BY

Lawrence E. Spivak *and* Charles Angoff

1944

THE BLAKISTON COMPANY

PHILADELPHIA

Printed at the COUNTRY LIFE PRESS, *Garden City,* **N.Y., U.S.A.**

COPYRIGHT, 1944, *by The American Mercury, Inc. No article may be reprinted in whole or in part without permission from the copyright owners*

CONTENTS

FOREWORD
THE MAN WHO KNEW COOLIDGE . . . . *Sinclair Lewis*   5
GO DOWN, DEATH! (*A Poem*) . . . . . . *James Weldon Johnson*   31
WILLIAM JENNINGS BRYAN . . . . *H. L. Mencken*   34
WHAT IS A STATESMAN? . . . . *Charles A. Beard*   38
DEATH IN THE WOODS (*A Story*) . . . . . *Sherwood Anderson*   42
REMEMBER US! . . . . *Ben Hecht*   51
TOM PAINE . . . . *William E. Dodd*   55
THE ANATOMY OF LONELINESS . . . . *Thomas Wolfe*   63
THAT EVENING SUN GO DOWN (*A Story*) . . . *William Faulkner*   70
WHITMAN AS HIS OWN PRESS-AGENT . . . . *Emory Holloway*   82
NO ONE MY GRIEF CAN TELL (*A Story*) . . . . . . *Nancy Hale*   91
PASSION (*A Poem*) . . . . *Walter de la Mare*   95
THE LAW TAKES ITS TOLL . . . . *Robert Blake*   96
BOY BABY (*A Poem*) . . . . *Carl Sandburg*   105
HIGH JOHN DE CONQUER . . . . *Zora Neale Hurston*   106
EMINENCE (*A Story*) . . . . *Ruth Suckow*   113
OUR ENEMY, THE CAT . . . . *Alan Devoe*   123
HE'S TAKEN HER BACK AGAIN (*A Poem*) . . . *Gwendolen Haste*   126
THE MORTICIAN . . . . *Elmer Davis*   127
HATRACK . . . . *Herbert Asbury*   138
HUSBANDS GROW ON TREES (*A Story*) . . . . . *Whitfield Cook*   144
ALL GOD'S CHILLUN GOT WINGS (*A Play*) . . . *Eugene O'Neill*   150
THE OVERCOAT (*A Story*) . . . . *Sally Benson*   176
THE BALLAD OF THE GALLOWS-BIRD (*A Poem*) . . *Edwin Markham*   179
ONE NIGHT AT CONEY (*A Story*) . . . . . . *Robert M. Coates*   191
LITANY (*A Poem*) . . . . *Charles Angoff*   196
CRUSADE FOR AIR POWER . . . . . *Major Alexander P. de Seversky*   197
TALES FROM OKLAHOMA (*Three Stories*) . . . . *George Milburn*   208
STEPHEN A. DOUGLAS . . . . *Edgar Lee Masters*   216

The Virginians Are Coming Again (*A Poem*)	Vachel Lindsay	230
Trial by Jury (*A Sketch*)	James M. Cain	233
Letter to Saint Peter (*A Poem*)	Elma Dean	239
Convention (*A Story*)	Theodore Dreiser	240
Americana		254
Two Poems	John McClure	258
Crazy Sunday (*A Story*)	F. Scott Fitzgerald	259
The Revolt of the Ghosts	Eugene Lyons	272
Myself Upon the Earth (*A Story*)	William Saroyan	277
Altar Boy (*A Story*)	John Fante	285
Aesthete: Model 1924	Ernest Boyd	296
At Breakfast (*A Poem*)	Grace Stone Coates	303
American Marriage (*Three Stories*)	Mary Austin	304
China Boy (*A Sketch*)	Idwal Jones	311
These Dark Hills (*A Poem*)	Jesse Stuart	320
We Rob a Bank	Ernest Booth	321
The Victor (*A Story*)	Freer Stalnaker	333
A Leaf-Treader (*A Poem*)	Robert Frost	338
The Lumberjacks Go Sissy	Stewart H. Holbrook	339
Bright Eyes	Jim Tully	343
The Theatre	George Jean Nathan	351
Happy Days	Raymond Clapper	357
The South Kills Another Negro	William Bradford Huie	363
Your Life Expectancy	Louis I. Dublin	372
Foolish About Windows (*A Poem*)	Carl Sandburg	378

Cartoons by: Arthur Szyk, Steinberg, Eric Peters, E. Schloss

ACKNOWLEDGMENTS

Cordial thanks are offered to all authors or their representatives for their cooperation in making this volume possible. Special credits:

"The Man Who Knew Coolidge," by Sinclair Lewis, later expanded into the book *The Man Who Knew Coolidge*, reprinted by permission of Harcourt, Brace & Company, Inc., copyright 1928 by Harcourt, Brace & Company, Inc.

"Go Down Death!" by James Weldon Johnson, later appeared in the book *God's Trombones*, copyright 1927 by, and used with the permission of, The Viking Press, Inc., New York.

"William Jennings Bryan," by H. L. Mencken, later expanded in the book *Prejudices: Fifth Series*, reprinted by permission of and special arrangement with Alfred A. Knopf, Inc., copyright 1926 by Alfred A. Knopf, Inc.

"Death in the Woods," by Sherwood Anderson, copyright 1926 by Eleanor Anderson, reprinted by permission of Mrs. Sherwood Anderson.

"Tom Paine," by William E. Dodd, reprinted by permission of William E. Dodd, Jr. and Martha Dodd Stern.

"The Anatomy of Loneliness," by Thomas Wolfe, later reprinted in the book *The Hills Beyond* (1941), published by Harper & Brothers, copyright 1941 by Maxwell Perkins as Executor.

"That Evening Sun Go Down," by William Faulkner, copyright 1931 by William Faulkner, used by permission of Random House, Inc.

"No One My Grief Can Tell," by Nancy Hale, reprinted by permission of Charles Scribner's Sons.

"The Law Takes Its Toll," by Robert Blake, reprinted by special permission of Mrs. J. H. Blake.

"Foolish About Windows" and "Chicago Boy Baby," by Carl Sandburg, later appeared in the book *Good Morning, America*, reprinted by permission of Harcourt, Brace & Company, Inc., copyright 1928 by Carl Sandburg.

"Eminence," by Ruth Suckow, later appeared in the book *Carry-Over*, copyright 1924, 1926, 1928, 1931, 1936 by Ruth Suckow and reprinted by permission of Farrar & Rinehart, Inc., publishers.

"Our Enemy, the Cat," by Alan Devoe, later appeared in the book *Down to Earth: A Naturalist Looks About*, reprinted by permission of Coward McCann, Inc., copyright 1937, 1938, 1939, 1940 by Alan Devoe.

"Hatrack," by Herbert Asbury, later appeared in the book *Up from Methodism*, reprinted by permission of and special arrangement with Alfred A. Knopf, Inc., copyright 1926 by Alfred A. Knopf, Inc.

"All God's Chillun Got Wings," by Eugene O'Neill, reprinted by permission of Random House, Inc., copyright 1924 by Eugene O'Neill.

"The Ballad of the Gallows-Bird," by Edwin Markham, reprinted by permission.

"Crusade for Air Power," by Major Alexander P. de Seversky, later expanded into the book *Victory Through Air Power*, copyright 1942 by Alexander P. de Seversky.

"Iron Filigree," "Yellow Paint," and "Those Seagrave Boys," by George Milburn, later appeared in the book *Oklahoma Town*, reprinted by permission of Harcourt, Brace & Company, Inc., copyright 1931 by George Milburn.

"The Virginians Are Coming Again," by Vachel Lindsay, later appeared in the book *The Selected Poems of Vachel Lindsay*, reprinted by permission of The Macmillan Company, publishers.

"Trial by Jury," by James M. Cain, later appeared in the book *Our Government*, reprinted by permission of and special arrangement with Alfred A. Knopf, Inc., copyright 1924, 1925, 1927, 1928, 1929, 1930 by James M. Cain.

"Convention," by Theodore Dreiser, later appeared in the book *Chains*, reprinted by permission of G. P. Putnam's Sons.

"Crazy Sunday," by F. Scott Fitzgerald, reprinted by permission of Charles Scribner's Sons.

"Myself Upon the Earth," by William Saroyan, later appeared in the book *The Daring Young Man on the Flying Trapeze*.

"Altar Boy," by John Fante, later appeared in the book *Dago Red*, reprinted by permission of the Viking Press, Inc., New York, copyright 1932, 1933, 1934, 1936, 1937, 1940 by John Fante.

"Papago Wedding," "The Way of a Woman," and "The Man Who Lied About a Woman," by Mary Austin, later appeared in the book *One-Smoke Stories*, reprinted by permission of Houghton Mifflin Company, copyright 1934 by Mary Austin.

"We Rob a Bank," by Ernest Booth, later appeared in the book, *Stealing Through Life*, reprinted by permission of and special arrangement with Alfred A. Knopf, Inc., copyright 1927, 1929 by Alfred A. Knopf, Inc.

"A Leaf-Treader," by Robert Frost, later appeared in the book *The Collected Poems of Robert Frost*, used by permission of Henry Holt and Company, Inc.

Excerpts from "Advice to a Young Critic" and "Fragmentary Meditations," by George Jean Nathan, reprinted by permission of and special arrangement with Alfred A. Knopf, Inc.

"The South Kills Another Negro," by William Bradford Huie, later appeared in the book *Mud on the Stars*, reprinted by permission of L. B. Fischer Publishing Corporation, copyright 1942 by L. B. Fischer Publishing Corporation.

FOREWORD

THE AMERICAN MERCURY made its first appearance in January, 1924, so that it is now in its third decade. This volume, containing a variety of distinguished articles, stories, sketches, poems and cartoons, forms a literary treasure trove of the past twenty years. It will, we believe, give an idea of the character and wide scope of the magazine and explain the influential and respected place it has won in American periodical journalism.

It was no easy task to make selections from more than two thousand pieces printed on more than thirty thousand pages. Dozens of other authors of equally high merit might just as well have been included. But our aim in the *American Mercury Reader* has been to offer representative material rather than just "the best." In the pages that follow you will find something from every period in the magazine's life and something from as many fields as possible.

From its very beginning under the editorship of H. L. Mencken, THE AMERICAN MERCURY has made significant contributions to contemporary journalism. Like all magazines, it has had its ups and downs — it has, alas, been on the wrong side of some issues, and it has published some things which it later regretted. But on the whole, during these twenty exciting and often tumultuous years, the magazine has consistently displayed a pioneering spirit and a gusto that have made it one of the most discussed and the most quoted periodicals in the country. It has changed with the years, but its zest, its ability to recognize new talent, its courage in handling vital issues, its accent on quality have remained constant. The new authors whom it has brought to light and helped establish add up to a "Who's Who" of current journalism and literature.

THE EDITORS

THE American Mercury READER

THE MAN WHO KNEW COOLIDGE

By Sinclair Lewis

I CERTAINLY do enjoy listening to you gentlemen and getting your views. That's one of the nice things about being on a Pullman like this: you can guarantee that you'll meet a lot of regular he-Americans with sound opinions and ideas.

And now let me tell you: the way I look at these things —

I don't mean to suggest for one second that I've got any better bean than the plain, ordinary, average citizen, but I've given a whole lot of attention to politics and such matters and — In fact, strikes me that it's the duty of all the better-educated citizens to take an interest in the affairs of the State, for what, after all, as a fellow was saying to us at the Kiwanis Club the other day — what is the government but the union of all of us put together for mutual advantage and protection?

And me — why, say, I read the political editorials in the *Advocate* — that's the leading paper in my town — Zenith — I read 'em like most folks read the sporting page. And as a result of all this, and certain personal information that I can't disclose the sources of, I've come to the firm conclusion —

Here's something maybe you gentlemen never thought of:

They can say all they want to about how President Coolidge — good old silent Cal Coolidge — isn't maybe as flashy as some of these statesmen. Maybe he isn't as much given to shooting off his mouth as certain other public figures that I could name. Maybe he isn't what my daughter would call Ritzy —

And say, by golly, it's beyond me where the young generation of today, taking them by and large, get all this slang that they pull. Why, here just the other day my daughter was talking to her

---

SINCLAIR LEWIS, *novelist and short story writer, was awarded the Nobel Prize in Literature in 1930. This long and hilarious story, which eventually became a book with the same title, displays Mr. Lewis in his glory.* (January, 1928)

brother, and Robby — That's the boy's name; only fifteen — three years younger than his sister, but smart's a whip. There's certainly one up-and-coming kid, if I do say so.

Why, say —

Now, I never put him up to it, y'understand. The Lord knows I can afford to give Robby the best the land affords, at least to a reasonable extent — I mean as much comfort and even luxury as is good for him. I'd never made a peep about his going out and earning a little money on the side. But he comes in one evening, just before supper — before dinnertime — with his hat on one side of his head, looking proud as Punch.

So I says to him, "Well, Robert Livingston —"

As a matter of fact, his middle name isn't Livingston at all, it's Otto, but we often call him Robert Livingston jokingly.

"Well, Robert Livingston," I says to him, "who do you think you are? Thomas Edison or Napoleon or somebody? Or maybe Red Grange! Sit down, Mr. Grange, and let me hang up your hat."

You know, jokingly.

Well, he just looks at me —

I'm afraid if the truth were known that kid is pretty gosh-awful fresh, but he's so darn' cute about it that you can't get sore at him, the darn' little cuss — just as up-and-coming as I was at his age. He just stands and looks at me and sticks his hands in his pants-pockets and then he says, "Dad," he says, "in me you behold the feline's *robe de nuit*. I've gone and —"

Mind you, 's I said, I'd never even suggested to him that he get a job out of school-hours and earn a little money. I most certainly do believe that it's a mighty fine thing for a boy to do a little work, no matter how well fixed his folks are, and learn the value of money; learn how doggone hard it is to sneak up on ole Mr. Dollar and get a stranglehold on him.

I swear, a lot of the young folks today seem to think the Old Man is simply made of money and don't have to sweat for every cent he makes. But same time, I hadn't figured it was time yet to explain this to Robby, though maybe that was a mistake on my part, and if it was, I'm perfectly willing to admit it — confession is good for the soul, as they say.

Maybe I should have drummed it into him long ago. I've got it on mighty straight inside information — in fact, one of my best friends is acquainted with a man who knows the Rockefellers intimately — and he tells me that the Rockefellers — people with all their jack — they bring up their families to be just as careful of money as any of us: *they* don't let their kids run away with the notion that it don't take any trouble to collect the dough.

Well, this gentleman related a significant little incident regarding the Rockefellers that he heard personally. Seems he was right there at the time. Here was old John D., probably with half the money-kings in the world waiting to see him, talking to young John D., just as simple and quiet as any of us. And he said, and I've never forgotten his words — in fact I repeated them to Robby that day — he looked at young John D., and prob'ly, I imagine, he put his hand on his shoulder, and he looked at him and said, "My boy, waste not, want not!"

Yes sir!

But anyway —

I'm afraid I'm getting a little off the subject of Coolidge, and if there's anything I hate it's a fellow that if he starts to talk about a subject he can't stick to it. I remember one time we had one of these book-authors speaking at the Kiwanis Club, and say, that fellow, maybe he could write all right (though at that I'd like to see him sit down and dictate a letter to some fellow that would make him pay his account and yet not make him sore!) —, I don't know anything about his writing, but when it came to *talking*, why say, he wandered all 'round Robin Hood's barn! Shows what a lack of business-training does to these fellows that think they're so gosh-awful smart and superior!

Well, as I say, Robby looks at me, and he says, "Well, Dad, I've got me a job in Zabriskie's drug-store for every Saturday afternoon, and I draw down one and one-half bucks for each and every said same!"

Pretty good, eh? I'll say it is! And him only fifteen!

But what I started to say was: The way that boy and his sister torture the English language to death just about gets my goat. Here him and his sister was talking one time, and he starts kidding her about some bird she was sweet on, and he says, "That guy's all wet."

But she come back at him, quick's a flash: "Yeh, he's wet like a Methodist Sunday-school!"

Yes sir, it beats the cars how this new generation takes the Queen's English like you and I were brought up to speak it in the good old-fashioned schools, where there was some thoroughness and not a lot of these flashy fads, and they just practically ruin it, and as I was saying, if Sister — that's what we often call my daughter — if *she* was talking about Coolidge, she'd probably say he wasn't Ritzy.

Well, if you want to look at it that way, all right. Maybe he isn't as highfalutin as some people I could name, but I wonder if any of you gentlemen ever thought of this?

He may not shoot off a lot of fireworks, but do you know what he is? He's SAFE.

II

Yes sir, Cal is the President for real honest-to-God Americans like us.

There's a lot of folks that pan him, but what are they? You can bet your sweet life he isn't popular with the bums, or yeggs, or anarchists, or highbrows, or cynics —

I remember our pastor saying one time, "A cynic is a man who sneers, and a man who sneers is setting himself up to tell God that he doesn't approve of God's handiwork!" No sir! You can bet Coolidge ain't popular with the Bolsheviks, or the lazy boob of a workman that wants fifteen bucks a day for doing nothing! No sir, nor with the cocaine fiends, or the drunkards, or the fellows that don't want the Prohibition law enforced —

Not that I never take a drink. What I say about Prohibition is: Once a law has been passed by the duly elected and qualified representatives of the people of these United States, in fact once it's on the statue books, it's *there*, and it's there to be enforced. There hadn't ought to be any blind pigs or illegal stills. But the same time, that don't mean you got to be a fanatic.

If a fellow feels like making some good home-brewed beer or wine, or if you go to a fellow's house and he brings out some hootch or gin that *you* don't know where he got it and it isn't any of your business, or if you have a business acquaintance coming to your house and you figure he won't loosen up and talk turkey without a little spot and you know a good dependable bootlegger that you can *depend* on, well then, that's a different matter, and there ain't any reason on God's green earth that *I* can see why you shouldn't take advantage of it, always providing you aren't setting somebody a bad example or making it look like you sympathized with law-breaking.

No, sir!

But now to come down to the point of my story, I hope to be able to give you gentlemen an agreeable little surprise.

I know Coolidge personally!

Yes sir! In fact, I was a classmate of his! Sure as I'm telling you! I'll give you gentlemen an inside view of him, not only as I saw him in college, but as I've studied him at the White House!

When I say I was a classmate of his —

Well, the fact is that certain unfortunate family circumstances that I needn't go into, and that wouldn't interest you, prevented me from completing my college course —

My father, and a fine, upstanding, cultured gentleman of the old school he was too, always ready with a helping hand for any mortal that needed it, a man of A 1 standing in his community — Fall River, Mass., that was; in fact I was born and brought up in Fall River, which is, as you may know, one of the most beautiful and enterprising and go-ahead communities in the fair State of Massachusetts — he was, in fact, the leading corn and feed merchant in his section of Fall River.

But I'm afraid he put a little too much confidence in the advice of an alleged friend.

Fact is, he invested his savings in a perpetual-motion machine company that had little or no value. He died, and it was quite sudden, in December of my freshman year, so I had to go back home and take up the burden of helping support the family.

But I certainly got a lot of value out of even that comparatively short time at Amherst, and the fellows at the Kiwanis Club tell me that they can see my educational advantages in the quality of such speeches or motions as I may be called upon to deliver at the club, and welcomes to speakers.

So it was at college that I was able to get an inside view of Cal Coolidge that has maybe been denied to even his more intimate associates in these later busy years, when he has been so engrossed with the cares of the nation.

I don't suppose I could have been called one of Cal's closest friends in college, but I knew him pretty well. In fact, we lived not far from each other, and I used to see him frequently. I'll admit that I never had any notion he'd climb to his present high position and international and historical fame, but even in those days you could see from the way he worked, and the way he looked at a thing from all sides before he went off half-cocked, that in whatever department of life he might choose, he would make his mark. And the next time you hear one of these birds criticizing Coolidge, you just tell 'em *that*, will you, from one who knew him in the days when he wasn't surrounded with adulations.

I can remember just's well as if it was yesterday, Cal and me happened to come out of a class together, and I said, "Well, it's going to be a cold winter," and he came right back, "Yep."

Didn't waste a lot of time arguing and discussing! He *knew*!

And another time: I never could get along any too good in Latin — my talent, you might say, is more along practical lines. I asked Cal — we happened to be going into class together, and I asked him, "Say, what's the Latin for 'defy'?"

"Don't know," he said. No beating around the bush and pretending and four flushing, but coming right out with it, bang! That's the kind of man he is, you take it from one who *knows* him!

Yes sir, I knew the boy and had the greatest affection and respect for him, like all of us who had the rare opportunity of *understanding* him!

And to think that I might not have gotten acquainted with him, if we hadn't been chums together in one of the smaller colleges!

I tell you, gentlemen, the way I figure it: the great, you might say the invincible advantage of the smaller educational institutions is that they throw the boys together in such intimate contact and — as Dr. Frank Crane says in one of his pieces somewhere — they provide that profound knowledge of human beings that fits a boy for supremacy in the future walks and struggles of life.

Still, the same time —

These great modern universities with their laboratories and stadiums and everything — They *do* have an advantage; and fact is, my son is preparing to enter the State university.

But anyway:

III

Naturally, considering that I had the privilege — through no virtue of my own, mind you — of being in my modest way rather chummy with Coolidge, I've watched his rise to world-wide fame with peculiar interest, and after he became President I often said to my wife, "By golly, I'd like to see the boy and just shake hands with him again."

Not, mind you, because he was President. After all, I've reached a position where I'm just as independent as the next fellow. An American citizen doesn't have to bow down and kowtow to anybody, whether it be the President, or a millionaire, or Queen Marie of Bulgaria, or —

By the way, Queen Marie made quite a stay at Zenith. She stopped over pretty near an hour between trains, and say, we certainly gave her a good time. The mayor read her an address and presented her with a gold-mounted polished cow's-foot combination ink-well, thermometer, and daily text calendar that I'll bet she's showing the folks in her palace right now. But I mean:

It wasn't because Cal was President, as I explained to the wife but —

"Besides," I said to her, "just between you and I, I bet it would give the boy a real kick, after having to associate with ambassadors and generals and Frank Kellogg and all those high-up guys, to be able to let down for a minute, and shake the mitt of a fellow that he used to laugh and joke with in the old care-free days before we both assumed the responsibilities of our present careers."

So here about six months ago, when we were planning to take a little trip to New York —

I had to go to New York to look over a new mimeographing machine. You see, I'm in the office-supply business, and let me tell you gentlemen that though I'm the first to respect other professions, though I honor the surgeon who can snatch you from the very gates of death, the lawyer who can so brilliantly argue your case — though personally I always think it's better to settle out of court — or the great banker or department-store owner, yet in all fairness, let me put this to you:

Who is it that enables these gentlemen to do business and get their great ideas across in an up-to-date, efficient, time-saving manner? Who is it but the office-supply man! Yes sir, I'm proud of my profession, and as a matter of fact, if I may say so, I have the honor of representing the office-supply classification in our great Zenith Kiwanis Club!

Just take filing-cabinets alone:

I always say, and sometimes the boys laugh at me at the Athletic Club — but good-naturedly, because I've got as fine a lot of friends as anybody I know, and believe me, I'm mighty good and proud of them, and I tell them, "Boys," I say, "excuse me if I get flowery, but you must always remember I'm a great reader of Colonel Bob Ingersoll, though I'm the first to deprecate the unfortunate religious ideas and skepticism that marred that otherwise great philosopher and public speaker, and probably it's from him that I got the idea of talking without having to resort to cheap and vulgar phrases, besides being a college man and —

"Excuse me if I get highfalutin," I often say to them — you know, at lunch at the Athletic Club — you know how a lot of fellows will get to reminiscing and chewing the rag when maybe they ought to be beating it back to their offices, but —

"Maybe you think I'm getting kind of woozy about it," I tell 'em, "but to me the beauties of modern filing-systems, which enable a man to instantly and without the least loss of time or effort find a letter on which, perhaps, depends the closing of an important deal, is in its practical way, to say nothing of the physical appearance of modern up-to-date filing-cabinets, no longer mere wooden boxes but whether in steel or fireproofed wood, the finest example of the cabinetmaker's art and imitating perfectly the rarest woods —

"To me," I often tell 'em, "these filing-systems are in every way as beautiful as the poet's song, as the flush on the maiden's cheek when she hears the first whispered words of love, or the soft chirp of the mother bird at eveningtide chirping to her birdlings! Yes sir, you bet your sweet life they are, and you can laugh all you want to!"

So as I say, I had to go on to New York to look over —

I usually do my buying in Chicago but this was a new caper that the wholesalers in Chicago hadn't got hold of yet. I'd been working pretty hard, and my wife was kind of a little rundown from the after-effects of the 'flu —

God, what a curse that is! I wonder if you gentlemen ever stopped to think that though the 'flu is in each individual case so much less fatal than diseases like the plague or brain-fever, yet considering the *number* of those afflicted with it — and after all, when you look at a subject, you've got to go into the statistics of it — of course, naturally an office-supply man has great advantages that way, being in the business — When you think how *many* folks get 'flu, it seems like one of the most important of all diseases.

I tell you, I'm as religious as the next fellow, and I'd never for one moment dream of criticizing the preachers' doctrines — let them figure out theology and religion, I say, and I'll stick to the office-supply business. But don't it sometimes almost make you question the workings of Providence when you see the mysterious way in which disease smites down the just with the unjust?

Why, my wife went on snivelling and subject to constant headaches for more than six weeks after the doctor *said* he'd got her all cured of the 'flu!

So I said to her, "Honey," as I often call her, "what say you and me and Almerine —"

Almerine, that's my daughter's name. Don't know, by the way, that I've introduced myself, Lowell Schmaltz is my name —

Funny! Whole lot of people take Schmaltz for a German name, but of course as a matter of fact when you look into the matter, it isn't German at all but Pennsylvania Dutch, which is almost the same as saying New England Yankee and —

Well, I figured Almerine could get away all right, because she's finished highschool.

I'd asked her if she wanted to go to college — I could perfectly well afford to send her, of course — but she thought it over, and she felt her talents lay more kind of along the musical line, and she was taking vocal and piano, but I figured she could drop them all right for a few weeks and I said —

Robby (that's my son), of course he couldn't get away, because he was in school, but —

I says to my wife, "Mamie, how'd it strike you — I've simply got to go to New York on a business trip, and things are kind of slack now, and how'd it be if Almerine and you went along and saw the Big Town?"

Say, she was tickled pink. She'd never seen New York, and of course —

Not that I'd want to live there. What I always say is: New York is a swell burg for a few days' visit, and theatres and all like that, but when it comes to living there — say, I wouldn't live there if they gave me Times Square and threw in Riverside Drive to boot. Compared with Zenith —

And believe me, gentlemen —

IV

I don't believe in going around boosting your own burg all the time. I don't suppose Zenith is any better, practically, than Minneapolis or Cincinnati or Pittsburgh, say. But it certainly is one high-class city, and you may or may not know that not only do we lead the world in the manufacture of loud speakers and overalls but we have, since Lindbergh's flight, made all the planes and raised quite a lot of the money to construct the largest and finest flying-field between Chicago and New York, excepting Detroit and Dayton of course, and we plan to have a restaurant there serving short-orders twenty-four hours a day.

And I must say the wife and I are pretty well fixed there. Believe me, we don't have to travel any to get ideas how to live. Just a couple of years ago I finished building a dandy little Italian villa style bungalow, with a Spanish mission entrance. We've got two bathrooms, and a fireplace, and everything fixed up first-rate, and in the basement I've installed an electric washing-machine and a garbage-incinerator, and we got something that you don't find in many houses: in both bathrooms I've got a slit in the wall, right by the stationary bowls, for the disposal of safety-razor blades.

And of course I drive a Chrysler myself and I gave my wife a Chevrolet coop —

Say, I certainly got a rise out of her. She's one darn' nice little woman, if I do say so: been an A 1 wife in every way, even if she does kick a little sometimes about my driving too fast. Well, here her last birthday I come home and I could see she was mooching around skittish as a wasp, because most always on her birthdays I've got something tucked in my inside pocket for her.

"Do you know what day this is?" I finally says to her, after I'd looked over the paper and listened in on the radio a little — though I remember there wasn't anything very interesting on then; nothing but the daily receipts reports from the Omaha stock-yards.

She brightens up and tries to look kittenish and makes out like she doesn't know, and she says, "No, what?"

"It's the day — or it will be the evening — of the Kid Milligan-Pooch Federstein fight, and we better invite in some of the folks and listen to the fight on the radio," I says.

Well sir, the poor kid, she certainly did look awful' down in the mouth. I didn't know whether she was going to be plucky or whether she'd bawl me out. But she was game and didn't say anything, and pretty soon, long about fifteen, maybe twenty minutes, I suggested we go out and have a little walk before dinner. Well, meantime, you get me, I'd had the fellow bring this Chevrolet coop around and park it right in front of the house.

"Here's a nice little car," I says. "Wonder how she runs."

And I goes and gets in and starts it!

Well sir — You know how women carry on. She cusses me out, and she beefs, and she gets on a rampage, and she says, "Why, Lowell Schmaltz, what do you mean! What'll the owner say?"

"I'll bet he'll do a lot of saying," I laughs, "if he — or she — happens to see me!"

"Why, I never *knew* you to do a thing like that!" she says. "You get right out of that car!"

Say, I had her wild!

"So that's how a fellow gets treated, is it?" I says, and I pretended to look hurt, and I gets out, and then I draws her attention to a little card that I'd had tied on the door handle — 'd tied it on myself, matter of fact — and it reads sort of like this: "To Mamie on her birthday from Woofums" — Woofums — nut name, but that's what she calls me every now and then when we're kind of fooling around.

Say, maybe she didn't pretty nearly keel over!

Yes sir, you bet, both of us have our own cars, though mine —

It ain't the fault of the Chrysler itself, I'm certain of that, but the garage got to fooling with it, and my car's got a squeak in it somewhere that I, by golly, simply can *not* locate, and say, if there's anything gets me wild when I'm driving —

I can stand the big gaff — Why say, when I had a Sweeney tire blow out on me after only two thousand miles — Any of you gentlemen ever try the Sweeney?

Well don't, that's my advice to you, and believe me I know! I've tried two of 'em, and in my opinion this monkey-business they advertise of wrapping the fabric crosswise or whatever it is is all the bugs; don't get the result they claim at all.

I can stand those big things, but say, even the littlest squeak, it simply drives me crazy when I'm driving.

Why, here just last Sunday I was driving the family out to a cousin of ours that lives in Elmwood for Sunday dinner, and it was as fine a day as you ever saw but just about the time I began to enjoy myself, and I was going past the Seven Corners and looking at the new filling-station they got there — Say, man, I'll bet that's one of the finest filling-stations in the United States: twelve pumps they got, and a comfort-station fixed up to look like an old-fashioned log cabin, and a supply store with a great big huge enormous fish-aquarium simply chucked full of goldfish right in the window. And geraniums!

And just when I was calling it to Mamie's attention — by golly, all of a sudden that squeak started again.

Well say, I couldn't enjoy anything all day. After dinner, I took Cousin Ed out for a drive, to see if he could locate the squeak, and we drove right down through a woods, a park they got there, mighty pretty and I'd of enjoyed it like the dickens — I always was a great believer in Nature — but every time I looked at a tree or a nice rustic bench or something, that darn' squeak would start in again, and Cousin Ed — he thinks he's such a wiz at cars, but Lord love you, he couldn't locate that squeak any more'n I could!

V

But 's I say: I guess we're about as well fixed as most folks, and don't have to get away from home to enjoy ourselves, but when I said to my wife, "I kind of got an idea you and Almerine might come along with me and give New York the once-over," why she looked like somebody'd left her a million dollars.

And Almerine, she just hollers, "Oh boy! I'll give those Manhattan cabarets a look at a live one for once!"

"And we might stop at Cousin Walter's in Troy, on the way," I says.

"Oh no, let's not," says my wife.

"But we *got* to go there! Ain't Cousin Walter living there?" I says.

"Well, what of that?" she says. "Haven't you and he always hated each other?"

"Well, maybe we have," I says, "but he's a *relative*, ain't he? And when you travel you got to look up your relatives, ain't you?"

Well, make a long story short, we decided to stop at Cousin Walter's for a few days — and then — man! — then I springs the BIG surprise!

"And after New York," I says, "we'll come home by way of Washington, and we'll stop in and call on the President!"

"Oh papa, we couldn't do *that!*" Almerine hollers.

"I'd like to know why not!" I says. "Ain't he and I classmates?"

"Yes, but maybe he wouldn't remember you," she says.

"Now you look here!" I says. "If you think for one moment that I wasn't just as important in college as he was, and maybe then some — they told me if I could of stayed till spring I'd of been on the track team —

"But that isn't the point! Let me tell you right now that words like that are a direct insult not to me, my fine young lady, but to the Great Executive himself! What is it that more than any other one quality distinguishes leaders of men like Cal? It isn't merely his profound thought, his immovable courage, his genial and democratic manners, but it's the fact that he's so close a student of human nature that he quickly but thoroughly studies each man as he meets him, and so never *can* forget him!

"Understand now," I says to them, "I understand that the President is one of the busiest men in the United States what with having to sign documents and shake hands with delegations and so on, and I certainly don't intend to intrude, but we'll just drop in and give him a pleasant surprise — think how many years it is since we've seen each other! — and just shake hands and pass on. And you, Almerine, you'll be able to tell your grandchildren that once you heard the voice of Calvin Coolidge!"

Well, of course when I made it all clear like that they were tickled to death at the prospect, and so we started making plans. Personally I was for just taking some suitcases, but my wife held out for the black trunk, and I must say — I'm always the first one to admit it when I'm licked, and Mamie certainly won that time — she pointed out I'd have to have my dress-suit in New York, and it wouldn't get wrinkled in a wardrobe trunk — and now say, while we're speaking of that, I'll bet it's struck you gentlemen as it has me: there's one of the highest class and most significant of modern inventions that do so much to make life happy, the wardrobe trunk, and what a lot it adds to ease of travel and seeing the world, yes sir, she sure won that time and —

And just then —

Say, isn't it funny how a fellow will remember comparatively unimportant details even regarding a critical moment? Happened just then that Robby — that's my son, he's only fifteen, and the little cuss had started smoking. Seems like I'd done everything I could to make him stop, but he's such a cute little beggar the way he comes back at you when you try to bawl him out that I never could get much more than a word in edgeways. Well, he comes in —

And besides, I must say I still ain't sold on the idea of cigarettes.

I think I can with justification call myself what you might call a modern, up-to-date, liberal man. I was the first fellow in my neighborhood to put in a radio, and I never did believe they ought to have hung Sacco and Vanzetti if they were innocent. But when it comes to smoking, I still prefer a pipe or a good cigar.

But's I was saying, he comes in smoking a cigarette, and Almerine — that's my daughter, a girl that I want to tell you gentlemen can in my judgment sing just as good right this minute as Schumann-Heink or Sophie Tucker or any of these famous prima donnas — and she hollers at him, "Say, Dad's going to take us to see President Coolidge!"

Well Robby gets fresh, and he says,

"Are you going to give him enough warning so he can get away?"

Well say, maybe I didn't light into him! I believe in giving kids their freedom, but I've told Robby time and time again that it's nice language and nice manners that enable a fellow to get along in this world, and if he'd study his mother and me a little more instead of a lot of these smart-aleck cigarette-sucking high-school fraternity yahoos, he'd be a lot better off! You bet! Every time!

Well, so we decided and got started. I don't want to bore you gentlemen with a lot of details of our trip. Of course what you want to hear about is the inside glimpse of Coolidge and the White House that I was privileged to have. So I'll cut it short and come right down to the real meat of the story.

VI

We got off on the noon train in about a week and — Say, it certainly is remarkable, ain't it, the conveniences of railroad travel today? In America, I mean. A fellow that knows every inch of Europe was telling me there ain't a what you might call really comfortable train in the whole length and breadth of the Old Country. But — there I sit in the club car, with every convenience and luxury — soft drinks (personally I always find the Loganberry highball the best drink on a Pullman) — soft drinks to be had just by touching a button, and a regular library of free magazines and everything, especially the *Saturday Evening Post*, which is, taking it by and large, my favorite magazine, especially the advertisements, now that they've taken to printing 'em in colors.

Say! they can keep their old masters; give me some of these advertisements!

Yes sir, it's wonderful what strides advertising has made these last few years. Of course I admire the really great and leading American authors — Mrs. Rinehart and Peter B. Kyne and Arthur Brisbane — but I doubt if even they can touch the fellows that get up these advertisements nowadays. And it was a mighty bright idea — I don't know who started it, but this idea of working in a girl with pretty legs in all sorts of ads; not only stocking ads, but auto ads, showing her climbing into a car; and machinery, showing her giving it the North and South, and so on. Yes sir, a fellow that wants to understand the United States, all he has to do is study the *Saturday Evening Post* ads, and he'll see why we're the most advanced nation in the world, and the most individual.

There's a lot of sorehead critics of America that claim we're standardized, but —

Well, to take an example, let me take the fellow that I happened to be lunching with just before I caught this train — just take the differences between him and me. We both belong to the Athletic Club, we both belong to service clubs, we have our offices in the same block, we live within a quarter of a mile of each other, we both like golf and a good lively jazz on the radio. And yet this fellow and me — his name is Babbitt, G. F. Babbitt, fellow in the real estate game — we're as different as Moses and Gene Tunney.

Where these poor devils of Europeans are crushed down and prevented from having their characters developed by the wide and free initiative so characteristic of American life, him and me can be friendly yet as different —

Well, like this, for instance: I drive a Chrysler, and Babbitt doesn't. I'm a Congregationalist, and Babbitt has no use whatsomever for anything but his old Presbyterian church. He wears these big round spectacles, and you couldn't hire me to wear anything but eyeglasses — much more dignified, *I* think. He's got so he likes golf for its own sake, and I'd rather go fishing, any day. And so on and so on. Yes sir, it's a wonderful thing how American civilization, as represented, you might say, by modern advertising, has encouraged the — as a speaker at the Kiwanis recently called it — the free play of individualism.

But as I say —

Make a long story short, we got to Cousin Walter's at Troy all right, and on to New York —

But say, Walt certainly did entertain us in fine style. I got to thinking he wasn't such a bad cuss after all. And he's got a new house that, and I'm the first to admit it, is just as modern as mine is. A modern homey home! Vacuum cleaner and gas clothes-dryer and one of these new noiseless electric refrigerators!

Man, what a convenience that is! I never could understand why they make so much fuss over Babe Ruth or even a real scientific pioneer like Lindbergh, when we haven't yet done anything to boost the honest-to-God master genius that invented the electric refrigerator!

Think of what it'll do! Give you every

sort of frozen dessert! Get rid of the iceman that tracks mud on the back porch! What I always say is: these fellows can have their big libraries, their blinking art galleries, their private pipe organs, their rose gardens, but give me the *practical* things that make a home an inspiration and a solid comfort to a real family!

And I got to admit that Walt's radio shades mine just the least little bit. And there's mighty few things that indicate a fellow's social rank and progress better than his radio.

And what an invention *that* is! *What* an invention! Talk about miracles —

Just think of it! Here you sit at home in the ole over-stuffed chair, happy as a clam at low tide (or is it high tide — whichever it is). You sit there and smoke your pipe and twiddle the knob and what do you get? *Think* of it! Right there at home you hear the best jazz bands in the country, bands in the best hotels in Chicago, and that wonderful orchestra at Zion City! Jokes by the best comedians in the country —

Say, I heard a crackajack over the radio the other day. Seems there was a couple of fellows sitting chinning in a Pullman, just like we are. "Haven't I met you in Buffalo?" one fellow says to the other, and the other says, "I've never been in Buffalo," and the first fellow says, "Neither have I — must o' been a couple o' other fellows!"

Yes sir! and then think of the instructive lectures you get on the radio — why say, just the other night I heard that in the eye of the ordinary house-fly there are several thousand, I think it was, separate lenses. Ever know that?

And then the sermons on Sunday morning. Why, that alone would make the radio one of the most world-revolutionizing inventions the world has ever known.

I tell you, it gives a real spiritual uplift to a poor devil that all week, excepting maybe at the Kiwanis lunch, he's had to toil and moil amid the dust of busy affairs and forget higher things. You bet! I'll never forget one sermon that I wouldn't ever've heard, if I hadn't had the radio, being way off in Youngstown, Ohio — Reverend Wayo on how he didn't want to say that every atheist was a bootlegger, but you could bet your sweet life every bootlegger was an atheist!

Cute idea for a sermon, eh? and —

But as I say, Walt's radio was every bit as good as mine, and we had some dandy drives around Troy and a big beer party Sunday evening — the only evening we stayed up late — I was mighty glad to find that Walt still kept regular hours and turned in about ten.

I tell you there never was a truer saying than "Early to bed, early to rise, makes a man healthy, wealthy, and wise." I've certainly found it true in my own case — and we drove out for a few rounds of golf —

Now you take golf. By golly, if anybody'd told me fifteen years ago that I'd ever be out on the links chasing a little white pill around, I'd 've told 'em they were crazy, but let me tell you, I've found one of the best ways to get acquainted with customers is to play 'round with 'em, and I've got so I like the game itself a good deal — take like my playing there at Troy, even when I wasn't making any contacts — and even though the weather was pretty chilly and —

Seems to me that on the whole the weather has gotten warmer than it used to be when we were kids. You read in the papers how it hasn't changed materially, but they can say what they want to, don't you remember how doggone cold it used to be mornings when we had to get up and chase off to school, and now it seems like we don't have any more old-fashioned winters? Maybe that's one reason why the kids today aren't as self-reliant as we were.

But to get back to my subject: As I say, I certainly did enjoy my stay with Walt, especially his stories and inside information about the war — he was a lieutenant in the quartermasters' corps at Camp Devon —

You know, there's a lot of false ideas about the war. I don't want to criticize General Pershing — I know he ranks among the greatest generals we've ever had, right along with Grant and Lee and Israel Putnam, but same time, what we ought to've done, what I'd 've done if I'd been running things, was to march right straight through to Berlin, and make them Germans suffer *good* — suffer like we did.

I was explaining this to my wife, and she says, "Why, Lowell T. Schmaltz," she says, "I'm ashamed of you! Don't we know some Germans that are awful' nice folks?"

"You don't know the Germans like I do," I says to her. "They haven't got any forward-looking ideas. They believe in rule by tyranny and despotism and compulsion and all that, and if they haven't understood our democratic ideas, they ought to of been *forced* to, that's what they ought to of been!" I told her. "But same time, you got to hand it to 'em — they certainly have buckled down to work ever since the war," I said. "Be a good thing if *our* workmen worked like that, 'stead of watching the clock and thinking about a raise all the time!"

But make a long story short, we certainly enjoyed our stay, and we went on to New York.

I was kind of sore all the time I was in New York though. These damn' New Yorkers — I hope none of you gentlemen come from New York — they seem to think they run the nation, and what I always say is, as a matter of fact New York is the most provincial town in the country! Give me Chicago every time!

You see, when I go to Chicago, in the first place I always stay at the Hotel Grand Imperial Palace, it's a nice quiet little place and the clerks *know* me and try to give me a little service; but in those big New York hotels, they're so darn' independent, you'd think they were doing you a favor.

Then when it comes to business —

In Chicago I usually do the bulk of my business, you might say, with Starbright, Horner, and Dodd; and Billy Dodd himself looks after me, and say, there's a man that it's a pleasure to do business with, a square-shooter if ever there was one, and always got a good story and a good cigar for you, and acts like he was glad to see you, and he isn't one of these fellows that throw seven kinds of cat-fits if maybe a fellow is temporarily a little short and wants an extension of a couple days or a month or so. Yes sir, and many's the good lunch I've had with Billy in the old Palmer House before they tore it down, and though of course this new Palmer House is you might say a regular palace, still, there was a kind of an atmosphere about the old place, and say, they certainly did know how to cook a steak and fried onions to a turn. But in New York —

All this darn' fancy French food, and the prices —

"My God," I says to one of these smart-aleck headwaiters, or maybe he was what they call a captain — anyway he was the fellow that takes the order and then hands it on to the regular waiter — "My God," I said to him, when I looked at the prices on the bill of fare, "I just come in here to eat," I says. "I don't want to buy the hotel!"

And just the same way in the business world.

Why say, the firm that was handling these new mimeograph machines, they said they were behind on their orders and they couldn't make a delivery right away. Oh, that's all right, I told 'em — why couldn't they fill my order and keep some other fellow waiting?

No sir, they said, they wouldn't do it. They were just naturally arbitrary, and when I tried to make 'em understand that with the class and volume of business that *I* do, they ought to be willing to make some concessions, they acted like a bunch of human icicles. Some day I'm going to write a letter to the New York papers and tell 'em what a real he-American from the Middle West thinks about their town.

The noise, and traffic so thick you can't get anywhere, and the outrageous prices and —

And no home life. Folks all out in the evening, hitting it up at these night clubs and everything. But back home — Now you take us, for instance. Evenings, except maybe when I have to be at the lodge or some Kiwanis committee meeting, or maybe Almerine or Robby are at the movies or a party or something, we all just settle down around the radio and have a real old-fashioned homey time together. But not in New York! No sir! I swear, I don't know what the nation's coming to —

And too many foreigners — fellows with wop names and hunky names and Lord knows what all — and all this corrupt politics —

Oh say, speaking of politics, if I may interrupt myself a moment and take the risk of straying from my story, I got to tell you what I heard at the Kiwanis luncheon just this past week. Our congressman, and I think it's pretty generally conceded even right in Washington that he's got one of the ablest minds in the entire House of Representatives, he got back from an extensive investigation of the European status — spent six weeks in Germany, France, and Italy, and he gave it as his measured opinion that all these countries are so prosperous now that we certainly ought to press for the payment of our debt in full! Why, he said that in the better class of hotels in those countries, you could get just as good food and nearly as expensive as in New York itself! And them complaining about being poor!

VII

But to get back to my story, I didn't think so much of New York, though we did have one dandy evening — we ran into some folks from home in the hotel lobby, and we all went to a Chink restaurant and got outside of some of the best chicken chow mein that I ever ate in my life, and then we went to a movie that I knew was good because I'd seen it in Zenith — Hoot Gibson in a crackajack Western film.

But Almerine, she liked New York, and my Lord, how that girl did keep nagging and teasing and complaining!

She wanted to go to one of these night clubs. I pointed out to her that while I had to work all day, talking to a lot of different firms, she and her mother were free to enjoy themselves all day — go to a matinée or look over the stores and shop a little (though I didn't encourage 'em to buy too much; "why not wait till you get back home — the stores there are just as up-to-date as New York, far's I can see," I pointed out to 'em). But she kept insisting, and her mother more or less agreed with her, and so one night I took 'em to a swell night club that was recommended to me by one of the bellboys at the hotel, cute little lad, knew the town like a book.

Well, thinks I, here's where I have a punk evening, but I want to admit that I was wrong. Not but what it was expensive, and I certainly wouldn't want to go to one of those places more'n once or twice a year, but say, that was some place!

First, we was all kind of disappointed. We drives up to a house in the Fifties, just an ordinary-looking place, and all dark.

"This can't be the place," I says to the taxi driver.

"Sure, this is the joint all right," he says.

"Are you sure?" I says.

"Sure, you bet," he says. "I've driven lots of folks here. You just ring that basement bell and they'll let you in," he says.

Well, I figured he probably knew his business, so my wife and Almerine and I, we all piled out of the taxi, and I went and rang the bell at the basement door — well, they call it the basement; it was really practically the ground floor, but this was one of those houses that they got so many of in New York, or used to have anyway, though now a lot of 'em are being torn down to make way for modern apartment houses — graystone houses they call 'em, and you go up a flight of steps from the street to the parlor floor, so the door to this basement floor, as they call it, was really kind of under these steps practically on the ground level, only of course you go down into a kind of areaway that's a step or maybe it might have been two steps below the pavement level but not more than that if I remember rightly, and there was a kind of iron grilled door but, 's I said, there weren't any lights or anything that *we* could see, and I wondered if the taxi-driver could of been right and —

But I rang the bell and pretty soon, sure enough, the door opened, and by golly, there was a fellow in one of these funny Lord High Admiral uniforms, and I says to him, "Is this the Nouvelle Desire?" That was the name of the joint I was looking for. "Is this the Nouvelle Desire?" I says.

"Yes, but I haven't the pleasure of knowing your face," he says — you know, some highfalutin comeback like that.

Well, I kidded him along — I told him it wasn't such a hard face to know when you put your mind to it. Almerine — she stood right back of me, and I must say, maybe it was just because she was my girl, but she wore a kind of light violet dress and shiny spangles and gold slippers and say, she certainly looked as elegant as anybody there that night, and my wife wasn't such a slouch herself, for a Midwestern girl and —

But as I was saying, Almerine was standing right near me, and she kind of whispers to me, "Say, you hadn't ought to kid the servants like that."

But I knew this guy in the uniform wasn't any ordinary servant and I wanted to show him I was just as used to the Gay Life as anybody (of course I was wearing my dress suit), and —

But anyway, he calls what I figured out to be the assistant manager — nice-looking fellow in a dress suit, kind of dark-complected, Italian I guess, but a nice-spoken fellow.

He explained that this Nouvelle Desire was a club and they couldn't let in nobody that didn't belong, but I introduced him to the wife and Almerine, and I explained we come from Zenith and was only in town for about a week, and I showed him my Elks card, and he looked us over good, and he said maybe he could fix it. The regular membership cost two hundred bucks a head a year, but finally he let me have a temporary membership for that week for only five bucks a head.

So we got in all safe and —

Maybe you couldn't see any lights outside, but inside, oh boy! It was fixed up as elegant as if it was the Vanderbilts' ballroom. They'd turned the whole parlor floor — that is, the floor above the basement — I guess they had the kitchen and all like that on the basement floor —

And here was a funny thing: this assistant manager — he and I got to be quite chummy; he told me to call him Nick, and I said he was to call me Low, but he said that was against the rules — and Nick told me something that may surprise you gentlemen as it certainly surprised me at the time: he told me that they did all their cooking by electricity!

Then, as I say, there was this kind of ballroom. Halfway up, the walls was all red satin or silk or something, with a lot of what they call Modern Art decoration, or that's what Nick called it — all kinds of zigzags and big flowers and everything in gold; and then above that the walls was all hung with flowers. I found they was artificial flowers, but they looked so real you had to touch 'em before you'd believe it.

And some of the tables was in kind of booths fixed up so they looked like grape arbors and all like that. And at the end of the room there was some great big yellow marble columns — it looked like real genuine marble, though it may not have been — in front of where the orchestra played — and say, the boys in that orchestra certainly were some jazz babies, all coons but they had a regular high-class musical education, Nick told me later; and the fellow that played the saxophone — say, if they got anybody better'n him in Paul Whiteman's band, I want to hear him, that's all — Why say, he could make that ole saxophone sound like a fog horn or anything he wanted.

Well, before we got settled down — there weren't many folks there yet — Nick took me aside and said they had a regular sure-enough old-fashioned bar on the floor above, and he thought he could fix it so that I could go up and throw in a little real liquor. The rules of the club, or so he said anyway, the rules of the club made every fellow buy wine at his table, and when it comes to fizz, of course it's a grand high-class wine, but it ain't got the authority like hootch, like the fellow says.

Well, make a long story short, he went away and he fixed it so we could go up to the bar.

I'd just intended to let Almerine and her mother have some ginger ale up there, but seems they didn't stock any soft drinks, and anyway, Almerine put up a holler.

"I want a cocktail," she says, "and I'll bet so does Mama, if she tells the truth. Maybe we'll never get to another night club again," she says. "And besides," she says, "you've let me taste a sip of your cocktail when you've had 'em at home. And think of what my bunch will say if I go back home and tell 'em we went to a night club and I couldn't have a cocktail. I'm not a kid," she says.

Well, anyway, I kicked, and I pointed out her mother didn't want any — my wife's a great believer in Prohibition — but her mother, doggone her, she went and laid right down on me and didn't back me up — just kind of giggled, and said she wouldn't mind one herself, just this once. So, make a long story short, we all had a cocktail — Mame took a Bronx, and Almerine took a side-car, if I remember rightly, and I ordered a Martini and then I said, "No sir, by golly, I believe I'll have a Manhattan. Must be five years since I've had a Manhattan cocktail." And so I had a Manhattan. And then I sneaked in a coupla highballs while Mame and the girl was in the ladies' dressing-room, and say, by that time I certainly did feel primed for one high, wide and fancy evening.

And I want to say that, think what you may of New York, we certainly had said evening.

Nick had fixed us up a nice little table almost right next to where they danced.

We looked around and there was a nice-looking lot of people there — they was just coming in. Almerine was just saying, "Oh, I wish we knew somebody here — I won't have anybody to dance with except you, Papa," and I was informing her that I was regarded as by golly just as good a dancer as anybody at the Country Club when — Say, you could've knocked me down with a feather! Yes sir, by golly I hears a familiar voice, and there stands Sam Geierstein, of the Mammoth Clothing Company of Zenith — fellow I'd often met at the Athletic Club.

Now, there's a whole lot of fellows I'd rather seen than Sam. To tell the truth, just between ourselves, he hasn't got any too good a reputation for square dealing, and I've heard some mighty queer rumors about the way him and his lady secretary carry on. But same time — you know how it is when you're away from home — especially in a city like New York where they're such a chilly lot of stiffs: familiar face sure does look good to you.

So we invites Sam to sit down, and say, I will say one thing for him, he certainly did insist on buying his share of wine and then some. And he sure could dance. I never did like his looks — kind of too dark and good-looking, and big black eyes like you don't really like to see in a real he-male, but he certainly did spin Almerine and even the wife around that ole floor all right. And me, after I'd got a little champagne into my system, I guess I wouldn't 've hardly beefed much even if he'd kissed Almerine —

Not that he did anything like that, you understand; he acted like a perfect gentlemen, you understand; and once when I was dancing with Mame and I kind of slipped and almost fell down — they had that floor altogether too slippery for any use — why, it was Sam that grabbed me and kept me from falling.

Though I don't like the way he's been hanging around the house since we been back in Zenith — seems he's got a wife somewhere, only they're separated. Almerine, she says I'm crazy. She says she just discusses music with Sam — seems he knows a lot about it. But I don't like her being out late —

Oh, I guess I'm an old crank. But Al is so young, and she thinks she knows everything, but she's innocent as a baby but — Oh, I'm a regular fusser, I guess. But anyway, we certainly did have one large round time that evening — evening, huh! Say, we certainly were high-rollers for once! I'll bet it was three o'clock before we hit the hay. I remember —

It was comic! Here was Mame — that's my wife — supposed to be a good respectable dame, and me, a deacon in the church, and us coming down Broadway at three G. M., singing "We Won't Go Home Until Morning!"

You see Sam — he's got the nerve of the Devil — he picked up a couple from Fort Worth, Texas (and maybe she wasn't some baby; say, she had all the regular New York dames there beat a mile!), and somehow, I don't exactly remember how, we got acquainted with another couple from San José, California, a gentleman that was in the fruit-ranching business, and his wife and son; he took a shine to Almerine; up in the bar I got to talking to a gentleman and lady from Kansas City, Missouri — or it may have been Kansas City, Kansas, I can't exactly remember, at this late date — and the whole lot of us carried on like we'd always known each other, dancing and laughing and drinking toasts and singing and drinking and cutting up — Say! But I hate to think of what it cost me. But as I told my wife, that's the way of it, in New York.

But I don't need to tell you gentlemen about New York. Probably you know it better'n I do, and you want me to sing my little song and get it finished and get on to Washington and my experiences at the White House. Yes sir, the less said about New York the better. Money-mad, that's what the New Yorkers are.

If I wanted to sacrifice other more worth-while things, like our home life and friendships and reading worth-while literature, and getting in a good fish every summer — And let me tell you that they can talk about Canada all they want to, but if they can show me any better fishing than I get up in Northern Michigan, right within you'd hardly call it more'n an overnight ride from Zenith, why just let 'em show it to me, that's all!

But the way I look at it, a fellow ought to be prosperous for his family's sake and that of his own position in the community, but money-making can be overdone, and what I always say is, Ideals before Dollars every time.

VIII

So that's what I think of New York and we packed up and went on to Washington, and say, Almerine pretended she didn't care, but she was so excited over the prospect of having a chat with the President that she couldn't hardly sit still. Well, so was I — hadn't seen Cal for so many years. I got to thinking maybe he might invite us to lunch or supper, but still, I knew that was unreasonable — having to entertain so many people — ambassadors and high officials of the Order of Moose and so on — but I guess I was pretty excited just the same.

I don't know how well you gentlemen know Washington, but the new station there is very handsome and up-to-date in every respect, with a great big open space — the Plaza I believe they call it — in front; and what I'd never known, you can see the dome of the Capitol right from the front of the station. I tell you I got a mighty big thrill out of that.

Well, Mame wanted us to get a room in the hotel first and get washed, but I says, "No sir, we better see the President first and see what his plans are; we'll just keep the taxi waiting and I don't care if it costs a dollar and a half; 'tisn't often in your life that you're going to sit in with a President of these United States!"

So we got into a taxi and we started off all het up and all of a sudden I says to my wife, "Say, do you notice anything funny about this taxi?"

"Why no," she says, "I don't know's I do; it looks all right to me. Why?"

"Looks all right!" I says, "I should say it does! Do you mean to tell me you don't notice something different about this taxi?"

"Why no," she says.

"Well, what make of car is it?" I says.

Of course Almerine has to horn in. "It's a Studebaker, isn't it?" she says.

"Oh it is, is it, Miss Smarty!" I says. "My God, and me teaching you to drive myself! It is not a Studebaker, and it isn't a Cadillac, no, and it isn't a flivver either! It's a Buick! See the significance?"

Well, they both stared at me — couldn't get the idea at all — just like women, even the brightest of 'em.

"Can't you see?" I says. "Here's the Buick, the biggest-selling six cylinder car in the United States, if not in the world.

And yet how often do you see a Buick taxi? Not very often. Ever think of that? Yes sir, it's a mighty peculiar thing, and I'm sure I don't know why it is. At least, I'm practically certain it's a Buick — of course, with a taxi body on it — I didn't happen to notice the hood, but from the looks of the dashboard — Anyway — "

So I tapped on the window, and the driver — he probably thought we were just ordinary tourists that wanted to see the town, and we were passing some building or other and he just hardly turns his head and says, "It's the Pensions Building." (Or it may have been the Patent Building — I didn't pay much attention, I was so worked up and excited about seeing the President, and I can't exactly remember at this late date.)

"No," I hollers at him, "what I want to know is: isn't this a Buick taxi?"

"Yeh," he says.

"There," I says to the girls, "what did I tell you!"

So we came to the White House and —

Now, even you gentlemen that've been to Washington and seen the White House may not know that the offices, including the President's own private office, are in wings stretching out on either side of the old main structure. The wings are new, I should think, and they're so low that you wouldn't hardly notice 'em from the street in front — not hardly know they were there unless you'd happened, like I was, to be privileged to enter 'em.

So we came up the driveway to that famous old place —

I tell you it was a mighty moving thing to think of the famous men that had inhabited that structure. Grant and McKinley and Harding and Garfield and everybody! By golly, as I told the Kiwanis when I addressed them about my trip, it certainly gave a fellow inspiration. For what, after all, is a greater inspiration than the lives of our heroes?

That reminds me that recently — why, in fact, it was just a couple of nights ago, and a neighbor and I were having a little visit, and he says to me, "Lowell, who do you think have been the greatest heroes of the United States since 1900, and the geniuses?"

Well, a question like that certainly makes a fellow think, and him and I, we began making lists, and it just happens I've still got mine in my pocket here, and here's how I figured out our leading intellects: Coolidge, Harding, Wilson (though I'm a Republican), Ford, Lindbergh, Billy Sunday, Pershing, Roosevelt, Judge Gary —

Now here's a couple more names that may surprise you gentlemen. Maybe you never looked at it like this. I figured that what you might call the Arts ought to be represented, and I put in Anne Nichols — say, the author of a play like "Abie's Irish Rose," that can run five years, is in my mind — maybe it's highbrow and impractical to look at it that way, but the way I see it, she's comparable to any business magnate. And besides, they say she's made as much money as Jack Dempsey!

And here's a name that may surprise you still more: Samuel Gompers!

Yes, I knew that would surprise you, my putting in a man that lots of folks think he merely stood for union labor and labor disturbances and all those kind of

Bolshevik activities. But it seems that Gompers — a fellow, some kind of professor he was, he was explaining this to us at the Kiwanis Club here just recently — Gompers stood right square against labor disturbances. He thought that laboring men ought to have their rights, and I suppose that's true, but the way he looked at it, he wanted employés and employers and the general public to join hands in one great brotherhood for the glory of the union and the extension of our markets into lands now unfairly monopolized by England and Germany. Yes sir!

So, as I say, we drove up to the White House —

I'd told the chauffeur to go right up to the front door — just like I'd expect Cal Coolidge to come right up to *my* front door, if he came to call on me in Zenith. I didn't understand then about the arrangement of the White House.

But there was some kind of cop at the gate and he says, "What do you want, please?"

"What do I want, officer?" I says. "What do I *want*? Why, I just want to call on the President!" I says. "I'm just an old friend of his, that's all!" I says.

Well, I explains, and he tells me the proper caper is to go round to the office entrance, so I says all right; I'd be the last, I says, as a friend of the President, to want to break any proper regulations.

Well, make a long story short, at last there we were, in one of the waiting-rooms to the President's own offices, and a gentleman came in — fine-looking gentleman he was, all dressed up like Sunday morning, in a cutaway coat and striped pants, and seems he was practically the President's first main secretary, and I presented my wife and Almerine to him, and I explained about the President and me being classmates.

"I know the President's a busy man, but it'd be nice to have a look at the old kid," I tells him, "and I kind of thought I'd like to have my wife and daughter shake hands with him."

Well sir, he understood perfectly.

He went right in and saw the President — didn't keep me waiting one minute, no sir, not hardly a minute.

He came back and said the President was awful' sorry he couldn't have us come in just that second, but seems he was all tied up with an important international conference about — I think it was about Geneva, he said — and would I wait? This secretary was mighty nice, too; he didn't let us sit there like bumps on a log; he sat and visited with us, and that's how I had the chance to get the real inside low-down on so many of the President's opinions and activities, but I don't want you gentlemen to give any of this stuff to the newspapers.

IX

I asked this secretary, Mr. Jones his name was — I said to him, "What does the President think about disarmament, Mr. Jones?"

"Well, it just happens," he says, "that I can tell you in the President's own words. I heard him talking to the Secretary of State," he says — say, maybe that didn't give me a kick, sitting in as it were on a conference between the President and the Secretary of State! But anyway: "I heard him talking to the Secretary," Mr. Jones told me, "and he said, 'Frank, big navies cost a lot of money, and in my opinion it would be a saving if we could get the different nations to reduce them.'"

"Well, well, I'm mighty glad to find that out, Mr. Jones," I said, "and it confirms my own opinion about disarmament. Say, tell me," I says, "how does the President live, in his personal life? What does he take for breakfast?"

Well, Mr. Jones explained that the President took a simple breakfast just like the rest of us — just some coffee and toast and eggs and porridge and so on. I was mighty proud and glad to hear that Cal was unspoiled by all his fame and was still just the same simple direct fellow he'd been when we were chums.

"What does the President think of the situation in China?" I asked Mr. Jones.

"Well I think I can say without violating any confidence that, in opposition to the opinion of certain Senators, the President feels the situation is serious and in fact almost critical, and that — but this musn't go any farther," Mr. Jones told me, "he feels decidedly that while the rights and properties of the Great Powers must be safeguarded, yet we must consider patiently and fairly the rights of the Chinese themselves."

"Well, sir, I certainly am interested to hear that," I told him. "There's no question about it. That's exactly how I feel myself."

You see, I'd had a kind of you might say special opportunity of getting the real inside dope about the Chinese situation and the Bolshevik influence there. I heard a missionary just recently back from the scene of disturbance in China, speak at the Wednesday Evening Supper at our church — the Pilgrim Congregational Church of Zenith — Dr. G. Prosper Edwards is the pastor, very famous pulpit orator, you've quite probably heard him on the radio, tunes in on WWWL every second Sunday morning at eleven-fifteen, very eloquent man and a ripsnorting good scholar, too — but very liberal. As he always says, he's more than ready to fellowship with any Christian body, no matter what their differences in theology are, providing they merely accept the fundamental and indisputable elements of Christianity, such as the Virgin Birth and the proven fact of afterlife.

I tell you how I feel about religion, anyway.

I'm a Congregationalist myself, and it isn't for one second just because I happened to be born one, as one of these smart-aleck agnostics was trying to prove to me one day, but because of my deep reverence for the great leaders of the church, like Jonathan Edwards and Roger Baldwin — no, come to think of it, he was a Baptist, wasn't he, that Rhode Island guy?

But anyway: just the same today: fellows like Newell Dwight Hillis and S. Parks Cadman, that during the World War they did as much to win the struggle for world-wide democracy as any soldier, the way they showed up the secret plans of Germany to dominate the world — and the way Dr. Cadman writes this column in the newspapers; say, he knows just about everything, and he can clear up your troubles about anything, whether it's an incurable sickness or who wrote Shakespeare — yes sir, a real big typical American leader.

But same time, way I look at it, the other denominations — the Methodists and Baptists and Presbyterians and Campbellites — they're all working together to make a greater and purer America.

Our generation, I guess we still got a lot of the Old Harry in us. Me, I admit, I smoke and I sometimes take a little drink — but never to excess; if there's anything I despise it's a man that can't hold his liquor. And I do like a nice drive on Sunday, and sometimes I cuss a little, and I guess I ain't above looking at a pretty ankle even yet. But it's my firm belief — maybe you gentlemen never thought about it this way — if we'll just support the churches and give the preachers a chance, a generation will come which won't even *want* to do those things, and then America will stand forth before the world such a nation as has never been seen, yes sir, and I'm mighty glad to fellowship with Methodists or —

Not that I think so much of these Christian Scientists and Seventh Day Adventists and all them, though. They carry things too far, and I don't believe in going to extremes in anything; and as for the Catholics — I hope none of you gentlemen are Catholics and I wouldn't want this to go any farther, but I've always felt the Catholics were too tolerant toward drinking and smoking, and so they aren't, you might say, really hardly typically American at all.

And as to religion in general, they tell me there's a lot of smart-aleck highbrows today that are calling the truth of Christianity in question. Well, I may not be any theologian, but I wish I could meet one of these fellows, and believe me, I'd settle his hash!

"Look here," I tell him; "in the first place it stands to reason, don't it, that fellows specially trained in theology, like the preachers, know more than us laymen, don't it? And in the second, if the Christian religion has lasted two thousand years and is today stronger than ever before — just look, for instance, at that skyscraper church they're building in New York — is it likely that a little handful of you smart galoots are going to be able to change it?"

I guess they never thought of that! Trouble with fellows like agnostics is that you simply can *not* get 'em to stop and think and use their minds!

And what have they got to put in the *place* of religion? Know what the trouble with those fellows is? *They're destructive and not constructive!*

But as I was saying, our church has a regular Wednesday Evening Supper before prayer-meeting, and say, the ladies of the church certainly do serve one of the nicest suppers you ever ate, and for only forty cents — Hamburg steak with Spanish sauce, or creamed chipped beef, or corn beef and cabbage, and sometimes ice cream for dessert, all A 1. And they usually have a speaker, and this evening I was speaking of, the speaker that spoke on China was a missionary, and he gave us the real lowdown on China, and he told us it was fierce the way the Chinks were carrying on, and not respecting either their trade treaties — and what a *damn* fool thing *that* was, because here they had a chance to get in contact with America and England and all, and get civilized, and give up worshipping idols — But he showed a real Christian spirit. He said that even though the Chinks had practically kicked him out, he believed they ought to be allowed to have another chance to try to run their own country.

Well, I could see that was fair, and I was real interested to see the President agreed with him, and then I asked Mr. Jones —

"Mr. Jones," I said, "what's the real truth about the President's fishing? Is he a good fisherman?" I asked.

"He's one of the best. His catch always compares favorably with that of any other member of the party, when he sets his mind to it, but you must remember that he's constantly weighed down by the cares of the world," Mr. Jones said.

"Yes, I can see that," I told him, "and personally, I think it's a shame for some of these newspapers that haven't got anything better to write to make fun of him. Say, another thing," I asked him, "does the President belong to any of the service clubs — Rotary and Kiwanis and so on?"

"No, in his position," Mr. Jones explained to me, "in his position he couldn't hardly discriminate between them, but I think I'm not betraying any secret when I say that the President has the highest admiration for the great service and ideals of all these organizations."

Well, I was mighty glad to hear that, and I think you gentlemen will be, too, whether you belong to 'em or not. For, after all, what organizations are doing a greater good and providing more real happiness today than the service clubs, all of them, though I myself am a Kiwanian and I can't help feeling that maybe our own organization has got the edge on the other fellows — we aren't as darned snobbish as these Rotarians, and yet we aren't you might say as common as the Civitans and the Lions and — Yes sir!

Think what these clubs provide. A chance for a lot of the most responsible and forward-looking men of the community to get together once a week, and not only have a high old time, with all the dignity of our positions checked at the door, calling each other by our first names — Think of what that means! Say here's some high muckamuck of a judge; for that hour or so I can call him "Pete," and slap him on the back and kid him about his family, and stands to reason that any man enjoys having a chance to let down and be human like that.

And then the good we do! Why say, just this past year our Zenith Kiwanians have put up not less than two hundred and sixty-three highway markers within forty miles of Zenith, and we gave the kids at an orphan asylum a dandy auto ride and free feed. And believe me it was one fine ad for the Kiwanians, because we took the kids out in trucks, and each one had on it a great big red sign: "Free Outing for the Unfortunate Kiddies, Provided Free by Zenith Kiwanis Club."

But be that as it may, I was mighty glad to hear the President speak like that and to get his real inside view, and so I asks Mr. Jones, "What's, uh — what's the President's views on taxation, if it isn't impertinent to ask?"

Now, you gentlemen will be interested to learn what Mr. Jones told me, because of course that's one of the most important topics of the day, and Jones spoke right up, without hesitation:

"I know for a fact," he told me, "that the President feels that the burdens of taxations should be so equably distributed that they shall lay no undue burden on the poor and unfortunate yet at the same time they must in no sense be so prejudicial to honest business interests as to cramp the necessary conduct and expansion of commerce."

And some soreheads claim the President isn't really a deep thinker!

And then —

Almerine had just been on pins and needles at the prospect of talking with the President; couldn't hardly keep still in her chair. Mr. Jones was real nice to her, and I certainly was proud of the way one of our home girls could answer up to a man in official position like that.

"So you come from Zenith," he says to her. "Do you like it?"

"Oh, you bet," she said. "I just think Zenith is the nicest city in America. Of course I'd rather live in New York, but my, do you know we have the finest park system in the United States?"

"Is that a fact!" he says. "No, I didn't know that. And I guess you like to Charleston," he says. "Or have you gone out for the Black Bottom? Do you like it?"

"Do I?" she says. "Oh boy! I'd show you, but I guess this isn't the place."

"No, I'm afraid it isn't," he says, and we all four bust right out laughing together — wasn't that a comical idea — to dance the Charleston in the President's office!

X

I was just going to ask Mr. Jones how the President felt about Socialism when there was a messenger boy come out and called Mr. Jones in and he was gone about a couple minutes, it couldn't have been more than that, and he come back, and say, he did look real sorry.

"I've got terrible news," he told me. "The President was just ready to see you when the British ambassador come in with some specially important business, and then he has to hustle down to the *Mayflower* — that's his yacht — and be gone maybe forty-five days, on an important secret conference. But he hopes you'll drop in any time you're in Washington."

So you gentlemen can see that it isn't by accident but by real thinking and good fellowship that President Coolidge — yes, or any other President we've had recently — maintains his position, and I hope I haven't bored you, and now I'll dry up and let some other fellow talk and —

But just to speak of Socialism a moment —

I'm willing to give every man a fair square deal, but when it comes to supporting a lot of loafers, the way I look at it is that constructive, practical people like ourselves, who control the country, ought, you might say —

GO DOWN, DEATH!

A Funeral Sermon

By James Weldon Johnson

Weep not, weep not,
  She is not dead;
She's resting in the bosom of Jesus.
Heart-broken husband — weep no more;
Grief-stricken son — weep no more;
Left-lonesome daughter — weep no more;
She's only just gone home.

Day before yesterday morning,
God was looking down from His great, high Heaven,
Looking down on all His children,
And His eye fell on Sister Caroline,
Tossing on her bed of pain.
And God's big heart was touched with pity,
With the everlasting pity.

And God sat back on His throne,
And He commanded that tall, bright angel standing at His right hand,
Call me Death!
And that tall, bright angel cried in a voice
That broke like a clap of thunder,
Call Death! Call Death!
And the echo sounded down the streets of Heaven
Till it reached away back to that shadowy place
Where Death waits with his pale, white horses.

JAMES WELDON JOHNSON, *who died in 1938, was among the top-rank Negro novelists and poets. His books include* The Autobiography of an Ex-Colored Man, The Book of American Negro Poetry *and* God's Trombones. *When "Go Down, Death!" first appeared it created an immediate sensation in literary circles and today, seventeen years after, it remains one of the most powerful poems in American literature.* (April, 1927)

And Death heard the summons,
And he leaped on his fastest horse,
Pale as a sheet in the moonlight.
Up the golden street Death galloped,
And the hoofs of his horse struck fire from the gold,
But they didn't make no sound.
Up Death rode to the great, white throne,
And waited for God's command.

And God said, Go down, Death, go down,
Go down to Savannah, Georgia,
Down in Yamacraw,
And find Sister Caroline.
She's borne the burden and heat of the day,
She's labored long in my vineyard,
And she's tired —
She's weary —
Go down, Death, and bring her to me.

And Death didn't say a word,
But he loosed the reins on his pale, white horse,
And he clamped the spurs to his bloodless sides,
And out and down he rode,
Through Heaven's pearly gates,
Past suns and moons and stars.
On Death rode,
And the foam from his horse was like a comet in the sky;
On Death rode,
Leaving the lightning's flash behind,
Straight on down he came.

While we were watching round her bed,
She turned her eyes and looked away,
She saw what we couldn't see;
She saw old Death. She saw old Death,
Coming like a falling star.
But Death didn't frighten Sister Caroline;
He looked to her like a welcome friend.
And she whispered to us, I'm going home,
And she smiled and closed her eyes.

GO DOWN, DEATH!

And Death took her up like a baby,
And she lay in his icy arms,
But she didn't feel no chill.
And Death began to ride again —
Up beyond the evening star,
Out beyond the morning star,
Into the glittering light of glory,
On to the great white throne.
And there he laid Sister Caroline
On the loving breast of Jesus.

And Jesus took His own hand and wiped away her tears,
And He smoothed the furrows from her face,
And the angels sang a little song,
And Jesus rocked her in His arms,
And kept a-saying, Take your rest,
Take your rest, take your rest!

Weep not — weep not,
She is not dead;
She's resting in the bosom of Jesus.

WILLIAM JENNINGS BRYAN

By H. L. Mencken

Has it been marked by historians that the late William Jennings Bryan's last secular act on this earth was to catch flies? A curious detail, and not without its sardonic overtones. He was the most sedulous flycatcher in American history, and by long odds the most successful. His quarry, of course, was not *Musca domestica* but *Homo neandertalensis*. For forty years he tracked it with snare and blunderbuss, up and down the backways of the Republic. Wherever the flambeaux of Chautauqua smoked and guttered, and the bilge of Idealism ran in the veins, and Baptist pastors dammed the brooks with the saved, and men gathered who were weary and heavy laden, and their wives who were unyieldingly multiparous and full of Peruna — there the indefatigable Jennings set up his traps and spread his bait.

He knew every forlorn country town in the South and West, and he could crowd the most remote of them to suffocation by simply winding his horn. The city proletariat, transiently flustered by him in 1896, quickly penetrated his buncombe and would have no more of him; the gallery jeered him at every Democratic national convention for twenty-five years. But out where the grass grows high, and the horned cattle dream away the lazy days, and men still fear the powers and principalities of the air — out there between the corn-rows he held his old puissance to the end. There was no need of beaters to drive in his game. The news that he was coming was enough. For miles the flivver dust would choke the roads. And when he rose at the end of the day to discharge his Message there would be such breathless attention, such a rapt and enchanted ecstasy, such a sweet rustle of amens as the world had not known since Johanan fell to Herod's headsman.

There was something peculiarly fitting in the fact that his last days were spent in a one-horse Tennessee village, and that death found him there. The man felt at home in such scenes. He liked people who sweated freely, and were not debauched by the refinements of the toilet. Making his progress up and down the Main street of little Dayton, surrounded by gaping primates from the upland valleys

---

H. L. MENCKEN'S *powers as a satirist and master of the English language are amply exemplified in this obituary of William Jennings Bryan. Mr. Mencken had attended the sensational "monkey trial" in Knoxville, Tennessee, where he heard Bryan, an orator, statesman and theologian of national reputation, oppose the teaching of evolution in the public schools, only to be verbally massacred by the late Clarence Darrow, counsel for the defence.* (October, 1925)

of the Cumberland Range, his coat laid aside, his bare arms and hairy chest shining damply, his bald head sprinkled with dust — so accoutred and on display he was obviously happy. He liked getting up early in the morning, to the tune of cocks crowing on the dunghill. He liked the heavy, greasy victuals of the farmhouse kitchen. He liked country lawyers, country pastors, all country people. I believe that this liking was sincere — perhaps the only sincere thing in the man.

His nose showed no uneasiness when a hillman in faded overalls and hickory shirt accosted him on the street, and besought him for light upon some mystery of Holy Writ. The simian gabble of a country town was not gabble to him, but wisdom of an occult and superior sort. In the presence of city folks he was palpably uneasy. Their clothes, I suspect, annoyed him, and he was suspicious of their too delicate manners. He knew all the while that they were laughing at him — if not at his baroque theology, then at least at his alpaca pantaloons. But the yokels never laughed at him. To them he was not the huntsman but the prophet, and toward the end, as he gradually forsook mundane politics for purely ghostly concerns, they began to elevate him in their hierarchy. When he died he was the peer of Abraham. Another curious detail: his old enemy, Wilson, aspiring to the same white and shining robe, came down with a thump. But Bryan made the grade. His place in the Tennessee hagiocracy is secure. If the village barber saved any of his hair, then it is curing gallstones down there today.

II

But what label will he bear in more urban regions? One, I fear, of a far less flattering kind. Bryan lived too long, and descended too deeply into the mud, to be taken seriously hereafter by fully literate men, even of the kind who write schoolbooks. There was a scattering of sweet words in his funeral notices, but it was no more than a response to conventional sentimentality. The best verdict the most romantic editorial writer could dredge up, save in the eloquent South, was to the general effect that his imbecilities were excused by his earnestness — that under his clowning, as under that of the juggler of Notre Dame, there was the zeal of a steadfast soul. But this was apology, not praise; precisely the same thing might be said of Mary Baker G. Eddy, the late Czar Nicholas, or Czolgosz. The truth is that even Bryan's sincerity will probably yield to what is called, in other fields, definitive criticism. Was he sincere when he opposed imperialism in the Philippines, or when he fed it with deserving Democrats in Santo Domingo? Was he sincere when he tried to shove the Prohibitionists under the table, or when he seized their banner and began to lead them with loud whoops? Was he sincere when he bellowed against war, or when he dreamed of himself as a tin-soldier in uniform, with a grave reserved among the generals? Was he sincere when he denounced the late John W. Davis, or when he swallowed Davis? Was he sincere when he fawned over Champ Clark, or when he betrayed Clark? Was he sincere when he pleaded for tolerance in

New York, or when he bawled for the fagot and the stake in Tennessee?

This talk of sincerity, I confess, fatigues me. If the fellow was sincere, then so was P. T. Barnum. The word is disgraced and degraded by such uses. He was, in fact, a charlatan, a mountebank, a zany without shame or dignity. What animated him from end to end of his grotesque career was simply ambition — the ambition of a common man to get his hand upon the collar of his superiors, or, failing that, to get his thumb into their eyes.

He was born with a roaring voice, and it had the trick of inflaming half-wits. His whole career was devoted to raising these half-wits against their betters, that he himself might shine. His last battle will be grossly misunderstood if it is thought of as a mere exercise in fanaticism — that is, if Bryan the Fundamentalist Pope is mistaken for one of the bucolic Fundamentalists. There was much more in it than that, as everyone knows who saw him on the field. What moved him, at bottom, was simply hatred of the city men who had laughed at him so long, and brought him at last to so tatterdemalion an estate. He lusted for revenge upon them. He yearned to lead the anthropoid rabble against them, to set *Homo neandertalensis* upon them, to punish them for the execution they had done upon him by attacking the very vitals of their civilization. He went far beyond the bounds of any merely religious frenzy, however inordinate. When he began denouncing the notion that man is a mammal even some of the hinds at Dayton were agape. And when, brought upon Darrow's cruel hook, he writhed and tossed in a very fury of malignancy, bawling against the baldest elements of sense and decency like a man frantic — when he came to that tragic climax there were snickers among the hinds as well as hosannas.

Upon that hook, in truth, Bryan committed suicide, as a legend as well as in the body. He staggered from the rustic court ready to die, and he staggered from it ready to be forgotten, save as a character in a third-rate farce, witless and in execrable taste. The chances are that history will put the peak of democracy in his time; it has been on the downward curve among us since the campaign of 1896.

He will be remembered, perhaps, as its supreme impostor, the *reductio ad absurdum* of its pretension. Bryan came very near being President of the United States. In 1896, it is possible, he was actually elected. He lived long enough to make patriots thank the inscrutable gods for Harding, even for Coolidge. Dullness has got into the White House, and the smell of cabbage boiling, but there is at least nothing to compare to the intolerable buffoonery that went on in Tennessee. The President of the United States doesn't believe that the earth is square, and that witches should be put to death, and that Jonah swallowed the whale. The Golden Text is not painted weekly on the White House wall, and there is no need to keep ambassadors waiting while Pastor Simpson, of Smithsville, prays for rain in the Blue Room. We have escaped something — by a narrow margin, but still safely.

III

That is, so far. The Fundamentalists continue at the wake, and sense gets a sort of reprieve. The legislature of Georgia, so the news comes, has shelved the anti-evolution bill, and turns its back upon the legislature of Tennessee. Elsewhere minorities prepare for battle — here and there with some assurance of success. But it is too early, it seems to me, to send the firemen home; the fire is still burning on many a far-flung hill, and it may begin to roar again at any moment. The evil that men do lives after them. Bryan, in his malice, started something that it will not be easy to stop. In ten thousand country towns his old heelers, the evangelical pastors, are propagating his gospel, and everywhere the yokels are ready for it. When he disappeared from the big cities, the big cities made the capital error of assuming that he was done for. If they heard of him at all, it was only as a crimp for real-estate speculators — the heroic foe of the unearned increment hauling it in with both hands. He seemed preposterous, and hence harmless. But all the while he was busy among his old lieges, preparing for a *jacquerie* that should floor all his enemies at one blow. He did the job competently. He had vast skill at such enterprises. Heave an egg out of a Pullman window, and you will hit a Fundamentalist almost anywhere in the United States today. They swarm in the country towns, inflamed by their pastors, and with a saint, now, to venerate. They are thick in the mean streets behind the gasworks. They are everywhere that learning is too heavy a burden for mortal minds, even the vague, pathetic learning on tap in little red schoolhouses. They march with the Klan, with the Christian Endeavor Society, with the Junior Order of United American Mechanics, with the Epworth League, with all the rococo bands that poor and unhappy folk organize to bring some light of purpose into their lives. They have had a thrill, and they are ready for more.

Such is Bryan's legacy to his country. He couldn't be President, but he could at least help magnificently in the solemn business of shutting off the Presidency from every intelligent and self-respecting man. The storm, perhaps, won't last long, as time goes in history. It may help, indeed, to break up the democratic delusion, now already showing weakness, and so hasten its own end. But while it lasts it will blow off some roofs and flood some sanctuaries.

WHAT IS A STATESMAN?

By Charles A. Beard

WHAT are the qualifications or characteristics which mark the statesman off from the great horde of more commonplace persons who concern themselves with government? What is it that gives him distinction and enduring fame? This is a question which has received little consideration at the hands of those who have written on the evolution of political society. Carlyle, it is true, stormed a great deal on the subject and ended with the general conclusion that the statesman is a genius, a hero, a sort of divine messenger sent now and then to set the weary world aright. The Marxians at the other end of the pole dismiss the statesman with a scoff as a mere automaton produced by a complex of economic forces. But neither of these answers is an answer. Each is a sort of categorical imperative: believe or be damned. Neither satisfies the requirements of the scientific spirit any more than the Miltonic account of creation or the Japanese myth of the Sun Goddess.

Trouble begins when inquiry is made as to who are the statesmen of any nation. At the very outset many of Carlyle's heroes and statesmen are dismissed by the special and the general as no heroes or statesmen at all, but mere evanescent windbags. It also appears, if popular esteem be taken into account, that the same person is a statesman to some part of the public and a demagogue and charlatan to the remainder. Still more curiously, a man who is celebrated as a statesman by one generation is dismissed from the school books and biographical dictionaries with a scant bow by the next generation. Are there not times when Napoleon the Great is the hero of France and other times when Pasteur receives the homage of the people? Was not John C. Calhoun the orator, statesman, and philosopher of the Far South and the incarnate demon of the Garrison-Phillips school? Bismarck, the Iron Chancellor, the maker of modern Germany, the successor of Frederick the Great, was a towering figure in the history books written between 1890 and 1914. He flouted the talkative members of the Frankfort Assembly — those loquacious professors who sought to make a national constitution out of paper instead of iron and

---

CHARLES A. BEARD, *dean of American historians, is the author of some two dozen books, the latest of which is* The Republic. *Perhaps the best known of his other books are* Economic Interpretation of the Constitution *and* The Rise of American Civilization, *the latter of which he wrote in collaboration with his wife,* Mary R. Beard. (April, 1924)

blood. He dismissed the windy Liberals of the Prussian Diet and built up a Prussian army in spite of their protests. He waged war on Austria and cleared that troublesome member out of the German Union. He made a constitution that gave Hans and Fritz a delusive representation in a national parliament. He outwitted Napoleon the Little in diplomacy and war; he created an Empire on the spot where Louis XIV once disported himself. Having launched the new state he guided its destinies until William the Small dismissed the safe pilot and ran the ship on the rocks. Surely here was a maker of great events out of his own wisdom and will. So it seems.

Yet there are many now who have grave doubts about the majesty of Bismarck, after all. If he had helped the Frankfort professors instead of kicking them down stairs, he might have made the transition to a constitutional democracy less tragic for the German nation. If he had picked no quarrel with Napoleon III, there would have been no *revanche*. With a characteristic gesture of omnipotence, he sought to silence Socialists first by clapping them into jail and then by stealing their thunder with social legislation. In vain. When puny big men had run his ship ashore in the autumn of 1918 it was only the hated Socialists who were prepared to take the hulk and keep her from pounding to pieces. In the light of cruel disillusionment, where does Bismarck stand?

Now take Gladstone. If all the school children throughout the English-speaking world were called upon to name two English statesmen of enduring fame, the Sage of Hawarden would be one of them. Yet how many who instinctively choose Gladstone could associate with his career one monumental achievement? What modern Liberal in England bases his appeal on the policies of Gladstone? In theological and scientific controversies he was a pigmy. In classical disputes he was approved principally by those who knew no Greek. He was a formidable debater, and yet to the Tories he was a man "intoxicated with the exuberance of his own verbosity." Liberal, humane, and evangelical, even when dealing with the Turk, Gladstone was idolized by those English bourgeois who refused to read a Sunday paper. Nevertheless in foreign and domestic policy, how far did he foresee the fate of England and prepare her for it? Even in his own sphere of Liberalism, it must be remembered, Disraeli dished him in 1867 by granting the suffrage to the working classes of England and later by formulating many enlightened measures of social legislation. The empire over the minds of men, which Gladstone built up in many long decades, vanished at his death. He left no heritage to his party, except that of defeat. And when the Liberal machine rose again to power in 1906 it was not his party but the party of the Welsh prestidigitator with his famous budget and his still more famous war. What and where is the Gladstone tradition? Even the friendly and facile Morley with three big volumes at his disposal could not create it. Read the speeches and books of young Liberals and see how few even refer to Gladstone — much less take inspiration from him.

II

Those who have carried on a long flirtation with the changeful Clio can readily show how fickle is the fame of any statesman. An ingenious mannerist like Strachey can even make the non-conformist conscience crackle with merriment over the downfall of the choicest gods. Indeed, the process has been carried forward with such zeal in every historical quarter that the satirist, Philip Guedalla, is driven to the conclusion that the fate of a politician depends upon the character of his exit from the stage of his labors! If he goes off with banners flying, orchestra thundering, and crowds roaring, his niche in history is likely to be secure. If he is shot by the villain in the last act, and the curtain goes down to soft music, with the heroine bending low over him, then he is sure to take a place among the national gods. But if, after a thrilling display of the histrionic arts, he catches his toe on a torn rug and falls flat on his face amid jeers and tears — of laughter — he is promptly shot into the lumber room.

Illustrations of Mr. Guedalla's ingenious theory may be taken from any historical arsenal. One trembles to think of what would have happened to the gentle and majestic Lincoln if he had lived through the grewsome days of Reconstruction, the Credit Mobilier, and the Star Route frauds, and spent his declining years, toothless and bald, tottering around the streets of Springfield, Illinois. How much poorer in spirit the American nation would be! One is dismayed in trying to imagine [Theodore] Roosevelt, full of zeal and ambition at the age of seventy, beating his restless soul against the iron bars of circumstance and commonplace with Coolidge and Daugherty grinning in the background. Suppose the would-be assassin who shot at Clemenceau during the Peace Conference had done the victim to death; imagine the funeral cortege of the Tiger passing under the Triumphal Arch, the tears of a grateful nation, and the orations by the saints of the *Action Libérale!*

Still, it is well to remember that many politicians and princes have been shot without winning a place on the honor roll. A president of France was assassinated a few years ago. Who remembers his name? Could all the stage managers in the world, from the age of Euripides to the age of Charles Chaplin, fix up a more tragic setting for the exit of a political leader than the immortal gods arranged for Maximilian of Mexico? A scion of royalty who, under the tutelage of Napoleon III, was to restore the balance of the world by setting up an empire is shot by a firing squad and his unhappy princess is swept down the stream of sixty years a hopeless maniac!

There is something in exits, but not much. Drums and funeral notes die away with unseemly haste and the rude janitor sweeps out the faded flowers.

If it is not the exit that makes the statesman, is it brains? Not brains alone. A man may be well equipped with powerful engines of logic and controversy and well stocked with knowledge, and yet, if he runs against the current of the long time, he passes away as grass that withers. How many read Bossuet now? And yet Bossuet was infinitely superior in intellect to Rousseau. Madison was one of the brainiest men in our Homeric Age; how many regard him as a statesman? In supercilious Boston he is more often remembered as the author of Mr. Madison's War which prevented business from going on as usual. If not brains, then is it morals? Well, Mr. Bryan's character is above reproach. Would anyone put him higher in the scale of fame than Benjamin Franklin, whose morals, to speak softly, were marred by a certain carelessness? Is it ideals clung to unflinchingly until death? For every martyr who achieves fame there are a thousand cranks stoned by the mob and consigned to oblivion.

After this negative review, let me hazard a guess. The statesman is one who divines the long future, foresees the place of his class and nation in it, labors intelligently to prepare his countrymen for their fate, combines courage with discretion, takes risks, has good luck, exercises caution where it is necessary, and goes off the stage with a reasonable degree of respectability. He must have brains — some, at least. He must have morals — some, at least. He must have ideals — but only those which are justified in the economy of Providence. He must be able to reconcile himself without complaining to the inexorable movement which the skeptical call the grand *pis aller* and the devout the divine plan. He must not only see; he must appear to be achieving in the current of things. Above all, he must be justified by events, that is, by good fortune. Perhaps beyond reason and understanding both Carlyle and Marx may be reconciled, a little bit. Meanwhile the mystery must not be entirely cleared up. Otherwise the game of politics would lose its savor.

DEATH IN THE WOODS

By Sherwood Anderson

She was an old woman and lived on a farm near the town in which I lived. All country and small town people have seen such old women, but no one knows much about them. Such an old woman comes into town driving an old worn-out horse or she comes afoot carrying a basket. She may own a few hens and have eggs to sell. She brings them in a basket and takes them to a grocer. There she trades them in. She gets some salt pork and some beans. Then she gets a pound or two of sugar and some flour.

Afterwards she goes to the butcher's and asks for some dog-meat. She may spend ten or fifteen cents, but when she does she asks for something. In my day the butchers gave liver to anyone who wanted to carry it away. In our family we were always having it. Once one of my brothers got a whole cow's liver at the slaughter-house near the fair-grounds. We had it until we were sick of it. It never cost a cent. I have hated the thought of it ever since.

The old farm woman got some liver and a soup-bone. She never visited with anyone and as soon as she got what she wanted she lit out for home. It made quite a load for such an old body. No one gave her a lift. People drive right down a road and never notice an old woman like that.

There was such an old woman used to come into town past our house one summer and fall when I was sick with what was called inflammatory rheumatism. She went home later carrying a heavy pack on her back. Two or three large gaunt-looking dogs followed at her heels.

The old woman was nothing special. She was one of the nameless ones that hardly anyone knows, but she got into my thoughts. I have just suddenly now, after all these years, remembered her and what happened. It is a story. Her name was, I think, Grimes, and she lived with her husband and son in a small unpainted house on the bank of a small creek four miles from town.

The husband and son were a tough lot. Although the son was but twenty-one, he had already served a term in jail. It was whispered about that the woman's husband stole horses and ran them off to

---

SHERWOOD ANDERSON, *who died in 1941, was one of the most accomplished short story writers this country has produced. His* Winesburg, Ohio *and* The Triumph of the Egg, *his two best known collections, will probably be read a hundred years from today. "Death in the Woods," here reprinted, was written later but it clearly belongs among his most brilliant stories.* (September, 1926)

some other county. Now and then, when a horse turned up missing, the man had also disappeared. No one ever caught him. Once, when I was loafing at Tom Whitehead's livery-barn, the man came there and sat on the bench in front. Two or three other men were there, but no one spoke to him. He sat for a few minutes and then got up and went away. When he was leaving he turned around and stared at the men. There was a look of defiance in his eyes. "Well, I have tried to be friendly. You don't want to talk to me. It has been so wherever I have gone in this town. If, some day, one of your fine horses turns up missing, well, then what?" He did not say anything actually. "I'd like to bust one of you on the jaw," was about what his eyes said. I remember how the look in his eyes made me shiver.

The old man belonged to a family that had had money once. His name was Grimes, Jake Grimes. It all comes back clearly now. His father, John Grimes, had owned a sawmill when the country was new and had made money. Then he got to drinking and running after women. When he died there wasn't much left.

Jake blew in the rest. Pretty soon there wasn't any more lumber to cut and his land was nearly all gone.

He got his wife off a German farmer, for whom he went to work one June day in the wheat harvest. She was a young thing then and scared to death. You see, the farmer was up to something with the girl — she was, I think, a bound girl and his wife had her suspicions. She took it out on the girl when the man wasn't around. Then, when the wife had to go off to town for supplies, the farmer got after her. She told young Jake that nothing really ever happened, but he didn't know whether to believe it or not.

He got her pretty easy himself, the first time he was out with her. He wouldn't have married her if the German farmer hadn't tried to tell him where to get off. He got her to go riding with him in his buggy one night when he was threshing on the place, and then he came for her the next Sunday night.

She managed to get out of the house without her employer's seeing, but when she was getting into the buggy he showed up. It was almost dark, and he just popped up suddenly at the horse's head. He grabbed the horse by the bridle and Jake got out his buggy-whip.

They had it out all right! The German was a tough one. Maybe he didn't care whether his wife knew or not. Jake hit him over the face and shoulders with the buggy-whip, but the horse got to acting up and he had to get out.

Then the two men went for it. The girl didn't see it. The horse started to run away and went nearly a mile down the road before the girl got him stopped. Then she managed to tie him to a tree beside the road. (I wonder how I know all this. It must have stuck in my mind from small town tales when I was a boy.) Jake found her there after he got through with the German. She was huddled up in the buggy seat, crying, scared to death. She told Jake a lot of stuff, how the German had tried to get her, how he chased her once into the barn, how another time, when they happened to be alone in the barn together, he tore her dress open clear down the front. The German, she said, might have got her that time if he hadn't heard his old woman drive in at the gate. She had been off to town for supplies. Well, she would be putting the horse in the barn. The German managed to sneak off to the fields without his wife seeing. He told the girl he would kill her if she told. What could she do? She told a lie about ripping her dress in the barn when she was feeding the stock. I remember now that she was a bound girl and did not know where her father and mother were. Maybe she did not have any father. You know what I mean.

II

She married Jake and had a son and daughter but the daughter died.

Then she settled down to feed stock. That was her job. At the German's place she had cooked the food for the German and his wife. The wife was a strong woman with big hips and worked most of the time in the fields with her husband. She fed them and fed the cows in the barn, fed the pigs, the horses and the chickens. Every moment of every day as a young girl was spent feeding something.

Then she married Jake Grimes and he had to be fed. She was a slight thing and when she had been married for three or four years, and after the two children were born, her slender shoulders became stooped.

Jake always had a lot of big dogs around the house, that stood near the unused sawmill near the creek. He was always trading horses when he wasn't stealing something and had a lot of poor bony ones about. Also he kept three or four pigs and a cow. They were all pastured in the few acres left of the Grimes place and Jake did little.

He went into debt for a threshing outfit and ran it for several years, but it did not pay. People did not trust him. They were afraid he would steal the grain at night. He had to go a long way off to get work and it cost too much to get there. In the winter he hunted and cut a little firewood, to be sold in some nearby town. When the boy grew up he was just like his father. They got drunk together. If there wasn't anything to eat in the house when they came home the old man gave his old woman a cut over the head. She had a few chickens of her own and had to kill one of them in a hurry. When they were all killed she wouldn't have any eggs to sell when she went to town, and then what would she do?

She had to scheme all her life about getting things fed, getting the pigs fed so they would grow fat and could be butchered in the fall. When they were butchered her husband took most of the meat off to town and sold it. If he did not do it first the boy did. They fought sometimes and when they fought the old woman stood aside trembling.

She had got the habit of silence anyway — that was fixed. Sometimes, when she began to look old — she wasn't forty yet — and when the husband and son were both off, trading horses or drinking or hunting or stealing, she went around the house and the barnyard muttering to herself.

How was she going to get everything fed? — that was her problem. The dogs had to be fed. There wasn't enough hay in the barn for the horses and the cow. If she didn't feed the chickens how could they lay eggs? Without eggs to sell how could she get things in town, things she had to have to keep the life of the farm going? Thank heaven, she did not have to feed her husband — in a certain way. That hadn't lasted long after their marriage and after the babies came. Where he went on his long trips she did not know. Sometimes he was gone from home for weeks and after the boy grew up they went off together.

They left everything at home for her to manage and she had no money. She knew no one. No one ever talked to her in town. When it was winter she had to gather sticks of wood for her fire, had to try to keep the stock fed with very little grain.

The stock in the barn cried to her hungrily, the dogs followed her about. In the winter the hens laid few enough eggs. They huddled in the corners of the barn and she kept watching them. If a hen lays an egg in the barn in the winter and you do not find it, it freezes and breaks.

One day in winter the old woman went off to town with a few eggs and the dogs followed her. She did not get started until nearly three o'clock and the snow was heavy. She hadn't been feeling very well for several days and so she went muttering along, scantily clad, her shoulders stooped. She had an old grain bag in which she carried her eggs, tucked away down in the bottom. There weren't many of them, but in winter the price of eggs is up. She would get a little meat for the eggs, some salt pork, a little sugar, and some coffee perhaps. It might be the butcher would give her a piece of liver.

When she had got to town and was trading in her eggs the dogs lay by the door outside. She did pretty well, got the things she needed, more than she had hoped. Then she went to the butcher and he gave her some liver and some dog-meat.

It was the first time anyone had spoken to her in a friendly way for a long time. The butcher was alone in his shop when she went in and was annoyed by the thought of such a sick-looking old woman out on such a day. It was bitter cold and the snow, that had let up during the afternoon, was falling again. The butcher said something about her husband and her son, swore at them, and the old woman stared at him, a look of mild surprise in her eyes as he talked. He said that if either the husband or the son were going to get any of the liver or the heavy bones with scraps of meat hanging to them that he had put into the grain bag, he'd see him starve first.

Starve, eh? Well things had to be fed. Men had to be fed, and the horses that weren't any good but maybe could be traded off, and the poor thin cow that hadn't given any milk for three months.

Horses, cows, pigs, dogs, men.

III

The old woman had to get back before darkness came if she could. The dogs followed at her heels, sniffing at the heavy grain bag she had fastened on her back.

When she got to the edge of town she stopped by a fence and tied the bag on her back with a piece of rope she had carried in her dress pocket for just that purpose. That was an easier way to carry it. Her arms ached. It was hard when she had to crawl over fences and once she fell over and landed in the snow. The dogs went frisking about. She had to struggle to get to her feet again but she made it. The point of climbing over the fences was that there was a short cut over a hill and through a wood. She might have gone around by the road, but it was a mile further that way. She was afraid she couldn't make it. And then, besides, the stock had to be fed. There was a little hay left, a little corn. Perhaps her husband and son would bring some home when they came. They had driven off in the only buggy the Grimes family had, a rickety thing, a rickety horse hitched to the buggy, two other rickety horses led by halters. They were going to trade horses, get a little money if they could. They might come home drunk. It would be well to have something in the house when they came back.

The son had an affair on with a woman at the county seat, fifteen miles away. She was a bad woman, a tough one. Once, in the summer, the son had brought her to the house. Both she and the son had been drinking. Jake Grimes was away and the son and his woman ordered the old woman about like a servant. She didn't mind much; she was used to it. Whatever happened she never said anything. That was her way of getting along. She had managed that way when she was a young girl at the German's and ever since she had married Jake. That time her son brought his woman to the house they stayed all night, sleeping together just as though they were married. It hadn't shocked the old woman, not much. She had got past being shocked early in life.

With the pack on her back she went painfully along across an open field, wading in the deep snow, and got into the woods.

There was a path, but it was hard to follow. Just beyond the top of the hill, where the wood was thickest, there was a small clearing. Had someone once thought of building a house there? The clearing was as large as a building lot in town, large enough for a house and a garden. The path ran along the side of the clearing and when she got there the old woman sat down to rest at the foot of a tree.

It was a foolish thing to do. When she got herself placed, the pack against the tree's trunk, it was nice, but what about getting up again? She worried about that for a moment and then quietly closed her eyes.

She must have slept for a time. When you are about so cold you can't get any colder. The afternoon grew a little warmer and the snow came thicker than ever. Then after a time the weather cleared. The moon even came out.

There were four Grimes dogs that had followed Mrs. Grimes into town, all tall, gaunt fellows. Such men as Jake Grimes and his son always keep just such dogs. They kick and abuse them, but they stay. The Grimes dogs, in order to keep from starving, had to do a lot of foraging for themselves, and they had been at it while the old woman slept with her back to the tree at the side of the clearing. They had been chasing rabbits in the woods and in adjoining fields and in their ranging had picked up three other farm dogs.

After a time all the dogs came back to the clearing. They were excited about something. Such nights, cold and clear and with a moon, do things to dogs. It may be that some old instinct, come down from the time when they were wolves and ranged the woods in packs on winter nights, comes back into them.

The dogs in the clearing, before the old woman, had caught two or three rabbits and their immediate hunger had been satisfied. They began to play, running in circles in the clearing. Round and round they ran, each dog's nose at the tail of the next dog. In the clearing, under the snow-laden trees and under the wintry moon they made a strange picture, running thus silently, in a circle their running had beaten in the soft snow. The dogs made no sound. They ran around and around in the circle.

It may have been that the old woman saw them doing that before she died. She may have awakened once or twice and looked at the strange sight with dim old eyes. She wouldn't be very cold now, just drowsy. Life hangs on a long time. Perhaps the old woman was out of her head. She may have dreamed of her girlhood at the German's, and before that, when she was a child and before her mother lit out and left her.

Her dreams couldn't have been very pleasant. Not many pleasant things had happened to her. Now and then one of the Grimes dogs left the running circle and came to stand before her. The dog thrust his face close to her face. His red tongue was hanging out.

The running of the dogs may have been a kind of death ceremony. It may have been that the primitive instinct of the wolf, having been aroused in the dogs by the night and the running, made them somehow afraid.

"Now we are no longer wolves. We are dogs, the servants of men. Keep alive, man! When man dies we become wolves again."

When one of the dogs came to where the old woman sat with her back against the tree and thrust his nose close to her face he seemed satisfied and went back to run with the pack. All the Grimes dogs did it at some time during the evening, before she died. I knew all about it afterward, when I grew to be a man, because once in a wood on another winter night I saw a pack of dogs act just like that. The dogs were waiting for me to die as they had waited for the old woman that night when I was a child, but when it happened to me I was a young man and had no intention whatever of dying.

The old woman died softly and quietly. When she was dead and when one of the Grimes dogs had come to her and had found her dead all the dogs stopped running.

They gathered about her.

Well, she was dead now. She had fed the Grimes dogs when she was alive, what about now?

There was the pack on her back, the grain bag containing the piece of salt pork, the liver the butcher had given her, the dog-meat, the soup bones. The butcher in town, having been suddenly overcome with a feeling of pity, had loaded her grain bag heavily. It had been a big haul for the old woman.

A big haul for the dogs now.

IV

One of the Grimes dogs sprang suddenly out from among the others and began worrying the pack on the old woman's back. Had the dogs really been wolves that one would have been the leader of the pack. What he did, all the others did.

All of them sank their teeth into the grain bag the old woman had fastened with ropes to her back.

They dragged the old woman's body out into the open clearing. The worn-out dress was quickly torn from her shoulders. When she was found, a day or two later, the dress had been torn from her body clear to the hips but the dogs had not touched her body. They had got the meat out of the grain bag, that was all. Her body was frozen stiff when it was found and the shoulders were so narrow and the body so slight that in death it looked like the body of some charming young girl.

Such things happened in towns of the Middle West, on farms near town, when I was a boy. A hunter out after rabbits found the old woman's body and did not touch it. Something, the beaten round path in the little snow-covered clearing, the silence of the place, the place where the dogs had worried the body trying to pull the grain bag away or tear it open — something startled the man and he hurried off to town.

I was in Main Street with one of my brothers who was taking the afternoon papers to the stores. It was almost night.

The hunter came into a grocery and told his story. Then he went to a hardware shop and into a drugstore. Men began to gather on the sidewalks. Then they started out along the road to the place in the wood.

My brother should have gone on about his business of distributing papers but he didn't. Everyone was going to the woods. The undertaker went and the town marshal. Several men got on a dray and rode out to where the path left the road and went into the woods, but the horses weren't very sharply shod and slid about on the slippery roads. They made no better time than those of us who walked.

The town marshal was a large man whose leg had been injured in the Civil War. He carried a heavy cane and limped rapidly along the road. My brother and I followed at his heels and as we went other men and boys joined the crowd.

It had grown dark by the time we got to where the old woman had left the road but the moon had come out. The marshal was thinking there might have been a murder. He kept asking the hunter questions. The hunter went along with his gun across his shoulders, a dog following at his heels. It isn't often a rabbit hunter has a chance to be so conspicuous. He was taking full advantage of it, leading the procession with the town marshal. "I didn't see any wounds. She was a beautiful young girl. Her face was buried in the snow. No, I didn't know her." As a matter of fact, the hunter had not looked closely at the body. He had been frightened. She might have been murdered and someone might spring out from behind a tree and murder him too. In a woods, in the late afternoon, when the trees are all bare and there is white snow on the ground, when all is silent, something creepy steals over the mind and body. If something strange or uncanny has happened in the neighborhood all you think about is getting away from there as fast as you can.

The crowd of men and boys had got to where the old woman crossed the field and went, following the marshal and the hunter, up the slight incline and into the woods.

My brother and I were silent. He had his bundle of papers in a bag slung across his shoulder. When he got back to town he would have to go on distributing his papers before he went home to supper. If I went along, as he had no doubt already determined I should, we would both be late. Either mother or our younger sister would have to warm our supper.

Well, we would have something to tell. A boy did not get such a chance very often. It was lucky we just happened to go into the grocery when the hunter came in. The hunter was a country fellow. Neither of us had ever seen him before.

Now the crowd of men and boys had got to the clearing. Darkness comes quickly on such winter nights but the full moon made everything clear. My brother and I stood near the trees, beneath which the old woman had died.

She did not look old, lying there frozen in that light. One of the men turned her over in the snow and I saw everything. My body trembled with some strange mystical feeling and so did my brother's. It might have been the cold.

Neither of us had ever seen a woman's body before. It may have been the snow, clinging to the frozen flesh, that made it look so white and lovely, so like marble. No woman had come with the party from town, but one of the men, he was the town blacksmith, took off his overcoat and spread it over her. Then he gathered her into his arms and started off to town, all the others following silently. At that time no one knew who she was.

V

I had seen everything, had seen the oval in the snow, like a miniature race-track, where the dogs had run, had seen how the men were mystified, had seen the white bare young-looking shoulders, had heard the whispered comments of the men.

The men were simply mystified. They took the body to the undertaker's, and when the blacksmith, the hunter, the marshal and several others had got inside they closed the door. If father had been there perhaps he could have got in, but we boys couldn't.

I went with my brother to distribute the rest of his papers and when we got home it was my brother who told the story.

I kept silent and went to bed early. It may have been I was not satisfied with the way he told it.

Later, in the town, I must have heard other fragments of the old woman's story. She was recognized the next day and there was an investigation.

The husband and son were found somewhere and brought to town and there was an attempt to connect them with the woman's death, but it did not work. They had perfect enough alibis.

However, the town was against them. They had to get out. Where they went I never heard.

I remember only the picture there in the forest, the men standing about, the naked girlish-looking figure, face down in the snow, the tracks made by the running dogs and the clear cold winter sky above. White fragments of clouds were drifting across the sky. They went racing across the little open space among the trees.

The scene in the forest had become for me, without my knowing it, the foundation for the real story I am now trying to tell. The fragments, you see, had to be picked up slowly, long afterwards.

Things happened. When I was a young man I worked on the farm of a German. The hired-girl was afraid of her employer. The farmer's wife hated her.

I saw things at that place. Once later, I had a half-uncanny, mystical sort of adventure with dogs in a forest on a clear, moonlit winter night. When I was a schoolboy, and on a summer day, I went with a boy friend out along a creek some miles from town and came to the house where the old woman had lived. No one had lived in the house since her death. The doors were broken from the hinges, the window lights were all broken. As the boy and I stood in the road outside, two dogs, just roving farm dogs no doubt, came running around the corner of the house. The dogs were tall, gaunt fellows and came down to the fence and glared through at us, standing in the road.

The whole thing, the story of the old woman's death, was to me as I grew older like music heard from far off. The notes had to be picked up slowly one at a time. Something had to be understood.

The woman who died was one destined to feed animal life. Anyway, that is all she ever did. She was feeding animal life before she was born, as a child, as a young woman working on the farm of the German, after she married, when she grew old and when she died. She fed animal life in cows, in chickens, in pigs, in horses, in dogs, in men. Her daughter had died in childhood and with her one son she had no articulate relations. On the night when she died she was hurrying homeward, bearing on her body food for animal life.

She died in the clearing in the woods and even after her death continued feeding animal life.

You see it is likely that, when my brother told the story, that night when we got home and my mother and sister sat listening, I did not think he got the point. He was too young and so was I. A thing so complete has its own beauty.

I shall not try to emphasize the point. I am only explaining why I was dissatisfied then and have been ever since. I speak of that only that you may understand why I have been impelled to try to tell the simple story over again.

REMEMBER US!

By Ben Hecht

WHEN the time comes to make peace, the men of many countries will sit around the table of judgment. The eyes of the German delegates will look into the eyes of Englishmen, Americans, Russians, Czechs, Poles, Greeks, Norwegians, Belgians, Frenchmen and Dutchmen. All the victims of the German adventure will be there to pass sentence — all but one. Absent from the table of judgment will be the Jew.

There are two reasons for this.

First is the fact that the Jews have only one unity — that of the target. They have lived in the world as a scattered and diverse folk who paid homage to many cultures, many ideologies, and called many flags their own. They had little in common but the Germans' rage against them. The pogrom restores their unity. The Germans have animated the myth of the Jewish menace beyond any of their predecessors and tried to prove their case by presenting the world with a larger pile of Jewish corpses than has ever before been introduced into the ancient argument. Despite this unity of death given the Jews, there will be no nation to represent them at the judgment table. There will be no one from the empire of nightmare in which for many years they dwelt in agony.

The second reason why they will not be represented at the peace conclave is an even more practical one. Outside the borders of Russia, there will not be enough Jews left in Europe to profit by representation were it given them. They will have been reduced from a minority to a phantom. There will be no representatives to make demands in behalf of the three million Jews who once lived in Poland, or of the nine hundred thousand who once lived in Rumania, or of the nine hundred thousand who once lived in Germany, or of the 750,000 who once lived in Hungary, or of the 150,000 who once lived in Czechoslovakia, or of the 400,000 who once lived in France, Holland and Belgium.

Of these six million Jews, almost a third have already been massacred by Germans, Rumanians and Hungarians and the most conservative of the scorekeepers estimate that before the war ends at least another third will have been done to death. These totals will not include Jews who died in the brief battles of the German blitzes. Nor will they include those who figured in the casualty lists

---

BEN HECHT, *whose short stories, novels and plays have won for him a sure place in the literary history of our times, has also done brilliant work in the field of journalism, as this highly moving article amply shows.* (February, 1943)

of the Russians. Of the three million Jews in Russia, more than seven hundred thousand have entered the Soviet armies and fought and bled on all the valorous battlefields of the Muscovites. These are the lucky Jews of Europe and are not to be counted in the tale of their nightmare.

In the hearts of the millions who were hanged, burned or shot, there was no dream of representation and no hope. They did not die dreaming, like the valorous Greeks, Dutchmen, Frenchmen and Czechs, of abasements to be avenged and homelands to be restored. These great sustaining powers in the human soul are unknown to the Jews. When they die in massacre, they look toward no tomorrow to bring their children happiness and their enemies disaster. They cannot gather strength out of any terrestrial past or future. For it is the whim of history, known to the Jews of Europe, that no homeland is ever theirs, no matter how long they live in it, how well they serve it or how many of its songs they learn to sing.[1]

When the plans for the new world are being threshed out at the peace conference, when the sentences are being passed and the guilt fixed and the plums distributed, there will be nothing for the Jews of Europe to say to the delegates around the judgment table but the faint, sad phrase, *"Remember us!"*

They will have only one political statement to offer and that will be that the manner of their dying must remain one of the measures of the German soul.

There will be wagon loads of savants on both sides, of economists, of metaphysicians, philosophers and financiers to plot the remaking of a world. The dead of many lands will speak for justice, but the Jew alone will have no one to speak for him. His voice will remain outside the hall of judgment, to be heard only when the window is opened and the sad, faint cry drifts in —

"Remember us! In the town of Freiburg in the Black Forest, two hundred of us were hanged and left dangling out of our kitchen windows to watch our synagogue burn and our rabbi flogged to death. In Mannheim and Hindenburg, the Germans drove us all into our burning churches where we knelt and prayed and died while they sang their German song outside,

Break the skulls of all the Jews
And Future glory win.
Proudly will our banners fly
When Jewish blood runs from our sabre.

"In the town in Szczucin in Poland on the morning of September 23rd, which was the Day set aside for our Atonement, we were all in our synagogues praying God to forgive us. All our village was there, our bakers, millers, harness-makers, our students, wives, mothers and sisters and every child that was old enough to pronounce the name of God. Above our prayers we heard the sound of the motor lorries. They stopped in front of our synagogue. The Germans tumbled out of them, torches in hand. The Germans set fire to us. When we ran out of the flames, they turned machine guns on us.

---

[1] In proportion to their numbers, there were more Jews who died in the first World War defending the Kaiser's Germany than there were Germans. The Jewish Soldier Cemetery outside Berlin, unless it has been plowed up and turned into a concentration camp, is witness to this.

They seized our women and undressed them and made them run naked through the market place before their whips. All of us were killed before our Atonement was done. *Remember us!*

"Remember us in Wloclawek. Here also the Germans came when we were at worship. The Germans tore the prayer shawls from our heads. Under whips and bayonets, they made us use our prayer shawls as mops to clean out German latrines. We were all dead when the sun set. *Remember us!*

"In Mogielnica, in Brzeziny, in Wengrow and in many such places where we lived obeying the law, studying to be wise, working for our bread and offering harm to no one, there also the Germans came with their bayonets and torches, debasing us first and then killing us slowly so they might longer enjoy the massacres.

"In Lublin, five hundred of our women and children were led to the market place and stood against the vegetable stalls they knew so well. Here the Germans turned machine guns on us and killed us all. But this was not as bad as in other places, for here we died quickly.

"In Warsaw, in the year 1941, we kept count and at the end of twelve months 72,279 of us had died. Most of us were shot but there were thousands of us who were whipped and bayoneted to death on the more serious charge of having been caught praying to God for deliverance.

"In the seven months after June 1941, there were sixty thousand of us massacred in Bessarabia and Bukhovina. There were more of us than that killed in Minsk. We hung from windows and burned in basements and were beaten to death in the market place and this was a time of great celebration for the Germans. *Remember us!*

"Remember us who were put in the freight trains that left France, Holland and Belgium and who rode standing up to the east. We died standing up for there was no food or air or water. Of the twenty thousand who made that trip, only a few hundred were taken alive from the boxcars. These were sent to Transnistria and in Transnistria we all died of hunger slowly and under the watchful eyes of the Germans and Rumanians.

"In Kiev no Jew young or old was left alive. We fill the waters of the Dnieper today with our bodies. There are thousands of us in the waters. And for a long time to come, no one will be able to drink from that river or to swim in it. For we are still there. And this, too, is held against us, that we have poisoned the waters of the Dnieper with our dead bodies.

"Remember us who were in the Ukraine. Here the Germans grew angry with us because we were costing them too much time and ammuniton to kill. They devised a less expensive method. They took our women into the roads and tied them together with their children. Then they drove their heavy motor lorries into us. Thousands of us died in this way, with the German military cars running back and forth over our broken bodies.

"In Chelm, Poland, the Germans paid special attention to our hospitals and orphan homes. They entered these places and hurled our sick and our children into the streets.

"Remember us in Ismail when the

Rumanians came. For two days, they were busy leading all the Jews to the synagogue. We were all finally locked inside it. The doors and windows were sealed. Then the Iron Guards blew us up with dynamite and threw torches at those of us who were not quite dead.

"In Odessa, the Germans led five thousand of us out into the country roads. We were mostly old men, old women and children — some too old and some too young to walk. Above our heads the Germans flew their bombers and dropped their bombs on us. The German officers yelled that we should be proud for we were serving Germany by helping their fliers improve their marksmanship. But their marksmanship was good. Of the five thousand, none of us remained alive.

"In Ungheni, Rumania, the Germans accused us of crimes against the police. Three thousand of us were tried. The Germans followed us to our homes. They had been forbidden to waste bullets on us. They obeyed their officers. We were old and unarmed but it took the Germans two days to club us all to death with their rifle butts and rip us into silence with their bayonets.

"In Riga, a thousand of us arrived on a transport from Germany as conscripted laborers. We had been traveling in sealed compartments for days without food. The Germans in Riga unlocked our compartment and looked us over. The Germans in Riga decided we were too weak to be of any use in the factories. They put us into large wagons, sealed the wagons and drove us into the fields and dynamited us. None of us was left alive. Remember us who were workingmen.

"Remember, too, those of us who were not killed by the Germans but who killed ourselves. Some say there were a hundred thousand of us, some say two hundred thousand. No count was kept. Our deaths accomplished little, but it made us happy to die quickly and to know that we were robbing the Germans of their sport."

These are only a few of the voices. There are many more and there will be more millions.

When the German delegates sit at the peace table with their monocles restored to their pale eyes, no sons or survivors or representatives of these myriad dead will be inside the hall to speak for them. And by that time, it will be seen that the Jews are Jews only when they fall under German rifle butts, before German motor lorries and hang from German belts out of their kitchen windows. It will be seen that the Jews are Jews only when they stand up for the hour of extermination. Once dead, it will be seen that they are left without a government to speak for their avenging and that there is no banner to fly in their tomorrow.

Only this that I write — and all the narratives like it that will be written — will be their voice that may drift in through the opened window of the judgment hall.

TOM PAINE

By William E. Dodd

Peoples show the transitoriness of their principles by the changing treatment which they accord to their benefactors. Of all the men who wrought desperately in the formative struggles of the American Republic, Thomas Paine was perhaps the most sincere. His contributions were little less than those of Washington or Franklin or Jefferson. But there is not a monument to him in Washington or in the capital of any State or elsewhere in the United States erected by official order.

The present form and democratic procedure of the English government are modeled almost exactly after the form set up and argued by Paine in the last decade of the Eighteenth Century. And the present drift of the modern world toward liberty of conscience and away from the religious autocracy of the Eighteenth Century follows the lines marked out by the man whose bones were not permitted decent sepulture either in England or in the United States. He whose ideas and precepts were written into the constitutions of all modern states and are observed in the behavior of liberal men everywhere today, was, before his death, and is now, an outcast — his memory unwelcome in a world which he did so much to create.

In the little village of Thetford in the ancient county of Norfolk, in southeastern England, there appeared in the late winter of 1737 an ill-clad child whose father, an humble, pious Quaker, took him early to the meetings of a score of his fellow worshippers in the little church by the doors of the jail, filled in those days by the victims of religious and governmental intolerance. After a varied experience as a staymaker at Dover, a private on a ship of war, an unpopular revenue collector, the husband of an early deceased wife and the victim of a second unhappy marriage, Paine appeared in the year 1774, at the age of thirty-seven, at the door of Benjamin Franklin, the wise and far-seeing representative of half a dozen American colonies in London, penniless, uncouth and nearly hopeless.

Like many another poverty stricken subject of the British crown, he sought passage across the stormy Atlantic, and the generous philosopher of Pennsylvania gave him a letter of introduction to his

WILLIAM E. DODD, *who died in 1940, was American ambassador to Germany in 1933–1937. He taught history for many years at the University of Chicago, specializing in the history of the United States, particularly the Old South and the Wilson era. His books include his celebrated* Diary, Statesmen of the Old South, Expansion and Conflict, Woodrow Wilson and His Work *and* Lincoln and Lee. (December, 1930)

son-in-law, Richard Bache, who might introduce him to a better world than he had ever hoped to enter on terms approaching equality. It was the last of November, and in six months the immigrant was the editor and maker of a monthly magazine with fifteen hundred subscribers.

The new world was entrancing. The Quakers were in command of the government of Pennsylvania. Baptists, New Light Presbyterians, German Dunkards, Episcopalians and even Catholics all lived and worshipped freely without persecution; and on the hills and in the valleys beyond the Schuylkill there dwelt a race of hardy Germans and Scotchmen who practised the democracy they preached. But the new world was astir in a struggle for free trade, for free lands for all who could improve them, and for free speech everywhere. On April 17, the British soldiers on a doubtful mission to Lexington, Mass., came into bloody conflict with New England farmers; in November of the same year the British Governor of Virginia called upon the slaves of his domain to rise against their masters. It was war. And the immigrant of twelve months' residence, out of his own consciousness and without aid from any other hand, formulated the thought of the thirteen infant States, and suggested the procedure of the seven years' war which was to follow.

On January 10 the somewhat stooping figure which bore the head of genius, according to John Adams, gave to the world the fifty-page pamphlet, *Common Sense*, which arrested the attention of rich and poor, of Quaker and Catholic, and speedily attained a circulation of two hundred thousand in a country that could hardly have had a million people able to read. Washington pored over its pages when he had a moment to spare in his desperate circumstances; and John Rutledge took it to the South Carolina Legislature where great aristocrats wondered whether to proclaim it as a challenge to the King of England, whom they hated, or to suppress it lest its pages corrupt the masses of South Carolinians, whom they feared.

But the little book stirred the world with its bullet-like epigrams: "Society in every state is a blessing, but government at best is but a necessary evil; Kings look upon themselves as born to reign, soon their minds are poisoned by importance; the palaces of Kings are built on the ruins of paradise; the birthday of a new world is at hand and a race of men, perhaps as numerous as all Europe contains, are to receive their portion of freedom." Such a writer had never been seen or heard in the colonies. Older and more learned men had long striven to voice American feeling. Here was the voice of a new and a simple people seeking what Locke and Rousseau and the rest had described as the natural rights of men. The half-educated but industrious student, just released from the hard life of peasant England, usurped the place of philosophers and statesmen.

Paine was a universal spirit. But unlike philosophers and statesmen he took upon himself the character of a private soldier and joined the ranks of Washington's army at the moment when thousands of older Americans were running away to their homes in New England or in the South lest they be caught in the doom that overhung Washington's courageous head. And Washington made the private an officer; and the officer, between marching and fighting, found time to write at the end of the sad year, 1776, *The Crisis*, an appeal which began with these historic words: "These are the times that try men's souls." It was read at the head of every lieutenant's command in the bedraggled army before it crossed the Delaware at night and captured from the English army in a day as many troops as it counted in its own ranks. The sales price of this widely read pamphlet, like that of *Common Sense*, was contributed by its poor author to the great cause he advocated.

At the end of the Revolution, with a home at Bordentown, N. J., and a three-hundred-acre farm in Westchester county, N. Y., the gift of the people, he felt the urge to join his fellow liberals in France and seek to repeat there what he had done in the United States. It was 1787, the year of the American and the French conventions. With a little money in his wallet for his aged mother, a secret allowance for his strangely ignorant wife, and with the blessings of Washington and Franklin upon his head, he arrived in Paris to talk with Jefferson and to plan the regeneration of Europe.

II

In a little while the rumblings of the great revolution in Paris were heard across the channel and the Atlantic; and Paine took ship for the land of his birth and impoverished youth. In London he became an intimate friend of Edmund Burke, Charles James Fox and other friends of the American cause and champions of a newer and better order in England. They formed a society in order that their influence might be spread, Paine the while building the first iron bridge that had ever been seen anywhere. But English statesmen feared the ideas which every traveling American brought across the Atlantic; and Burke was beginning to hesitate when those ideas flowered into the Revolution of France.

On November 1, 1790, the great English champion of popular rights in America published *Reflections on the French Revolution*, which was at once taken as the greatest possible defense of the old and unjust régimes of the Bourbon and the Hanover Kings of France and England. It was read as gospel in every reactionary home of the time; it was bought, handsomely bound and circulated as the precious literary possession of the crowned heads of the Continent. Fox hardly knew what to say to his fallen friend; Paine declared war. The people of England were astir as the people of the thirteen colonies had been in 1774. The social system of centuries was under attack. England was ripe for regeneration; and Thomas Paine undertook to write for the country of his birth the unanswerable gospel of the United States.

The Rights of Man appeared in 1791. It was his reply to Burke; and in a year a hundred thousand copies of the pamphlet were circulated, and the entire proceeds of the sale at two shillings six pence a copy were given to the cause he advocated. Burke's answer was a demand for its suppression and the prosecution of its author — as great a tribute to its effectiveness as might have been asked. The traitor of Pennsylvania was now as well known in England as he had been known in North America. The members of Washington's Cabinet sought to recall their famous friend and make him postmaster-general. The French translated *The Rights of Man*, and Sieyès, Lanthenas and Condorcet read the new book with enthusiasm, and its author's name became a household word.

But the year 1791 brought danger of arrest and imprisonment in England to the man who recommended and outlined the very reforms which England now accepts as the highest scheme of human government, and which most of the world takes for granted. *The Rights of Man* proclaimed a new freedom, a freer trade with all the world, friendly association between nations, the abolishing of war, the maintenance of sound money, a kingship without the veto, a House of Lords without power to thwart the House of Commons, representation of all the people in legislation, popular suffrage and a Cabinet responsible to the people's representatives. There was not a radical idea in this system, as men look at government today, not even the abolition of war; and the masses of England were strongly inclined to take the Paine as against the Burke view of things. William Pitt said to Lady Hester Stanhope, "Tom Paine is right; but what am I to do?"

He determined to arrest and try the troublesome author for treason; and Paine, unwilling to retreat from a trial before a jury, prepared for the ordeal. As the news of English treatment seeped into France, the American writer rose in popularity to the rank of a statesman. Burke and his friends in the British Cabinet now outlawed him, set a price on his head and scoured the country in the hope of bringing him to the gallows. Twenty minutes before the King's posse hurried into the town of Dover to prevent their victim from taking ship for Paris, a hurrying traveler stood before the customs officer. Paine's baggage was seized; but the inspector came upon a letter from George Washington and hesitated to arrest a man with such credentials. The traveler was allowed to take ship and the King's posse hurried to the wharf a little later only to see the traitor's boat disappear. It was a narrow call.

Elected to a seat in the French constitutional convention, then gathering in Paris, from Calais and Versailles, the author of the terrible English book chose to sit for the northernmost borough of France and on September 19, 1792, took his place in the famous convention. Paine, Sieyès and Condorcet were promptly appointed to draw a constitution for France. The author of *Common Sense* would now write the law for the United States of Europe! Before the constitution was drawn the Jacobins, whom Paine distrusted, took steps to behead Louis XVI and Marie Antoinette.

The *Américain* protested that the death of the King would anger Washington and alienate the American people, the only allies of France. But all the efforts of the English Quaker proved vain. The King was beheaded on January 21, and henceforth the life of Paine was at the mercy of his bitter enemies, Gouverneur Morris, the minister of the United States, seeking by shrewd indirections to bring his fellow revolutionist of 1776 into prison, if not to the guillotine. Strangely enough, members of the American Cabinet encouraged Morris and furthered their party cause by deceiving Washington as to the facts.

III

Despairing now of the republic of Europe which he endeavored to model upon that of the United States, the aging liberal turned once more to his pen. He took an obscure house in St. Denis, associated himself there with a few Americans who loved him, and set about the last of his great books, *The Age of Reason*.

As the Spring and Summer of 1793 advanced, Paine saw his greater French friends go to prison or to the guillotine. His writings were anathema in England; his friends there were in jail; his own effigy was hanged or burned in a score of market places; while the appearance of his *Rights of Man* in the United States all but caused a Cabinet crisis.

Every day he expected the agents of Robespierre to hurry him off to prison; and Robespierre was not unwilling to have him assassinated if Gouverneur Morris and George Washington were unwilling to claim him as an American citizen. Even the unparalleled optimism of Thomas Paine faltered. It was then that he took to his cups and gave opportunity to Morris to call him a filthy drunkard, which an American President of our day dinned into the ears of a generation that had forgotten the benefactor of their fathers.

As the first part of *The Age of Reason* was taking shape in the mind of the author, he wrote: "My friends were falling as fast as the guillotine could cut their heads off and, as I expected every day the same fate, I resolved to begin my work. I had not finished the first part more than six hours before I was arrested and taken to prison." The text of the new book was: "The moral duty of man consists in imitating the moral goodness of God; and everything of persecution and revenge between man and man, and everything of cruelty to animals, is a violation of moral duty." The book began thus:

> To my fellow citizens of the United States. I put the following work under your protection. I have always supported the right of every man to his opinion. He who denies to another this right makes a slave of himself to his present opinion. The most formidable weapon against error is reason. I have never used any other.
>
> Your affectionate fellow, the Luxembourg prison, Paris.

Sick and imprisoned, the minister of the United States steering clear of his cell, Paine sent these pages to the press of New York, which soon put them before the audience which had eagerly read his *Common Sense*. There was an immediate cry of horror. Eminent deists, whose faith was that of Paine, turned upon him with a venom which delighted at the prospect of his approaching death. John Adams, whose popularity in Europe had been enhanced in 1779 because he was supposed to be Paine, could hardly call his name but in wrath. Washington refused to claim as a citizen the man who had shared his own privations at Valley

Forge. It is one of the sorrowful tales of American history. A change had come over the country of Franklin.

The Age of Reason was a destructive criticism of the Old Testament. It made scornful attack upon the cruelties and superstitions of a book which religious leaders till that time thought they must revere and defend *verbatim*. It also dwelt upon the beauties and the tenderness of the career and teachings of Jesus, who, he thought, had never proclaimed Himself a messiah. The reasoning of Thomas Paine in his last book was the reasoning of William E. Channing and Ralph Waldo Emerson thirty years later. Paine was always impatient with those who impose upon, and profit from, the credulity of simple folk, and he hated superstition dressed in ecclesiastical authority. Channing and Emerson felt the same impulses, but spoke gently, and worked out for a limited sect a deistical creed and practical faith identical with that of the author of *The Age of Reason*.

The former appealed to the masses to overthrow arrogant church authority; the latter appealed to a circle of educated men to do the same thing. The former was anathematized; the latter were proclaimed great thinkers and friends of the race. His method was his fault, but it was not the crime for which insincere men crucified him. Paine's ideal of religion was that man's relation to the deity was single. No priest or intermediary was necessary or even admissible, and no man should affect to pray for another, least of all set up a hierarchy or charge a fee. To think clearly, live simply and do good to men and animals was the whole duty of man.

IV

Ill and in bed, the physician visited Paine one afternoon and, noting the chalked sign on the sick man's door that he was to be taken out for execution that night, he by accident or design left the door open and the sign was not visible when the agents of death came. Thomas Paine was thus spared the fate of a thousand others, and a few weeks later the new American minister, James Monroe, a slave master of Virginia, claimed the author of *Common Sense* and the first secretary of the first American committee of foreign relations as a citizen of the United States; and he was free. He was nursed to health again in the family of the minister; but angry that Washington had not inquired during the ten months of imprisonment, he wrote that terrible indictment of the first President which will ever be read with distress by the friends of both.

When Bonaparte was about to become Napoleon, Paine's loyal friend, Nicholas Bonneville, a friend in the convention of 1792, now editor and owner of a paper in Paris, was put under surveillance by the police, and France became again a dangerous home for such as Paine, Monroe having been recalled for his sympathy with radical Europe. On the other side of the Atlantic Thomas Jefferson rose at last to the presidency and offered to send a ship to bring home the weary and homeless champion of liberty. Unwilling to subject his presidential friend to the criticism of his passage at public expense, Paine waited till the peace of Amiens, and then slipped off in a private vessel to

Baltimore, the English now unable to seize him at sea. It was October 30, 1802.

Paine hurried to the President's house. A happy winter followed, Jefferson and he walking and riding about the little capital, all the world looking on and hesitating to attack the generous act of a great man. But the tide of a cultivated public hatred could not long be resisted. Paine felt that the cause of his friend was injured by his presence; and I think Jefferson himself did not press him to remain longer the guest of a nation which loved the one and hated the other. One sometimes abandons a friend for a cause and yet wins the verdict of history.

Paine journeyed to Philadelphia, the scene of his early exploits. There Dr. Benjamin Rush, friend and radical of earlier days, refused to meet or greet him. He went to his own house in Bordentown, where Kitty Nicholson, now the wife of the retired Georgia Senator, William Few, and an intimate friend in 1787, refused so much as to acknowledge his existence. He sought to mount a stage for New York, but the passengers pushed him off. On another stage that did take him toward the new metropolis, he was obliged to look upon placards along the roadside picturing himself in the clutches of the Devil taking him off to the lake of everlasting fire.

In New York he was as unwelcome as he had been in New Jersey. Neither Hamilton nor Burr, fellows in the days that tried men's souls, and themselves deists of his own faith, paid him the honorable devoir of recognition; and lesser men threw mud where the greater scowled. He went to the farm in Westchester which represented the generous act of 1787 and there went to the polls in 1806 to cast his ballot.

Elisha Ward, a Tory who had lived under the English flag in New York while Paine fought for the country, presided at the election. He denied Paine citizenship and cited Gouverneur Morris's conduct in Paris to sustain the denial. As much the author of modern political civilization as any man then living, Paine was thus outlawed by England, pushed out of France by Napoleon, and denied a rightful place in the United States. More angry than he usually allowed himself to become, he applied to Congress for proof of his service as the secretary of foreign affairs in 1777; and although the proof was on every page of the official record, a committee of the national Legislature declined to authenticate the fact. One of the authors of the Declaration of Independence thus remained an Ishmael on a tract of land given him for that service.

V

As the weary years wore on, Madame Bonneville migrated to New York and came to nurse Paine in his last illness as she had nursed him when he was released from the Luxembourg in Paris. As the end approached, pious Christians looked daily for a recantation of his *Age of Reason* or for the physical presence of the Devil hovering about his room in New York City. It was the Spring of 1808. Father Fenwick, later the Bishop of Boston, tried to approach his bedside to hear and record the recantation or to report the presence of Satan himself.

There was a Quaker churchyard in Westchester county. Paine requested the brethren of that gentle sect to permit his bones to rest in their hallowed ground. The brethren refused.

He died as he had lived, faithful to his ideal of the deity, an honorable physician witness to the disputed fact. Father O'Brian, of the red nose, knelt over the dead body of the great man to say: "Oh, you ugly drunken beast." And the Presbyterian divine who had proclaimed the sanctity of Alexander Hamilton said: "Ah, Tom, thou'll get the frying in Hell; they'll roast thee like a herring."

> They'll put thee in the furnace hot,
> And on thee bar the door:
> How the devils will laugh
> To hear thee burst and roar.

On June 8 a little cortège wound its way to a corner of the farm at New Rochelle. Madame Bonneville and Willet Hicks, the reformed Quaker, some Irishmen of little wealth, and two Negroes, walked or rode behind the corpse: humble men taking the remains of their friend to the grave which they had prepared on the remnant of Paine's land. It was not to be the end. Eleven years later William Cobbett, a former enemy who had himself denounced the author of *The Age of Reason*, to make amends and to serve the cause of human freedom in England, took up the coffin, carried it to Liverpool, whence he hoped to carry it at the head of processions, and then place it under a fitting monument among plain people who had never quite repudiated him. But Richard Carlile, the friend of Paine, was that year put into prison and fined $7,500 for selling *The Rights of Man*. The town crier of Bolton went to jail for nine weeks for announcing the arrival of Paine's dead body.

Cobbett failed in his endeavor. The government and the churches of England refused the remains of the reformer sepulture either in hallowed or unhallowed ground; and his bones were in the possession of an old day-laborer in 1844, from whom they passed into the storeroom of B. Tilley, a furniture dealer, at 13 Bedford Square, near the British Museum and a little way from the bronze effigy of Paine's more lucky friend, Charles James Fox, at the entrance of Bloomsbury park.

Such in brief is the story of one of the makers of modern history. Denied a resting place in the land he loved most, his bones were scattered about the country of his birth, Christian men everywhere willing that it should be so. But wherever man looks about him thoughtfully today, he beholds something of the work of Paine and more of the spirit of *Common Sense* and *The Rights of Man*.

THE ANATOMY OF LONELINESS

By Thomas Wolfe

My life, more than that of anyone I know, has been spent in solitude and wandering. Why this is true, or how it happened, I cannot say; yet it is so. From my fifteenth year — save for a single interval — I have lived about as solitary a life as a modern man can have. I mean by this that the number of hours, days, months, and years that I have spent alone has been immense and extraordinary. I propose, therefore, to describe the experience of human loneliness exactly as I have known it.

The reason that impels me to do this is not that I think my knowledge of loneliness different in kind from that of other men. Quite the contrary. The whole conviction of my life now rests upon the belief that loneliness, far from being a rare and curious phenomenon, peculiar to myself and to a few other solitary men, is the central and inevitable fact of human existence. When we examine the moments, acts, and statements of all kinds of people — not only the grief and ecstasy of the greatest poets, but also the huge unhappiness of the average soul, as evidenced by the innumerable strident words of abuse, hatred, contempt, mistrust, and scorn that forever grate upon our ears as the manswarm passes us in the streets — we find, I think, that they are all suffering from the same thing. The final cause of their complaint is loneliness.

But if my experience of loneliness has not been different in kind from that of other men, I suspect it has been sharper in intensity. This gives me the best authority in the world to write of this, our general complaint, for I believe I know more about it than anyone of my generation. In saying this, I am merely stating a fact as I see it, though I realize that it may sound like arrogance or vanity. But before anyone jumps to that conclusion, let him consider how strange it would be to meet with arrogance in one who has lived alone as much as I. The surest cure for vanity is loneliness. For, more than other men, we who dwell in the heart of solitude are always the victims of self-doubt. Forever and forever in our loneliness, shameful feelings of inferiority will rise up suddenly to overwhelm us in a poisonous flood of horror, disbelief, and desolation, to sicken and corrupt our

---

THOMAS WOLFE, *who died in 1938, achieved national and international fame with his first novel,* Look Homeward, Angel, *which was published in 1929. "The Anatomy of Loneliness," probably more than any other single essay of his, gave his public an insight into the magnificent solitary turbulence that rocked him and propelled him to write as he did.* (October, 1941)

health and confidence, to spread pollution at the very root of strong, exultant joy. And the eternal paradox of it is that if a man is to know the triumphant labor of creation, he must for long periods resign himself to loneliness, and suffer loneliness to rob him of the health, the confidence, the belief and joy which are essential to creative work.

To live alone as I have lived, a man should have the confidence of God, the tranquil faith of a monastic saint, the stern impregnability of Gibraltar. Lacking these, there are times when anything, everything, all or nothing, the most trivial incidents, the most casual words, can in an instant strip me of my armor, palsy my hand, constrict my heart with frozen horror, and fill my bowels with the gray substance of shuddering impotence.

Sometimes it is nothing but a shadow passing on the sun; sometimes nothing but the torrid milky light of August, or the naked, sprawling ugliness and squalid decencies of streets in Brooklyn fading in the weary vistas of that milky light and evoking the intolerable misery of countless drab and nameless lives. Sometimes it is just the barren horror of raw concrete, or the heat blazing on a million beetles of machinery darting through the torrid streets, or the cindered weariness of parking spaces, or the slamming smash and racket of the El, or the driven manswarm of the earth, thrusting on forever in exacerbated fury, going nowhere in a hurry.

Again, it may be just a phrase, a look, a gesture. It may be the cold, disdainful inclination of the head with which a precious, kept, exquisite princeling of Park Avenue acknowledges an introduction, as if to say: "You are nothing." Or it may be a sneering reference and dismissal by a critic in a high-class weekly magazine. Or a letter from a woman saying I am lost and ruined, my talent vanished, all my efforts false and worthless — since I have forsaken the truth, vision, and reality which are so beautifully her own.

And sometimes it is less than these — nothing I can touch or see or hear or definitely remember. It may be so vague as to be a kind of hideous weather of the soul, subtly compounded of all the hunger, fury, and impossible desire my life has ever known. Or, again, it may be a half-forgotten memory of the cold wintry red of waning Sunday afternoons in Cambridge, and of a pallid, sensitive, esthetic face that held me once in earnest discourse on such a Sunday afternoon in Cambridge, telling me that all my youthful hopes were pitiful delusions and that all my life would come to naught, and the red and waning light of March was reflected on the pallid face with a desolate impotence that instantly quenched all the young ardors of my blood.

Beneath the evocations of these lights and weathers, and the cold, disdainful words of precious, sneering, and contemptuous people, all of the joy and singing of the day goes out like an extinguished candle, hope seems lost to me forever, and every truth that I have ever found and known seems false. At such a time the lonely man will feel that all the evidence of his own senses has betrayed him, and that nothing really lives and moves on earth but creatures of the death-in-life — those of the cold, constricted heart and the sterile loins, who exist forever in the red waning light of March and Sunday afternoon.

All this hideous doubt, despair, and dark confusion of the soul a lonely man must know, for he is united to no image save that which he creates himself, he is bolstered by no other knowledge save that which he can gather for himself with the vision of his own eyes and brain. He is sustained and cheered and aided by no party, he is given comfort by no creed, he has no faith in him except his own. And often that faith deserts him, leaving him shaken and filled with impotence. And then it seems to him that his life has come to nothing, that he is ruined, lost, and broken past redemption, and that morning — bright, shining morning, with its promise of new beginnings — will never come upon the earth again as it did once.

He knows that dark time is flowing by him like a river. The huge, dark wall of loneliness is around him now. It encloses and presses in upon him, and he cannot escape. And the cancerous plant of memory is feeding at his entrails, recalling hundreds of forgotten faces and ten thousand vanished days, until all life seems as strange and insubstantial as a dream. Time flows by him like a river, and he waits in his little room like a creature held captive by an evil spell. And he will hear, far off, the murmurous drone of the great earth, and feel that he has been forgotten, that his powers are wasting from him while the river flows, and that all his life has come to nothing. He feels that his strength is gone, his power withered, while he sits there drugged and fettered in the prison of his loneliness.

Then suddenly, one day, for no apparent reason, his faith and his belief in life will come back to him in a tidal flood. It will rise up in him with a jubilant and invincible power, bursting a window in the world's great wall and restoring everything to shapes of deathless brightness. Made miraculously whole and secure in himself, he will plunge once more into the triumphant labor of creation. All his old strength is his again: he knows what he knows, he is what he is, he has found what he has found. And he will say the truth that is in him, speak it though the whole world deny it, affirm it though a million men cry it is false.

At such a moment of triumphant confidence, with this feeling in me, I dare now assert that I have known Loneliness as well as any man, and will now write of him as if he were my very brother, which he is. I will paint him for you with such fidelity to his true figure that no man who reads will ever doubt his visage when Loneliness comes to him hereafter.

II

The most tragic, sublime, and beautiful expression of human loneliness which I have ever read is the Book of Job; the grandest and most philosophical, Ecclesiastes. Here I must point out a fact which is so much at variance with everything I was told as a child concerning loneliness and the tragic underweft of life that, when I first discovered it, I was astounded and incredulous, doubting the overwhelming weight of evidence that had revealed it to me. But there it was, as solid as a rock, not to be shaken or denied; and as the years passed, the truth of this discovery became part of the structure of my life.

The fact is this: the lonely man, who is also the tragic man, is invariably the man who loves life dearly — which is to say, the joyful man. In these statements there is no paradox whatever. The one condition implies the other, and makes it necessary. The essence of human tragedy is in loneliness, not in conflict, no matter what the arguments of the theater may assert. And just as the great tragic writer (I say, "the tragic writer" of tragedies, for certain nations, the Roman and French among them, have had no great tragic writers, for Virgil and Racine were none, but rather great writers of tragedy): just as the great tragic writer — Job, Sophocles, Dante, Milton, Swift, Dostoevski — has always been the lonely man, so has he also been the man who loved life best and had the deepest sense of joy. The real quality and substance of human joy is to be found in the works of these great tragic writers as nowhere else in all the records of man's life upon the earth. In proof of this, I can give here one conclusive illustration:

In my childhood, any mention of the Book of Job evoked instantly in my mind a long train of gloomy, gray, and unbrokenly dismal associations. This has been true, I suspect, with most of us. Such phrases as "Job's comforter," and "the patience of Job," and "the afflictions of Job," have become part of our common idiom and are used to refer to people whose woes seem uncountable and unceasing, who have suffered long and silently, and whose gloom has never been interrupted by a ray of hope or joy. All these associations had united to make for me a picture of the Book of Job that was grim, bleak, and constant in its misery. But any reader of intelligence and experience who has read that great book in his mature years will realize how false such a picture is.

For the Book of Job, far from being dreary, gray, and dismal, is woven entire, more than any single piece of writing I can recall, from the sensuous, flashing, infinitely various, and gloriously palpable material of great poetry; and it wears at the heart of its tremendous chant of everlasting sorrow the exulting song of everlasting joy.

In this there is nothing strange or curious, but only what is inevitable and right. It is the sense of death and loneliness, the knowledge of the brevity of his days, and the huge impending burden of his sorrow, growing always, never lessening, that makes joy glorious, tragic, and unutterably precious to a man like Job. Beauty comes and passes, is lost the moment that we touch it, can no more be stayed or held than one can stay the flowing of a river. Out of this pain of loss, this bitter ecstasy of brief having, this fatal glory of the single moment, the tragic writer will therefore make a song for joy. That, at least, he may keep and treasure always. And his song is full of grief because he knows that joy is fleeting, gone the instant that we have it, and that is why it is so precious, gaining its full glory from the very things that limit and destroy it.

He knows that joy gains its glory out of sorrow, bitter sorrow, and man's loneliness, and that it is haunted always with the certainty of death, dark death, which stops our tongues, our eyes, our living breath, with the twin oblivions of dust and nothingness. Therefore a man like Job will make a chant for sorrow, too, but it will still be a song for joy as well, and one more strange and beautiful than any other that man has ever sung:

> Hast thou given the horse strength? Hast thou clothed his neck with thunder? Canst thou make him afraid as a grasshopper? The glory of his nostrils is terrible.
> He paweth in the valley, and rejoiceth in his strength: he goeth on to meet the armed men.
> He mocketh at fear, and is not affrighted; neither turneth he back from the sword.
> The quiver rattleth against him, the glittering spear and the shield.
> He swalloweth the ground with fierceness and rage; neither believeth he that it is the sound of the trumpet.
> He saith among the trumpets, Ha, ha; and he smelleth the battle afar off, the thunder of the captains, and the shouting.

That is joy — joy solemn and triumphant; stern, lonely, everlasting joy, which has in it the full depth and humility of man's wonder, his sense of glory, and his feeling of awe before the mystery of the universe. An exultant cry is torn from our lips as we read the lines about that glorious horse, and the joy we feel is wild and strange, lonely and dark like death, and grander than the delicate and lovely joy that men like Herrick and Theocritus described, great poets though they were.

III

Just as the Book of Job and the sermon of Ecclesiastes are, each in its own way, supreme histories of man's loneliness, so do all the books of the Old Testament, in their entirety, provide the most final and profound literature of human loneliness that the world has known. It is astonishing with what a coherent unity of spirit and belief the life of loneliness is recorded in those many books — how it finds its full expression in the chants, songs, prophecies, and chronicles of so many men, all so various, and each so individual, each revealing some new image of man's secret and most lonely heart, and all combining to produce a single image of his loneliness that is matchless in its grandeur and magnificence.

The total, all-contributary unity of this conception of man's loneliness in the books of the Old Testament becomes even more astonishing when we begin to read the New. For, just as the Old Testament becomes the chronicle of the life of loneliness, the gospels of the New Testament, with the same miraculous and unswerving unity, becomes the chronicle of the life of love. What Christ is saying always, what he never swerves from saying, what he says a thousand times and in a thousand different ways, but always with a central unity of belief, is this: "I am my Father's son, and you are my brothers." And the unity that binds us all together, that makes this earth a family, and all men brothers and the sons of God, is love.

The central purpose of Christ's life, therefore, is to destroy the life of loneliness and to establish here on earth the life of love. It should be obvious to everyone that when Christ says: "Blessed are the poor in spirit: for theirs is the kingdom of heaven," "Blessed are they that mourn: for they shall be comforted," "Blessed are the merciful: for they shall obtain mercy," — Christ is not here extolling the qualities of humility, sorrow and mercy as virtues sufficient in themselves, but he promises to men who have these virtues the richest reward that men were ever offered — a reward that promises not only the inheritance of the earth, but the kingdom of heaven as well.

Such was the final intention of Christ's life, the purpose of his teaching. And its total import was that the life of loneliness could be destroyed forever by the life of love. Or such, at least, has been the meaning which I read into his life. For in these recent years when I have lived alone so much, and known loneliness so well, I have gone back many times and read the story of this man's words and life to see if I could find in them a meaning for myself, a way of life that would be better than the one I had. I read what he had said, not in a mood of piety or holiness, not from a sense of sin, a feeling of contrition, or because his promise of a heavenly reward meant very much to me. But I tried to read his bare words nakedly and simply, as it seems to me he must have uttered them, and as I have read the words of other men — of Homer, Donne, and Whitman, and the writer of Ecclesiastes — and if the meaning I have put upon his words seems foolish or extravagant, childishly simple or banal, mine alone are no different from what ten million other men have thought, I have only set it down here as I saw it, felt it, found it for myself, and have tried to add, subtract, and alter nothing.

And now I know that though the way and meaning of Christ's life is a far, far better way and meaning than my own, yet I can never make it mine; and I think that this is true of all the other lonely men that I have seen or known about — the nameless, voiceless, faceless atoms of this earth as well as Job and Everyman and Swift. And Christ himself, who preached the life of love, was yet as lonely as any man that ever lived. Yet I could not say that he was mistaken because he preached the life of love and fellowship, and lived and died in loneliness; nor would I dare assert his way was wrong because a billion men have since professed his way and never followed it.

I can only say that I could not make his way my own. For I have found the constant, everlasting weather of man's life to be, not love, but loneliness. Love itself is not the weather of our lives. It is the rare, the precious flower. Sometimes it is the flower that gives us life, that breaches the dark walls of all our loneliness and restores us to the fellowship of life, the family of the earth, the brotherhood of man. But sometimes love is the flower that brings us death; and from it we get pain and darkness; and the mutilations of the soul, the maddening of the brain, may be in it.

How or why or in what way the flower of love will come to us, whether with life or death, triumph or defeat, joy or madness, no man on this earth can say. But I know that at the end, forever at the end for us — the houseless, homeless, doorless, driven wanderers of life, the lonely men — there waits forever the dark visage of our comrade, Loneliness.

But the old refusals drop away, the old avowals stand — and we who were dead have risen, we who were lost are found again, and we who sold the talent, the passion, and belief of youth into the keeping of the fleshless dead, until our hearts were corrupted, our talent wasted, and our hope gone, have won our lives back bloodily, in solitude and darkness. And we walk the Bridge alone with you, stern friend, the one to whom we speak, who never failed us. Hear:

"Loneliness forever and the earth again! Dark brother and stern friend, immortal face of darkness and of night, with whom the half part of my life was spent, and with whom I shall abide now till my death forever — what is there for me to fear as long as you are with me? Heroic friend, have we not gone together down a million ways, have we not coursed together the great and furious avenues of night, have we not crossed the stormy seas alone, and known strange lands, and come again to walk the continent of night and listen to the silence of the earth? Have we not been brave and glorious when we were together, friend? Have we not known triumph, joy, and glory on this earth — and will it not be again with me as it was then, if you come back to me?

"Come to me in the secret and most silent heart of darkness. Come to me as you always came, bringing to me again the old invincible strength, the deathless hope, the triumphant joy and confidence that will storm the earth again."

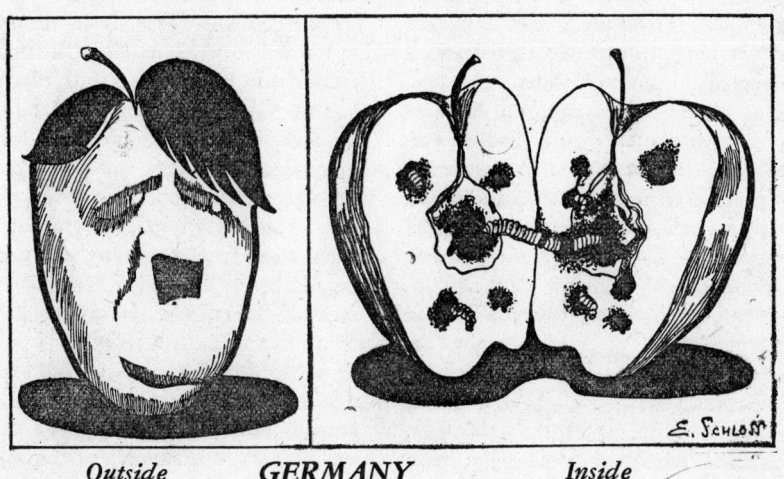

Outside   **GERMANY**   *Inside*
(*February, 1943*)

THAT EVENING SUN GO DOWN

By William Faulkner

Monday is no different from any other week day in Jefferson now. The streets are paved now, and the telephone and the electric companies are cutting down more and more of the shade trees — the water oaks, the maples and locusts and elms — to make room for iron poles bearing clusters of bloated and ghostly and bloodless grapes, and we have a city laundry which makes the rounds on Monday morning, gathering the bundles of clothes into bright-colored, specially made motor-cars: the soiled wearing of a whole week now flees apparition-like behind alert and irritable electric horns, with a long diminishing noise of rubber and asphalt like a tearing of silk, and even the Negro women who still take in white peoples' washing after the old custom, fetch and deliver it in automobiles.

But fifteen years ago, on Monday morning the quiet, dusty, shady streets would be full of Negro women with, balanced on their steady turbaned heads, bundles of clothes tied up in sheets, almost as large as cotton bales, carried so without touch of hand between the kitchen door of the white house and the blackened wash-pot beside a cabin door in Negro Hollow.

Nancy would set her bundle on the top of her head, then upon the bundle in turn she would set the black straw sailor hat which she wore winter and summer. She was tall, with a high, sad face sunken a little where her teeth were missing. Sometimes we would go a part of the way down the lane and across the pasture with her, to watch the balanced bundle and the hat that never bobbed nor wavered, even when she walked down into the ditch and climbed out again and stooped through the fence. She would go down on her hands and knees and crawl through the gap, her head rigid, up-tilted, the bundle steady as a rock or a balloon, and rise to her feet and go on.

Sometimes the husbands of the washing women would fetch and deliver the clothes, but Jubah never did that for Nancy, even before father told him to stay away from our house, even when Dilsey was sick and Nancy would come to cook for us.

And then about half the time we'd have to go down the lane to Nancy's house and tell her to come on and get breakfast. We would stop at the ditch, because father told us to not have anything to do with Jubah — he was a short

---

WILLIAM FAULKNER, *author of the celebrated novels* The Sound and the Fury, Sanctuary, *and* As I Lay Dying, *has also written many first-rate stories, and this one is universally regarded as one of his most effective.* (March, 1931)

black man, with a razor scar down his face — and we would throw rocks at Nancy's house until she came to the door, leaning her head around it without any clothes on.

"What yawl mean, chunking my house?" Nancy said. "What you little devils mean?"

"Father says for you to come and get breakfast," Caddy said. "Father says it's over a half an hour now, and you've got to come this minute."

"I ain't studying no breakfast," Nancy said. "I going to get my sleep out."

"I bet you're drunk," Jason said. "Father says you're drunk. Are you drunk, Nancy?"

"Who says I is?" Nancy said. "I got to get my sleep out. I ain't studying no breakfast."

So after a while we quit chunking the house and went back home. When she finally came, it was too late for me to go to school.

So we thought it was whiskey until that day when they arrested her again and they were taking her to jail and they passed Mr. Stovall. He was the cashier in the bank and a deacon in the Baptist church, and Nancy began to say:

"When you going to pay me, white man? When you going to pay me, white man? It's been three times now since you paid me a cent——" Mr. Stovall knocked her down, but she kept on saying, "When you going to pay me, white man? It's been three times now since ——" until Mr. Stovall kicked her in the mouth with his heel and the marshal caught Mr. Stovall back, and Nancy lying in the street, laughing. She turned her head and spat out some blood and teeth and said, "It's been three times now since he paid me a cent."

That was how she lost her teeth, and all that day they told about Nancy and Mr. Stovall, and all that night the ones that passed the jail could hear Nancy singing and yelling. They could see her hands holding to the window bars, and a lot of them stopped along the fence, listening to her and to the jailer trying to make her shut up. She didn't shut up until just before daylight, when the jailer began to hear a bumping and scraping upstairs and he went up there and found Nancy hanging from the window bar. He said that it was cocaine and not whiskey, because no nigger would try to commit suicide unless he was full of cocaine, because a nigger full of cocaine was not a nigger any longer.

The jailer cut her down and revived her; then he beat her, whipped her. She had hung herself with her dress. She had fixed it all right, but when they arrested her she didn't have on anything except a dress and so she didn't have anything to tie her hands with and she couldn't make her hands let go of the window ledge. So the jailer heard the noise and ran up there and found Nancy hanging from the window, stark naked.

When Dilsey was sick in her cabin and Nancy was cooking for us, we could see her apron swelling out; that was before father told Jubah to stay away from the house. Jubah was in the kitchen, sitting behind the stove, with his razor scar on his black face like a piece of dirty string. He said it was a watermelon Nancy had under her dress. And it was winter, too.

"Where did you get a watermelon in the winter?" Caddy said.

"I didn't," Jubah said. "It wasn't me that give it to her. But I can cut it down, same as if it was."

"What makes you want to talk that way before these chillen?" Nancy said. "Whyn't you go on to work? You done et. You want Mr. Jason to catch you hanging around his kitchen, talking that way before these chillen?"

"Talking what way, Nancy?" Caddy said.

"I can't hang around white man's kitchen," Jubah said. "But white man can hang around mine. White man can come in my house, but I can't stop him. When white man want to come in my house, I ain't got no house. I can't stop him, but he can't kick me outen it. He can't do that."

Dilsey was still sick in her cabin. Father told Jubah to stay off our place. Dilsey was still sick. It was a long time. We were in the library after supper.

"Isn't Nancy through yet?" mother said. "It seems to me that she has had plenty of time to have finished the dishes."

"Let Quentin go and see," father said. "Go and see if Nancy is through, Quentin. Tell her she can go on home."

I went to the kitchen. Nancy was through. The dishes were put away and the fire was out. Nancy was sitting in a chair, close to the cold stove. She looked at me.

"Mother wants to know if you are through," I said.

"Yes," Nancy said. She looked at me. "I done finished." She looked at me.

"What is it?" I said. "What is it?"

"I ain't nothing but a nigger," Nancy said. "It ain't none of my fault."

She looked at me, sitting in the chair before the cold stove, the sailor hat on her head. I went back to the library. It was the cold stove and all, when you think of a kitchen being warm and busy and cheerful. And with a cold stove and the dishes all put away, and nobody wanting to eat at that hour.

"Is she through?" mother said.

"Yessum," I said.

"What is she doing?" mother said.

"She's not doing anything. She's through."

"I'll go and see," father said.

"Maybe she's waiting for Jubah to come and take her home," Caddy said.

"Jubah is gone," I said. Nancy told us how one morning she woke up and Jubah was gone.

"He quit me," Nancy said. "Done gone to Memphis, I reckon. Dodging them city *po*-lice for a while, I reckon."

"And a good riddance," father said. "I hope he stays there."

"Nancy's scaired of the dark," Jason said.

"So are you," Caddy said.

"I'm not," Jason said.

"Scairy cat," Caddy said.

"I'm not," Jason said.

"You, Candace!" mother said. Father came back.

"I am going to walk down the lane with Nancy," he said. "She says Jubah is back."

"Has she seen him?" mother said.

"No. Some Negro sent her word that he was back in town. I won't be long.'

THAT EVENING SUN GO DOWN

"You'll leave me alone, to take Nancy home?" mother said. "Is her safety more precious to you than mine?"

"I won't be long," father said.

"You'll leave these children unprotected, with that Negro about?"

"I'm going, too," Caddy said. "Let me go, father."

"What would he do with them, if he were unfortunate enough to have them?" father said.

"I want to go, too," Jason said.

"Jason!" mother said. She was speaking to father. You could tell that by the way she said it. Like she believed that all day father had been trying to think of doing the thing that she wouldn't like the most, and that she knew all the time that after a while he would think of it. I stayed quiet, because father and I both knew that mother would want him to make me stay with her, if she just thought of it in time. So father didn't look at me. I was the oldest. I was nine and Caddy was seven and Jason was five.

"Nonsense," father said. "We won't be long."

Nancy had her hat on. We came to the lane. "Jubah always been good to me," Nancy said. "Whenever he had two dollars, one of them was mine." We walked in the lane. "If I can just get through the lane," Nancy said, "I be all right then."

The lane was always dark. "This is where Jason got scared on Hallowe'en," Caddy said.

"I didn't," Jason said.

"Can't Aunt Rachel do anything with him?" father said. Aunt Rachel was old. She lived in a cabin beyond Nancy's, by herself. She had white hair and she smoked a pipe in the door, all day long; she didn't work any more. They said she was Jubah's mother. Sometimes she said she was and sometimes she said she wasn't any kin to Jubah.

"Yes, you did," Caddy said. "You were scairder than Frony. You were scairder than T.P. even. Scairder than niggers."

"Can't nobody do nothing with him," Nancy said. "He say I done woke up the devil in him, and ain't but one thing going to lay it again."

"Well, he's gone now," father said. "There's nothing for you to be afraid of now. And if you'd just let white men alone."

"Let what white men alone?" Caddy said. "How let them alone?"

"He ain't gone nowhere," Nancy said. "I can feel him. I can feel him now, in this lane. He hearing us talk, every word, hid somewhere, waiting. I ain't seen him, and I ain't going to see him again but once more, with that razor. That razor on that string down his back, inside his shirt. And then I ain't going to be even surprised."

"I wasn't scaired," Jason said.

"If you'd behave yourself, you'd have kept out of this," father said. "But it's all right now. He's probably in St. Louis now. Probably got another wife by now and forgot all about you."

"If he has, I better not find out about it," Nancy said. "I'd stand there and every time he wropped her, I'd cut that arm off. I'd cut his head off and I'd slit her belly and I'd shove ——"

"Hush," father said.

"Slit whose belly, Nancy?" Caddy said.

"I wasn't scared," Jason said. "I'd walk right down this lane by myself."

"Yah," Caddy said. "You wouldn't dare to put your foot in it if we were not with you."

II

Dilsey was still sick, and so we took Nancy home every night until mother said, "How much longer is this going to go on? I to be left alone in this big house while you take home a frightened Negro?"

We fixed a pallet in the kitchen for Nancy. One night we waked up, hearing the sound. It was not singing and it was not crying, coming up the dark stairs. There was a light in mother's room and we heard father going down the hall, down the back stairs, and Caddy and I went into the hall. The floor was cold. Our toes curled away from the floor while we listened to the sound. It was like singing and it wasn't like singing, like the sounds that Negroes make.

Then it stopped and we heard father going down the back stairs, and we went to the head of the stairs. Then the sound began again, in the stairway, not loud, and we could see Nancy's eyes half way up the stairs, against the wall. They looked like cat's eyes do, like a big cat against the wall, watching us. When we came down the steps to where she was she quit making the sound again, and we stood there until father came back up from the kitchen, with his pistol in his hand. He went back down with Nancy and they came back with Nancy's pallet.

We spread the pallet in our room. After the light in mother's room went off, we could see Nancy's eyes again. "Nancy," Caddy whispered, "are you asleep, Nancy?"

Nancy whispered something. It was oh or no, I don't know which. Like nobody had made it, like it came from nowhere and went nowhere, until it was like Nancy was not there at all; that I had looked so hard at her eyes on the stair that they had got printed on my eyelids, like the sun does when you have closed your eyes and there is no sun. "Jesus," Nancy whispered. "Jesus."

"Was it Jubah?" Caddy whispered. "Did he try to come into the kitchen?"

"Jesus," Nancy said. Like this: Jeeeeee-eeeeeeeeesus, until the sound went out like a match or a candle does.

"Can you see us, Nancy?" Caddy whispered. "Can you see our eyes too?"

"I ain't nothing but a nigger," Nancy said. "God knows. God knows."

"What did you see down there in the kitchen?" Caddy whispered. "What tried to get in?"

"God knows," Nancy said. We could see her eyes. "God knows."

Dilsey got well. She cooked dinner. "You'd better stay in bed a day or two longer," father said.

"What for?" Dilsey said. "If I had been a day later, this place would be to rack and ruin. Get on out of here, now, and let me get my kitchen straight again."

Dilsey cooked supper, too. And that night, just before dark, Nancy came into the kitchen.

"How do you know he's back?" Dilsey said. "You ain't seen him."

"Jubah is a nigger," Jason said.

"I can feel him," Nancy said. "I can

feel him laying yonder in the ditch."

"Tonight?" Dilsey said. "Is he there tonight?"

"Dilsey's a nigger too," Jason said.

"You try to eat something," Dilsey said.

"I don't want nothing," Nancy said.

"I ain't a nigger," Jason said.

"Drink some coffee," Dilsey said. She poured a cup of coffee for Nancy. "Do you know he's out there tonight? How come you know it's tonight?"

"I know," Nancy said. "He's there, waiting. I know. I done lived with him too long. I know what he fixing to do fore he knows it himself."

"Drink some coffee," Dilsey said. Nancy held the cup to her mouth and blew into the cup. Her mouth pursed out like a spreading adder's, like a rubber mouth, like she had blown all the color out of her lips with blowing the coffee.

"I ain't a nigger," Jason said. "Are you a nigger, Nancy?"

"I hell-born, child," Nancy said. "I won't be nothing soon. I going back where I come from soon."

She began to drink the coffee. While she was drinking, holding the cup in both hands, she began to make the sound again. She made the sound into the cup and the coffee sploshed out on to her hands and her dress. Her eyes looked at us and she sat there, her elbows on her knees, holding the cup in both hands, looking at us across the wet cup, making the sound.

"Look at Nancy," Jason said. "Nancy can't cook for us now. Dilsey's got well now."

"You hush up," Dilsey said. Nancy held the cup in both hands, looking at us, making the sound, like there were two of them: one looking at us and the other making the sound. "Whyn't you let Mr. Jason telefoam the marshal?" Dilsey said. Nancy stopped then, holding the cup in her long brown hands. She tried to drink some coffee again, but it sploshed out of the cup, on to her hands and her dress, and she put the cup down. Jason watched her.

"I can't swallow it," Nancy said. "I swallows but it won't go down me."

"You go down to the cabin," Dilsey said. "Frony will fix you a pallet and I'll be there soon."

"Won't no nigger stop him," Nancy said.

"I ain't a nigger," Jason said. "Am I, Dilsey?"

"I reckon not," Dilsey said. She looked at Nancy. "I don't reckon so. What you going to do, then?"

Nancy looked at us. Her eyes went fast, like she was afraid there wasn't time to look, without hardly moving at all. She looked at us, at all three of us at one time. "You member that night I stayed in yawls' room?" she said. She told about how we waked up early the next morning, and played. We had to play quiet, on her pallet, until father woke and it was time for her to go down and get breakfast. "Go and ask you maw to let me stay here tonight," Nancy said. "I won't need no pallet. We can play some more," she said.

Caddy asked mother. Jason went too. "I can't have Negroes sleeping in the house," mother said. Jason cried. He cried until mother said he couldn't have any dessert for three days if he didn't stop. Then Jason said he would stop if Dilsey would make a chocolate cake. Father was there.

"Why don't you do something about it?" mother said. "What do we have officers for?"

"Why is Nancy afraid of Jubah?" Caddy said. "Are you afraid of father, mother?"

"What could they do?" father said. "If Nancy hasn't seen him, how could the officers find him?"

"Then why is she afraid?" mother said.

"She says he is there. She says she knows he is there tonight."

"Yet we pay taxes," mother said. "I must wait here alone in this big house while you take a Negro woman home."

"You know that I am not lying outside with a razor," father said.

"I'll stop if Dilsey will make a chocolate cake," Jason said. Mother told us to go out and father said he didn't know if Jason would get a chocolate cake or not, but he knew what Jason was going to get in about a minute. We went back to the kitchen and told Nancy.

"Father said for you to go home and lock the door, and you'll be all right," Caddy said. "All right from what, Nancy? Is Jubah mad at you?" Nancy was holding the coffee cup in her hands, her elbow on her knees and her hands holding the cup between her knees. She was looking into the cup. "What have you done that made Jubah mad?" Caddy said. Nancy let the cup go. It didn't break on the floor, but the coffee spilled out, and Nancy sat there with her hands making the shape of the cup. She began to make the sound again, not loud. Not singing and not un-singing. We watched her.

"Here," Dilsey said. "You quit that, now. You get a-holt of yourself. You wait here. I going to get Versh to walk home with you." Dilsey went out.

We looked at Nancy. Her shoulders kept shaking, but she had quit making the sound. We watched her. "What's Jubah going to do to you?" Caddy said.

"He went away."

Nancy looked at us. "We had fun that night I stayed in yawls' room, didn't we?"

"I didn't," Jason said. "I didn't have any fun."

"You were asleep," Caddy said. "You were not there."

"Let's go down to my house and have some more fun," Nancy said.

"Mother won't let us," I said. "It's too late now."

"Don't bother her," Nancy said. "We can tell her in the morning. She won't mind."

"She wouldn't let us," I said.

"Don't ask her now," Nancy said. "Don't bother her now."

"They didn't say we couldn't go," Caddy said.

"We didn't ask," I said.

"If you go, I'll tell," Jason said.

"We'll have fun," Nancy said. "They won't mind, just to my house. I been working for yawl a long time. They won't mind."

"I'm not afraid to go," Caddy said. "Jason is the one that's afraid. He'll tell."

"I'm not," Jason said.

"You are," Caddy said. "You'll tell."

"I won't tell," Jason said. "I'm not afraid."

"Jason ain't afraid to go with me," Nancy said. "Is you, Jason?"

"Jason is going to tell," Caddy said. The lane was dark. We passed the pasture gate. "I bet if something was to jump out from behind that gate, Jason would holler."

"I wouldn't," Jason said. We walked down the lane. Nancy was talking loud.

"What are you talking so loud for, Nancy?" Caddy said.

"Who; me?" Nancy said. "Listen at Quentin and Caddy and Jason saying I'm talking loud."

"You talk like there was four of us here," Caddy said. "You talk like father was here too."

"Who; me talking loud, Mr. Jason?" Nancy said.

"Nancy called Jason 'Mister'," Caddy said.

"Listen how Caddy and Quentin and Jason talk," Nancy said.

"We're not talking loud," Caddy said. "You're the one that's talking like father——"

"Hush," Nancy said; "hush, Mr. Jason."

"Nancy called Jason 'Mister' aguh——"

"Hush," Nancy said. She was talking loud when we crossed the ditch and stooped through the fence where she used to stoop through with the clothes on her head. Then we came to her house. We were going fast then. She opened the door. The smell of the house was like the lamp and the smell of Nancy was like the wick, like they were waiting for one another to smell. She lit the lamp and closed the door and put the bar up. Then she quit talking loud, looking at us.

"What're we going to do?" Caddy said.

"What you all want to do?" Nancy said.

"You said we would have some fun," Caddy said.

There was something about Nancy's house; something you could smell. Jason smelled it, even. "I don't want to stay here," he said. "I want to go home."

"Go home, then," Caddy said.

"I don't want to go by myself," Jason said.

"We're going to have some fun," Nancy said.

"How?" Caddy said.

Nancy stood by the door. She was looking at us, only it was like she had emptied her eyes, like she had quit using them.

"What do you want to do?" she said.

"Tell us a story," Caddy said. "Can you tell a story?"

"Yes," Nancy said.

"Tell it," Caddy said. We looked at Nancy. "You don't know any stories," Caddy said.

"Yes," Nancy said. "Yes I do."

She came and sat down in a chair before the hearth. There was some fire there; she built it up; it was already hot. You didn't need a fire. She built a good blaze. She told a story. She talked like her eyes looked, like her eyes watching us and her voice talking to us did not belong to her. Like she was living somewhere else, waiting somewhere else. She was outside the house. Her voice was there and the shape of her, the Nancy that could stoop under the fence with the bundle of clothes balanced as though without weight, like a balloon, on her head, was there. But that was all. "And so this here queen come walking up to the ditch, where that bad man was hiding. She was walking up the ditch, and she say, 'If I can just get past this here ditch,' was what she say. . . ."

"What ditch?" Caddy said. "A ditch like that one out there? Why did the queen go into the ditch?"

"To get to her house," Nancy said. She looked at us. "She had to cross that ditch to get home."

"Why did she want to go home?" Caddy said.

III

Nancy looked at us. She quit talking. She looked at us. Jason's legs stuck straight out of his pants, because he was little. "I don't think that's a good story," he said. "I want to go home."

"Maybe we had better," Caddy said. She got up from the floor. "I bet they are looking for us right now." She went toward the door.

"No," Nancy said. "Don't open it." She got up quick and passed Caddy. She didn't touch the door, the wooden bar.

"Why not?" Caddy said.

"Come back to the lamp," Nancy said. "We'll have fun. You don't have to go."

"We ought to go," Caddy said. "Unless we have a lot of fun." She and Nancy came back to the fire, the lamp.

"I want to go home," Jason said. "I'm going to tell."

"I know another story," Nancy said. She stood close to the lamp. She looked at Caddy, like when your eyes look up at a stick balanced on your nose. She had to look down to see Caddy, but her eyes looked like that, like when you are balancing a stick.

"I won't listen to it," Jason said. "I'll bang on the floor."

"It's a good one," Nancy said. "It's better than the other one."

"What's it about?" Caddy said. Nancy was standing by the lamp. Her hand was on the lamp, against the light, long and brown.

"Your hand is on that hot globe," Caddy said. "Don't it feel hot to your hand?"

Nancy looked at her hand on the lamp chimney. She took her hand away, slow. She stood there, looking at Caddy, wringing her long hand as though it were tied to her wrist with a string.

"Let's do something else," Caddy said.

"I want to go home," Jason said.

"I got some popcorn," Nancy said. She looked at Caddy and then at Jason and then at me and then at Caddy again. "I got some popcorn."

"I don't like popcorn," Jason said. "I'd rather have candy."

Nancy looked at Jason. "You can hold the popper." She was still wringing her hand; it was long and limp and brown.

"All right," Jason said. "I'll stay a while if I can do that. Caddy can't hold it. I'll want to go home, if Caddy holds the popper."

Nancy built up the fire. "Look at Nancy putting her hands in the fire," Caddy said. "What's the matter with you, Nancy?"

"I got popcorn," Nancy said. "I got some." She took the popper from under the bed. It was broken. Jason began to cry.

"We can't have any popcorn," he said.

"We ought to go home, anyway," Caddy said. "Come on, Quentin."

"Wait," Nancy said; "wait. I can fix it. Don't you want to help me fix it?"

"I don't think I want any," Caddy said. "It's too late now."

"You help me, Jason," Nancy said. "Don't you want to help me?"

"No," Jason said. "I want to go home."

"Hush," Nancy said; "hush. Watch. Watch me. I can fix it so Jason can hold it and pop the corn." She got a piece of wire and fixed the popper.

"It won't hold good," Caddy said.

"Yes it will," Nancy said. "Yawl watch. Yawl help me shell the corn."

The corn was under the bed too. We shelled it into the popper and Nancy helped Jason hold the popper over the fire.

"It's not popping," Jason said. "I want to go home."

"You wait," Nancy said. "It'll begin to pop. We'll have fun then." She was sitting close to the fire. The lamp was turned up so high it was beginning to smoke.

"Why don't you turn it down some?" I said.

"It's all right," Nancy said. "I'll clean it. Yawl wait. The popcorn will start in a minute."

"I don't believe it's going to start," Caddy said. "We ought to go home, anyway. They'll be worried."

"No," Nancy said. "It's going to pop. Dilsey will tell um yawl with me. I been working for yawl long time. They won't mind if you at my house. You wait, now. It'll start popping in a minute."

Then Jason got some smoke in his eyes and he began to cry. He dropped the popper into the fire. Nancy got a wet rag and wiped Jason's face, but he didn't stop crying.

"Hush," she said. "Hush." He didn't hush. Caddy took the popper out of the fire.

"It's burned up," she said. "You'll have to get some more popcorn, Nancy."

"Did you put all of it in?" Nancy said.

"Yes," Caddy said. Nancy looked at Caddy. Then she took the popper and opened it and poured the blackened popcorn into her apron and began to sort the grains, her hands long and brown, and we watching her.

"Haven't you got any more?" Caddy said.

"Yes," Nancy said; "yes. Look. This here ain't burnt. All we need to do is ——"

"I want to go home," Jason said. "I'm going to tell."

"Hush," Caddy said. We all listened. Nancy's head was already turned toward the barred door, her eyes filled with red lamplight. "Somebody is coming," Caddy said.

Then Nancy began to make that sound again, not loud, sitting there above the fire, her long hands dangling between her knees; all of a sudden water began to come out on her face in big drops, running down her face, carrying in each one a little turning ball of firelight until it dropped off her chin.

"She's not crying," I said.

"I ain't crying," Nancy said. Her eyes

were closed. "I ain't crying. Who is it?"

"I don't know," Caddy said. She went to the door and looked out. "We've got to go home now," she said. "Here comes father."

"I'm going to tell," Jason said. "You all made me come."

The water still ran down Nancy's face. She turned in her chair. "Listen. Tell him. Tell him we going to have fun. Tell him I take good care of yawl until in the morning. Tell him to let me come home with yawl and sleep on the floor. Tell him I won't need no pallet. We'll have fun. You remember last time how we had so much fun?"

"I didn't have any fun," Jason said. "You hurt me. You put smoke in my eyes."

IV

Father came in. He looked at us. Nancy did not get up.

"Tell him," she said.

"Caddy made us come down here," Jason said. "I didn't want to."

Father came to the fire. Nancy looked up at him. "Can't you go to Aunt Rachel's and stay?" he said. Nancy looked up at father, her hands between her knees. "He's not here," father said. "I would have seen. There wasn't a soul in sight."

"He in the ditch," Nancy said. "He waiting in the ditch yonder."

"Nonsense," father said. He looked at Nancy. "Do you know he's there?"

"I got the sign," Nancy said.

"What sign?"

"I got it. It was on the table when I come in. It was a hog bone, with blood meat still on it, laying by the lamp. He's out there. When yawl walk out that door, I gone."

"Who's gone, Nancy?" Caddy said.

"I'm not a tattletale," Jason said.

"Nonsense," father said.

"He out there," Nancy said. "He looking through that window this minute, waiting for yawl to go. Then I gone."

"Nonsense," father said. "Lock up your house and we'll take you on to Aunt Rachel's."

"'Twon't do no good," Nancy said. She didn't look at father now, but he looked down at her, at her long, limp, moving hands.

"Putting it off won't do no good."

"Then what do you want to do?" father said.

"I don't know," Nancy said. "I can't do nothing. Just put it off. And that don't do no good. I reckon it belong to me. I reckon what I going to get ain't no more than mine."

"Get what?" Caddy said. "What's yours?"

"Nothing," father said. "You all must get to bed."

"Caddy made me come," Jason said.

"Go on to Aunt Rachel's," father said.

"It won't do no good," Nancy said. She sat before the fire, her elbows on her knees, her long hands between her knees. "When even your own kitchen wouldn't do no good. When even if I was sleeping on the floor in the room with your own children, and the next morning there I am, and blood all ——"

"Hush," father said. "Lock the door and put the lamp out and go to bed."

"I scared of the dark," Nancy said. "I scared for it to happen in the dark."

"You mean you're going to sit right here, with the lamp lighted?" father said. Then Nancy began to make the sound again, sitting before the fire, her long hands between her knees. "Ah, damnation," father said. "Come along, chillen. It's bedtime."

"When yawl go, I gone," Nancy said. "I be dead tomorrow. I done had saved up the coffin money with Mr. Lovelady——"

Mr. Lovelady was a short, dirty man who collected the Negro insurance, coming around to the cabins and the kitchens every Saturday morning, to collect fifteen cents. He and his wife lived in the hotel. One morning his wife committed suicide. They had a child, a little girl. After his wife committed suicide Mr. Lovelady and the child went away. After a while Mr. Lovelady came back. We would see him going down the lanes on Saturday morning to the Baptist church.

Father carried Jason on his back. We went out Nancy's door; she was sitting before the fire. "Come and put the bar up," father said. Nancy didn't move. She didn't look at us again. We left her there, sitting before the fire with the door opened, so it wouldn't happen in the dark.

"What, father?" Caddy said. "Why is Nancy scared of Jubah? What is Jubah going to do to her?"

"Jubah wasn't there," Jason said.

"No," father said. "He's not there. He's gone away."

"Who is it that's waiting in the ditch?" Caddy said. We looked at the ditch. We came to it, where the path went down into the thick vines and went up again. "Nobody," father said.

There was just enough moon to see by. The ditch was vague, thick, quiet. "If he's there, he can see us, can't he?" Caddy said.

"You made me come," Jason said on father's back. "I didn't want to."

The ditch was quite still, quite empty, massed with honeysuckle. We couldn't see Jubah, any more than we could see Nancy sitting there in her house, with the door open and the lamp burning, because she didn't want it to happen in the dark. "I done got tired," Nancy said. "I just a nigger. It ain't no fault of mine."

But we could still hear her. She began as soon as we were out of the house, sitting there above the fire, her long brown hands between her knees. We could still hear her when we had crossed the ditch, Jason high and close and little about father's head.

Then we had crossed the ditch, walking out of Nancy's life. Then her life was sitting there with the door open and the lamp lit, waiting, and the ditch between us and us going on, dividing the impinged lives of us and Nancy.

"Who will do our washing now, father?" I said.

"I'm not a nigger," Jason said.

"You're worse," Caddy said, "you are a tattletale. If something was to jump out, you'd be scairder than a nigger."

"I wouldn't," Jason said.

"You'd cry," Caddy said.

"Caddy!" father said.

"I wouldn't," Jason said.

"Scairy cat," Caddy said.

"Candace!" father said.

WHITMAN AS HIS OWN PRESS-AGENT

By Emory Holloway

Years ago, in a newspaper, I ran across a casual allusion to Walt Whitman's having been at one time connected with Alexander H. Shephard's Washington *Chronicle*. When recently the opportunity arrived for running the matter down, I found that the writer had his facts somewhat mixed. The *Chronicle* was friendly to Whitman and appears to have printed articles from his pen, anonymously; but it was never owned by Shephard. Yet Shephard was one of the owners of the Washington *Evening Star*, which, about 1870, was a sturdy champion of the poet.

The first editions of *Leaves of Grass* had no publisher except the author, who, to make headway against the prevailing ridicule and indifference, found it advisable to act as his own press-agent. Accordingly, he explained his new verse, not only in a classic preface to the poems themselves, but also through anonymous reviews in various newspapers. Throughout his remaining years he continued to exert an influence on what his friends, at least, should print about him. His guiding or restraining hand in the books by Burroughs, Bucke, and Traubel, for instance, is well known. Though he was pretty well advertised, if not widely read, by 1869, through the sale of the 1860 and 1867 editions, and the laudation of his friends Burroughs and O'Connor, he did not feel satisfied with the headway he was making with American critics. He saw no better way to remedy matters than to keep before the public eye the image of the picturesque personage of whom the book was an expression.

This he did in many indirect ways. Sometimes he would criticize himself, or merely describe himself, in the third person, inserting little harmless phrases of doubt or criticism as a smoke-screen to conceal his authorship; or he would write something purporting to be an interview with himself; again, he would quote morsels from friendly European reviews. It is hard to tell just how many of the editorials about him in the *Star* and the *Chronicle* were directly inspired by him or how many were actually written by him, though in one or two cases we have, not only internal evidence as a guide, but the copy in his own manuscript. There is no such manuscript of the follow-

---

EMORY HOLLOWAY *is perhaps the country's leading authority on Walt Whitman. He has written extensively on the poet, and his* Walt Whitman — An Interpretation in Narrative *was awarded the Pulitzer Prize in 1926. He has contributed to the* Cambridge History of American Literature *and the* Encyclopedia Britannica. (December, 1929)

ing, so far as I know, but it can hardly fail to impress the reader who is intimately acquainted with his style as coming from his pen. It appeared in the *Chronicle* on Sunday, May 9, 1869.

Walt Whitman, the poet, will complete the fiftieth year of his age the current May 31, 1869, having been born on that date, 1819. His friends in New York, Brooklyn, and elsewhere, will be pleased to learn that, on the verge of becoming half a centenarian, he retains his accustomed health, eats his rations regularly, and keeps his weight well toward 190 pounds.

Of the poetical merits and demerits of the subject of our item, concerning which the contest still rages in literary circles, we desire to say nothing. We will only mention here, for what it is worth, the judgment of a late German critic,[1] (Mr. Whitman's poetry has been translated and published in Germany), who characterizes him as "the most radically *Christian* and *Socratic* poet of any modern writer," inasmuch as he adopts for the chief reliance and ground-plan of individual and public excellence the elements of friendship, personal purity, and disinterestedness, the cultivation of "the inner light," and the like; and also in his treatment of the whole material frame of things, in its particulars and in its aggregate, as but the gateway, through death and decay, to spiritual existence, the only substantial one, and the purport, according to him, of all material objects and persons, and also the true key to all science.

We may add that the poems, *Leaves of Grass*, originally published in New York about fourteen years ago, and since added to, and republished time and again in various cities, are still considered unfinished by their author. But we understand that the collection, revised, and including his new verses on religious themes, and forming probably the final digest and edition of the book, will be printed the ensuing summer. *Democratic Vistas*, a small prose book, will also be published during the summer.

The article then proceeds to a more personal tone:

Mr. Whitman, at the present date, continues to occupy a third-class clerkship in the Attorney-General's office, where, since the close of the war, he has been employed successively under Attorney-Generals Speed, Stanbery, Bowning, Evarts, and Hoar. An inveterate pedestrian, and, like a true Greek, living much in the open air, he has long become a familiar figure in our city, and amid the varied and picturesque scenery of the District.

In times past, in New York, he frequented the top of the Broadway omnibuses, and became a well-known pet of the drivers. Here he has to content himself with the platform of the street-cars, often riding out to Georgetown, or to the Eastern Branch. On Pennsylvania avenue or Seventh street or Fourteenth street, or perhaps of a Sunday, along the suburban roads toward Rock creek, or across on Arlington Heights, or up the shores of the Potomac, you will meet moving along at a firm but moderate pace, a robust figure, six feet high, costumed in blue or gray, with drab hat, broad shirt-collar, gray-white beard, full and curly, face like a red apple, blue eyes, and a look of animal health more indicative of hunting or boating than the department office or author's desk. Indeed the subject of our item, in his verse, his manners, and even his philosophy, evidently draws from, and has reference to, the influences of the sea and sky and woods and prairies, with their laws, and man in his relation to them; while neither the conventional parlor nor library has cast its spells upon him.

Possessing singular personal magnetism, and frequently beloved at sight, yet Walt Whitman's nonchalance, large adhesive-

---

[1] Ferdinand Freiligrath, in the Augsburg *Allgemeine Zeitung*, May 10, 1868. Freiligrath introduced Whitman to the Germans.

ness,[2] and a certain silent defiance both in his poetry and appearance, have long laid him open to caricature and sarcastic criticism. Then there have been imputations of a virulent description, such as ignorance, drunkenness, and lust, to which mental aberration and moral obliquity have been strenuously added. Very little, however, do these charges trouble the subject of them.

"In early years," said Mr. Whitman, lately in conversation, "I suffered much at the fate of being misrepresented and misunderstood — at the lies of enemies and still more the complacent fatuity of those I loved. But I see now that it is no detriment to a hardy character, but is perhaps the inevitable price of freedom, and a vigorous training and growth; and that even slanders mean something to every real student of himself, and as it were betray to the commander of the fort where his embankments are openest to the enemy, and most need strengthening and the guard."

There are numerous pictures, frontispieces, photographic, and other pretended likenesses of Walt Whitman, whose great bulky head, wooly beard, carmine cheeks, and open throat attract the artists. Most of these pictures are bad, some of them comically monstrous (as in Hotten's London edition of Walt Whitman's poems). Mr. Gardiner, on Seventh street, however, has a capital photo, taken in 1863. Messrs. Seybold & Tarisse, on the Avenue, below Sixth, have a good head, just taken, very strong in shade and light. William Kurtz, New York, has two or three noble photos. Charles Hine, the artist, same city, has a fine portrait in oil, life size.

Since Lowell's publication of Whitman's "Bardic Symbols" in the *Atlantic Monthly* nearly a score of years before, nothing from the latter's pen had found a welcome there, until, in February, 1869, he placed "Proud Music of the Sea Storm" for one hundred dollars. The manuscript was presented to the editor, James T. Fields, not directly, but through Emerson, who, according to Whitman, had offered his services in the matter. The incident has interest as showing both the relation of Whitman and Emerson at the time and the precaution Whitman was taking not to have the poem rejected by the magazine which was more or less the arbiter of literary elegance in America. Nor did he lose any time in capitalizing his success, if we may judge by the comment of the *Star* on January 18, probably before the magazine was on the Washington newsstands:

> The claims of Walt Whitman to the position of a poet are so far recognized by the literary set in Boston, who consider their *dicta* supreme law in matters pertaining to letters, that the *Atlantic* for February contains a long poem from his sturdy pen, and one of the very best, to our notion, that he has yet written. Between *Blackwood* and the *Atlantic* he is now pretty well endorsed on both continents — a circumstance that may be very gratifying to his friends, but which, we suspect, matters very little to him.

During the editorship of Professor Bliss Perry the *Atlantic* printed a number of things about Whitman, but during the last ten years I have had several articles on the poet returned with a courteous announcement that the magazine was closed to all articles about him. Whitman wished the public to believe him as indifferent to criticism, friendly or hostile, as the great poet he had described in his verse — an answerer of the profound

---

[2] A phrenological term which Whitman was fond of using to designate a personal attraction between men that is stronger than ordinary friendship. The "Calamus" poems celebrate it.

questions of life, but not one to notice a critical attack. In the flush of his first inspiration he had boasted, with the boundless hope of youth:

> I exist as I am, that is enough,
> If no other in the world be aware I sit content,
> And if each and all be aware I sit content.
> One world is aware and by far the largest to me, and that is myself,
> And whether I come to my own today or in ten thousand or ten million years,
> I can cheerfully take it now, and with equal cheerfulness I can wait.

But if all the references to his indifference concerning fame to be found in the Washington papers were inspired by him, that indifference was rather too vocal and insistent to be convincing. When Bayard Taylor and others travestied his American Institute poem in 1871, the *Evening Star*, using information it could hardly have had except from Whitman or his friends, countered thus:

> The newspapers still keep up their talk about Walt Whitman. Here now comes the announcement that Roberts Brothers, of Boston, are to publish his late American Institute utterance in small book form. From abroad, we learn that the English poet and critic, Roden Noel, of aristocratic and Lord Byron lineage, has prepared a lengthy review of Whitman for *Dark Blue*, the new Oxonian magazine.
>
> The truth about Whitman, as author not only of this American Institute piece but all else, is that his contempt for the "poets" and "poetry" of the day, his presentation of thoughts and things at first hand instead of second or third hand, his sturdy and old-fashioned earnestness, and his unprecedented novelty, make him a capital target for the smart writers and the verbal fops engaged in manufacturing items and "criticism." Then besides, to be candid, Walt Whitman *is* a pretty hard nut to crack. His involved sentences, always hiding at least half their meaning, his kangaroo leaps as if from one crag to another, his appalling catalogues, (enough to stagger the bravest heart,) his unheard of demand for brains in the reader as well as in the thing read, and then his scornful silence, never explaining anything nor answering any attack, all lay him fairly open to be misunderstood, to slur, burlesque, and sometimes spiteful innuendo; and will probably continue to do so.
>
> Like his own "Kosmos," he can be viewed from many and partial points of view, among the rest, from one or two whence he certainly appears gross, repellant, and dangerous. But his complete and permanent character — and that is the only just method of comprehending him — is nevertheless healthy, free, manly, attractive, and of a purity and strength almost beyond example. The basis of his principal poetry is the intuitional and emotional, actuated by what the phrenologists term self-esteem and adhesiveness. Like all revolutionists and founders, he himself will have to create the growth by which he is to be fully understood and accepted. This will be a slow and long work, but sure.

The reader who is familiar with Whitman's diction, phraseology, psychology and methods of anonymous self-defense will not be led by the candor of this passage hastily to assume that he had nothing to do with its compostion. But the *Evening Star* took pains to present him in other lights than that of the misunderstood bard indifferent whether the laurel wreath should grace his good gray brow. Here is a little anecdote, from the issue of January 18, 1869, which I have never seen reprinted:

> A moderate-sized oil painting has been placed in the window of Mohum & Bestor's

store, on the Avenue today, that calls for special notice from all lovers of perfect art. It is called "The Cavalry Picket," and represents, in the midst of a lonesome winter scene, probably in Virginia, in a bleak and freezing snow-storm, drifted, the ground white, a cavalry soldier, numbed and dead, fallen from his horse, extended on his back, a thin veil of snow drifted over his face, and the horse (a fine piece of drawing and painting) standing by, and peering over the dead soldier. The picture is by Mr. McLeod, of this city, and is a work that will make its own reputation.

We saw Walt Whitman standing before the window this morning, looking at it long. The tears fell down his cheeks, called forth by many sad reminiscences. "Write something about it," he said, "and tell the painter how profoundly it has affected me. I consider it, in its way, unsurpassed in all technical requirements, from the point of view of art merely. A typical incident of the great war; then mounting above, and spreading wide, it touches the universal human heart, and is as strong as it is manly and tender."

Not long ago a leading dealer in autographs said to me: "American writers rank thus — Poe, Whitman, Hawthorne; for collectors will pay for their manuscripts in that order." He seriously urged using the manuscript prices current as an index of literary merit. The *Evening Star* must have been familiar with this yardstick for the measurement of genius, for, getting its facts from Whitman or his friends, it tried to show that Walt Whitman, Unlimited, was a going concern. For example:

Walt Whitman on a Gold Basis. — The ever-increasing favor the American poet finds in Europe oddly contrasts with the treatment he has received in the past in his own country. No less striking a parallel is afforded between the offishness of publishers toward his writings here and the high pecuniary value set upon them by the same class abroad. For the group of poems from his pen, entitled "Whispers of Heavenly Death," which appeared in the last number of the English *Broadway Magazine*, the proprietors paid Mr. Whitman twenty-five dollars a page *in gold*. This amounts to about seventy-five dollars in currency for the whole — the composition occupying two [*sic*] pages of the magazine. It is needless to add that no other poet except Tennyson commands such a price in England.

When the Philadelphia *Bulletin* asserted that Whitman "never had an income of over $900 a year," the *Evening Star*, joining battle on the facts, replied:

Oh, yes. The Blue Book puts him down: "W. Whitman, New York. Clerk, Attorney-General's office. Salary, $1600."

Though Whitman had been receiving this salary for five years, this information seems to have struck the current journalistic mind as having news value, for in September, 1871, the New York *Evening Post* ran the following:

Walt Whitman receives a salary of $1600 a year as clerk in the office of the Attorney-General and is said to be the richest man in Washington, because he never wants what he does not have. His philosophy is better than his poetry.

II

But Whitman did want what he did not have — increasing recognition at home, if not for himself at least for his poetry. He thought he was beginning to get it when he was invited to deliver a commencement poem at Dartmouth in 1872;

but though he conquered when he came, Professor Bliss Perry has shown that the invitation itself was a student joke at the expense of a rather conservative faculty. Whitman used the occasion not only to send copies to the press but to write an anonymous eulogy of his poem for a newspaper, though we do not know that it saw print. However, the *Evening Star's* leader on the Dartmouth poem is so full of Whitmanisms of thought, expression and even punctuation, as to convince me that either Whitman wrote it or someone so familiar with *Democratic Vistas* as to have caught both the gist of its meaning and its style. Here, in part, is the article:

> Peculiar in literary form, echoing Whitman's fervid patriotism for the whole country, and totally unlike the classic or sentimental reminiscences of such occasions, its key-note seems to be an earnest conviction that the loftiest and most binding union and truest pride and glory of the United States (after the establishment of their material interests, which he thinks already permanently provided for,) are to to be sought in new moral, patriotic, national literary development, on a scientific and spiritual basis, and always with a realizing sense of physical health, and finest and handsomest offspring.
>
> For Walt Whitman, as we understand, while he admits the merits of the scientific and journalistic press of the day, avowedly views the whole tribe of poets and novelists with contempt. His notion is that for imaginative purposes the modern time, and the United States especially, can only fitly express and justify their vital and characteristic elements by new and native lyric, artistic, and even religious forms, and that, for present and future use, current poetry, art and ecclesiasticisms, however serviceable for their time in Europe and the past, are impotent for America, and incompatible with her genius.

Similarly, in the preceding year, Whitman had been elated to receive an invitation from the managers of the American Institute to deliver an orginal poem at the opening of their annual fair in New York. Perhaps he did not know that Horace Greeley, the president of the Institute, was the regular attraction on opening day, but that busy with a presidential bee in his bonnet, the sage of Chappaqua was electioneering in the Middle West. Whitman came to New York and, on September 7, read his poem, "After All, Not to Create Only." Two days later, having found that much of the metropolitan press was disposed to make merry over his only half-inspired effort, he sent his own account of the occasion to the Washington *Chronicle* for publication as an anonymous letter from New York.

> Imagine yourself inside a huge barn-like edifice of a couple of acres, spanned by immense arches, like the ribs of some leviathan ship, (whose skeleton hull inverted the structure might be said to resemble,) & this building, crowded & crammed with incipient displays of goods and machinery — everything that grows & is made — & a thousand men actually engaged at work, in their shirt-sleeves, putting the said goods & machinery in order — all with a noise, movement, & variety as if a good-sized city was in process of being built.
>
> In the middle of this, to an audience of perhaps two or three thousand people, with a fringe on the outside of perhaps five or six hundred partially-hushed workmen, carpenters, machinists, & the like, with saws, wrenches, or hammers in their hands, Walt Whitman, last Thursday, gave his already celebrated poem before the American Institute. His manner was at first sight coldly quiet, but you soon

felt a magnetism & felt stirred. His great figure was clothed in gray, with white vest, no necktie, & his beard was as unshorn as ever. His voice is magnificent, & is to be mentioned with Nature's oceans & the music of forests and hills.

His gestures are few, but significant. Sometimes he stands with his hands in his breast pockets; once or twice he walked a few steps to & fro. He did not mind the distant noises & the litter & machinery, but doubtless rather enjoyed them. He was perfectly self-possessed. His apostrophe to the Stars and Stripes which floated above him, describing them in far different scenes in battle, was most impassioned. Also his "Away with War itself!" & his scornful "Away with novels, plots, & plays of foreign courts!"

A few of his allusions were in a playful tone, but the main impression was markedly serious, animated, & earnest. He was applauded as he advanced to read, besides several times throughout, & at the close. He did not respond in the usual way by bowing. All the directors & officers of the Institute crowded around him & heartily thanked him. He extricated himself, regained his old Panama hat & stick, and, without waiting for the rest of the exercises, made a quiet exit by the steps at the back of the stand.

The real audience of this chant of peace, invention, & labor, however, was to follow. Of the New York & Brooklyn evening and morning dailies, twelve out of seventeen published the poem in full the same evening or the next morning.

So much for the picture Whitman wished the public to have of his performance. His own words make clear how careful he was to create a pose and to maintain it, the trademark of the new poetry. He had no doubt supplied copies of the poem to the press in advance, and I have found that a good many of them did print it, in whole or in part. But this does not mean that they all took it seriously. A humorous contrast to Whitman's description appeared in the *World's* report (September 8) captioned "Poetry and Ploughs." The reporter failed to see the thousands to which Whitman refers. (The *Tribune* estimated that there were 200–300 present.) "The vacancy caused by the absence of Mr. Greeley," said the *World,* "was regarded with painful emotion." The police were so little able to quiet the workmen's hubbub, even for the prayer of invocation, that it was impossible for Whitman's voice to carry more than fifteen feet. "After prayer the poet was introduced. The managers were all provided with printed proofs, which enabled them to follow the author as he recited his verses and put in the applause where it was proper to do so. No one among the meeting house benches could have heard anything the poet said." The report was accompanied by an editorial entitled "A Whitmaniacal Catalogue." The editor saw no "playful tone" in the poem, but satirized its prosaic formlessness, which is, of course, its weakest point.

Dropping the hand of the amiable Muse with a rude suddenness, born probably of a recollection of his duties as a compiler of a catalogue, Mr. Whitman returns to his work, and gives in rapid succession a list of everything on exhibition at the fair. Even when fairly in the midst of this prosaic task the painful confusion of his intellect is frequently manifest. He arbitrarily groups coffee-mills, mowing-machines, and anti-malarious pills under the singular heading of "rills of civilization," and boldly prophesies that these strangely composite rills will ultimately become pyramids and obelisks, upon which "pow-

erful matrons" will gaze in admiration. It is true he expressly states that these matrons of the future will be
> Vaster than all the old;

but why the vastness of a matron should induce her to regard rills of mowing-machines as identical with obelisks does not appear. Even the famous fat lady of Barnum's former museum, who, if not a matron, was at all events the vastest of modern females, would have repelled with indignation the idea that she could not tell a rill from a pyramid.

Even the Brooklyn *Eagle*, which Whitman had edited a quarter of a century before, though admitting that he had his points, was disposed to treat him rather as a freak, properly exhibited at a fair.

> The most of it [the Institute poem], however, will be pronounced by the average reader hard, commonplace, realistic, prosaic, when it is not simple jargon — word-piling with no obvious purpose. Whether Whitman is to remain on view throughout the exhibition the advertizements do not state. If he is engaged permanently we advise the citizens of Brooklyn to go and see him. He has a special and local, as well as a general and national, reputation.

III

But it was the *Tribune* that saw in the occasion opportunity for mirth unconfined. Bayard Taylor, who was the next year to defend American publishers, in the so-called Buchanan War, against what he termed the "intellectual convexity" of Whitman's ardent sponsors, sat down and composed parodies of the four poets most in the public eye — Bret Harte, John Hay, Joaquin Miller and Whitman. These the managing editor connected with a prose burlesque, representing the four poets as contending for first honors at the fair, each by celebrating himself. The tone of the Whitman travesty [3] is well represented by the opening lines:

> Who was it sang of the procreant urge, recounted sextillions of subjects?
> Who but myself, the Kosmos, yawping abroad, concerned not at all about either the effect or the answer.

But there were editors to praise Whitman's poem, including those of the Brooklyn *Standard*, the New York *Sun* and the faithful Washington *Star*, which blamed the *Tribune's* attitude on the jealousy of its own "kept poet." Altogether Whitman did create a stir, which may have been as much as he hoped for. Taylor doubtless never appreciated the full greatness of the man, yet one who has studied the record must appreciate the point he made in 1876 in answer to the charge that there was a literary cabal against Whitman among American publishers and editors:

> The charge of a cabal among any portion of the authors of America, to persecute and suppress Walt Whitman, or anybody else, is an absurdity and an impertinence. Other writers have their contributions returned by magazine editors, and do not whine about it. Hawthorne was ignored during his best years, Emerson abused and ridiculed, and their friends never dreamed of imagining a conspiracy against them. No man in this country has ever been so constantly and skillfully advertised by his disciples as Walt Whitman. They have not only been sleeplessly watchful for attack, but they have resented indifference. They

---
[3] Reprinted, with the others, in Taylor's "The Echo Club and Other Literary Diversions" and in Henry S. Saunders' "Walt Whitman Parodies."

deny, for his sake, the right of a critic to be honest, the right of an editor to select, or the right of a publisher to refuse. Not patient for the final and irreversible decision of time, they angrily claim immediate acceptance of a theory of formlessness in literature which would send the world's great authors to the shade. If their master's new venture should fail, they will be chiefly to blame. He has wisely held himself aloof from their aggressive championship; and we heartily commend the silence and apparent indifference of "the good gray poet" to the imitation of his good green friends.

Whitman did often restrain his impetuous friends, less shrewd than he, and he professed not to have started the Buchanan War, though I cannot find that he was displeased with it. In fact, he made himself often enough the same charges against American publishers that Buchanan made when he opened hostilities. And had Taylor been able to see Whitman's practiced hand behind such articles for instance, as I have quoted here, I doubt if he would have drawn a line between the good gray poet and his good green friends.

If there was jealousy in the heart of Taylor, there is, on the other hand, room to believe that Whitman found in him a natural rival and enemy. When Taylor was asked to write the poem for the Centennial Exposition in Philadelphia in 1876, Whitman was disappointed. He renamed the American Institute piece "Song of the Exposition" and further celebrated the occasion by issuing a Centennial Edition of his poems. Concerning these two occasions when his ambitions crossed those of Taylor, he afterward said to Horace Traubel:

It rather staggered me at the time to receive the invitation to make this poem: I was everywhere, practically everywhere, disavowed — hated, ridiculed, lampooned, parodied; rejected by the notables everywhere. Then this invitation came. Of course my inviters were criticized for inviting, I was criticized for being invited — for accepting — all kinds of impolite things were said, mostly for my benefit: I even got a few anonymous letters from people who wanted to tell me "the plain truth," as one of them said. But the thing went off — went of all right — yes: was its own kind of success.

I've only had a few such occasions to take care of. William [O'Connor] told Eldridge or somebody that I should have had the poem for the Centennial — that Bayard Taylor was unfit — that no one but Walt Whitman could have proved equal to the exigency: but William found few to take his view of the matter. I do not seem to belong to great show events — I am more like nobody than like somebody, — I was more used to being kicked out than asked in: I always went to the big pow-wows with the crowd, to look on, not with the nabobs, to perform.

Even here Whitman is trying to launch the idea that only prejudice and bad luck prevented him from being a literary lion. His unhappiness lay in his effort to be both journalist and poet, sensationalist and seer. He was an occasional poet, and our greatest; but the only occasion to which he could fitly respond, as in the case of his threnody on Lincoln's death, was some sudden and unpredictable eruption of his own emotions. The calendar had nothing to do with his creative impulses. It is a pity that he felt he had to advertise himself or go under; and that, if he must be his own press-agent, he injudiciously called attention to his worst poetry as well as his most sublime.

NO ONE MY GRIEF CAN TELL

By Nancy Hale

Amanda lay inert and burning hot in the sand on the little beach, under a huge red July sun like a fat zinnia in the blue sky. The sky made the sun look redder and the sun made the sky look bluer. She stared at the sun through slitted eyes and watched it get smaller, contract, and then burst open redder than ever, so hot that she could imagine that it sang, a sizzling, piercing hum of heat.

She turned herself over in the lazy yellow sift of sand and felt her backbone burn and melt, her limbs slide sensuously against the dry warmth under. Her pale green bathing suit was still wet, hot wet, and she imagined herself lying there with a drift of condensing steam rising up from her into the sun, all damp darkness and vicious liquids leaving her and rising, leaving her as clean and hard and chalky dry as a piece of coral. Her head lay resistlessly on her hand, sidewise, and in her upper ear she heard the hissing song of the sun and in her under ear the interminable whisper and shift of grains of sand.

Ten feet away from her, her child played with fearful concentration, leaning over a big log of driftwood, his little yellow jersey backside making a small hummock along the beach, while his carroty head bent lower and lower and lower over the sea-shells, or whatever objects gripped him with this absorption. He could stand there for hours in this position, legs straight and fat, trunk suddenly tipped downward from baby loins, his head nearly as low as his feet. His lips were tightly compressed, his face red, and he breathed violently through his nose, so that Amanda could just hear the loud whiffling sound of his concentration. He was four years old.

Part of me, she thought vaguely, playing with sea-shells. The loosened cell growing to be itself. The sun bakes him to a dry coral baby, dry and clean and well; the sun dries him from the pervading dampness of his beginning. He is being dried and cleared and healed from the wet wound of me, and lightened from the deep darkness of me, and he is becoming his wound-healed and complete self. As I am healed of him. O loop cut from my skein and once an undifferentiated strand within my skein, flap of my flesh cut away and healed again! He has no rawness where the knife once was, he is round and finished and without seam. And I am healed, but there is scar-tissue that will

NANCY HALE, *author of the highly popular* The Prodigal Women, *achieved her first success in the realm of the short story, of which this one is an excellent example.* (October, 1932)

not whiten, and a seam that is wrinkled and pursed. I cannot forget that something was a bubble of me that now is round and seamless and floats alone.

She pushed herself up on her elbow and held one hand flat shelved above her eyes and called, "Baby! Are your feet wet?"

The yellow jersey hummock caved in slowly and reluctantly; the baby stood up, scowling furiously.

"Unh-*unh*." He stared at her with infant resentment for a minute and then jerked himself around, expressively, back to the log and again addressed himself with ferocity to his sea-shells.

Let him alone. Let him swell and bubble. Let the sun dry away the primordial dampness and make him coral. What in the world did I call him for? How would his feet possibly get wet? The old scar itches, the flesh presses uselessly against that which once it owned, pressing and pressing, but they are two flesh. You are of me, but I am not of you. How is that, and how and why?

The sun got small again before her eyes, a far off point of light, and she watched it spring back near and huge and red, with a humming and a clash of brass. She lay on her back again so that the sun burned at all that was within the round trench of her bones, as though the top had been lifted and she lay broiling, the damp meat within the spiny carcass. Dry those damp and intricate darknesses within me, wither those dark and caverned sources of hate and revulsion and cunning, of furious possession and the corruption that it is to be a woman.

After a while she stood up and slapped at the crust of sand along her thighs.

II

She began to run along the beach, first through the soft deep sand, then down across the sharp mesh of dry seaweed, and then along the dark hard sand nearest the sea, marked with a Chinese tracery of the little waves that had now receded with the tide.

She raced near the edge of the water, running as fast as she had ever been able to run, and as neatly, taking long clean bounds and feeling her toes and the balls of her feet jab into the damp grittiness in sharp even rhythm. She could run as fast, her neck was as straight and firm, as ever. But she could not feel the same, or as free, or as ruthlessly young. It was no use. She put her head down into the light sea-wind and sprinted, running away.

At the end of the beach she came to a mounting pile of brown rocks, spattered with white barnacles and netted with seaweed. She sat on the wet slippery summit. She slid her eyes back and forth along the knife-edge of the horizon where two blues met.

I love a beach and I love the sea. And a pirate ship came galloping straight over the horizon, bound for the beach, bulging with buccaneers hanging out both sides, and on top a fat square white sail and the black flag. Maxfield Parrish, with the sea the color of an alcohol flame. No ocean looks its best without a sail showing somewhere. What the well-dressed ocean will wear. Steamships — bad ocean fashions, the sea would do well to sink them all.

And the beaches. The yellow sands of the New World, and the chalk cliffs of

Dover, the pink beaches of the far Bermudas, the dark and sinister dunes where up climbed the pirates carrying hooped chests under the tropical sun that gave them fever. Where stood Miranda all alone, staring out to sea — come unto these yellow sands. The marooned and the exiled. (My child? Don't look, you must try to become whole, that he can become whole. Don't look, think your own thoughts about yourself, or your thoughts about him will kill him.) Drake in the Pacific, Westward Ho, Salvation Yeo. He said, Sail On, Sail On! Sir Richard Grenville lay. In Flores in the Azores. While the hollow oak our fortress is, our heritage the sea. We — something something, balked the eternal sea. To hell with it!

She had to stand up to see where her child was. Way up the beach a small yellow dot, bright against the straw-yellow of the sand, walked next to white trousers and a blue coat. That was Oliver, his father. The afternoon train was in. The family man had come home and had joined his litt-le femily on th' beach and was taking his litt-le son for a walk, so sweet. We, meant to founder, something something, balked the eternal sea.

Should I never go back now, should I swim out into the gargantuan deeps, into the deep indigo darkness, what? Should I never return now, never walk back across the beach into the hot buzzing little box where live I, but with one paroxysm of desire, throw myself into depth and darkness and majestic oblivion, what? Home is where the heart is, ha ha! And the heart lies deep in beaded wells of forgetfulness and in the august and oblivious sea. The heart is drowned in yesterday, in fathoms deep of accumulated years and talking too much and always getting a little farther and a little farther from the early and fragile truth. Where is the truth, and where is the heart? Dropped into the shifting strata of the sea, and floating downward through interminable fathoms. Far, far away, and never to be regained.

Since life can never be brought back to beauty, and since the way has led off and away from faith or the slightest knowledge of what it is all about, why try to mend the way, why try to love what is intolerable? And all the things that life was going to be have dissolved, somehow, into the rest of impractical youth, like all good things. Now there is only existing and taking care of things and looking at faces and listening to people and talking and talking and talking.

All but my child. He is young and whole and an unseamed bubble and as pure and hard of heart as coral; he is beauty and he is mine, but I want him too much. Because, in the end, there is nothing left but dust and talk, all that I gave to myself and to ineffable and impossible dreaming and to the core of the world in me, all this must go somewhere. And there is nowhere for it to go but to him. It will possess him. He will become mine and the receptacle of my love. And the receptacle of my hate.

Is it fair? It is not fair. No one can contain more than he is himself, for if there is more than that given to him, he must throw away his own dreams and himself, for there is no room for them. He will become utterly the violin of me, and he will be utterly mine, for I will fill him with more passion than he can understand, and it will possess him.

All the time she had been walking back along the beach, lifting her feet and setting them into the sand delicately and disdainfully. She looked up, and saw the sun upon its downward course, drifting, still hot and quivering, down the sky. I hate to see — that evening sun go down. It takes away the heat, and when the heat is gone I become all damp again, dark with liquid corruption which is possessive love. The sea was a little mauve now, and gulls flew along in scalloped lines.

"Hi!" Oliver called when she was within calling distance.

"Hi!" she called back. "Isn't it a swell day?"

He began to laugh as she got near him.

"You ought to see yourself," he said. "You've got a burn like a house afire. You're a beet. Did you know it?"

"I lay out here all day," she said. "It doesn't hurt."

"It doesn't?" He threw back his arm and gave her a terrific slap between the shoulder blades. "I bet that hurt."

"Sure it hurt," she said, laughing.

"The kid's burned too. For God's sake, why didn't you put a hat on him?"

"It's supposed to be good for him. He likes it."

The baby, released, had gone back to his sea-shells, and was singing, an interminable, noteless wail, in the late afternoon quiet. Oliver lay down in the sand and closed his eyes. He took a long breath.

"Nice, darling?" Amanda dropped down beside him and put her hand in his. He took his away and scratched his nose.

"By the way," he said, and then closed his mouth as if he had finished a sentence.

"What?"

"I'll be out to dinner."

"Who? Beatrice?"

"I don't know why you say it in that tone of voice."

"No reason."

"I'll be home early."

"All right."

"Well, I *will* be home early."

"All *right*, I said."

III

The evening sun kept going down. Amanda got up and put a sweater on the baby. He was so fat his arms had to be squeezed into the stretchy knitted sleeves.

The baby was sleepy and pushed his head back comfortably into her breast. He was a nice fat size, and felt warm and delicious in her arms. She felt at last relaxed and untormented. She dug her chin gently into the top of his head and looked out to sea, feeling healed and well with her child against her. He stopped all pain, closed all wounds. It was as easy as that. He rolled his head around luxuriously. "Mmmmmmh," he murmured, half asleep. His response and unconscious love were so agonizingly right to her that she could not help drawing her arms tighter around him, with a stabbing knot tied inside her. He smelt so good. Everything in her ached to be given to him, to pour love and love upon his round head. There was so much pent inside her and so much that beat to get out.

Oliver got up.

"I've got to dress sometime," he said. "Coming?"

"I guess so. I hate to put the baby down, you know," she grinned up at him.

He burst out laughing again.

"God, you look like hell. Your nose is glittering, it's so shiny."

"Darling," she said, "I wish you'd stick around tonight."

He looked at her and gave another of his laughs.

"Well, baby, so that's the way you feel? We got the rest of our lives for seeing each other. Got to live, you know, get around, do things before we're old."

He gave her a little cheerful kick with his foot, and started up the beach.

The baby stirred again and threw one arm violently around her. She tightened her arms wildly about him. The old scar aches, the tissue is not healed. This flesh that was mine, returns to me, but closer, closer.

All that I have so long, so much, take it; let the ancient blood flow back between us once more. I love you, my own flesh, and I love nothing else in the world. I can give to nobody else.

He lay perfectly still against her, swelling with his baby breathing. He was so warm, so terribly alive and new. She let her eyes seek the indefinite horizon, thinking of nothing, wanting nothing, letting her love and her need and her beating want flow into him, as though no knife had ever cut them, as if there had been no wound and no scar. She held him a little tighter for a minute before she got up to go, for it was turning a little chill, the sun bobbed like a bubble above the horizon.

PASSION

By Walter de la Mare

Passion's a flame that, leaping up apace,
 Will in blind fury its own being efface;
Squand'ring its fuel in a deadening dust,
Not for the wishing, but because it must.

(December, 1940)

THE LAW TAKES ITS TOLL

By Robert Blake

THE PLACE
The Death House in the Texas State Penitentiary at Huntsville.
THE TIME
A day and night in April, 1929. The dialogue begins eighteen hours before the time set for an execution.
THE PERSONS
NUMBER ONE, *a Mexican sentenced to death.*
NUMBER TWO, *a white man sentenced to death.*
NUMBER FIVE, *a white man sentenced to death.*
NUMBER SIX, *a white man sentenced to die at midnight tonight.*
NUMBER SEVEN, *a white man sentenced to death.*
NUMBER NINE, *a white man sentenced to death, but reprieved because he has gone crazy.*
Prison officials, guards, a priest, Protestant chaplains, newspaper reporters, etc.
There are nine cells in the condemned row, but only six of them are occupied. They are so constructed that no condemned man can see another, but each can hear whatever any of the others says. There is a corridor in front of the cells, and at one end of it is a green door leading into the execution chamber.

SIX — Well, boys, this is my last day.
TWO — No, I think you'll get a stay.
FIVE — Yeah, you'll get a stay all right. No one has ever gone down here without at least one stay. Why should you be an exception?
SIX — Well, just the same, I don't expect it, or the Governor would have given it to me when he gave Two his stay.
FIVE — It'll come at the last minute. He refused to commute your sentence, but he would appoint a sanity commission to investigate your sanity if you had the priest wire him.
TWO — When does the priest come around?
ONE — Oh, he comes whenever you write for him or ask for him.
NINE [*In a loud, wailing voice, idiotically*] — Jo————nes!
SIX [*Humorously*] — I guess maybe I'd better start yelling Jones!
SEVEN — Too late now. You ought to done that long ago.

~~~~~~

ROBERT BLAKE *here attempted to set down, as literally as possible, the conversation among his fellow condemned men in the Death House of the State Penitentiary at Huntsville, Texas, on a day when one of them was to die. He himself was executed a week after he completed "The Law Takes Its Toll." It was later dramatized into* The Last Mile, *by John Wexley, and had a long run on Broadway.* (July, 1929)

THE LAW TAKES ITS TOLL

Two — Here comes breakfast!
Six — It had better be a good one. It's to be my last, I guess.
One [*The Mexican*] — Oh, you don' know. I think you get stay all right, too.
Six — Well, by God I'd better! He's given every nigger that ever went down a stay. He's a nigger-lover if he don't.
Two — Here's the mail.
Voice from Outside — Give these cigars to Six.
Guard — Here's some cigars for you.
Six — Who sent 'em?
Guard — Some of the guards.
Six — Hell! That's more than I'll ever smoke!
One — Send 'em on down to me!
Six — Aw, go to Hell! I'm goin' to ask 'em to let me hold your hand tonight, or you can sit on my lap.
One — Damn if I will!
Six — Sure you will, and I'll take you to Hell with me.
One — Shut up!
Nine [*A horrible howl*] — Jo ——nes! Jo—nes! Jo-o-o-o-nes!
Seven [*Breaking into verse*] —
The death house is where they come and go;
They linger just a short time
Before they are taken to the electric chair,
Accused of some crime.
One — Shut up, you ——!
Six — Forget that!
Seven [*Going on doggedly*] —
I have seen them come, I have seen them go;
I have heard the death warrants read,
And when I see the bright lights go dim —
In the electric chair another soul is dead!
Six — For Christ's sake, Seven, have a heart!
Seven —
When I hear the lonesome hum of the motor
That sends the high voltage to your death,
I have a sad unexplainable sensation
Running through my breast.
What is your feelings when your head is shaved,
And you are dressed out for death —
Six — I'm going to come back and haunt you, if you don't shut up.
Seven [*A poet and proud of it, he refuses to be daunted*] —
When your time grows near — less than one hour —
And you get a reprieve of a little more rest?
Six — Now you're talking sense.
Seven —
Why do they pull a black cap over your face,
And let it remain until you're dead?
Because the high voltage of electricity
Will make your eyes pop out of your head!

When I am speaking of the Midnight Special,
You probably don't understand what I mean;
It's the horrid electric chair of injustice
That burns the blood of human flesh!

But when you're riding the Midnight Special,

You won't ride it for long;
Just hope you'll ride it to Heaven
Where you'll hear the sweetest of songs.

But the trains run in two directions;
One goes to Heaven and one to Hell;
And when you're riding the Midnight Special,
Which train you'll ride is hard to tell.

When the warden tightens the head screws
That fits the copper helmet over your head,
And pulls the lever of injustice —
In one minute you are dead!
NINE — Jo——nes!
GUARD [*Whispering*] — Here is the paper. Read this and don't say anything to Six.
Two — All right.
He reads: CLEMENCY REFUSED; SLAYER TO DIE FRIDAY; GOVERNOR NOT TO ACT. The Governor will decline to extend clemency for Jack Henderson, under sentence of electrocution for the murder of a twelve-year-old girl. . . .
The door leading into the death chamber slams. The motor beyond begins to hum. The lights grow dim.
ONE — Hey! Hey! They're testing the Midnight Special for Six.
Two — That causes cold chills to run up and down my spine.
NINE — Jo——nes! O——h!
SEVEN —
And when I see the bright lights go dim —
In the electric chair, another soul is dead!
Look at those lights go dim!
SIX — Oh, my God!

FIVE — They're playing with that thing. I guess that they'll play with it all day, now, until your stay comes.
SIX — Say! you goddam monkeys, get the hell out of my house! Jeez! That makes me sick.
Two — I can't stand a whole lot of that. I'd rather be anywheres than here.
ONE — Me too!
SIX — My stomach got a funny sensation then. Kinda burnin' like.
FIVE — The worst is to come yet. Wait until he really gets up tight.
NINE — Jo——nes!
Two — Fellows, it is no joke, I'd like to be some place else today.
FIVE — You'd have been some place if you hadn't got that stay.
Two — How well I know it! But, honest, I hate to be here when a man is going to be electrocuted.
FIVE — Aw, you'll get used to it, before long. You'll probably get some more stays and see several more go. We can't all miss it. With the protests that some of us are going to get, we can't all miss it.
SIX — Play that phonograph.
The guard is changed. Lunch is served. Less than twelve hours remain to SIX.
SEVEN — What did you tell them you wanted for dinner, Six?
SIX — I ordered pork chops, fried potatoes, jelly, bread and butter and some milk. Why?
SEVEN — That was plenty.
ONE — You must be goin' on a long trip.
SIX — Yes, I guess I'll get hungry before I get to Hell.
Two — I don't believe that I could eat.
SIX — You're crazy. I got a chance to

get a big feed. I oughta ordered chicken and all the trimmin's.

FIVE — They'd give you anything that you wanted to eat. [*Oracularly.*] Any reasonable request that you would make now would not be refused you.

SIX — You're right about that chair making your stomach turn over, One.

ONE — Hey! Lordy! I know!

SIX — That reporter told me that they expected me to tell 'em the whole story tonight. That's a crazy idea they've got. It wouldn't do me a damn bit of good. Don't think I will. No one needs to know.

ONE — Say, Six, keep everyone out but the State witness. I wouldn't let 'em in if I was you.

SIX — Aw, I don't care who sees it.

ONE — I wouldn't let a nigger in.

SIX — I won't.

NINE — Jo——nes! Jo-o-o-o-nes!

SIX — Anyone want these shoes? Anyone want these socks? Who am I going to give this money to? Well, say something, you damn guys!

ONE — Send dat money on down here!

SIX — I'll send it before they shake me down. I remember when you sent me everything that you had, money and all, when you were gettin' ready to go, and the Governor gave you a stay and I had to give you everything back. I sure did cuss.

ONE — Oh, I send you ever'thing back tomorrow.

SIX — Two, do you want these cigarettes? I've got seven packs.

TWO — Keep 'em, Six, and you can smoke them tomorrow.

SIX — I hope so!

TWO — The Governor will grant you a stay, I'm sure.

SIX — Maybe so. I'm going to have the priest wire him when he comes.

Two o'clock. Three o'clock. An ominous silence reigns over death row. The keys rattle in the door. A stay? No, the chaplain.

SIX — Who is that?

TWO — The chaplain and a guard.

CHAPLAIN — Good evening, boys. How are you today?

The chaplain stands in front of the cell occupied by SIX *and reads a chapter from the Bible; then prays. The guard laughs and jokes with* ONE.

SIX — I have sent for the priest.

CHAPLAIN — He may be here now. I have not seen him, but I heard that he was coming down.

SIX — Well, I want to see him.

The chaplain and guard leave.

SIX — Did you hear that goddam guard laugh while the chaplain was praying?

FIVE — He's dizzy. Don't pay any attention to that.

NINE — Jo——nes! Jo-o-o-nes!

TWO — Six, here comes the warden's secretary with a telegram. Maybe it is a stay. *The warden's secretary sends the telegram to* SIX *by the guard on duty in the corridor.*

SIX — Tell 'em I said "Hell no!"

SECRETARY — All right.

SIX — That telegram was from a sheriff of some damn county, wanting to know if he and some justice of the peace who want to come to see me electrocuted can get my permission to do it. If they mess with me, I won't let anyone in that the State will let me keep out.

FIVE — Don't let 'em come!
SIX — You heard me tell him to wire them and say "Hell no," didn't you?
FIVE — What reporters are you going to let in?
SIX — I don't know.
FIVE — Let the boys from the *Press* and *Chronicle* in if they come.
SIX — Yeah, that's a pretty good bunch, I think.
FIVE — They've treated us white.
SIX — You see, they explained everything to me up in the warden's office. They told me that there would be five witnesses for the State and the guards, and that I could have any five that I wanted for my witnesses, but that if I didn't want anyone else, I could keep out all that the State doesn't require.

4 p.m. The priest arrives.

PRIEST — How are you, boys?

The priest has the guard ring for the keys to the cells, and when the keys come he goes into the cell with SIX and administers the rites of the Catholic Church. The guard is relieved and dinner is served.

VOICE FROM OUTSIDE — Boss!
GUARD — Yes, right here!
VOICE FROM OUTSIDE — We want to get the measurements for the shroud for Six.
GUARD — Oh! He weighs about a hundred and forty-five and is about six feet tall.
PRIEST — Well, boy, how are you feeling?
TWO — Very well, thank you.
PRIEST — I have saved his soul. It is not possible to save his life or body because the Governor has refused to extend any clemency. I am coming back tonight to deliver Holy Communion to Six. I will stay with him during his last hour. It will calm his nerves and a man needs someone. I always walk to the chair with the man that I prepare for death and deliver the last rites to. That keeps him steady and the guards don't get to touch him.
TWO — That's good.
PRIEST — I will talk to you again tonight. I have to go get my supper now. I'll be back.
ONE — *Que dice*, Six?
SIX — *Nada, señor, nada!*
NINE — Jo——nes!

6 p.m. The guards arrive with the barber and shroud. They are shaving SIX. He is out of his cell in the corridor.

SIX — Here are some oranges that I can't take with me.
TWO — Thanks, Six. Say, Six——
SIX — What d'ya say?
TWO — Stay with 'em, old boy.
SIX — I will. I'll be waiting for you in Hell the fifteenth.
TWO — Forget that!

SIX is now getting his head shaved.

SIX — All right, up there, Two. Play that phonograph of yours.
TWO — What do you want to hear?
SIX — Any damn thing, as long as it is music. Say, I'm getting up tight. If something doesn't happen damn quick, I'm going to give up hope.

The clock strikes seven.

SIX — What was that, seven o'clock?
GUARD — Yes.
SIX — Whooie! My time is short! Why in the hell don't you play that phonograph, Two?
NINE — Jo——nes!

SIX has now bathed and has donned his

THE LAW TAKES ITS TOLL

shroud. *A guard cuts a trouser leg from knee to cuff. The barber is shaving his leg. Seven guards are in the corridor.*

SIX — One, they are going to fix that chair up for you next.

ONE — Quit singin' those blues aroun' here, suh!

SIX — Aw, hell, I'll be waiting for you, *Six has been placed in an empty cell. No furniture, just two blankets to sit on. The death watch has begun. All of the guards are gone but one.*

SIX — I'm sick at my stomach.

TWO — I'll send you one of these oranges to eat.

SIX — It isn't that, boys, I just hate to go. I didn't know that I hated anything so bad. I hate to leave you boys.

SEVEN — This old life isn't very good anyway, old boy. Let's just hope that you'll go to a better one. Maybe there's a better place, somewhere.

The guard blows his nose and wipes his eyes with his handkerchief. There are tears in his eyes. He must be human, after all.

SIX — Boys, I'm about to the end of my rope. I have stood up pretty good so far, but I can't make it much longer.

SEVEN — Stay right there, Six!

NINE — Jo——nes!

SIX — Well, just stick with me, boys. I'll build an air castle or something to get my mind off of the chair. Let's start that old revolution going, One.

ONE — Leave me alone, you fellows. I'm prayin' for Six.

SIX — Keep up the good work, One! Wish I had a drink of good liquor.

GUARD — Boys, I've never been up against this before. It touches me.

NINE — Jo——nes!

Four guards and the assistant warden come in. The assistant warden reads the death warrant.

ASSISTANT WARDEN — Now, Six, anything that you want to say, you can tell me. Your mother has asked me to get your last words for her.

SIX — I'll give them to the priest.

ASSISTANT WARDEN — Is there anything that you want that I can get for you? If there is, just name it, and I'll do my best to get it for you.

SIX — No, I guess not. I did ask for some coffee to come a little later on. Will it come?

ASSISTANT WARDEN — I'll sure see that you get it. Is there anything else that you want?

SIX — No, thank you.

NINE — Jo——nes! O—h!

ASSISTANT WARDEN — Well, we'll go now and if that coffee doesn't come in a few minutes, ring for me and I'll see that you get it.

The assistant warden and the four guards leave.

NINE — Jo——nes!

A guard and a convict come in with a pot of coffee. The convict serves all of the inmates.

SIX — Two, you were lucky to get that thirty-five-day stay, old boy. I wish I had one. Looks like I'd get one stay, anyway.

TWO — If it was possible for me to do it, I'd give you half of mine, and we'd both have seventeen and a half days. I wish I could.

SIX — Don't try to kid me. You wouldn't do that.

Two — Of course, I have no way to prove it to you. I know that you don't believe me, but just the same, I would do it. I wish it was possible, because I hate to see you go, Six.
Six — I wish you could do it.
Convict — He'd do it, I believe!
Guard — Yep, I believe he would.

The guard and the convict leave with the coffee-pot. Another guard and a hospital attendant enter with a bottle of alcohol and take Six out of his cell. They strap his arms to his side and put him in the barber chair. The hospital attendant washes Six's head and leg with the alcohol.

Six — Boy, howdy! I'd like to have a drink of that.
Hospital Attendant — It is denatured, Six.
Guard — Well, what do you think about it, boy?
Two — Maybe he will get a stay.
Guard — No, I don't think so. I'd bet money that he don't.
Hospital Attendant — I think that he will get a stay. The priest is working on it and has wired the Governor.

The guard and hospital attendant leave and the priest comes in.

Nine — Jo——nes! O——h! Jo——nes!
The priest takes a table, candle and a crucifix into the cell with Six. He comes out and takes his handbag in.

Six — Light me a cigarette, Two. I'm afraid my head will catch on fire with all of this alcohol on it if I strike a match.
Two — Sure.

The priest comes out of the cell and talks to One in Spanish.

Seven — Well, Six, it looks like you are going. I hate to see you go, but there must be something for you to look forward to. It must be better than this life or it wouldn't be worth much. I don't think that any of us are going to lose much when we go to that chair, for there's bound to be a Heaven and everyone has an opportunity to get right with God.
Six — Well, I hope there is some place else. I may not have to go tonight, yet.

A man and a woman, who say that they are Pentecostal missionaries, come in with a guard.

Pentecostal Woman — When I read of your impending execution, I just had to come to see you and find out if you were saved in God's way.
Six — Yes, I'm ready, but I'm still hoping until the last minute that my life will be spared.
Nine — Jo——nes.
Pentecostal Woman — Oh, I'm so glad that you are ready!
Six — Well, I'm glad that I'm not leaving a wife and kids. I'm glad that I never married.
Pentecostal Man — Yes, it is easier where there is no one else concerned but yourself.
Nine — Jo——nes!
Pentecostal Woman — What is that?
Six — That's a crazy man back there. He's harmless. He can't get to you. Well, I hate to leave mother. It hurts her, I know.
Pentecostal Woman — It will be so much easier for her to bear knowing that when you went that you were all right with God.

The man and woman leave.

Six — Light me a cigarette, Two.

Three newspaper reporters enter with a guard and SIX *recounts his crime to them. The reporters leave and* SIX *asks for more coffee.*

TWO — Wonder what time it is, One.

ONE — Must be ten-thirty.

SIX — Say, boys, wouldn't I be tickled to get a thirty-day stay! I have more hopes now than I did two hours ago. I was pretty low then. The warden's secretary sent me word that he would stay by the telephone.

TWO — Yeah, you'll get a stay.

SIX — I still have hopes.

The clock strikes eleven.

SIX — Say, that clock striking makes me feel funny around my middle.

PRIEST — When were you born, and so on?

SIX *gives him his nativity and life's history.*

SIX — I would wire mother if I had the money, but I gave it all to One.

ONE — Here's some.

TWO — I'll pay for it, Six.

PRIEST — No, you boys keep your money. I'll send the wire. What do you want to tell her?

SIX — Tell her that I'm laughing and joking and thinking of her. Tell her that I'm all right and that my thoughts are all of her.

PRIEST — I'll surely do it.

SIX — Do you want these slippers, Two?

TWO — No, thanks, I have a pair.

SIX — Give me some more coffee, Boss, if they's left any. Light me a cigarette, Two.

NINE — Jo——nes!

The priest leaves and the guard changes at eleven-thirty.

SIX [*Singing*] — A little white light will lead you to my blue Heaven. A smiling face, a fireplace, a cozy room.... [*Stops abruptly.*]

SEVEN — Stay right in there and pitch, Six! That Governor is liable to give you a stay, yet. Maybe he's just letting you get up tight to scare you. You see, the Legislature's in session and he won't go to bed before midnight. He may wire or telephone in here any minute, now.

SIX — Well, the priest wired him and I may get some action on that. If I don't get a stay, though, I'm going to try to set an example for white men here. They say that a white man has never died here who didn't show weakness. I'm going to show them that I can. I can, all right, I can!

SEVEN — I hate to see you go, but if you do have to go, it is better to take it like a man. Don't weaken.

SIX — I hate to go.

FIVE — Well, if you get one stay, you've got a chance. You won't burn if the Legislature passes that bill abolishing capital punishment. That would have some provision in it commuting all sentences to life imprisonment. Just one stay, and you got a chance to miss burning.

TWO — Here's the keys!

SIX — Who is it?

TWO — The priest.

The priest goes into the cell with SIX *and gives him Holy Communion.*

SIX — I hate to go, but it looks like it's got to be done.

SEVEN — Don't give up hope.

SIX — I still have hopes, but they are getting weak.

Two Protestant chaplains, white and

colored, enter. They stand against the wall and watch the priest. The white chaplain reads the Bible and bows his head in silent prayer.

NINE — Jo——nes!

The clock strikes twelve.

SIX — Twelve o'clock!

The guard watches the door.

SIX — Light me a cigarette, Two.

There is a hush, an expectant air. They are all waiting to hear footsteps approaching.

SIX — Let me out with the boys, Boss. I want to tell them all good-bye.

GUARD — I can't do it. I would if I could, but it would be against the rules. I'm sorry.

SIX — Oh, I don't care. 'Sall right. They split my pants leg, and I don't like that. This is a new style, boys. How do you like it? Light me a cigarette, Two. I'm not taking it as hard as I thought I would. I'm nervous, though; I've never had anything to do with electricity before. Wonder how it will feel. I hope it won't take long. Wonder if a fellow knows anything after the first shot hits him. I don't think I will.

FIVE — Aw, a fellow never knows what hits him. It's all over in a few shakes. Brace up!

SIX — You know, it's funny. I was worse at my trial than I am here. I almost broke down there at the trial. I lost fifteen pounds when my trial was going on. Give me some more coffee, Boss. [*The guard brings coffee.*] Ha! Well, here's to the old penitentiary, boys!

Six guards and the assistant warden come in and unlock the cell door.

GUARD — All right, boy, let's go!

Two guards strap his arms to his side. Six steadily walks out of his cell with the priest holding his arm.

SIX — I want to say good-bye to the boys.

ASSISTANT WARDEN — Certainly. Come up here to the front and start back.

SIX *walks in front of* ONE's *cell.*

SIX — Good-bye, Mex. I won't shake hands. That's bad luck.

ONE — Good-bye, Six.

SIX [*As he walks in front of* Two's *cell*]— Give me that cigarette, Two.

Two gives SIX *the cigarette. He has to bend his head almost to his waist to get the cigarette in his mouth.*

SIX — Good-bye, Two.

TWO — Good-bye, Six. Say — stay with them, Six!

SIX — I got 'em. I'll make it now.

FIVE — Good-bye, Six.

SIX — Good-bye, Five. Good-bye, Seven.

NINE — Jo——nes! O——h!

SEVEN — Good-bye, old Doctor Six. Stay right in there.

SIX — I think I'm doing about as well as you would do.

SEVEN — I *know* you are!

The guard has some difficulty in unlocking the door to the death chamber. He yanks and rattles the lock.

SIX — Can't get the door open, Seven.

SEVEN — Take those keys and open the door for them, Six.

SIX — I'd stay here until next Christmas before I'd open that door for 'em. Well, the door is open. I'll say good-bye to everybody again.

TWO — Good-bye, Six!

SIX — Good-bye, Two!

These lines are written while SIX *is being*

strapped into the chair. *The door between the death chamber and death row is open.*
SIX — I hope I am the last one that ever sits in this chair. Tell my mother that my last words were of her.
The lights go dim as we hear the whine of the motor when the switch is turned on.
TWO — Oh, my God!
SEVEN — Old Doctor Six is gone!
The lights go dim twice more. Someone is running along the walk outside.
TWO — Who's that?
ONE — Oh, that's reporters. They hurry to 'phone the paper.

FIVE — They're giving him the juice again. Wonder what they're trying to do, cook him?
ONE — He stay in there longer than that nigger.
NINE — Jo——nes!
TWO — I won't be able to sleep for a week!
FIVE — I'm going to sleep now. You'll be able to sleep all right. Forget about it.
SEVEN — Good-night, boys.
ONE — I can't sleep, either, Two.
NINE — Jo——nes! Jo-o-o-o-o-nes!

BOY BABY

BY CARL SANDBURG

THE baby picked from an ash-barrel by the night police
came to the hospital of the Franciscan brothers
in a diaper and a white sheet.

It was a windy night in October, leaves and geese scurrying across the north sky, and the curb pigeons more ravenous than ever for city corn in the cracks of the street stones.

The two policemen who picked the baby from the ash-barrel are grayheads; they talk about going on the pension list soon; they talk about whether the baby, surely a big man now, votes this year for Smith or Hoover.

(*October, 1928*)

HIGH JOHN DE CONQUER

By Zora Neale Hurston

MAYBE, now, we used-to-be black African folks can be of some help to our brothers and sisters who have always been white. You will take another look at us and say that we are still black and, ethnologically speaking, you will be right. But nationally and culturally, we are as white as the next one. We have put our labor and our blood into the common causes for a long time. We have given the rest of the nation song and laughter. Maybe now, in this terrible struggle, we can give something else — the source and soul of our laughter and song. We offer you our hopebringer, High John de Conquer.

High John de Conquer came to be a man, and a mighty man at that. But he was not a natural man in the beginning. First off, he was a whisper, a will to hope, a wish to find something worthy of laughter and song. Then the whisper put on flesh. His footsteps sounded across the world in a low but musical rhythm as if the world he walked on was a singing-drum. The black folks had an irresistible impulse to laugh. High John de Conquer was a man in full, and had come to live and work on the plantations, and all the slave folks knew him in the flesh.

The sign of this man was a laugh, and his singing-symbol was a drumbeat. No parading drum-shout like soldiers out for show. It did not call to the feet of those who were fixed to hear it. It was an inside thing to live by. It was sure to be heard when and where the work was the hardest, and the lot the most cruel. It helped the slaves endure. They knew that something better was coming. So they laughed in the face of things and sang, "I'm so glad! Trouble don't last always." And the white people who heard them were struck dumb that they could laugh. In an outside way, this was Old Massa's fun, so what was Old Cuffy laughing for?

Old Massa couldn't know, of course, but High John de Conquer was there walking his plantation like a natural man. He was treading the sweat-flavored clods of the plantation, crushing out his drum tunes, and giving out secret laughter. He walked on the winds and moved fast. Maybe he was in Texas when the lash fell on a slave in Alabama, but before the blood was dry on the back he was there. A faint pulsing of a drum like a goatskin stretched over a heart, that came nearer and closer, then somebody in the sad-

---

ZORA NEALE HURSTON *has achieved a reputation in anthropology as a folklorist and for a time headed the Drama Department at North Carolina College for Negroes. Her most recent book is the autobiographical* Dust Tracks on the Road. *(October, 1943)*

dened quarters would feel like laughing, and say, "Now, High John de Conquer, Old Massa couldn't get the best of *him*. That old John was a case!" Then everybody sat up and began to smile. Yes, yes, that was right. Old John, High John could beat the unbeatable. He was top-superior to the whole mess of sorrow. He could beat it all, and what made it so cool, finish it off with a laugh. So they pulled the covers up over their souls and kept them from all hurt, harm and danger and made them a laugh and a song. Night time was a joke, because daybreak was on the way. Distance and the impossible had no power over High John de Conquer.

He had come from Africa. He came walking on the waves of sound. Then he took on flesh after he got here. The sea captains of ships knew that they brought slaves in their ships. They knew about those black bodies huddled down there in the middle passage, being hauled across the waters to helplessness. John de Conquer was walking the very winds that filled the sails of the ships. He followed over them like the albatross.

It is no accident that High John de Conquer has evaded the ears of white people. They were not supposed to know. You can't know what folks won't tell you. If they, the white people, heard some scraps, they could not understand because they had nothing to hear things like that with. They were not looking for any hope in those days, and it was not much of a strain for them to find something to laugh over. Old John would have been out of place for them.

Old Massa met our hope-bringer all right, but when Old Massa met him, he was not going by his right name. He was traveling, and touristing around the plantations as the laugh-provoking Brer Rabbit. So Old Massa and Old Miss and their young ones laughed with and at Brer Rabbit and wished him well. And all the time, there was High John de Conquer playing his tricks of making a way out of no-way. Hitting a straight lick with a crooked stick. Winning the jack pot with no other stake but a laugh. Fighting a mighty battle without outside-showing force, and winning his war from within. Really winning in a permanent way, for he was winning with the soul of the black man whole and free. So he could use it afterwards. For what shall it profit a man if he gain the whole world, and lose his own soul? You would have nothing but a cruel, vengeful, grasping monster come to power. John de Conquer was a bottom-fish. He was deep. He had the wisdom tooth of the East in his head. Way over there, where the sun rises a day ahead of time, they say that Heaven arms with love and laughter those it does not wish to see destroyed. He who carries his heart in his sword must perish. So says the ultimate law. High John de Conquer knew a lot of things like that. He who wins from within is in the "Be" class. *Be* here when the ruthless man comes, and *be* here when he is gone.

Moreover, John knew that it is written where it cannot be erased, that nothing shall live on human flesh and prosper. Old Maker said that before He made any more sayings. Even a man-eating tiger and lion can teach a person that much. His flabby muscles and mangy hide can teach an emperor right from wrong. If the emperor would only listen.

There is no established picture of what sort of looking-man this John de Conquer was. To some, he was a big, physical-looking man like John Henry. To others, he was a little, hammered-down, low-built man like the Devil's doll-baby. Some said that they never heard what he looked like. Nobody told them, but he lived on the plantation where their old folks were slaves. He is not so well known to the present generation of colored people in the same way that he was in slavery time. Like King Arthur of England, he has served his people, and gone back into mystery again. And, like King Arthur, he is not dead. He waits to return when his people shall call again. Symbolic of English power, Arthur came out of the water, and with Excalibur, went back into the water again. High John de Conquer went back to Africa, but he left his power here, and placed his American dwelling in the root of a certain plant. Only possess that root, and he can be summoned at any time.

II

"Of course, High John de Conquer got plenty power!" Aunt Shady Anne Sutton bristled at me when I asked her about him. She took her pipe out of her mouth and stared at me out of her deeply wrinkled face. "I hope you ain't one of these here smart colored folks that done got so they don't believe nothing, and come here questionizing me so you can have something to poke fun at. Done got shamed of the things that brought us through. Make out 'tain't no such thing no more."

When I assured her that that was not the case, she went on.

"Sho John de Conquer means power. That's bound to be so. He come to teach and tell us. God don't leave nobody ignorant, you child. Don't care where He drops you down, He puts you on a notice. He don't want folks taken advantage of because they don't know. Now, back there in slavery time, us didn't have no power of protection, and God knowed it, and put us under watch-care. Rattlesnakes never bit no colored folks until four years after freedom was declared. That was to give us time to learn and to know. 'Course, I don't know nothing about slavery personal like. I wasn't born till two years after the Big Surrender. Then I wasn't nothing but a infant baby when I was born, so I couldn't know nothing but what they told me. My mama told me, and I know that she wouldn't mislead me, how High John de Conquer helped us out. He had done teached the black folks so they knowed a hundred years ahead of time that freedom was coming. Long before the white folks knowed anything about it at all.

"These young Negroes reads they books and talk about the war freeing the Negroes, but Aye, Lord! A heap sees, but a few knows. 'Course, the war was a lot of help, but how come the war took place? They think they knows, but they don't. John de Conquer had done put it into the white folks to give us our freedom, that's what. Old Massa fought against it, but us could have told him that it wasn't no use. Freedom just *had* to come. The time set aside for it was there. That war was just a sign and a symbol of the thing. That's the truth! If I tell the truth about everything as good as I do about that, I can go straight to Heaven without a prayer."

Aunt Shady Anne was giving the inside feeling and meaning to the outside laughs around John de Conquer. He romps, he clowns, and looks ridiculous, but if you will, you can read something deeper behind it all. He is loping on off from the Tar Baby with a laugh.

Take, for instance, those words he had with Old Massa about stealing pigs.

Old John was working in Old Massa's house that time, serving around the eating table. Old Massa loved roasted young pigs, and had them often for dinner. Old John loved them too, but Massa never allowed the slaves to eat any at all. Even put aside the left-over and ate it next time. John de Conquer got tired of that. He took to stopping by the pig pen when he had a strong taste for pig-meat, and getting himself one, and taking it on down to his cabin and cooking it.

Massa began to miss his pigs, and made up his mind to squat for who was taking them and give whoever it was a good hiding. So John kept on taking pigs, and one night Massa walked him down. He stood out there in the dark and saw John kill the pig and went on back to the "big house" and waited till he figured John had it dressed and cooking. Then he went on down to the quarters and knocked on John's door.

"Who dat?" John called out big and bold, because he never dreamed that it was Massa rapping.

"It's me, John," Massa told him. "I want to come in."

"What you want, Massa? I'm coming right out."

"You needn't to do that, John. I want to come in."

"Naw, naw, Massa. You don't want to come into no old slave cabin. Youse too fine a man for that. It would hurt my feelings to see you in a place like this here one."

"I tell you I want to come in, John!"

So John had to open the door and let Massa in. John had seasoned that pig *down*, and it was stinking pretty! John knowed Old Massa couldn't help but smell it. Massa talked on about the crops and hound dogs and one thing and another, and the pot with the pig in it was hanging over the fire in the chimney and kicking up. The smell got better and better.

Way after while, when that pig had done simbled down to a low gravy, Massa said, "John, what's that you cooking in that pot?"

"Nothing but a little old weasly possum, Massa. Sickliest little old possum I ever did see. But I thought I'd cook him anyhow."

"Get a plate and give me some of it, John. I'm hungry."

"Aw, naw, Massa, you ain't hongry."

"Now, John, I don't mean to argue with you another minute. You give me some of that in the pot, or I mean to have the hide off of your back tomorrow morning. Give it to me!"

So John got up and went and got a plate and a fork and went to the pot. He lifted the lid and looked at Massa and told him, "Well, Massa, I put this thing in here a possum, but if it comes out a pig, it ain't no fault of mine."

Old Massa didn't want to laugh, but he did before he caught himself. He took the plate of brownded-down pig and ate it up. He never said nothing, but he gave John and all the other house servants roast pig at the big house after that.

III

John had numerous scrapes and tight squeezes, but he usually came out like Brer Rabbit. Pretty occasionally, though, Old Massa won the hand. The curious thing about this is, that there are no bitter tragic tales at all. When Old Massa won, the thing ended up in a laugh just the same. Laughter at the expense of the slave, but laughter right on. A sort of recognition that life is not one-sided. A sense of humor that said, "We are just as ridiculous as anybody else. We can be wrong, too."

There are many tales, and variants of each, of how the Negro got his freedom through High John de Conquer. The best one deals with a plantation where the work was hard, and Old Massa mean. Even Old Miss used to pull her maids' ears with hot firetongs when they got her riled. So, naturally, Old John de Conquer was around that plantation a lot.

"What we need is a song," he told the people after he had figured the whole thing out. "It ain't here, and it ain't no place I knows of as yet. Us better go hunt around. This has got to be a particular piece of singing."

But the slaves were scared to leave. They knew what Old Massa did for any slave caught running off.

"Oh, Old Massa don't need to know you gone from here. How? Just leave your old work-tired bodies around for him to look at, and he'll never realize youse way off somewhere, going about your business."

At first they wouldn't hear to John, that is, some of them. But, finally, the weak gave in to the strong, and John told them to get ready to go while he went off to get something for them to ride on. They were all gathered up under a big hickory nut tree. It was noon time and they were knocked off from chopping cotton to eat their dinner. And then that tree was right where Old Massa and Old Miss could see from the cool veranda of the big house. And both of them were sitting out there to watch.

"Wait a minute, John. Where we going to get something to wear off like that. We can't go nowhere like you talking about dressed like we is."

"Oh, you got plenty things to wear. Just reach inside yourselves and get out all those fine raiments you been toting around with you for the last longest. They is in there, all right. I know. Get 'em out, and put 'em on."

So the people began to dress. And then John hollered back for them to get out their musical instruments so they could play music on the way. They were right inside where they got their fine raiments from. So they began to get them out. Nobody remembered that Massa and Miss were setting up there on the veranda looking things over. So John went off for a minute. After that they all heard a big sing of wings. It was John come back, riding on a great black crow. The crow was so big that one wing rested on the morning, while the other dusted off the evening star.

John lighted down and helped them, so they all mounted on, and the bird took out straight across the deep blue sea. But it was a pearly blue, like ten squillion big pearl jewels dissolved in running gold. The shore around it was all grainy gold itself.

Like Jason in search of the golden fleece, John and his party went to many places, and had numerous adventures. They stopped off in Hell where John, under the name of Jack, married the Devil's youngest daughter and became a popular character. So much so, that when he and the Devil had some words because John turned the dampers down in old Original Hell and put some of the Devil's hogs to barbecue over the coals, John ran for High Chief Devil and won the election. The rest of his party was overjoyed at the possession of power and wanted to stay there. But John said no. He reminded them that they had come in search of a song. A song that would whip Old Massa's earlaps down. The song was not in Hell. They must go on.

The party escaped out of Hell behind the Devil's two fast horses. One of them was named Hallowed-Be-Thy-Name, and the other, Thy-Kingdom-Come. They made it to the mountain. Somebody told them that the Golden Stairs went up from there. John decided that since they were in the vicinity, they might as well visit Heaven.

They got there a little weary and timid. But the gates swung wide for them, and they went in. They were bathed, robed, and given new and shining instruments to play on. Guitars of gold, and drums, and cymbals and wind-singing instruments. They walked up Amen Avenue, and down Hallelujah Street, and found with delight that Amen Avenue was tuned to sing bass and alto. The west end was deep bass, and the east end alto. Hallelujah Street was tuned for tenor and soprano, and the two promenades met right in front of the throne and made harmony by themselves. You could make any tune you wanted to by the way you walked. John and his party had a very good time at that and other things. Finally, by the way they acted and did, Old Maker called them up before His great work-bench, and made them a tune and put it in their mouths. It had no words. It was a tune that you could bend and shape in most any way you wanted to fit the words and feelings that you had. They learned it and began to sing.

Just about that time a loud rough voice hollered, "You Tunk! You July! You Aunt Diskie!" Then Heaven went black before their eyes and they couldn't see a thing until they saw the hickory nut tree over their heads again. There was everything just like they had left it, with Old Massa and Old Miss sitting on the veranda, and Massa doing the hollering.

"You all are taking a mighty long time for dinner," Massa said. "Get up from there and get on back to the field. I mean for you to finish chopping that cotton today if it takes all night long. I got something else, harder than that, for you to do tomorrow. Get a move on you!"

They heard what Massa said, and they felt bad right off. But John de Conquer took and told them, saying, "Don't pay what he say no mind. You know where you got something finer than this plantation and anything it's got on it, put away. Ain't that funny? Us got all that, and he don't know nothing at all about it. Don't tell him nothing. Nobody don't have to know where us gets our pleasure from. Come on. Pick up your hoes and let's go."

They all began to laugh and grabbed up their hoes and started out.

"Ain't that funny?" Aunt Diskie laughed and hugged herself with secret laughter. "Us got all the advantage, and Old Massa think he got us tied!"

The crowd broke out singing as they went off to work. The day didn't seem hot like it had before. Their gift song came back into their memories in pieces, and they sang about glittering new robes and harps, and the work flew.

IV

So after a while, freedom came. Therefore High John de Conquer has not walked the winds of America for seventy-five years now. His people had their freedom, their laugh and their song. They have traded it to the other Americans for things they could use like education and property, and acceptance. High John knew that that was the way it would be, so he could retire with his secret smile into the soil of the South and wait.

The thousands upon thousands of humble people who still believe in him, that is, in the power of love and laughter to win by their subtle power, do John reverence by getting the root of the plant in which he has taken up his secret dwelling, and "dressing" it with perfume, and keeping it on their person, or in their houses in a secret place. It is there to help them overcome things they feel that they could not beat otherwise, and to bring them the laugh of the day. John will never forsake the weak and the helpless, nor fail to bring hope to the hopeless. That is what they believe, and so they do not worry. They go on and laugh and sing. Things are bound to come out right tomorrow. That is the secret of Negro song and laughter.

So the brother in black offers to these United States the source of courage that endures, and laughter. High John de Conquer. If the news from overseas reads bad, and the nation inside seems like it is stuck in the Tar Baby, listen hard, and you will hear John de Conquer treading on his singing-drum. You will know then, that no matter how bad things look now, it will be worse for those who seek to oppress us. Even if your hair comes yellow, and your eyes are blue, John de Conquer will be working for you just the same. From his secret place, he is working for all America now. We are all his kinfolks. Just be sure our cause is right, and then you can lean back and say, "John de Conquer would know what to do in a case like this, and then he would finish it off with a laugh."

White America, take a laugh out of our black mouths, and win! We give you High John de Conquer.

EMINENCE

By Ruth Suckow

Mr. AND Mrs. WATKINS were going to church on Christmas Eve. Mr. Watkins was proudly carrying Florentine. Her little white legs, dangling, bumped against his coat. Her curls were carefully covered. Mrs. Watkins was carrying, wrapped from the snow, the star and crown of silver paper.

"Be careful of her slippers, daddy!"

"I'm being careful."

Florentine took one bare hand from her muff and stretched it out to the snow flakes. They were like dim soft little stars. They melted with a cool delicious tingle upon her warm skin. The flimmer of misty snow hushed for a moment the high excitement of being on the programme.

"Oh, keep your hands covered, darling!"

The church was brilliant with lighted windows in the snowfall. With preoccupied faces, taking only an instant to smile and half nod to this one and that, Mr. and Mrs. Watkins made their way through the people flocking up the church steps. They were thrillingly aware of the whispers all around them. A man called out jovially, "What's that you've got there, Watkins?" Mr. Watkins said proudly, "That's part of the programme!" Above all the heads was Florentine's small pale face with starry eyes.

They went straight to the Infant Room, where the children who were going to take part on the programme were crowded. Instantly they were surrounded. "Oh, here she is! They've brought her!" Faces of Sunday-school teachers, of older girls, delighted, eager, were all around them. Boys watched, while they pretended not to, with aloof and silent admiration. At the edge of the group, withdrawn, solemn and watchful, were the other little girls in Florentine's class.

Mr. Watkins set Florentine on her feet. Mrs. Watkins sent him to find seats for them in the audience room. Her face was tensely absorbed as she laid aside Florentine's white wavy furs, drew off her white coat, and undid the scarf. She brushed out the pale-gold curls that were flattened, the little fine surface hairs roughened and glinting, from the pressure. She knelt to place the crown of silver paper, tipped at the center with a

---

RUTH SUCKOW, *one of the most highly praised short story writers of our time, has contributed to many magazines and won public acclaim with her novel,* The Folks. *"Eminence" displays her art at its best.* (March, 1927)

star, upon Florentine's head. Florentine was all in white. She wore white slippers and stockings and a little white silk dress with puffed sleeves.

"How darling! How dear! Mrs. Watkins, what is she?"

"The Christmas Fairy," Mrs. Watkins said.

She led Florentine over to the register, murmuring, "Come, darling, you must get warm!" The girls from the older classes circled around her in delight, with coos and cries of ecstasy, reaching out adoring fingers to brush Florentine's floating curls, to fondle her little soft wrists, and touch her silken skirts. "Oh, Mrs. Watkins, can't we look after her?" Florentine Watkins was the prettiest child in the Sunday-school. She stood on the register, a little princess, small, calm and sure of herself, but her face pale and her eyes like dark blue stars. She let one hold her hand and another lay all her curls straight, with one curl over each shoulder. Beneath her little smile, the glory of the occasion, of the moment, of the worship, was shining and singing through her — almost ready to break into fiery sparkles, as when she dragged her feet across the rug and touched the cat's fur. She was well aware of being the star of the evening. The scarf her mother had anxiously put about her floated and clung to her puffed sleeves and her small chilly arms. The heat from the register billowed out her full silk skirt, that clung like milkweed floss to the fingers of the girls when they pushed it down. All the boys were aware of her, but awed, looking sidelong at her and standing apart.

"Mrs. Watkins, let us take care of her!"

"Will you stay with the girls, darling?" Florentine consented royally.

"You remember your piece, darling. You remember what to do."

"I remember."

Still on the edge of the group stood the other girls in the class. Lola, Kitty, Amy, Mary Louise. They were in their Winter dresses, black stockings and high shoes. They had walked to the church. Their hair was crimped or braided, and they wore big red hair ribbons. They eyed Florentine.

The noise in the audience room was growing louder. It was almost time for the programme to begin. The teachers were beginning to marshal the classes. "Now, Miss Morrison's class!" That was the one to which Florentine belonged. She stepped into line with a thrill of shining fear and expectation.

Lola, Kitty, Amy and Mary Louise huddled together behind her with giggles and excited whispers. They clung to each other. "What if I should forget!" "I know your part. I'll prompt you." Florentine stood at the head. Now her fear had become a great cold blankness that left her, in the midst of the envy and the worship, all alone. The girls looked at her, but did not cling to her. Her face was white and her eyes dark under her silver star. If she forgot, none of them could help her. She had the principal part. The exercise depended upon her.

The organ was almost hidden behind the Christmas tree, dark glistening green, laden with white packages, shredded over with sparkles of tinsel. The opening march sounded out through the branches.

It spread through the air heated from the big registers and chilled by the wintry drafts from the door, spiced with evergreen, thick with the odors of the crowd in their winter clothing damp from the snow. All the heads turned to watch the Sunday-school march in.

Mr. and Mrs. Watkins sat near the front. Their eyes were set in a glaze of expectation. Mrs. Watkins clasped her hands until the knuckles were strained to white. In all the marching ranks — little boys and little girls, bigger, smaller, fair-haired, black-haired, awkward, pretty — they could see only one child. "There comes Florentine!" She had a little space to herself, as if made by the shining of her silver star and the dainty floating of her silken skirts. That made everyone look at her. Just for one transported instant the little face passed them, pale, unconscious of them, under the silver star. Then they sat back. With shovings, rustlings, scuffings, and orders from teachers, the Sunday-school was seated. She was lost to them among the other children.

II

The exercises began.

"Joy *to* the world, the Lord has come. . . ."

The music roared through the branches of the Christmas tree and filled the room. When the audience sat down again, the front seats reserved for the Sunday-school quivered with hair ribbons.

All bowed their heads, but they were not listening to the minister's prayer. It was just something that came at this time on the programme. Parents were craning and straining their eyes to see their own children. The children had their eyes on the packages heaped about the tree. They nudged one another to see that big package propped at its foot. "Wonder whose that is?" The prayer ended, the audience moved and shuffled, and the superintendent stepped forward and announced the first real number of the programme. Now those who were to take part became self-conscious, looked down and twisted their shaking fingers, with their lips silently repeating the opening lines of their pieces.

"A song by the Infant Department."

Pulling back, stopping and wandering, whimpering or looking about with widely innocent eyes, the infants were herded upon the platform. The little ones were pulled to their places in front. Some were too large and awkward among the others. A shock-headed boy, with holes in his stockings that showed white patches of winter underwear, stood grinning at the end of the line. The little threads of voices followed the voice of the primary teacher, on and off the key. When the song was over none of the infants knew enough to go down. They stood smiling with engaging foolishness at the audience until the teacher marshalled them off the platform. Some wandered down, others came with quick little steps, while the audience laughed and clapped, the men grinning, but ashamed, at the exhibition of ingenuousness.

Mr. and Mrs. Watkins smiled slightly and clapped perfunctorily. They could not give ready applause until Florentine had had hers.

Exercises, songs and recitations — pieces by children whose mothers would be offended if they were left off the programme. Good or bad, the audience clapped. Here a clear little voice got a momentary sharpness of applause; or a lisp or a stutter drew a ripple of laughter. Mrs. Watkins listened, clasping her hands. Once she was angry. It was when Howard Hopkins "forgot." He stood staring at the audience with a bright bold, unabashed gaze, and when he could not go on, suddenly grinned and said, "Guess that's all!" and marched nonchalantly down. The roar of laughter and appreciation beat upon Mrs. Watkins' jealous ears. It was not fair. It did not really belong to the programme. This boy had no right to come in, not even able to speak his piece, and take away some of the applause from Florentine.

In the third row from the front, Miss Morrison's class waited, all crowded together. Their exercise came near the end of the programme. It was the principal one. They were old enough now to know how to do things, but still small enough to be "cute." And then, they had Florentine Watkins. They wiggled and squirmed through the earlier numbers. The other girls whispered together. But Florentine sat still, her eyes brightly fixed, whispering over and over to herself with rapt intentness the first line of her piece. At times she forgot about it, and it fled away from her, and then, after a cold moment when the world shook, it sounded clear and true in her mind. She felt all the eyes upon her silver star. Through the earlier part of the programme, that elated her and made her hold her small golden head high. But now it quivered through her with terror. Her turn was almost here. She was Florentine Watkins. The whole church expected her to do well. The teacher depended upon her. The girls would wait for her. Her mother and father were listening. Her lines started to vanish and her mind made a leap and caught them. The lights and the sparkles on the Christmas tree dazzled together. She could not breathe or live until this was over. She moistened her lips and moved one cold little hand. She was the most miserable one on the programme. If she could be Kitty, with only four lines to speak, that girl in front of her who had already given her recitation — be a child of whom no one expected anything — Beany Watters, that boy with the holes in his stockings! The shining of the silver star on her forehead was a bright terror. The next . . . her heart began to thump. . . .

" 'The Christmas Fairy' — an exercise by Miss Morrison's class."

Florentine rose at the head of her line, made her way daintily down the aisle and up the steps, padded with white and bordered with evergreen, and crossed the enormous space of the platform. Her knees were trembling, but a strange spacious coolness was upon her. She would get through her part, and then die.

In shaking silence the little girls took their places about Florentine. Mr. and Mrs. Watkins were staring straight ahead. Mr. Watkins cleared his throat. Mrs. Watkins saw her child through a wavering shimmer of dizziness: little delicate white figure in the flimsy shine of the silken dress, silver star tipping the golden head — was the dress all right? long enough? the crown straight on her head? Mrs. Watkins dug her nails in ecstatic agony into her palms. Then silence. Florentine stepped forward. Her voice came out clear and small, tremulous — like the shaking of a tiny bell — in the rustling hush of the room.

> Dear children all, I heard your wishes,
> And o'er the world I flew
> To bring my happy Christmas message
> To all the world and you. . . .

Her mother's eyes were fixed in an agony of watchfulness on that small face. Every word seemed to turn and twist in her own heart.

Florentine was getting through it. Her little bell-like voice rang out the words small and clear and pure. Her knees had stopped trembling. Her coolness was fired with happiness. Why, it was going to be over too soon! In a blaze of elation she wanted to go all through it again. Now the eyes upon her were a bright intoxication. Just for this little moment, she was the Fairy — silver star and white slippers, silken gown and silver crown — herself and beyond herself. . . . It was over. She had spoken the last word. She was standing — she was going down the steps — sliding into her pew. The applause was a roaring sea in her ears. It was not until she was seated, breathing quickly and clasping her warm trembling hands in her silken lap, that she realized in a burning glory that the applause was for her!

Mr. Watkins was smiling broadly, unable to hold in his pride. Mrs. Watkins' heart steadied into a happy, elated beat as she drank in the applause. Their child, their child — the best on the whole programme! Moisture stung in her eyes, and warmth flowed over her. Now she could be happy. Now she could be easy. She could smile at the rest of the programme.

III

The children were growing restless. They did not want to hear the superintendent's announcements. They were watching, turning — but the little ones shrieked when they heard a jingle of bells from the entry and a stamping of feet. Santa Claus came running down the aisle. He shouted in an enormous jovial voice, "Well, children, Merry Christmas! Did you think old Santy wouldn't come?"

Clapping, laughter and cat-calls answered him.

"Well, Santy pretty near thought so himself. I'll tell you how it was. One of Santy's reindeer got a stone in its hoof and we had to stop and see the blacksmith down there at Grover. Well sir, and all the presents I was bringing to the good little girls and boys in Mahaska — Santy don't give any presents to bad children, no sir, but you're all good, ain't you? [A little trusting voice piped up, 'Yes, Santy!'] Sure you are! I knew it! Well, all the presents rolled out, and those children in Grover — I guess they hadn't seen any things like those — they came pretty near getting the whole lot of them."

The little children sat with starry eyes of wonder and expectation. It was Mr. Heggy. The big boys were whispering that it was only Mr. Heggy. And yet, could they be sure? There were the buffalo coat and the fur cap, the white woolly beard and rosy cheeks, the jingle of sleighbells from up his sleeve.... They watched breathlessly while the first presents were taken from the Christmas tree. "Aw, it ain't either Santy. It's just Mr. Heggy. Because there's another Santy at the Methodists'. They ain't two Santys, is they?" Still the little ones were not convinced. They murmured, "I bet it *could* be Santy, though!"

The big boys in Mr. Pendleton's class were distributing the candy — hard Christmas candy, little colored curleycues and squares and round white logs with flowers in the center glistening red and sticky white. Every child — visitors and all — got one of the little cardboard packages. Florentine accepted hers. She was glad to sit back for a little while in the obscurity that Santa's speech made for her, but still with the radiance of her great moment warmly upon her.

Santa had come to the packages. He was reading the names in a loud voice as he took them from the tree.

"'Helen Vincent'! Anybody know Helen? Oh, that's Helen, is it? Hold up your hand, Helen, this looks like a pretty nice present.... 'Mamie Runkle'! Now I wonder who could have given Mamie a present like that? Must have been someone who liked her pretty well!... 'Mrs. Peabody. From her Sunday-school class'! Well, well, I guess those boys know a good teacher when they get one."

The boys rushed about, waving the packages, sending them down the aisles from hand to hand. Children were gnawing at the hard candy, with loud snaps, as if teeth were breaking. Papers were strewed untidily over the church. The Christmas tree was shining but disheveled. Santa was just calling the names now. The big box at the foot of the tree had not yet been given out. It had been saved for the last. The children were still pointing to it, and hoping and whispering about it.

Santa lifted it. A hush in the buzzing and talking and rustling followed. The package was big enough to catch the last jaded attention of the audience. He looked it all over for a name. The room became still. Respectful, wondering eager glances were turned toward the box. Santa took his time.

"Well, this is quite a little bundle! Glad Santy didn't have to carry this very far. Guess this must go to Santy himself — must be a token of appreciation.... No, sir! I'm mistaken there. This seems to belong to a little girl. I'd oughta brought my specs along from the North Pole to read this. Let's see if I can make it out.... 'Florentine Watkins'! Well, well! A big box for a little girl! Here, boys! The little girl with the silver star on her head."

The sound of wonder, envy, disappointment, and excited laughter swelled. Mr. and Mrs. Watkins sat suffused with happy pride. Florentine's face was pale as she held out her arms to take the package. "Open it, open it!" She heard the whispers all around her. The girls pressed close. Someone had to help her untie the string.... The string was loose, the white paper off — tissue paper, crackling and soft, and wadded into it, an enormous doll!... There was a long sigh from the children crowding to see. The doll lay revealed — closed, waxy-lidded eyes and golden-brown lashes upon pink bisque cheeks, golden curls matted upon its cold bisque forehead, dress of pink satin, pink stockings, gold buckles on its tiny shoes. . . . "Oh, look!" A moan came from the girls. They crowded about to touch the hair and the satin gown. "Florentine, will you let me see? Is she jointed all over? Can I just *touch* her?" Heads through the audience craned to see, people half rose, the room was a buzz.

Florentine sat holding the big box. She was mute with a surfeit of bliss. Nothing else could happen after this.

IV

In the loud hubbub of leaving, people were all crowded and talking at the door. Children came running on padding little feet up the sloping aisles, and bumped joyously into parents. "Oh, here you are, are you?" A father put his arm around a little shoulder, squeezed a flaxen head against him and held it there while he went on talking, and the other persons smiled. "See all the things I got, papa!" "Well, well!" He didn't really see them. "Santy Claus was pretty good to you!" Mothers had gone down to the front rows to find their own infants. They sat down in convenient pews and tried to drag small, stiff, black overshoes over little feet limp in their laps. The white sheeting on the platform was marked all over with footprints, the evergreen trimmings were pulled out from their tacks. The Christmas tree stood sparkling but denuded. From it spread the odors of pine needles, hot wax, popcorn and paper.

Mrs. Watkins had taken Florentine at once into the Infant Room to find her wraps. Mr. Watkins waited in the audience room near the register. He talked in a manly way with Mr. Hollister — also waiting — about the effect this snow would have upon the ground; but his ears were straining with shamed eagerness for the words that were occasionally spoken to him: "I should think you'd be pretty proud of that little girl tonight, Mr. Watkins!"

In the Infant Room, where tired mothers were finding wraps in the piled mountain shaking and toppling on an old discarded pew — "How can we *ever* find our own things in this jam!" — Mrs. Watkins took down Florentine's white wraps from their special hook. "Are you tired, darling?" she mourned. Even when she was drawing on the little coat, and her back was turned to the room, she was tinglingly aware of the notice of the others and the glory shed upon her by her child. She pretended to think only of the hurry of getting home. As soon as she turned toward the room, she expected the congratulations to break out. With careful, proud, reluctant hands she lifted off the silver crown and star.

A woman came searching through the Infant Room with a big-eyed little child clinging to her hand. "Oh, here she is!" She encouraged the child, "Ask her! I think she will!"; and then to Mrs. Watkins, "Here's a little girl, Mrs. Watkins, who thinks she can't go home until she's seen Florentine Watkins' big doll!"

"Why, of course!" Mrs. Watkins said with radiant graciousness. "It's in the other room. Mr. Watkins has it. You come in with us, Lucy. Florentine will show it to you."

"I want to see that, too! Mamma, I want to see it, too! I want to see the big doll."

Now all the crowd who had been pawing over the wraps and staying away from Mrs. Watkins and Florentine out of respect, diffidence and envy, came flocking around them.

"These children want to see the doll, daddy!"

"Want to see the doll?"

Mr. Watkins opened the box. The little children gave great sighs. Mothers had to clutch little reaching hands and warn, "Oh, musn't touch!" while Mrs. Watkins smiled graciously, but alertly. Mr. Watkins set the box upright, and the bright blue eyes of the doll flew open between its golden-brown lashes. Lola Hollister cried with an anguish of longing, "Oh, mamma, look! The doll's got *real* little gold buckles on its shoes!" Mrs. Hollister said in a slight, withdrawn voice, "Yes, I see!", and gave a painful little smirk. She compared this doll with the doll Lola was going to get in the morning. Her heart was rent with a painful anguish of jealousy for her child. Mr. Hollister tried to be admiring, but it shamed him, shamed his adequacy as a father, when he too compared this doll with Lola's doll, which he had bought. Some of the crowding faces were artlessly adoring. Others had a look of reserve which Mrs. Watkins' alert eyes caught. At last all the wondering childish eyes were satiated with the vision. Hands of mothers drew little figures gently back and voices murmured: "Well, are you satisfied? Have you seen the big doll?"

Long-drawn sighs answered them.

But there was something that made Florentine wonder. Mary Louise did not come to look at the doll. "I saw it before!" she said snippily to Lola, and ran off. The doll was too much. The Watkinses, on the very peak of glory in showing it off, did not know. Even some of the admiring ones went away from the church saying: they shouldn't have bought the doll; they shouldn't have put it on the Christmas tree; it was too expensive for a little girl; the Watkinses made them tired trotting out that child; next year they hoped some other child would get a chance.

The chief families of the church, with the minister and his wife, stood talking at the door. Mr. Watkins had set Florentine in a pew, and she stood leaning against him while he kept his arm around her. As people passed him, going to the door, they stopped. "My, but you must be proud of her tonight!" Florentine touched his cheek with a little princess air. The great doll was asleep in its closed box. The room glittered in tinsel and evergreen, and her presents were heaped on the pew beside her.

Freddy Parkins, being dragged out by a father who wanted to get home, called back eagerly, "G'night, Flor'ntine!"

"Goodnight!" she answered with starry graciousness.

Old ladies moving slowly to the door, stopping to pat her little woolly sleeve with thin fingers, murmured, "Wasn't she dear? Just *like* a little fairy!" Florentine accepted the homage with sweet, childish royalty. But in her mind, under all the glory, was a tremulous, shining wonder that craved to be reassured.

Mrs. Watkins was flushed. She drank down the praise that burned her like a fiery wine. "She was simply perfect, Mrs. Watkins!" "I know you're proud to-night!" But the first perfect bliss of the applause that followed Florentine's exercise was marred. Florentine had won, and yet there were people who went away unconvinced, who seemed to have other, strange values. Already the atmosphere of universal praise had slackened. She was jealous of the laughter that still followed any mention of Howard Hopkins. "Wasn't that kid funny? Say, he was great!" Could there be people who had enjoyed him more than Florentine? She hated the minister's wife, who kept repeating, with effervescing tactfulness, "They were *all* good!"

V

It was time to close up the church. The people who were talking over the programme, the expenses, the success of the evening, began to look about for their children; and the Watkinses were beginning to realize that they had heard all the praise they were likely to hear for this evening. Lola and Mary Louise and Kitty were playing a game, chasing each other through the pews and down the aisles. "Come! It's time to go home! Remember, tomorrow is Christmas!" They came scampering up to the register, flushed, with disordered hair, panting and giggling together. "What are you little girls up to?" someone asked tolerantly. Kitty pinched Lola, and they laughed; but when they looked at Florentine, their eyes grew sober and aloof, considering.

"You go get your wraps on, young lady!"

Kitty ran off. She turned to call back to Mary Louise, "Don't you forget about tomorrow!" Mary Louise answered, "I won't! Don't *you* forget, Lola!" "I won't." They were going to see each other's presents. Lola gave a timid look at Florentine, but did not ask her to come. Florentine's big doll was so wonderful — finer than anything they would get. Florentine, in her white dress and slippers, noticed by everyone, was no longer one of them.

Florentine stood silent and cool. She could not make a move toward the other girls, but she looked after them with a strange loneliness; and all at once it seemed to her that they had been having the most fun in the world playing together. She was suddenly very tired. Her eyes blinked under the dazzle of the lights. She no longer cared what people said to her. The programme was over. She had her doll. What more was there? Christmas would be nothing after this evening.

Mrs. Watkins said commiseratingly, "Hurry up, daddy. She's tired."

Mr. Watkins picked Florentine up in his arms again. As they went outside the warm church into the snow, her disheveled little head drooped upon his shoulder.

Mrs. Watkins was carrying the doll,

and she was saying with anxious caution, "I was so afraid some of those children would do something to this doll! Daddy and mother had to send away off for it. It isn't to play with every day — just on special occasions. And Florentine, you must never let any of the girls handle it, no matter if they do ask you. You can't trust other children with it. Remember how Kitty ruined your little piano! This doll is much too expensive for that."

Florentine did not answer. All down the silent street — it had stopped snowing now, the ground where the corner light shone was covered with a soft, white, diamondy fluff — she snuggled down against her father's shoulder. To be carried by her father, and give way to the strong shelter of his arms, was all she wanted now. When they came up onto their own porch, stamping the snow from their rubbers, he set her down. They were going into the house, proud, happy and satisfied; but by the hall light they saw her sleepy face under the bright dishevelment of hair, drunk with the glories of the evening, forlorn now and bewildered, able to bear no more. Her eyes were almost closed. It was as if they had never realized until now how small she was.

Her father said heartily, "Well, the big night's over!"

But her mother cried, in an anguish of adoring pity: "She must go to bed this minute! She'll be all tired out if she doesn't. We mustn't forget that tomorrow will be here."

OUR ENEMY, THE CAT

By Alan Devoe

WE TIE bright ribbons around their necks, and occasionally little tinkling bells, and we affect to think that they are as sweet and vapid as the coy name "kitty" by which we call them would imply. It is a curious illusion. For, purring beside our fireplaces and pattering along our back fences, we have got a wild beast as uncowed and uncorrupted as any under heaven.

It is five millenniums since we snared the wild horse and broke his spirit to our whim, and for centuries beyond counting we have been able to persuade the once-free dog to fawn and cringe and lick our hands. But a man must be singularly blind with vanity to fancy that in the three — ten? — thousand years during which we have harbored cats beneath our roof-trees, we have succeeded in reducing them to any such insipid estate. It is not a "pet" (that most degraded of creatures) that we have got in our house, whatever we may like to think. It is a wild beast; and there adheres to its sleek fur no smallest hint of the odor of humanity.

It would be a salutary thing if those who write our simpering verses and tales about "tabby-sit-by-the-fire" could bring themselves to see her honestly, to look into her life with eyes unblurred by wishful sentiment. It would be a good thing — to start at the beginning — to follow her abroad into the moonlight on one of those raw spring evenings when the first skunk-cabbages are thrusting their veined tips through the melting snow and when the loins of catdom are hot with lust.

The love-play of domestic creatures is mostly a rather comic thing, and loud are the superior guffaws of rustic humans to see the clumsy, fumbling antics that take place in the kennels and the stockpen. But the man had better not laugh who sees cats in their rut. He is looking upon something very like aboriginal passion, untainted by any of the overlaid refinements, suppressions, and modifications that have been acquired by most of mankind's beasts. The mating of cats has neither the bathetic clumsiness of dogs' nor the lumbering ponderousness of cattle's, but — conducted in a lonely secret place, away from human view — is marked by a quick concentrated intensity of lust that lies not far from the borderline of agony. The female, in the tense

ALAN DEVOE, *whose writings appeal to an ever-widening public, has been called the Thoreau of twentieth century America. His monthly nature essays have been the most consistently popular feature in the entire magazine. As a philosopher and as a writer of quiet and strangely moving prose, he occupies a unique position in contemporary American letters.* (December, 1937)

moment of the prelude, tears with her teeth at her mate's throat, and, as the climax of the creatures' frenzy comes, the lean silky-furred flanks quiver vibrantly as a taut wire. Then quietly, in the spring night, the two beasts go their ways.

It will be usually May before the kittens come; and that episode, too, will take place secretly, in its ancient feline fashion, where no maudlin human eye may see. Great is the pique in many a house when "pussy", with dragging belly and distended dugs, disappears one night — scorning the cushioned maternity-bed that has been prepared for her — and creeps on silent feet to the dankest cranny of the cellar, there in decent aloneness to void her blood and babies. She does not care, any more than a lynx does, or a puma, to be pried upon while she licks the birth-hoods from her squirming progeny and cleans away the membrane with her rough pink tongue.

A kitten is not a pretty thing at birth. For many days it is a wriggling mite of lumpy flesh and sinew, blind and unaware, making soft sucking noises with its wet, toothless mouth, and smelling of milk. Daily, hourly, the rough tongue of the tabby ministers to it in its helplessness, glossing the baby-fur with viscid spittle, licking away the uncontrolled dung, cleaning away the crumbly pellet of dried blood from its pointed ears. By that tenth or fourteenth day when its eyes wholly unseal, blue and weak in their newness, the infant cat is clean to immaculateness, and an inalienable fastidiousness is deep-lodged in its spirit.

It is now — when the kitten makes its first rushes and sallies from its birthplace, and, with extraordinary gymnastics of its chubby body, encounters chair-legs and human feet and other curious phenomena — that it elicits from man those particular expressions of gurgling delight which we reserve for very tiny fluffy creatures who act very comically. But the infant cat has no coy intent to be amusing. If he is comic, it is only because of the incongruity of so demure a look and so wild a heart. For in that furry head of his, grim and ancient urges are already dictating.

Hardly larger than a powder-puff, he crouches on the rug and watches a fleck of lint. His little blue eyes are bright, and presently his haunches tense and tremble. The tiny body shivers in an ague of excitement. He pounces, a little clumsily perhaps, and pinions the fleeting lint-fleck with his paws. In the fractional second of that lunge, the ten small needles of his claws have shot from their sheaths of flesh and muscle. It is a good game; but it is not an idle one. It is the kitten's introduction into the ancient ritual of the kill. Those queer little stiff-legged rushes and prancings are the heritage of an old death-dance, and those jerkings of his hind legs, as he rolls on his back, are the preparation for that day when — in desperate conflict with a bigger beast than himself — he will win the fight by the time-old feline technique of disembowelment. Even now, in his early infancy, he is wholly and inalienably a cat.

While he is still young he has already formulated his attitude toward the human race into whose midst he has been born. It is an attitude not easily described, but compounded of a great pride, a great reserve, a towering integrity. It is even to be fancied that there is something in it of a sort of bleak contempt. Solemnly the cat watches these great hulking two-legged creatures into whose strange tribe he has unaccountably been born — and who are so clumsy, so noisy, so vexing to his quiet spirit — and in his feline heart is neither love nor gratitude. He learns to take the food which they give him, to relish the warmth and the comfort and the caresses which they can offer, but these profferments do not persuade his wild mistrustful heart to surrender itself. He will not sell himself, as a dog will, for a scrap of meat; he will not enter into an allegiance. He is unchangeably and incorruptibly a cat, and he will accommodate himself to the ways and spirit of mankind no more than the stern necessity of his unnatural environment requires.

II

Quietly he dozes by the fire or on a lap, and purrs in his happiness because he loves the heat. But let him choose to move, and if any human hand tries to restrain him for more than a moment he will struggle and unsheath his claws and lash out with a furious hate. Let a whip touch him and he will slink off in a sullen fury, uncowed and outraged and unrepenting. For the things which man gives to him are not so precious or essential that he will trade them for his birthright, which is the right to be himself — a furred four-footed being of ancient lineage, loving silence and aloneness and the night, and esteeming the smell of rat's blood above any possible human excellence.

He may live for perhaps ten years; occasionally even for twenty. Year after year he drinks the daily milk that is put faithfully before him, dozes in laps whose contours please him, accepts with casual pleasure the rubbing of human fingers under his chin — and withdraws, in every significant hour of his life, as far away from human society as he is able. Far from the house, in a meadow or a woods if he can find one, he crouches immobile for hours, his lithe body flattened concealingly in the grass or ferns, and waits for prey.

With a single pounce he can break a rabbit's spine as though it were a brittle twig. When he has caught a tawny meadow-mouse or a mole, he has, too, the ancient cat-ecstasy of toying and playing with it, letting it die slowly, in a long agony, for his amusement. Sometimes, in a dim remembrance from the remote past of his race, he may bring home his kill; but mostly he returns to the house as neat and demure as when he left, with his chops licked clean of blood.

Immaculate, unobtrusive, deep withdrawn into himself, he passes through the long years of his enforced companionship with humanity. He takes from his masters (how absurd a word it is) however much they may care to give him; of himself he surrenders nothing. However often he be decked with ribbons and cuddled and petted and made much over, his cold pride never grows less, and his grave calm gaze — tinged perhaps with a gentle distaste — is never lighted by adoration. To the end he adores only his own gods, the gods of mating, of hunting, and of the lonely darkness.

One day, often with no forewarning whatever, he is gone from the house and never returns. He has felt the presaging shadow of death, and he goes to meet it in the old unchanging way of the wild — alone. A cat does not want to die with the smell of humanity in his nostrils and the noise of humanity in his delicate peaked ears. Unless death strikes very quickly and suddenly, he creeps away to where it is proper that a proud wild beast should die — not on one of man's rugs or cushions, but in a lonely quiet place, with his muzzle pressed against the cold earth.

HE'S TAKEN HER BACK AGAIN
By Gwendolen Haste

She has come back,
And we peer behind the curtains,
And whisper in the store.
She has come back
And has washed her curtains,
And is buying flour and butter at the store.
She has friendly hazel eyes,
And a little smile.
Now she irons, sweeps and fries,
And hangs out clothes on Monday.
For marriage time is reckoned from Sunday to Sunday,
And for her who has returned
It is all one day;
With curtains between her and a time that is dead,
And trips to the store for a loaf of bread.

(September, 1927)

THE MORTICIAN

By Elmer Davis

> For not Life's joys alone I sing, repeating — the joy of Death. — *Walt Whitman*.
>
> The advancement of any people can be measured by the honor which they show to those who are departed. — *Dr. Frank Crane*.

BELIEVE it or not, but there was a time, not so very remote, when only one café in New York stayed open all night. (That, of course, was before Prohibition.) To this famous institution, maintained by the late John Dunston at Sixth avenue and Forty-third street, there came in the early hours of a certain morning a man of letters (not the author of these observations) who was disconsolate and depressed. He was there because he had had a row with his wife and could not go home; and he proceeded to plant his foot on the rail, prop himself Atlas-like against the bar, and endeavor to wash his sorrows into oblivion.

Presently, as will happen, he found himself engaged in conversation with another gentleman, who was helping him out in the public-spirited enterprise of keeping the bar from falling over; and when confidences had been exchanged in due course it appeared that this other gentleman also had had a row with his wife, and was at Jack's because he was afraid to go home. In celebration of this singular coincidence a few more drinks were had, and the party of the second part glowed with a brilliant idea. They were, he observed with cogency, in a hell of a fix; and for him (he dropped a furtive tear) there was no hope. But fortunately he was able to fix up everything for his friend the man of letters; yes, sir. He was going to send him home to his wife in such style that she would be glad to see him, and would promptly forgive him all. "Yes, sir. You leave it to me."

The man of letters, by that time, was only too glad to leave it to anybody; he had barely strength enough left to whisper an address before he passed out completely and was left in the hands of his new-found friend. But no hands could have been gentler or defter, more dexterous or more sanitary — for the other gentleman was one of New York's most celebrated morticians.

ELMER DAVIS, *director of the Office of War Information, was formerly news analyst for the Columbia Broadcasting System, and before that was for ten years a member of the staff of the New York* Times. *He showed immense courage as an article writer, and this essay was such strong meat for the times, strange as it may seem today, that a quality magazine, which frequently published his essays, rejected it.* (May, 1927)

He was, moreover, as good as his word. At dawn the man of letters went home in style, in the somber opulence of the best hearse in New York, drawn by six black horses adorned with nodding black plumes, escorted by a retinue of silk-hatted gentlemen funereally clad, their faces decently downcast in grief endured with manly fortitude. The hearse stopped before the door; a sumptuous rosewood casket was carried into the apartment; and when the lid was removed, there lay the man of letters, his limbs gracefully arranged against a background of pink satin — not dead, but sleeping.

If this were fiction I could set forth the successive emotions that harrowed the inhospitable wife — her bitter penitence at the thought that the harsh words lately spoken could never more, in this life, be wiped out; her rapturous joy when she discovered that her husband was not gone forever, but had been restored to her loving arms; the hallowed bliss of their reconciliation. . . . But unfortunately it is fact; and fact (luckily for us fiction writers who live by selling something more agreeable) rarely comes out with the pat neatness that could be desired. The address whispered by the man of letters, in that last moment of semi-consciousness, was not his own, but that of a bachelor friend who was accustomed to offer him asylum on the frequent occasions when he dared not go home. And the bachelor friend, perceiving before he was thoroughly waked up that the man of letters was not defunct after all, merely observed, "What the hell, he is drunk again," and went back to sleep.

None the less the whole incident breathes a spirit of fraternal coöperation that is none too common in this self-centered age; and it shows furthermore that the mortician, whom the general public is apt to eye a little distrustfully through no fault of his own, but merely because he is the inevitable and predestined receiver of us all, is a man of like passions with ourselves, with his private sorrows and his generous impulses to benevolence. And by way of proof that under the just order of the universe benevolence is suitably rewarded, it may be added that a few weeks later the man of letters died, and was embalmed and laid away by his friend the mortician, at the usual rates.

II

It is a cause of much grief to morticians and funeral directors — there are no undertakers any more, or if there are, they are men of so little vision as not to be worth considering — that the public is inclined to regard their profession with levity. They argue, and quite reasonably, that the disposal of the dead is a function that has to be performed, and one, moreover, which the surviving relatives usually feel must be performed with a certain amount of ceremony and parade.

But to the philosophic observer it does not appear that the customer can wholly be blamed; the fault is in the nature of things. However doctors and nurses may regard it, death close at hand still has a gruesome strangeness to the rest of us; ancient emotions revive against our will, suggesting that the corpse is something unnatural and ominous, that some sort of tabu hangs about the man whose business it is to do away with it.

Morticians themselves, of course, can reconcile their public and private characters by the easy process which enables every man to reconcile whatever may have to be reconciled if he is to make his living and retain his peace of mind. But the effort to make the public take the mortician naturally is more arduous, and it is this that has led the mortuary industry into refinements of euphemism that would have aroused the helpless admiration of the Attic tragedians.

Consider the word mortician itself. "Undertaker," says one of the leading morticians of the country, "is a message of yesterday, gruesome and repulsive." I personally cannot see why; it is a general word, with nothing in it to connect it with the idea of death from which all modern mortuary publicity shies away. However, it is out of favor; anybody with any spirit at all now calls himself a funeral director, and if he does not yet call himself a mortician, he soon will. The word, one learns, owes its origin chiefly to Frank Fairchild of Brooklyn and Harry Samson of Pittsburgh, distinguished members of the profession; and those who use it want to make it connote a standard of efficiency.

It is not a patented or exclusive word; there is a body known as the National Select Morticians, including only some 200 of the 24,000 funeral directors of the United States, and these in the main the leaders of the profession; but the word mortician is not restricted to its members as the word realtor is restricted to the members of certain associations, or would be if these genuine blown-in-the-glass realtors could persuade a callous public to respect the decencies of nomenclature. "An undertaker," says George W. Olinger of Denver, head of the Public Relations Committee of the National Select Morticians, "is a man who waits for somebody to die and then tries to grab him. A mortician is a trained professional worker who realizes that a certain number of people are bound to die within a given period, by the law of averages, and prepares himself to give the Service that is required and give it as well as possible." It would seem, then, that a funeral director becomes a mortician as he increases in wisdom and stature and elevates his standards of Service.

Nevertheless the word has failed to make the impression on the public that its inventors hoped. That low imitator, bootician, has involved it in some discredit. Realtor has passed into the spoken language, though not as the title of nobility which it was originally meant to be, but a mortician is never called a mortician by anybody but another mortician. "The word," says a member of the profession with entire accuracy, "is perfect in its meaning and derivation." Nevertheless it has lately roused the fury of that captious purist, Mr. Aldous Huxley, who wants to know by what right the embalmers of the dead class themselves with such persons as mathematicians and academicians. Mr. Huxley, whose erudition is universal but not always accurate, forgets that the functions of morticians and academicians are essentially not very different.

Mortician, however, is only one of the euphemisms now current in the trade. The corpse is not a corpse nor does it wear a shroud. It is the body, or the remains; indeed it is not referred to at all when possible; and the garment in which it is wrapped, when there is one aside from ordinary clothing, is a negligée. The body is placed on a slumber-cot and removed from the home in an ambulance to the mortuary, where it is prepared for burial by sanitarians. What was once the ice-box, the cooler, or the morgue is now the preparation room; and thereafter the body is left in a slumber room until the services in the mortuary chapel. Coffin and hearse and cemetery are obsolete words; the body is placed in a casket which is conveyed by a funeral coach to the memorial park.

Death grins out from the very word mortician, but it seems to be bad form for a bearer of that title to mention death in any other way. This ritual reticence, this indirection, this avoidance of words of ill omen suggests the Neolithic savage; it seems a deliberate revival of primitive tabus. Yet the morticians might point out that they are not the only ones who are trying to prettify the language. Realtors are notorious offenders, and the trades that beautify the person seem to feel under obligation to bestow elegance on the vocabulary as well. A woman who used to buy her underwear and shoes and stockings at specialty shops now purchases lingerie and footwear and hosiery at salons devoted to exclusivities; once she wore dresses that made her look thin, now she is costumed in gowns that slenderize. And so on. Even in my own business, the trade term spiritual autobiography describes a type of novel which is pretty apt to be, in fact, an extremely carnal autobiography.

For yielding to this universal tendency the morticians have more excuse than most people, for their relations to the public labor under an inevitable and incurable burden. As a candid speaker confessed at a recent convention, "the public is not attracted by the nature of the work a funeral director does."

So hard is it to strike just the right note that that brisk trade journal, the *Casket and Sunnyside*, maintains a special department of comment and advice on advertising and publicity. The conductor of this page passed some sharp criticism on a mortician's advertisement under the figure of a black-winged angel, remarking that "there is a clammy finality about this advertisement that is appalling."

More chipper are the advertisements of the various mausoleums, cloisters, burial abbeys, and so on (before long they will probably be calling them memorial cathedrals) which have sprung up of late years. Here the cult of the departed rises to heights never touched by any primitive chthonic worship; nor does it seem to be supported by any authoritative Christian doctrine on the resurrection of the body. Ground burial, one learns, is out of date and barbarous; mausoleum entombment is modern, progressive, and humanitarian, "as sanitary as cremation and as sentimental as a churchyard." When sentiment blends with sanitation, who can resist the joint appeal? "Here your departed loved ones will rest in permanent peace in an individual white marble tomb or crypt high above the ground, where neither water, damp, nor mold can enter." And again: "You have the choice of just two things: the one typifying death in darkness, looking down, always down, into the grave; the other typifying death in light, death in sunshine and brightness, death in the hope of the Resurrection."

One mausoleum near New York, not satisfied with taking the sting out of death, exerted itself to free the blessed hereafter from another sting that grievously pricks some people in their lives below. It was pointed out that families of great social distinction had already purchased space in the mausoleum, and that those who bought now would enjoy the privilege of parking their remains next to those of persons of quality, with whom they would never have had a chance to associate in the world of the living. Upon which an anonymous newspaper bard observed:

> Here in the body pent
> I love the rich but never see 'em;
> Yet nightly pitch my moving tent
> A day's march nearer the mausoleum.

Yet mortuary advertising can be done, and done well. Readers of the New York papers will remember the series of pastels in prose dealing with the charms of a local mortuary which appeared, a few years ago, under the title of "The Heaven of Sorrow." If the late Dr. Berthold Baer, who wrote them, ever had a superior in the arts of euphemism and suaviloquence, the name escapes me. Consolation dripped from him like holy oil that runneth down upon the beard, even Aaron's beard; it speaks well for the stability of our national character that hundreds of people did not forthwith commit suicide, in order to enjoy the ineffable bliss of being buried by Dr. Baer's employer.

III

Among themselves, however, the morticians unbend. When the National Selected Morticians, and shortly afterward the National Funeral Directors' Association, met at Washington last fall, bright eyes and smiling faces were seen everywhere; the opening of each session of the latter and larger body was in the hands of a community song expert, who "pepped up the crowd with stunt singing;" delegates and their wives did the sights, ascended the Washington Monument, made their pilgrimage to Mount Vernon, and in all ways behaved as normal Americans.

The National Selected Morticians did indeed meet with a misfortune traceable to the habit of euphemism; they had an engagement to shake hands *en masse* with President Coolidge and when they appeared at the White House and announced themselves as the morticians, word was passed down the line till it came to some uneducated person (uneducated, or perchance malicious) who transmuted the title into bricklayers. As bricklayers they were received by the President, as bricklayers they shook his hand; but no doubt the presidential handclasp was just as fervent under one name as another; a bricklayer's vote counts for just as much as a mortician's.

How high this merry spirit can rise

when exoteric persons are not around to cramp the mortician's style is shown by the menu of a dinner at Kokomo, Ind., which concluded a convention of the funeral directors of surrounding counties:

        Blood Solvent
       Embalmers' Delight
    Whipped Plaster of Paris
    Carbohydrate Compound
Face Cosmetics with Cold-Cream Dressing
    Carbonaceous Compound
        Cavity Filler
      Embalming Fluid
       Cavity Fluid
       Disinfectants

What actual foods are described by these allegorical titles I do not know, nor would it make much difference to the non-mortuary diner with a weak stomach who saw that card set before him. The morticians, however, seem to have confronted it without a qualm; which suggests that the habit of euphemism is not yet so ingrained that it need be maintained in private.

And the trade journals call a spade a spade. Look over their advertising pages, intended only for the professional eye, and you will find cheerful references to "our fast-selling line;" slogans such as "Making good is the best method of getting repeat orders." (You and I and all of us are destined to be those repeat orders.) Pleasant in its conjunction of the personal touch with business acumen is the advertisement of a memorial crucifix, which "will develop your word-of-mouth good will in a manner perfectly consistent with good taste and Catholic doctrine. Given as your tribute to the bereaved family, the profit will take care of itself."

Indeed, with the best will in the world, the profession can hardly take the same view of its work as do those who are fated in due time to become its raw material. A recent editorial in the *Casket* dealt with the need for the more general adoption of higher standards of embalming. With this praiseworthy aspiration to technical efficiency no one can quarrel, yet it is rather disconcerting to the lay reader to find it set forth in such language as this: "If the embalming is of so low grade as to cause patrons to shudder as they for the last time look on the face of their departed, then the whole funeral is a total loss from the viewpoint of satisfaction."

I can think of a number of funerals that I might contemplate from the viewpoint of satisfaction, but they are not those at which I am likely to appear in the character of patron.

IV

To bridge this gap as adequately as possible, to make the consumer (inevitably destined, in the course of time, to become the consumed) understand the problems, the merits, and the deserts of the mortician, is the greatest worry of the leading men in the profession at the present moment. And it would seem that it is not the occasional irreverence of the public that worries them so much as a practical, and, the morticians would argue, an undeserved resentment.

Last summer the Metropolitan Life Insurance Company threw something of a shock into the entire profession by announcing that it was about to undertake an investigation into the cost of funerals — the actual cost, and the reasonable or proper cost. Along with the announcement appeared some newspaper stories about the cost of certain funerals, which the mortician regards as outrageously exceptional and which he is afraid the public will take as average specimens. But the profession ought to be aware by this time that the high cost of funerals is always news. For example, the papers lately carried a story that the government was about to investigate the funeral of an Osage Indian enriched by oil royalties, which cost $3,000, including a $1,600 casket. The mortician might well have remarked that everybody trims the Osages and that it was unfair to pick on a single offender. For just as there are morticians and morticians, so there are funerals and funerals. They may cost comparatively little, or they may cost as much as you like; and if the mortician tries to sell you the more expensive rather than the cheaper goods, he is doing only what most other merchants will do in his place, given the mortician's advantage of knowing that the customer cannot very well walk out without buying anything at all.

But — the mortician who tries to sell off his costly goods hereafter, unless he knows that the customer can afford them, is going against the explicit ethical codes of his own profession. The National Funeral Directors' Association, in its convention last October, adopted a resolution that it is "criminal to take advantage of a family in its hour of grief by knowingly overselling merchandise or service." A week or two earlier the National Select Morticians had adopted a code of ethics which pledged its members to give "professional service in keeping with the living standards of the deceased" and to make its charges "commensurate with the services rendered, with business soundness, and with the economic self-respect of our members." This last stipulation may seem superfluous, and indeed the members of the National Selected Morticians are men who have reached their positions by taking care of their economic self-respect; but in the lower strata of the profession there are a good many men whose economic self-respect is so low as to lead them to advertise cheap funerals in language suited to very sumptuous funerals indeed.

None the less the announcement of the investigation disturbed the industry considerably. Promptly the national associations offered to coöperate, and their representatives were appointed on the supervisory committee; but it was evident from remarks made at the October conventions that there was a good deal of disquiet. This was less apparent among the National Selected Morticians, and naturally; these men, generally speaking, are the leaders, they are good enough technicians and good enough business men to be able to make a profit without extortion. Farther down the scale everything becomes vaguer and uncertain; there is more overcharging and less profit. "In trading for profit," said Past President Ferd P. Schoedinger to the National Funeral Directors' Association, "the funeral director has too often sacrificed future opportunity." That is, he has killed the goose that laid the golden eggs; he has missed his chance of getting repeat orders. And yet he may have overcharged because he thought he had to overcharge, because he found he was running behind; and the chances are that he was running behind because he did not know his own business.

That is why this Metropolitan investigation, which in considering the cost of funerals will no doubt make allowance for difference in ground rental, cost of materials, and cost of labor in different parts of the country, may turn out to be the best thing that ever happened to the industry.

V

For, if the outsider may trust the speeches made at last fall's conventions and the editorial comment on them in the trade papers, the chief trouble of the mortuary profession is inefficiency. That is probably true of most industries, and of society at large; and it will be true so long as the general run of humanity is possessed of only moderate brain power. But the mortuary business also suffers from overproduction — and overproduction to meet a relatively fixed demand. The death-rate fluctuates slightly but its general tendency is downward; the enrollment in the mortuary industry goes steadily upward. Only a great epidemic could enable its plant to run at full capacity, and the doctors rather hope we have got rid of great epidemics.

There are, or were when the last census was taken in 1920, altogether some 24,000 morticians, funeral directors and undertakers in the United States. That is three times as many as there were thirty years ago; the population is less than twice what it was thirty years ago, and the total number of deaths not much more than a third larger. In 1890, the average mortician took care of 124 funerals a year; in 1920 he had only 56. That means more costly funerals and less prosperity among the general run of morticians.

Of these 24,000 only a little more than 7,000 belong to the National Funeral Directors' Association; add the three State associations not affiliated with the national body, and still two-thirds of them are left out. This unorganized two-thirds is, of course, in the main, the less competent two-thirds; it includes the marginal morticians, many of them hanging on the ragged edge. At the last NFDA convention it was roundly declared that the 24,000 ought to be cut down to 10,000; the best ten thousand of the lot could do good jobs and make comfortable living without overcharges. What would become of the other fourteen thousand is another matter nor need it be gone into now; for they are going to stay in the business until or unless dire poverty forces them out.

But even in the higher grades there are a good many men who hardly know what it is all about. The last NFDA convention was much concerned over cost accounting. The subject had been brought up a year before and several hundred members had expressed receptivity to a cost accounting system; but it appears that only eighteen of all the thousands had in the meantime actually installed it.

Cost accounting, like Service, is an

idea that can be overdone; but it would seem that most people are in no present danger of overdoing it. A survey of a considerable number of representative morticians by a firm of cost accountants showed that these men, in the higher grades of the profession, handled half their cases at an actual loss. Naturally they did not know they were handling cases at a loss; they did not understand their own business, did not comprehend their actual costs or their actual capital investment. No doubt many a mortician would as soon think of including the good will and the plant of a business inherited from his father in the capital items on which he must earn a return as would the average farmer of including the capital value of the farm which his grandfather homesteaded. Farmer and mortician alike wallow in the fat years with no idea of laying up a reserve for depreciation and replacement, and then wonder why hard times hit them with such violence.

And because they do not know what they must earn to break even they do not know what to charge or how to charge. John M. Byrne, commissioner of the Casket Manufacturers' Association, told the convention that the average funeral director's method was simply to multiply the cost of the casket by five or six and set that down as the total cost of the funeral. On the bill, of course, it is itemized; but as likely as not the distribution will be fanciful, and the mortician himself will not know what actual costs a given item covers. A man who bills his customers thus cannot be fair to them or to himself except by happy accident.

This simple economic ignorance, rather than evil intent, probably accounts for a practice against which the national associations are fighting — the custom of advertising this and that feature of the funeral as free; free chapel accommodations, free use of certain rooms, even, occasionally, free casket-coach service. All of these services cost the mortician something, and, the economists of the profession argue, if he gives them away free he is a poor business man. As a matter of fact, he does not give them away; he adds a rough estimate of their cost to some other item.

VI

All of which has an interest for you and me, the general public. Sooner or later we are certain to be consumers of the mortician's services, and it is good news that he is on the way to charging for them more reasonably and more intelligently. For when it comes to the cost of a funeral the conscience of the mortician seems likely to be his only guide for some time to come. The customer, though he may buy with at least some intelligence in another market, procrastinates and shies away from a cool-headed examination of the wares of the mortician; he waits till the funeral is over and then cries out that all undertakers are thieves.

Mr. Olinger, before he undertook to look after the public relations of the National Selected Morticians, issued a booklet about his own business in Denver which leaves little enough vagueness and mystery about mortuary costs and services. He argues that a man who has foresight enough to budget his income, to lay aside so much for insurance, so much for payments on his house, so much for savings or investment, might reasonably lay aside a certain amount to pay for the funerals which are going to occur to all of us some day. (The example of Enoch and Elijah seems unlikely to be repeated in our time.) "Eighty-five per cent of the families where death occurs," one reads, "do not have $500 in cash." The cost usually comes out of the insurance, of course, but most families need the insurance for other things. It is only good sense to start a burial fund; and it is only good sense, as Mr. Olinger recommends, to shop around while there is time, to look over various mortuaries, price the different grades of service, and decide at leisure what you want.

Unless you do that, "the next-door neighbor, the family physician, or the nurse, are usually the ones who call the mortician. Naturally they favor their friends and it is a well known fact that in many instances unscrupulous parties recommend undertakers who never fail to compensate them for their trouble, and this bill the family eventually pays in settling their funeral expenses." True enough; and equally true that any man of sense will make up his mind now whether he wants a $300 funeral or an $800 funeral and find out where he can get one that suits him at the price.

But in these matters, as in some others, the human race is not addicted to reasonable behavior. That man is rare who will devote solicitous attention to plans for his own funeral, still less for his wife's. We all let it go till somebody dies, and then — why, then, thinking over the tabulated meannesses of the last ten or twenty or forty years for which it is too late to apologize, we decide that the best is none too good.

The average rosewood casket, it may reasonably be conjectured, is offered in reparation for countless snarls across the breakfast table. The funeral usually effects some discharge of the accumulated emotion; and when the bill presently comes along we look it over and decide that the mortician is a robber with no bowels of mercy.

He will sell us what we want, and sometimes it comes high. How high? Well, pending the Metropolitan report, Mr. Olinger is not afraid to let light into dark places; in an establishment which will go as low as $125 or as high as you like, "the average expense for a modern funeral today," he says, "including a simple dignified casket of quality, embalming service, newspaper notices, music, and in fact all details of service, including the use of two limousines and motor hearse, will be from $200 to $300." That, of course, is a Denver price; it would have to be boosted for New York or Chicago. But even in New York and Chicago it does not have to run up into the thousands unless you take off the limit, or let the mortician do it with your eyes open.

But who has the hardihood to order a cheap funeral? One might do it for one's self, if one could ever grasp the idea that one is mortal; but not for a wife, a husband, a parent, a child. In certain Italian circles a funeral is no funeral without a brass band; this folkway can hardly be blamed on the mortician, nor is he wholly to blame for the cult of the costly casket. Even beside the grave, perhaps especially beside the grave, one must keep up with the neighbors.

I knew a man, an employer of labor — poorly paid labor with ideas beyond its means. To do away with false modesty, I may say that he was a newspaper owner; to avoid misconception, I may add that he never was my employer. When one of his employés died, he who paid the salaries knew well that the family could not afford an expensive funeral; so he was accustomed to go to the widow and tell her that he had influence with a casket manufacturer, and could get her an excellent coffin below cost price.

This was a pious fraud; the coffins he got were made out of pine wood, decently covered with the proper black cloth; he paid forty dollars apiece for them, and at that price, in those days, the manufacturer made a profit. But nobody knew that underneath the black cloth was only a pine box; the widow paid forty dollars for a forty-dollar coffin, and enjoyed all the satisfaction of believing that she had a casket that would retail for two or three hundred. She had the satisfaction, the coffin manufacturer had his profit, and everybody was happy. . . . But if she had known that her husband was actually being laid away in a forty-dollar coffin she would have dropped dead on the spot in grief and shame.

So the pride and belated contrition of the human race is the mortician's standing temptation to overselling; he can hardly be blamed for resenting the general tendency to regard him as a despoiler of the widow and orphan. It is hard to see what can be done about it; people will go on ordering extravagant funerals without looking around to see what they can get at a reasonable price; and the mortician will go on taking the blame.

Nor does it appear that the mortician has much hope of attaining his other desire, of being treated with a properly reverent solemnity. He might evoke a little less levity if he would leave the art of euphemism to the realtors and the garment trade, and go back to calling a hearse a hearse and a coffin a coffin; but a gruesome humor will play about him and his calling till the end of time. There never was a keener reader of the public mind than William Shakespeare, and he knew that a gravedigger was always good for a laugh. For sooner and later the mortician and his retinue are going to get us, each and every one; at which prospect we might as well laugh, for that is all we can do about it.

HATRACK

By Herbert Asbury

WHEN I was a boy in Farmington, Missouri, it was the custom of our pastors and pious brethren, and of the professional devil-chasers who were imported as reinforcements from time to time, to proclaim loudly and incessantly that our collective morals were compounded of a slice of Sodom and a cut of Gomorrah, with an extract of Babylon to flavor the stew. They worried constantly and fretfully over our amorous activities; they regarded every man except the very aged and decrepit as a potential seducer, and every young girl as a prospective daughter of sin, whose salvation depended almost entirely upon the volume of noise they themselves could make.

In their more feverish discourses appeared significant references to the great difficulty of remaining pure, and in effect they advised our young women to go armed to the teeth, prepared to do battle in defense of their virginity. These gloomy predictions of the inevitability of seduction naturally had a tremendous effect upon young minds; very likely it was after she had heard the ravings of such an evangelist that the little girl of the fable, requested by her teacher to define a virgin, replied, "A female person under five years of age."

In all the small towns of the Middle West this sort of thing was the principal stock in trade of those who would lead their brethren to the worship of the current God. I do not recall ever having heard an evangelist, whether professional or amateur, who did not assure his hearers that their town was overrun by harlots, and that brothels abounded in which leading citizens abandoned themselves to shameful orgies while church attendance dwindled, and collections became smaller and smaller, and chicken appeared less and less frequently upon the ministerial table. Their tirades were generally in this fashion:

> Shall we permit these painted daughters of Jezebel, these bedizened hussies, to stalk the streets of this fair city and flaunt their

HERBERT ASBURY *leaped into the national spotlight literally overnight with the appearance of "Hatrack," which the New England Watch and Ward Society and other bluenoses denounced as "salacious." For a time they managed to have it barred from public sale and banned from the mails. The editor of the one magazine that dared to publish it personally went to Boston and had himself arrested, as a test case, on Boston Common for selling the issue. There ensued a long series of litigations, during which "Hatrack" achieved a popularity probably unequaled in the history of periodical journalism. The article may appear somewhat tame now, but that is only because the public attitude toward "salacious" literature has considerably matured.* (April, 1926)

sin in the face of the Lord? Shall we permit them to lure our sons and brothers into their vile haunts and ply their nefarious trade in the very shadow of the House of God? No! I say NO! Jesus Christ must live in this town!

Immediately everyone shouted, "Amen, Brother!" and "Praise the Lord!" But it was sometimes difficult to determine whether the congregation praised the Lord for inspiring the evangelist to so courageously defy the harlots, or for permitting him to discover them. If the Man of God could find them, why not the damned too? Certainly there were always many who wondered if the brother had acquired any good addresses or telephone numbers since coming to town. Not infrequently, indeed, he was stealthily shadowed home by young men eager to settle that question.

These charges and denunciations were repeated by the evangelist at the meetings for men only which were always a most interesting feature of the revivals. At similar gatherings for women, or ladies, as we called them in small town journalism, his wife or a devout sister discussed the question from the feminine viewpoint. What went on at these latter conclaves I do not know, though I can guess, for I have often seen young girls coming out of them giggling and blushing. The meetings for men only were juicy indeed. The evangelist discussed all angles of the subject, and in a very free manner. His own amorous exploits before he became converted were recited in considerable detail, and he painted vivid word pictures of the brothels he had visited, both as a paying client and in the course of his holy work. Almost invariably they were subterranean palaces hung with silks and satins, with soft rugs upon the floor, and filled with a vast multitude of handsome young women, all as loose as ashes. Having thus intimated, with some smirking, that for many years he was almost the sole support of harlotry, he became confidential. He leaned forward and said:

"There are such Dens of the Devil right here in your town!"

This was first-class information, and immediately there was a stir in the audience, many of his hearers betraying an eagerness to be gone. But before they could get away the evangelist thundered:

"Shall we permit them to continue their wicked practices?"

I always hoped to be present some day when the audience forgot itself and answered that question with the reply that was so plainly in its mind, namely, "Yes!" But alas, I never heard it, although there was much shouting of "Amen!" and "Glory to God!" These meetings for men only were generally held in the afternoon, and their net result was that the business of the drugstore increased immediately, and when night fell bands of young good-for-nothings scurried hither and yon about the town, searching feverishly for the Dens of the Devil. They searched without fear, confident that modern science would save them from any untoward consequences, and knowing that no matter what they did they would go to heaven if they permitted a minister to intercede for them in the end, or a priest to oil them with holy unguents.

But the Dens of the Devil were not found, neither in Farmington nor in any other small town in that region, for the very good reason that they did not exist. The evangelist did not know what he was talking about; he was simply using stock blather that he had found by experience would excite the weak-minded to both sexual and religious emotions, which are very similar. He knew that when they were thus upset they would be less likely to question his ravings — that they would be more pliable in his hands and easier to convert. It is, in fact, well-nigh impossible to convert anyone who can keep his head and retain control of his emotions. Such a person is likely to giggle during the most solemn moments, and nothing is more destructive of evangelical fervor than a hearty giggle.

II

Our small towns were not overrun by harlots for the plain reason that harlotry could not flourish in a small town. It was economically impossible; there were not enough cash customers to make the scarlet career profitable. Also, the poor girls had to meet too much competition from emotional ladies who had the professional spirit but retained their amateur standing by various technicalities. And harlots, like the rest of us, had to live; they required the same sort of raiment and food that sufficed their virtuous sisters; it was not until they died that they wore nothing but the smoke of hell and were able to subsist on a diet of brimstone and sulphur.

Many men who in larger communities would have patronized the professionals could not do so in a small town. They could not afford to; it was too dangerous. The moment a woman was suspected of being a harlot she was watched eagerly by everyone from the mayor down to the preachers, and the name of every man seen talking to her, or even looking at her, went winging swiftly from mouth to mouth, and was finally posted on the heavenly bulletin board as that of an immoral wretch. A house in which harlotry was practiced was picketed day and night by small boys eager to learn the forbidden mysteries, and by brethren and sisters hopefully sniffing. It was not possible for a harlot to keep her clientèle secret, for the sexual life of a small town is an open book, and news of amorous doings could not travel faster if each had a tabloid newspaper.

Exact statistics, of course, are not available, but it is probably true that no small American town has ever harbored a harlot whose professional income was sufficient to feed and clothe her. Few if any such towns have ever been the abode of more than one harlot at a time. When I was a boy every one had its own harlot, just as it had its town sot (this, of course, was before drunkards became extinct), and its town idiot. But she was generally a poor creature who was employed by day as a domestic servant and practised her ancient art only in her hours of leisure. She turned to it partly for economic reasons, and partly because of a great yearning for human companionship, which she could obtain in no other way. She remained in it because she was almost instantly branded a Daughter of

Satan, and shunned by good and bad alike. She seldom, if ever, realized that she was doing wrong; her moral standards were those of a bed bug. She thought of harlotry in terms of new ribbons and an occasional pair of shoes, and in terms of social intercourse; she was unmoral rather than immoral, and the proceeds of her profession, to her, were just so much extra spending money.

Small town men who occasionally visited the larger cities, and there thought nothing of spending from ten to fifty dollars in metropolitan brothels, were very stingy in dealing with the town harlot. They considered a dollar an enormous price for her, and frequently they refused to give her anything. Many small communities were not able to support even a part-time harlot; consequently some members of the craft went from town to town, taking secular jobs and practicing harlotry as a side line until driven out by the godly or until the inevitable business depression occurred. I recall one who made several towns along the O. K. Railroad in Northeastern Missouri as regularly as the shoe drummers. Her studio was always an empty box car on the town siding, and she had a mania for inscribing in such cars the exact dates and hours of her adventures, and her honoraria. It was not unusual to find in a car some such inscription as this:

Ten p.m., July 8. Fifty cents.

These writings, scrawled in lead pencil or with a bit of chalk, were signed "Box Car Molly." Once, in a car from which I had unloaded many heavy bags of cement, I came across what seemed to be a choice bit of very early, and apparently authentic Box-Car-Molliana. On the wall was this:

I was ruined in this car May 10.
Box Car Molly

III

Our town harlot in Farmington was a scrawny creature called variously Fanny Fewclothes and Hatrack, but usually the latter in deference to her figure. When she stood with her arms outstretched she bore a remarkable resemblance to the tall hatracks then in general use in our homes, and since she was always most amiable and obliging, she was frequently asked to pose thus for the benefit of drummers and other infidels. In time, she came to take a considerable pride in this accomplishment; she referred to herself as a model, and talked vaguely of abandoning her wicked life and going to St. Louis, where she was sure she could make a living posing for artists.

Six days a week Hatrack was a competent and more or less virtuous drudge employed by one of our best families, but Sunday was her day off, and she then, in turn, offered her soul to the Lord and went to the devil. For the latter purpose she utilized the Masonic and Catholic cemeteries, which were side by side, although their occupants presumably went to different heavens. Hatrack's regular Sunday night parade, her descent from righteousness to sin, was one of the most fascinating events of the week, and promptly after supper those of us who did not have engagements to take young ladies to church (which was practically equivalent to publishing the banns), went downtown to the loafing place in front of the Post Office and waited impatiently.

On week days Hatrack turned a deaf ear to the blandishments of our roués, but on Sunday night she was very gracious and receptive. This, however, was not until she had gone to church and had been given to understand, tacitly but none the less clearly, that there was no room for her in the Kingdom of Heaven. Our Sunday night services usually began about eight o'clock, following the meetings of the various young people's societies. At seven thirty, regardless of the weather, the angular figure of Hatrack could be discerned coming down the hill from the direction of the cemeteries. She lived somewhere in that section and worked by the day. She was always dressed in her best, and in her eyes was the light of a great resolve. She was going to church, and there was that in her walk and manner which said that thereafter she was going to lead a better life.

There was always a group of men waiting for her around the Post Office. But although several always muttered, "Here she comes!" it was not good form to speak to her then, and she walked past them as though she had not seen them. But they, with their wide knowledge of the vagaries of the agents of the Lord, grinned hopefully and settled down to wait. They knew she would be back. She went on up the street past the Court House and turned into the Northern Methodist Church, where she took a seat in the last row. All about her were empty seats; if they were not empty when she got there they were soon vacated. No one spoke to her. No one asked her to come to Jesus. No one held out a welcoming hand. No one prayed for her. No one offered her a hymn-book. At the protracted meetings and revivals, which she invariably attended, none of the brothers and sisters tried to convert her; she was a Scarlet Woman and belonged to the devil. There was no place for her in a respectable congregation. They could not afford to be seen talking to her, even in church, where God's love, by their theory, made brothers and sisters of us all.

It was painful to watch her; she listened to the Word with such rapt attention; she sang the hymns with such fanatical fervor, and she plainly yearned for the comforts of that barbaric religion and the blessings of easy intercourse with decent people. But she never got them. From the Christians and their God she got nothing but scorn. Of all the sinners in our town Hatrack would have been the easiest to convert; she was so eager for salvation. If a preacher, or a brother, or a sister, had so much as spoken a kind word to her she would have dropped to her knees and given up her soul. And her conversion, in all likelihood, would have been permanent, for she was not mentally equipped for a struggle against the grandiose improbabilities of revealed religion. If someone had told her, as I was told, that God was an old man with long whiskers, she would not have called him "Daddy," as some of her more flippant city sisters might have done; she would have accepted Him and gloried in Him

But she was not plucked from the burning, for the workers for the Lord would have nothing to do with her, and by the end of the service her eyes had grown sullen and her lip had curled upward in a sneer. Before the final hymn was sung and the benediction pronounced upon the congregation she got to her feet and left the church. None tried to stop her; she was not wanted in the House of God. I have seen her sit alone and miserably unhappy while the preacher bellowed a sermon about forgiveness, with the whole church rocking to a chorus of "Amens" as he told the stories of various Biblical harlots, and how God had forgiven them.

But for Hatrack there was no forgiveness. Mary Magdalene was a Saint in heaven, but Hatrack remained a harlot in Farmington. Every Sunday night for years she went through the same procedure. She was hopeful always that someone would speak to her and make a place for her, that the brothers and sisters who talked so volubly about the grace and the mercy of God would offer her some of the religion that they dripped so freely over everyone else in town. But they did not, and so she went back down the street to the Post Office, swishing her skirts and offering herself to all who desired her. The men who had been waiting for her, and who had known that she would come, leered at her and hailed her with obscene speech and gesture. And she gave them back leer for leer, meeting their sallies with giggles, and motioning with her head toward the cemeteries.

And so she went up the hill. A little while later a man left the group, remarking that he must go home. He followed her. And a moment after that another left, and then another, until behind Hatrack was a line of men, about one to a block, who would not look at one another, and who looked sheepishly at the ground when they met anyone coming the other way. As each man accosted her in turn Hatrack inquired whether he was a Protestant or a Catholic. If he was a Protestant she took him into the Catholic cemetery; if he was a Catholic they went into the Masonic cemetery.

They paid her what they liked, or nothing, and she was grateful for whatever she received. It was Hatrack who made the remark that was famous in our town for many years. To a stranger who offered her a dollar she said:

"You know damned well I haven't got any change."

HUSBANDS GROW ON TREES

By Whitfield Cook

THE manner in which the Likely sisters acquired a husband was one of the more notable events in the history of West Haddam — in fact, the only truly notable event since Nathan Hale taught there in 1774. For one hundred and sixty-four years the town slumbered quietly in obscurity and then suddenly became famous as the birthplace of Vincent, that ideal man, who relieved the Likely sisters of the embarrassments of spinsterhood.

Until Vincent's coming, the Likely girls had been unobtrusive old maids. Rose had a good mind and buck teeth, and Sybil just had buck teeth. They lived quietly in their late father's Victorian house, where the most exciting events were the semi-annual dusting of the cupola and the spring rub-down given the iron deer. Every Sunday they rode to church on their bicycles, prayer books tied firmly on behind. Nobody bothered to wonder what went on beneath their greying, old-fashioned pompadours. The general assumption was that if they thought at all it must be of roses and piano duets, to both of which they were devoted.

So West Haddam would have been surprised to learn that the Likely sisters thought furiously about husbands. About all sorts and conditions of husbands: light husbands, dark husbands, husbands in the raw, and husbands pickled. About Mrs. Hawley's husband, for instance. The Hawleys lived next door to the Likelys, and Mr. Hawley had long been a thorn in the Likely girls' sides. When Mr. Hawley left for the bank in the morning, Mrs. Hawley would kiss him good-bye right where the Likelys couldn't help but see her from their dining room window. When Mrs. Hawley came over for a quiet afternoon of sewing, it was always her husband's socks or shirts on which she was working. And her conversation was, of course, entirely about him. Sometimes she'd say, "Oh, I'm *so* lucky to have Jim. Good husbands don't grow on trees, you know." And then she'd look smug. It was all so intimate and wifely; and the Likely girls could only retaliate with a few remarks about their canary's molting. But what is there particularly intimate about a canary's molting! It was humiliating; and it rankled in their minds.

The first hint the town had of Vincent's existence was the sisters' appear-

WHITFIELD COOK *is one of the younger short story writers who has been encouraged by this magazine and whose work has won wide acclaim.* (September, 1939)

ance in Gregg's men's store, where they asked to see some shoes, socks, underwear, shirts, collars, ties, suits, gloves, and hats. Mr. Gregg, who had lived all his life in West Haddam and was therefore unprepared for any unusual event, was thrown into a panic. For an hour he and the Likely sisters went from confusion to greater confusion. In the first place, the girls weren't sure about the sizes they wanted.

"Though we *do* know," said Rose Likely firmly, "that he has large hips and a 36 bust."

"Yes," agreed Sybil, "that we *do* know."

Which only made matters worse.

Mr. Gregg suggested in desperation that the gentleman, whoever he might be, come in and purchase his own clothes.

"That," said Rose, "would be impossible. He cannot appear as yet in public. He hasn't a stitch to his name."

Finally they left, worn but triumphant, having purchased one complete masculine outfit.

Of course, Mr. Gregg lost no time in spreading his astounding story. The townspeople were divided into schools of varying opinions. One school thought the Likelys must have gone stark staring mad. Hadn't their grandfather been a bit cracked? Another school thought they were simply getting ready for a masquerade. But if that were the case, asked the others, who was Vincent? A third group, more imaginative than the rest, thought the Likelys might be harboring an escaped convict and helping him evade the police with a new suit of clothes. It was Mrs. Eben Berryman, the wife of the Congregational minister, who finally asked outright about it. She encountered the Likelys one morning in front of the post office.

"Is it true," she asked, looking sternly from Rose to Sybil and back again, "that you are harboring a man in your house?"

"Oh, I wouldn't put it that way," said Rose.

"Then there *is* a man there?" pressed Mrs. Berryman.

"Only our husband," said Sybil casually.

And that's all Mrs. Berryman learned, for before she could recover enough to ask further questions, the Likely girls had swung onto their bicycles and with a gay ringing of their bells were off down the street.

Vincent made his first public appearance the very next day. He came out of the house and was taken for a little walk, a Likely sister on either side of him. Though the girls tried to be very casual, they were as happy and self-conscious as brides, which, indeed, they were. They had wanted a husband for thirty years, and now they had one. Only one, to be sure; but that was enough. They would share him, for surely half of a perfect husband was better than all of an imperfect one. And as far as they were concerned, Vincent was absolutely perfect. He didn't drink or smoke. He didn't snore. He was never boring or cross. He was a tireless listener. And — as it turned out later — he was even a good provider. Of course, his figure was a little strange, but that was because the Likely sisters had made him out of an old dressmaker's form, great-uncle Samuel's cork legs, and the head of a large china doll, the latter carefully repainted by Sybil, who in her time had been very handy with watercolors. She had given Vincent a mustache for, as she often said to Rose, there was nothing quite like a man with a mustache. Besides, Mrs. Hawley's husband had a mustache.

II

The town's reaction to Vincent was immediate. Children followed after him and giggled, dogs barked, neighbors gaped with amazement and whispered with alarm and indignation. Through all this the Likelys moved with slow unconcern, chattering on to Vincent about the weather and the condition of his sinus and supporting his light weight easily between them.

For the next few days the air was electric with critical discussions. The men were amused, but their wives were annoyed and upset. Vincent was a public scandal, a disgrace, an insult. If this was a joke, it was a little too-pointed a joke, and the Likelys carried it too far. They took Vincent to church with them (he rode on Sybil's handlebars); and whereas the Likelys usually had to listen to at least a dozen women talk about their husbands, they now turned the tables and talked to those same women about Vincent.

"I don't believe you've met Vincent, Mrs. Oglethorpe. Our husband, you know. You must excuse him for not being more cordial. He's bothered so with his sinus this morning. And you know what men are. Can't stand the least bit of pain. Just like grown-up children, aren't they? And he's tired, too. He's been working so hard on his book. Yes, he writes. Historical things. His new one is to be called *The Monetary Systems of Ancient Civilizations*."

The Likely sisters went out more than usual now that they had Vincent to escort them, and the town gradually became accustomed to seeing the three of them sitting sedately on a bench in the park while Rose read aloud from Jean Jacques Rousseau (for Vincent had widened their literary horizons). After a time, it no longer seemed strange to have a man's shirts and underwear hanging conspicuously on the Likely clothesline or to hear from Rose or Sybil that Vincent's intestines were troubling him or that he was hard on socks or that he had descended from a fine old Boston family.

The women of the town, though they were still indignant over Vincent, began to grow just a little envious. It seemed as though the sisters now enjoyed all the advantages of married life without having to suffer the disadvantages. They had a husband who would go with them wherever they wanted, who never complained, and who never brought anyone home unexpectedly to dinner. To be sure, his appearance was decidedly comic, but weren't there several human husbands in the town who looked just as funny? On one point only did Vincent fall down. He couldn't support the Likely girls. And, remembering that, every wife in the town, no matter how shiftless her husband, still felt superior. But that state of affairs lasted only a short while, for Vincent soon proved his earning power.

A bored young man came to West Haddam to write an article for a New York paper on the Nathan Hale schoolhouse; but his boredom fled when he saw the Likely girls out walking with Vincent, who was looking particularly dashing that day in a new tweed suit. He moved along the street jauntily, an arm on each girl's shoulder, while they held him up casually by the seat of his trousers.

The girls told the reporter all the things about Vincent which the town had heard time and again. The young man jotted all this down joyfully, took a picture of Vincent and the girls, and dashed back to New York. And in due time an article appeared all over the country. It was headed WEST HADDAM SISTERS FIND PERFECT HUSBAND. Overnight Vincent became famous.

A short while later the Likelys announced that they were going away for an indefinite length of time. Their publicity was growing, and they admitted not too reluctantly that their public was demanding them. Mrs. Hawley, when she heard this, went right over. She found Rose and Sybil putting dust covers on the parlor furniture, while Vincent sat quietly in a chair and looked on.

"Well," said Mrs. Hawley, "Vincent isn't helping you much."

"We refuse to let him," said Sybil. "He tires so easily, the lamb."

"I understand you're going away," said Mrs. Hawley. "Are you going far?"

"To New York," said Sybil.

"We don't want to go at all," said Rose, "but they're clamoring for Vincent. And offering him *so* much money. And if Vincent has to go, we shall go, too. A wife's duty is by her husband's side. That's what *we* always say. Of course, we don't particularly approve of night clubs," she added, hanging Vincent on the chandelier and backing off to admire him. "But who are we to stand in the way of our husband's career?"

"I thought his career was writing," said Mrs. Hawley.

A wicked gleam came into the eyes of Rose and Sybil. "It is. But he has *other* careers, too. He's *amazingly* versatile. Now suppose Mr. Hawley wanted to leave his position at the bank, could *he* entertain in a night club?"

"Ho hum," said Sybil casually, as she pushed Vincent to and fro and watched him swing gracefully through the air.

"Just look at him," said Rose. "He certainly is in fine form, if I do say it myself." She turned condescendingly to Mrs. Hawley. "How is *your* husband on a chandelier?" she asked.

Mrs. Hawley had no answer for that. She said good-bye and left.

III

In New York Vincent began making really big money. All he had to do at the Krazy Kwilt Klub, for that was the night club which had secured his talents, was appear in smartly-tailored evening clothes between the conservatively dressed Likelys and look pleasant while the girls sang a group of old-fashioned songs. This was not too difficult for him, even though Sybil usually was slightly off key. After the songs, Rose would give a short talk on

The Care and Raising of Husbands. Certain high points pleased her audiences enormously: "They may be a bit more trouble, but husbands in the long run are more satisfactory than dogs or climbing roses. . . . Always brag about your husband's intellectual qualities, even though you know his head is hollow. . . . When supporting your husband, do so by a firm hold on the seat of his trousers, thus making him appear to stand on his own feet. . . . Give your husband a few slight imaginary ailments. If you don't, your friends will imagine worse ones. . . . If you are bored with him, hang him in a closet for a while; you'll be surprised how delightful he'll seem afterward."

This simple routine endeared the three of them to the hearts of New Yorkers. They were wined, dined, photographed, and interviewed. They had a new cocktail and a new nervous disease named after them. The mayor gave them the keys to the city — and a certain old political institution even offered to give them the mayor. In short, they were a huge success.

Altogether, it was over a year before they saw West Haddam again, and it was unfortunate for Vincent that they ever went back for it was then that the incident occurred which led directly to his spectacular demise. Returning to their home town with new glory and increased wealth, and every woman now openly envious of their capable husband, the Likelys set up housekeeping on a more elaborate scale. They even hired a maid.

Her name was Josephine, and she seemed an able girl. But she had weaknesses, one of which was drink. Before long Rose and Sybil realized they would have to dismiss her. But they didn't do so soon enough. One afternoon the Likelys went to a meeting of the Woman's Club and left Vincent at home, supposedly hard at work on *The Monetary Systems of Ancient Civilizations*. When they returned they found Josephine and Vincent in an aroma of liquor, asleep together on the sofa. Of course, Josephine had folded Vincent up and jammed him into a corner and was using him as a pillow; nevertheless the Likelys considered the evidence damning enough. As far as they were concerned, Vincent had been caught *in flagrante delicto*.

They were quite excited over it. Now they could feel equal not only to Mrs. Hawley and Mrs. Berryman, whose husbands were virtuous, but also to Mrs. Dixon and Mrs. Frost, whose husbands were sinners. Now was the time, the Likely sisters felt, to illustrate the final and greatest advantage of a husband like Vincent. Within a week engraved cards were sent to all their acquaintances. They read:

> Rose and Sybil Likely
> take Pleasure in Announcing
> that because of
> his Habitual Infidelity
> They are Burning their Husband
> with the Rubbish
> Tuesday, May 17   Four to Six

They had been unable to resist the temptation to use the word "habitual." Vincent, after all, was supposed to excel in everything.

Vincent's last day was warm and clear. Although no townspeople came openly to the services, the Likelys knew that houses facing their backyard were filled with the curious. A newspaper reporter and a photographer were the only people on the grounds when, at four o'clock, Rose and Sybil came out of the house with Vincent between them. They were dressed in deep mourning, but they moved with nervous haste, as they knew widows often did when anxious to get through the ceremony and read the will. They doubled Vincent over and placed him neatly in the wire rubbish basket; then they lit the kindling beneath him. Soon he was hidden by flames, but he took a long time to burn and his smoke was rather unpleasant. The reporter and photographer left and Rose and Sybil were definitely bored long before he was completely consumed. Finally, however, there were enough ashes to gather up in a large jar and take into the house. (Even his ashes proved superior to those of other husbands, for the following year Sybil used them with great success on the climbing roses.)

They placed the jar in the center of the parlor mantel and stood off and looked at it with appropriate expressions.

"Well," said Rose, "that's the end of the best husband *this* town will ever see."

The town settled back into its undisturbed life once more, and the Likely sisters, sobered by their widowhood, returned to comparative normalcy. All might have continued that way, had Mrs. Hawley not presented her husband with a child. But she did; and the Likelys took it as a direct challenge. The next day they appeared in the town, each with a baby (cloth body and china head) in her arms.

"Posthumous twins," said Sybil to the first person they met. "And don't they look exactly like their dear late papa?"

ALL GOD'S CHILLUN GOT WINGS

By Eugene O'Neill

CHARACTERS
JIM HARRIS
MRS. HARRIS, *his mother*
HATTIE, *his sister*
ELLA DOWNEY
SHORTY
JOE
MICKEY
Whites and Negroes

Act One

SCENE ONE — *A corner in lower New York. Years ago. End of an afternoon in spring.*
SCENE TWO — *The same. Nine years later. End of an evening in spring.*
SCENE THREE — *The Same. Five years later. A night in spring.*
SCENE FOUR — *The street before a church in the same ward. A morning weeks later.*

Act Two

SCENE ONE — *A flat in the same ward. A morning two years later.*
SCENE TWO — *The same. At twilight some months later.*
SCENE THREE — *The same. A night some months later.*

Act I

Scene 1

A corner in lower New York, at the edge of a colored district. Three narrow streets converge. A triangular building in the rear, red brick, four-storied, its ground floor a grocery. Four-story tenements stretch away down the skyline of the two streets. The fire escapes are crowded with people. In the street leading left, the faces are all white; in the street leading right, all black. It is hot spring. On the sidewalk are eight children, four boys and four girls. Two of each sex are white, two black. They are playing marbles. One of the black boys is JIM HARRIS. *The little blonde girl, her complexion rose and white, who sits behind his elbow and holds his marbles is* ELLA DOWNEY. *She is eight. They play the game with concentrated attention for a while. People pass, black and white, the Negroes frankly participants in the spirit of spring, the whites laughing constrainedly, awkward in natural emotion. Their words are lost. One only hears their laughter. It expresses the difference in race. There are street noises — the clattering roar of the Elevated, the puff of its locomotives, the ruminative lazy sound of a horse-car. From the street of the whites a high-pitched, nasal tenor sings the chorus of "Only a Bird in a Gilded Cage." On the street of the blacks a Negro strikes up the chorus of: "I Guess I'll Have to Telegraph My Baby." As this singing*

EUGENE O'NEILL *was awarded the Pulitzer Prize for drama in 1920, 1922, and 1928, and in 1936 he was awarded the Nobel Prize for literature. "All God's Chillun Got Wings" was first presented to the public, even before its stage production, in this magazine.* (February, 1924)

ends, there is laughter, distinctive in quality, from both streets. Then silence. The light in the street begins to grow brilliant with the glow of the setting sun. The game of marbles goes on.]

WHITE GIRL — [*Tugging at the elbow of her brother*] Come on, Mickey!

HER BROTHER — [*Roughly*] Aw, gwan, youse!

WHITE GIRL — Aw right, den. You kin git a lickin' if you wanter. [*Gets up to move off.*]

HER BROTHER — Aw, git off de eart!

WHITE GIRL — De old woman'll be madder'n hell!

HER BROTHER — [*Worried now*] I'm comin', ain't I? Hold your horses.

BLACK GIRL — [*To a black boy*] Come on, you Joe. We gwine git frailed too, you don't hurry.

JOE — Go long!

MICKEY — Bust up de game, huh? I gotta run! [*Jumps to his feet.*]

OTHER WHITE BOY — Me, too. [*Jumps up.*]

OTHER BLACK GIRL — Lawdy, it's late!

JOE — Me for grub!

MICKEY — [*To* JIM HARRIS] You's de winner, Jim Crow. Yeh gotta play tomorrer.

JIM — [*Readily*] Sure ting, Mick. Come one, come all! [*He laughs.*]

OTHER WHITE BOY — Me too! I gotta git back at yuh.

JIM — Aw right, Shorty.

LITTLE GIRLS — Hurry! Come on, come on! [*The six start off together. Then they notice that* JIM *and* ELLA *are hesitating, standing awkwardly and shyly together. They turn to mock.*]

JOE — Look at dat Jim Crow! Land sakes, he got a gal! [*He laughs. They all laugh.*]

JIM — [*Ashamed*] Ne'er mind, you Chocolate!

MICKEY — Look at de two softies, will yeh! Mush! Mush! [*He and the two other boys take this up.*]

LITTLE GIRLS — [*Pointing their fingers at* ELLA] Shame! Shame! Everybody knows your name! Painty Face! Painty Face!

ELLA — [*Hanging her head*] Shut up!

LITTLE WHITE GIRL — He's been carrying her books!

COLORED GIRL — Can't you find nuffin' better'n him, Ella? Look at de big feet he got! [*She laughs. They all laugh.* JIM *puts one foot on top of the other, looking at* ELLA.]

ELLA — Mine yer own business, see! [*She strides toward them angrily. They jump up and dance in an ecstasy, screaming and laughing.*]

ALL — Found yeh out! Found yeh out!

MICKEY — Mush-head! Jim Crow de Sissy! Stuck on Painty Face!

JOE — Will Painty Face let you hold her doll, boy?

SHORTY — Sissy! Softy! [ELLA *suddenly begins to cry. At this they all howl.*]

ALL — Cry-baby! Cry-baby! Look at her! Painty Face!

JIM — [*Suddenly rushing at them, with clenched fists, furiously*] Shut yo' moufs! I kin lick de hull of you! [*They all run away, laughing, shouting, and jeering, quite triumphant now that they have made him, too, lose his temper. He comes back to* ELLA, *and stands beside her sheepishly, stepping on one foot after the other. Suddenly he blurts out:*] Don't bawl no more. I done chased 'em.

ELLA — [*Comforted, politely*] Tanks.

JIM — [*Swelling out*] It was a cinch. I kin wipe up de street wid any one of dem. [*He stretches out his arms, trying to bulge out his biceps*] Feel dat muscle!

ELLA — [*Does so gingerly — then with admiration*] My!

JIM — [*Protectingly*] You mustn't never be scared when I'm hanging round, Painty Face.

ELLA — Don't call me that, Jim — please!

JIM — [*Contritely*] I didn't mean nuffin'. I didn't know you'd mind.

ELLA — I do — more'n anything.

JIM — You oughtn't to mind. Dey's jealous, dat's what.

ELLA — Jealous? Of what?

JIM — [*Pointing to her face*] Of dat. Red 'n' white. It's purty.

ELLA — I hate it!

JIM — It's purty. It's — outa sight!

ELLA — I hate it. I wish I was black like you.

JIM — [*Sort of shrinking*] No you don't. Dey'd call you Crow, den — or Chocolate — or Smoke.

ELLA — I wouldn't mind.

JIM — [*Somberly*] Dey'd call you nigger sometimes, too.

ELLA — I wouldn't mind.

JIM — [*Humbly*] You wouldn't mind?

ELLA — No, I wouldn't mind. [*An awkward pause.*]

JIM — [*Suddenly*] You know what, Ella? Since I been tuckin' yo' books to school and back, I been drinkin' lots o' chalk 'n' water tree times a day. Dat Tom, de barber, he tole me dat make me white, if I drink enough. [*Pleadingly*] Does I look whiter?

ELLA — [*Comfortingly*] Yes — maybe — a little bit —

JIM — [*Trying a careless tone*] Reckon dat Tom's a liar, an' de joke's on me! Dat chalk only makes me feel kinder sick inside.

ELLA — Why do you want to be white?

JIM — Because — just because — I lak dat better.

ELLA — I wouldn't. I like black. Let's you and me swap. I'd like to be black. [*Clapping her hands*] Gee, that'd be fun, if we only could!

JIM — [*Hesitatingly*] Yes — maybe —

ELLA — Then they'd call me Crow, and you'd be Painty Face!

JIM — They wouldn't never dast call you nigger, you bet! I'd kill 'em! [*A long pause. Finally she takes his hand shyly. They both keep looking as far away from each other as possible.*]

ELLA — I like you.

JIM — I like you.

ELLA — Do you want to be my feller?

JIM — Yes.

ELLA — Then I'm your girl.

JIM — Yes. [*Then grandly*] You kin bet none o' de gang gwine call you Painty Face from dis out! I lam' 'em good! [*The sun has set. Twilight has fallen on the street. An organ grinder comes up to the corner and plays "Annie Rooney." They stand hand-in-hand and listen. He goes away. It is growing dark.*]

ELLA — [*Suddenly*] Golly, it's late! I'll git a lickin'!

JIM — Me, too.

ELLA — I won't mind it much.

JIM — Me nuther.

ELLA — See you going to school tomorrow.

JIM — Sure.
ELLA — I gotta skip now.
JIM — Me, too.
ELLA — I like you, Jim.
JIM — I like you.
ELLA — Don't forget.
JIM — Don't you.
ELLA — Good-by.
JIM — So long. [*They run away from each other — then stop abruptly, and turn as at a signal.*]
ELLA — Don't forget.
JIM — I won't, you bet!
ELLA — Here! [*She kisses her hand at him, then runs off in frantic embarrassment.*]
JIM — [*Overcome*] Gee! [*Then he turns and darts away as*

THE CURTAIN FALLS

Scene 2

The same corner. Nine years have passed. It is again late spring at a time in the evening which immediately follows the hour of Scene 1. Nothing has changed much. One street is still all white, the other all black. The fire escapes are laden with drooping human beings. The grocery-store is still at the corner. The street noises are now more rhythmically mechanical, electricity having taken the place of horse and steam. People pass, white and black. They laugh as in Scene 1. From the street of the whites the high-pitched nasal tenor sings: "Gee, I Wish That I Had a Girl," and the Negro replies with "All I Got Was Sympathy." The singing is followed again by laughter from both streets. Then silence. The dusk grows darker. With a spluttering flare the arc-lamp at the corner is lit and sheds a pale glare over the street. Two young roughs slouch up to the corner, as tough in manner as they can make themselves. One is the SHORTY *of Scene 1; the other the Negro,* JOE. *They stand loafing. A boy of seventeen or so passes by, escorting a girl of about the same age. Both are dressed in their best, the boy in black with stiff collar, the girl in white.*

SHORTY — [*Scornfully*] Hully cripes! Pipe who's here! [*To the girl, sneeringly*] Wha's matter, Liz? Don't yer recernize yer old fr'ens?
GIRL — [*Frightenedly*] Hello, Shorty.
SHORTY — Why de glad rags? Goin' to graduation? [*He tries to obstruct their way but, edging away from him, they turn and run.*]
JOE — Har-har! Look at dem scoot, will you! [SHORTY *grins with satisfaction.*]
SHORTY — [*Looking down other street*] Here comes Mickey.
JOE — He won de semi-final last night easy?
SHORTY — Knocked de bloke out in de thoid.
JOE — Dat boy's suah a-comin'! He'll be de champeen yit.
SHORTY — [*Judicially*] Got a good chanct — if he leaves de broads alone. Dat's where he's wide open. [MICKEY *comes in from the left. He is dressed loudly, a straw hat with a gaudy band cocked over one cauliflower ear. He has acquired a typical "pug's" face, with the added viciousness of a natural bully. One of his eyes is puffed, almost closed, as a result of his battle the night before. He swaggers up.*]
BOTH — Hello, Mickey.
MICKEY — Hello.
JOE — Hear you knocked him col'.
MICKEY — Sure. I knocked his block off. [*Changing the subject*] Say. Seen

'em goin' past to de graduation racket?

SHORTY — [*With a wink*] Why? You int'rested?

JOE — [*Chuckling*] Mickey's gwine roun' git a good conduct medal.

MICKEY — Sure. Dey kin pin it on de seat o' me pants. [*They laugh*] Listen. Seen Ella Downey goin'?

SHORTY — Painty Face? No, she ain't been along.

MICKEY — [*With authority*] Can dat name, see! Want a bunch o' fives in yer kisser? Den nix! She's me goil, understan'?

JOE — [*Venturing to joke*] Which one? Yo' number ten?

MICKEY — [*Flattered*] Sure. De real K.O. one.

SHORTY — [*Pointing right — sneeringly*] Gee! Pipe Jim Crow all dolled up for de racket.

JOE — [*With disgusted resentment*] You mean tell me dat nigger's graduatin'?

SHORTY — Ask him. [JIM HARRIS *comes in. He is dressed in black, stiff white collar, etc. — a quiet-mannered Negro boy with a queerly-baffled, sensitive face.*]

JIM — [*Pleasantly*] Hello, fellows. [*They grunt in reply, looking over him scornfully.*]

JOE — [*Staring resentfully*] Is you graduatin' tonight?

JIM — Yes.

JOE — [*Spitting disgustedly*] Fo' Gawd's sake! You *is* gittin' high-falutin'!

JIM — [*Smiling deprecatingly*] This is my second try. I didn't pass last year.

JOE — What de hell does it git you, huh? Whatever is you gwine do wid it now you gits it? Live lazy on yo' ol' woman?

JIM — [*Assertively*] I'm going to study and become a lawyer.

JOE — [*With a snort*] Fo' Chris' sake, nigger!

JIM — [*Fiercely*] Don't you call me that — not before them!

JOE — [*Pugnaciously*] Does you deny you's a nigger? I shows you —

MICKEY — [*Gives them both a push — truculently*] Cut it out, see! I'm runnin' dis corner. [*Turning to* JIM *insultingly*] Say, you! Painty Face's gittin' her ticket tonight, ain't she?

JIM — You mean Ella —

MICKEY — Painty Face Downey, dat's who I mean! I don't have to be perlite wit' her. She's me goil!

JIM — [*Glumly*] Yes, she's graduating.

SHORTY — [*Winks at* MICKEY] Smart, huh?

MICKEY — [*Winks back — meaningly*] Willin' to loin, take it from me! [JIM *stands tensely as if a struggle were going on in him.*]

JIM — [*Finally blurts out*] I want to speak to you, Mickey — alone.

MICKEY — [*Surprised — insultingly*] Aw, what de hell —!

JIM — [*Excitedly*] It's important, I tell you!

MICKEY — Huh? [*Stares at him inquisitively — then motions the others back carelessly and follows* JIM *down front.*]

SHORTY — Some noive!

JOE — [*Vengefully*] I gits dat Jim alone, you wait!

MICKEY — Well, spill de big news. I ain't got all night. I got a date.

JIM — With — Ella?

MICKEY — What's dat to you?

JIM — [*The words tumbling out*] What —

I wanted to say! I know — I've heard — all the stories — what you've been doing around the ward — with other girls — it's none of my business, with them — but she — Ella — it's different — she's not that kind —

MICKEY — [*Insultingly*] Who told yuh so, huh?

JIM — [*Draws back his fist threateningly*] Don't you dare — ! [MICKEY *is so paralyzed by this effrontery that he actually steps back.*]

MICKEY — Say, cut de comedy! [*Beginning to feel insulted*] Listen, you Jim Crow! Ain't you wise I could give yuh one poke dat'd knock yuh into next week?

JIM — I'm only asking you to act square, Mickey.

MICKEY — What's it to yuh? Why, yuh lousy goat, she wouldn't spit on yuh even! She hates de sight of a coon.

JIM — [*In agony*] I — I know — but once she didn't mind — we were kids together —

MICKEY — Aw, ferget dat! Dis is *now!*

JIM — And I'm still her friend always — even if she don't like colored people —

MICKEY — *Coons*, why don't yuh say it right! De trouble wit' you is yuh're gittin' stuck up, dat's what! Stay where yeh belong, see! Yer old man made coin at de truckin' game and yuh're tryin' to buy yerself white — graduatin' and law, for Hell's sake! Yuh're gittin yerself in Dutch wit' everyone in de ward — and it ain't cause yer a coon neider. Don't de gang all train wit' Joe dere and lots of others? But yuh're tryin' to buy white and it won't git yuh no place, see!

JIM — [*Trembling*] Some day — I'll show you —

MICKEY — [*Turning away*] Aw, gwan!

JIM — D'you think I'd change — be you — you dirty white —!

MICKEY — [*Whirling about*] What's dat?

JIM — [*With hysterical vehemence*] You act square with her — or I'll show you up — I'll report you — I'll write to the papers — the sporting writers — I'll let them know how white you are!

MICKEY — [*Infuriated*] Yuh damn nigger, I'll bust yer jaw in [*Assuming his ring pose he weaves toward* JIM, *his face set in a cruel scowl.* JIM *waits helplessly but with a certain dignity.*]

SHORTY — Cheese it! A couple bulls! And here's de Downey skoit comin', too.

MICKEY — I'll get yuh de next time! [ELLA DOWNEY *enters from the right. She is seventeen, still has the same rose and white complexion, is pretty but with a rather repelling bold air about her.*]

ELLA — [*Smiles with pleasure when she sees* MICKEY] Hello, Mick. Am I late? Say, I'm so glad you won last night. [*She glances from one to the other as she feels something in the air*] Hello! What's up?

MICKEY — Dis boob. [*He indicates* JIM *scornfully.*]

JIM — [*Diffidently*] Hello, Ella.

ELLA [*Shortly, turning away*] Hello. [*Then to* MICKEY] Come on, Mick. Walk down with me. I got to hurry.

JIM — [*Blurts out*] Wait — just a second. [*Painfully*] Ella, do you hate — colored people?

MICKEY — Aw, shut up!

JIM — Please answer.

ELLA — [*Forcing a laugh*] Say! What is this — another exam?

JIM — [*Doggedly*] Please answer.

ELLA — [*Irritably*] Of course I don't! Haven't I been brought up alongside — Why, some of my oldest — the girls I've been to public school the longest with —

JIM — Do you hate me, Ella?

ELLA — [*Confusedly and more irritably*] Say, is he drunk? Why should I? I don't hate anyone.

JIM — Then why haven't you ever hardly spoken to me — for years?

ELLA — [*Resentfully*] What would I speak about? You and me've got nothing in common any more.

JIM — [*Desperately*] Maybe not any more — but — right on this corner — do you remember once —?

ELLA — I don't remember nothing! [*Angrily*] Say! What's got into you to be butting into my business all of a sudden like this? Because you finally managed to graduate, has it gone to your head?

JIM — No, I — only want to help you, Ella.

ELLA — Of all the nerve! You're certainly forgetting your place! Who's asking you for help, I'd like to know? Shut up and stop bothering me!

JIM — [*Insistently*] If you ever need a friend — a true friend —

ELLA — I've got lots of friends among my own — kind, I can tell you. [*Exasperatedly*] You make me sick! Go to — hell! [*She flounces off. The three men laugh.* MICKEY *follows her.* JIM *is stricken. He goes and sinks down limply on a box in front of the grocery-store.*]

SHORTY — I'm going to shoot a drink. Come on, Joe, and I'll blow yuh.

JOE — [*Who has never ceased to follow every move of* JIM'S *with angry, resentful eyes*] Go long. I'se gwine stay here a secon'. I got a lil' argyment. [*He points to* JIM.]

SHORTY — Suit yerself. Do a good job. See yuh later. [*He goes, whistling.*]

JOE — [*Stands for a while glaring at* JIM, *his fierce little eyes peering out of his black face. Then he spits on his hands aggressively and strides up to the oblivious* JIM. *He stands in front of him, gradually working himself into a fury at the other's seeming indifference to his words*] Listen to me, nigger: I got a heap to whisper in yo' ear! Who is you, anyhow? Who does you think you is? Don't yo' old man and mine work on de docks togidder befo' yo' old man gits his own truckin' business? Yo' ol' man swallers his nickels, my ol' man buys him beer wid dem and swallers dat — dat's de on'y diff'rence. Don't you'n' me drag up togidder?

JIM — [*Dully*] I'm your friend, Joe.

JOE — No, you isn't! I ain't no fren o' yourn! I don't even know who you is! What's all dis schoolin' you doin'? What's all dis dressin' up and graduatin' an' sayin' you gwine study be a lawyer? What's all dis fakin' an' pretendin' and swellin' out grand an' talkin' soft and perlite? What's all dis denyin' you's a nigger — an' wid de white boys listenin' to you say it! Is you aimin' to buy white wid yo' ol' man's dough like Mickey say? What is you? [*In a rage at the other's silence*] You don't talk? Den I takes it out o' yo' hide!

[*He grabs* JIM *by the throat with one hand and draws the other fist back*] Tell me befo' I wrecks yo' face in! Is you a nigger or isn't you? [*Shaking him*] Is you a nigger, Nigger? Nigger, is you a nigger?

JIM — [*Looking into his eyes — quietly*] Yes, I'm a nigger. We're both niggers. [*They look at each other for a moment.* JOE's *rage vanishes. He slumps onto a box beside* JIM's. *He offers him a cigarette.* JIM *takes it.* JOE *scratches a match and lights both their cigarettes.*]

JOE — [*After a puff, with full satisfaction*] Man, why didn't you 'splain dat in de fust place?

JIM — We're both niggers. [*The same hand-organ man of Scene 1 comes to the corner. He plays the chorus of "Bon Bon Buddie, the Chocolate Drop." They both stare straight ahead listening. Then the organ man goes away. A silence.* JOE *gets to his feet.*]

JOE — I'll go get me a cold beer. [*He starts to move off — then turns*] Time you was graduatin', ain't it? [*He goes.* JIM *remains sitting on his box staring straight before him as*

THE CURTAIN FALLS

Scene 3

The same corner five years later. Nothing has changed much. It is a night in spring. The arc-lamp discovers faces with a favorless cruelty. The street noises are the same but more intermittent and dulled with a quality of fatigue. Two people pass, one black and one white. They are tired. They both yawn, but neither laughs. There is no laughter from the two streets. From the street of the whites the tenor, more nasal than ever and a bit drunken, wails in high barber-shop falsetto the last half of the chorus of "When I Lost You." The Negro voice, a bit maudlin in turn, replies with the last half of "Waitin' for the Robert E. Lee." Silence. SHORTY *enters. He looks tougher than ever, the typical gangster. He stands waiting, singing a bit drunkenly, peering down the street.*

SHORTY — [*Indignantly*] Yuh bum! Ain't yuh ever comin'? [*He begins to sing:* "And sewed up in her yeller kimona, She had a blue-barrelled forty-five gun, For to get her man who'd done her wrong." *Then he comments scornfully*] Not her, dough! No gat for her. She ain't got de noive. A little sugar. Dat'll fix her. [*Ella enters. She is dressed poorly, her face is pale and hollow-eyed, her voice cold and tired.*]

SHORTY — Yuh got de message?

ELLA — Here I am.

SHORTY — How yuh been?

ELLA — All right. [*A pause. He looks at her puzzledly.*]

SHORTY — [*A bit embarrassedly*] Well, I s'pose yuh'd like me to give yuh some dope on Mickey, huh?

ELLA — No.

SHORTY — Mean to say yuh don't wanter know where he is or what he's doin'?

ELLA — No.

SHORTY — Since when?

ELLA — A long time.

SHORTY — [*After a pause — with a rat-like viciousness*] Between you'n me, kid, you'll get even soon — you'n all de odder dames he's tossed. I'm on de inside. I've watched him trainin'. His next scrap, watch it! He'll go! It won't be the odder guy. It'll be all youse dames he's kidded — and de ones what's kidded him. Youse'll all be in de odder guy's corner. He won't need no odder seconds. Youse'll trow water on him, and sponge his face, and take de kinks out of his socker — and Mickey'll catch it on de button — and he won't be able to take it no more —'cause all your weight — you and de odders — 'll be behind dat punch. Ha ha! [*He laughs an evil laugh*] And Mickey'll go — down to his knees first—[*He sinks to his knees in the attitude of a groggy boxer.*]

ELLA — I'd like to see him on his knees!

SHORTY — And den — flat on his pan — dead to de world — de boidies singin' in de trees — ten — out! [*He suits his action to the words, sinking flat on the pavement, then rises and laughs the same evil laugh.*]

ELLA — He's been out — for me — a long time. [*A pause*] Why did you send for me?

SHORTY — He sent me.

ELLA — Why?

SHORTY — To slip you dis wad o' dough. [*He reluctantly takes a roll of bills from his pocket and holds it out to her.*]

ELLA — [*Looks at the money indifferently*] What for?

SHORTY — For you.

ELLA — No.

SHORTY — For de kid den.

ELLA — The kid's dead. He took diphtheria.

SHORTY — Hell yuh say! When?

ELLA — A long time.

SHORTY — Why didn't you write Mickey—?

ELLA — Why should I? He'd only be glad.

SHORTY — [*After a pause*] Well — it's better.

ELLA — Yes.

SHORTY — You made up wit yer family?

ELLA — No chance.

SHORTY — Livin' alone?

ELLA — In Brooklyn.

SHORTY — Workin'?

ELLA — In a factory.

SHORTY — You're a sucker. There's lots of softer snaps fer you, kid —

ELLA — I know what you mean. No.

SHORTY — Don't yuh wanter step out no more — have fun — live?

ELLA — I'm through.

SHORTY — [*Mockingly*] Jump in de river, huh? T'ink it over, baby. I kin start yuh right in my stable. No one'll bodder yuh den. I got influence.

ELLA — [*Without emphasis*] You're a dirty dog. Why doesn't someone kill you?

SHORTY — Is dat so! What're you? They say you been travelin' round with Jim Crow.

ELLA — He's been my only friend.

SHORTY — A nigger!

ELLA — The only white man in the world! Kind and white. You're all black — black to the heart!

SHORTY — Nigger-lover [*He throws the money in her face. It falls to the street*] Listen, you! Mickey says he's off of yuh for keeps. Dis is de finish! Dat's what he sent me to tell you. [*Glances at her searchingly — a pause*] Yuh won't make no trouble?

ELLA — Why should I? He's free. The kid's dead. I'm free. No hard feelings — only — I'll be there in spirit at his next fight, tell him! I'll take your tip — the other corner — second the punch — nine — ten — out! He's free! That's all. [*She grins horribly at* SHORTY] Go away, Shorty.

SHORTY — [*Looking at her and shaking his head — maudlinly*] Groggy! Groggy! We're all groggy! Gluttons for punishment! Me for a drink. So long. [*He goes. A Salvation Army band comes toward the corner. They are playing and singing "Till We Meet at Jesus' Feet." They reach the end as they enter and stop before* ELLA. THE CAPTAIN *steps forward.*]

CAPTAIN — Sister —

ELLA — [*Picks up the money and drops it in his hat — mockingly*] Here. Go save yourself. Leave me alone.

A WOMAN SALVATIONIST — Sister —

ELLA — Never mind that. I'm not in your line — yet. [*As they hesitate, wonderingly*] I want to be alone. [*To the thud of the big drum they march off.* ELLA *sits down on a box, her hands hanging at her sides. Presently* JIM HARRIS *comes in. He has grown into a quietly-dressed, studious-looking Negro with an intelligent yet queerly-baffled face.*]

JIM — [*With a joyous but bewildered cry*] Ella! I just saw Shorty —

ELLA — [*Smiling at him with frank affection*] He had a message from Mickey.

JIM — [*Sadly*] Ah!

ELLA — [*Pointing to the box behind her*] Sit down. [*He does so. A pause — then she says indifferently*] It's finished. I'm free, Jim.

JIM — [*Wearily*] We're never free — except to do what we have to.

ELLA — What are you getting gloomy about all of a sudden?

JIM — I've got the report from the school. I've flunked again.

ELLA — Poor Jim.

JIM — Don't pity me. I'd like to kick myself all over the block. Five years — and I'm still plugging away where I ought to have been at the end of two.

ELLA — Why don't you give it up?

JIM — No!

ELLA — After all, what's being a lawyer?

JIM — A lot — to me — what it means. [*Intensely*] Why, if I was a Member of the Bar right now, Ella, I believe I'd almost have the courage to —

ELLA — What?

JIM — Nothing. [*After a pause — gropingly*] I can't explain — just — but it hurts like fire. It brands me in my pride. I swear I know more'n any member of my class. I ought to, I study harder. I work like the devil. It's all in my head — all fine and correct to a T. Then when I'm called on — I stand up — all the white faces looking at me — and I can feel their eyes — I hear my own voice sounding funny, trembling — and all of a sudden it's all gone in my head — there's nothing remembered — and I hear myself stuttering — and give up — sit down — They don't laugh, hardly ever. They're kind. They're good people. [*In a frenzy*] They're considerate, damn them! But I feel branded!

ELLA — Poor Jim!

JIM — [*Going on painfully*] And it's the same thing in the written exams. For weeks before I study all night. I can't sleep anyway. I learn it all, I see it, I understand it. Then they give me the paper in the exam room. I look it over, I know each answer — perfectly. I take up my pen. On all sides are white men starting to write. They're so sure — even the ones that I know know nothing. But I know it all — but I can't remember any more — it fades — it goes — it's gone. There's a blank in my head — stupidity — I sit like a fool fighting to remember a little bit here, a little bit there — not enough to pass — not enough for anything — when I know it all!

ELLA — [*Compassionately*] Jim. It isn't worth it. You don't need to —

JIM — I need it more than anyone ever needed anything. I need it to live.

ELLA — What'll it prove?

JIM — Nothing at all much — but everything to me.

ELLA — You're so much better than they are in every other way.

JIM — Then — you understand?

ELLA — Of course. [*Affectionately*] Don't I know how fine you've been to me! You've been the only one in the world who's stood by me — the only understanding person — and all after the rotten way I used to treat you.

JIM — But before that — way back so high — you treated me good. [*He smiles.*]

ELLA — You've been white to me, Jim. [*She takes his hand.*]

JIM — White — to you!

ELLA — Yes.

JIM — All love is white. I've always loved you. [*This with the deepest humility.*]

ELLA — Even now — after all that's happened!

JIM — Always.

ELLA — I like you, Jim — better than anyone else in the world.

JIM — That's more than enough, more than I ever hoped for. [*The organ grinder comes to the corner. He plays the chorus of "Annie Laurie." They sit listening, hand in hand.*]

JIM — Would you ever want to marry me, Ella?

ELLA — Yes, Jim.

JIM — [*As if this quick consent alarmed him*] No, no, don't answer now. Wait! Turn it over in your mind! Think what it means to you! Consider it — over and over again! I'm in no hurry, Ella. I can wait months — years —

ELLA — I'm alone. I've got to be helped. I've got to help someone — or it's the end — one end or another.

JIM — [*Eagerly*] Oh, I'll help — I know I can help — I'll give my life to help you — that's what I've been living for —

ELLA — But can I help you? Can I help you?

JIM — Yes! Yes! We'll go abroad where a man is a man — where it don't make that difference — where people are kind and wise to see the soul under skins. I don't ask you to love me — I don't dare to hope nothing like that! I don't want nothing — only to wait — to know you like me — to be near you — to keep harm away — to make up for the past — to never let you suffer any more — to serve you — to lie at your feet like a dog that loves you — to kneel by your bed like a nurse that watches over you sleeping — to preserve and protect and shield you from evil and sorrow — to give my life and my blood and all the strength that's in me to give you peace and joy — to become your slave! — yes, be your slave! — your black slave that adores you as sacred! [*He has sunk to his knees. In a frenzy of self-abnegation, as he says the last words he beats his head on the flagstones.*]

ELLA — [*Overcome and alarmed*] Jim! Jim! You're crazy! I want to help you, Jim — I want to help —

CURTAIN

Scene 4

Some weeks or so later. A street in the same ward in front of an old brick church. The church sets back from the sidewalk in a yard enclosed by a rusty iron railing with a gate at center. On each side of this yard are tenements. The buildings have a stern, forbidding look. All the shades on the windows are drawn down, giving an effect of staring, brutal eyes that pry callously at human beings without acknowledging them. Even the two tall, narrow church windows on either side of the arched door are blanked with dull green shades. It is a bright, sunny morning. The district is unusually still, as if it were waiting, holding its breath.

From the street of the blacks to the right a Negro tenor sings in a voice of shadowy richness — the first stanza with a contented, childlike melancholy —

Sometimes I feel like a mourning dove,
Sometimes I feel like a mourning dove,
    I feel like a mourning dove.

The second with a dreamy, boyish exultance —

Sometimes I feel like an eagle in the air,
Sometimes I feel like an eagle in the air,
    I feel like an eagle in the air.

The third with a brooding, earthbound sorrow —

Sometimes I wish that I'd never been born,
Sometimes I wish that I'd never been born,
    I wish that I'd never been born.

As the music dies down there is a pause of waiting stillness. This is broken by one startling, metallic clang of the church bell. As if it were a signal, people — men, women, children — pour from the two tenements, whites from the tenement to the left, blacks from the one to the right. They hurry to form into two racial lines on each side of the gate, rigid and unyielding, staring across at each other with bitter hostile eyes. The halves of the big church door swing open and JIM *and* ELLA *step out from the darkness within into the sunlight. The doors slam behind them like wooden lips of an idol that has spat them out.* JIM *is dressed in black,* ELLA *in white, both with extreme plainness. They stand in the sunlight, shrinking and confused. All the hostile eyes are now concentrated on them. They become aware of the two lines through which they must pass; they hesitate and tremble; then stand there staring back at the people as fixed and immovable as they are. The organ grinder comes in from the right. He plays the chorus of "Old Black Joe." As he finishes the bell of the church clangs one more single stroke, insistently dismissing.*

JIM — [*As if the sound had awakened him from a trance, reaches out and takes her hand*] Come. Time we got to the steamer. Time we sailed away over the sea. Come, Honey! [*She tries to answer* but her lips tremble; she cannot take her eyes off the eyes of the people; she is unable to move. He sees this and, keeping the same tone of profound, affectionate kindness, he points upward in the sky, and gradually persuades her eyes to look up] Look up, Honey! See the sun! Feel his warm eye lookin' down! Feel how kind he looks! Feel his blessing deep in your heart, your bones! Look up, Honey! [*Her eyes are fixed on the sky now. Her face is calm. She tries to smile bravely back at the sun. Now he pulls her by the hand, urging her gently to walk with him down through the yard and gate, through the lines of people. He is maintaining an attitude to support them through the ordeal only by a terrible effort, which manifests itself in the hysteric quality of ecstasy which breaks into his voice.*] And look at the sky! Ain't it kind and blue! Blue for hope! Don't they say blue's for hope? Hope! That's for us, Honey. All those blessings in the sky! What's it the Bible says? Falls on just and unjust alike? No, that's the sweet rain. Pshaw, what am I saying? All mixed up. There's no unjust about it. We're all the same — equally just — under the sky — under the sun — under God — sailing over the sea — to the other side of the world — the side where Christ was born — the kind side that takes count of the soul — over the sea — the sea's blue, too —. Let's not be late — let's get that steamer! [*They have reached the curb now, passed the lines of people. She is looking up to the sky with an expression of trancelike calm and peace. He is on the verge of collapse, his face twitching, his eyes staring. He calls hoarsely:*] Taxi! Where is he? Taxi!

CURTAIN

Act II
Scene 1

Two years later. A flat of the better sort in the Negro district near the corner of Act 1. This is the parlor. Its furniture is a queer clash. The old pieces are cheaply ornate, naïvely, childishly gaudy — the new pieces give evidence of a taste that is diametrically opposed, severe to the point of somberness. On one wall, in a heavy gold frame, is a colored photograph — the portrait of an elderly Negro with an able, shrewd face but dressed in outlandish lodge regalia, a get-up adorned with medals, sashes, a cocked hat with frills — the whole effect as absurd to contemplate as one of Napoleon's Marshals in full uniform. In the left corner, where a window lights it effectively, is a Negro primitive mask from the Congo — a grotesque face, inspiring obscure, dim connotations in one's mind, but beautifully done, conceived in a true religious spirit. In this room, however, the mask acquires an arbitrary accentuation. It dominates by a diabolical quality that contrast imposes upon it.

There are two windows on the left looking out in the street. In the rear, a door to the hall of the building. In the right, a doorway with red and gold portières leading into the bedroom and the rest of the flat. Everything is cleaned and polished. The dark brown wallpaper is new, the brilliantly figured carpet also. There is a round mahogany table at center. In a rocking chair by the table Mrs. Harris *is sitting. She is a mild-looking, gray-haired Negress of sixty-five, dressed in an old-fashioned Sunday-best dress. Walking about the room nervously is* HATTIE, *her daughter,* JIM's *sister, a woman of about thirty with a high-strung, defiant face — an intelligent head showing both power and courage. She is dressed severely, mannishly.*

It is a fine morning in spring. Sunshine comes through the windows at the left.

MRS. HARRIS — Time dey was here, ain't it?

HATTIE — [*Impatiently*] Yes.

MRS. H. — [*Worriedly*] You ain't gwine ter kick up a fuss, is you — like you done wid' Jim befo' de weddin'?

HATTIE — No. What's done is done.

MRS. H. — We mustn't let her see we hold it agin her — de bad dat happened to her wid dat no-count fighter.

HATTIE — I certainly never give that a thought. It's what she's done to Jim — making him run away and give up his fight —!

MRS. H. — Jim loves her a powerful lot, must be.

HATTIE — [*After a pause — bitterly*] I wonder if she loves Jim!

MRS. H. — She must, too. Yes, she must, too. Don't you forget dat it was hard for her — mighty, mighty hard — harder for de white dan for de black!

HATTIE — [*Indignantly*] Why should it be?

MRS. H. — [*Shaking her head*] I ain't talkin' of shoulds. It's too late for shoulds. Dey's o'ny one should. [*Solemnly*] De white and de black shouldn't mix dat close. Dere's one road where de white goes on alone; dere's anudder road where de black goes on alone —

HATTIE — Yes if they'd only leave us alone.

MRS. H. — Dey leaves your Pa alone. He comes to de top till he's got his own business, lots o' money in de bank, he owns a building even befo' he died. [*She looks up proudly at the picture.* HATTIE *sighs impatiently — then her mother goes on*] Dey leaves me alone. I bears four children into dis worl', two dies, two lives, I helps you two grow up fine an' healthy and eddicated wid schoolin' and money fo' yo' comfort —

HATTIE — [*Impatiently*] Ma!

MRS. H. — I does de duty God set for me in dis worl'. Dey leaves me alone. [HATTIE *goes to the window to hide her exasperation. The mother broods for a minute — then goes on*] The worl' done change. Dey ain't no satisfaction wid nuffin' no more.

HATTIE — Oh! [*Then after a pause*] They'll be here any minute now.

MRS. H. — Why didn't you go meet 'em at de dock like I axed you?

HATTIE — I couldn't. My face and Jim's among those hundreds of white faces — [*With a harsh laugh*] It would give her too much advantage.

MRS. H. — [*Impatiently*] Don't talk dat way! What makes you so proud? [*Then after a pause — sadly*] Hattie.

HATTIE — [*Turning*] Yes, Ma.

MRS. H. — I want to see Jim again — my only boy — but — all de same I'd ruther he stayed away. He say in his letter he's happy, she's happy, dey likes it dere, de folks don't think nuffin' but what's natural at seeing 'em married. Why don't dey stay?

HATTIE — [*Vehemently*] No! They were

cowards to run away. If they believe in what they've done, then let them face it out, live it out here, be strong enough to conquer all prejudice!

MRS. H. — Strong? Dey ain't many strong. Dey ain't many happy neider. Dey was happy ovah yondah.

HATTIE — We don't deserve happiness till we've fought the fight of our race and won it! [*In the pause that follows there is a ring from back in the flat*] It's the door bell! You go, Ma. I — I — I'd rather not. [*Her mother looks at her rebukingly and goes out agitatedly through the portières.* HATTIE *waits, nervously walking about, trying to compose herself. There is a long pause. Finally the portières are parted and* JIM *enters. He looks much older, graver, worried.*]

JIM — Hattie!

HATTIE — Jim! [*They embrace with great affection.*]

JIM — It's great to see you again! You're looking fine.

HATTIE — [*Looking at him searchingly*] You look well, too — thinner maybe — and tired. [*Then as she sees him frowning*] But where's Ella?

JIM — With Ma. [*Apologetically*] She sort of — broke down — when we came in. The trip wore her out.

HATTIE — [*Coldly*] I see.

JIM — Oh, it's nothing serious. Nerves. She needs a rest.

HATTIE — Wasn't living in France restful?

JIM — Yes, but — too lonely — especially for her.

HATTIE — [*Resentfully*] Why? Didn't the people there want to associate —?

JIM — [*Quickly*] Oh, no indeedy, they didn't think anything of that. [*After a pause*] But — she did. For the first year it was all right. Ella liked everything a lot. She went out with French folks and got so she could talk it a little — and I learned it — a little. We were having a right nice time. I never thought then we'd ever want to come back here.

HATTIE — [*Frowning*] But — what happened to change you?

JIM — [*After a pause — haltingly*] Well — you see — the first year — she and I were living around — like friends — like a brother and sister — like you and I might.

HATTIE — [*Her face becoming more and more drawn and tense*] You mean — then —? [*She shudders — then after a pause*] She loves you, Jim?

JIM — If I didn't know that I'd have to jump in the river.

HATTIE — Are you sure she loves you?

JIM — Isn't that why she's suffering?

HATTIE — [*Letting her breath escape through her clenched teeth*] Ah!

JIM — [*Suddenly springs up and shouts almost hysterically*] Why d'you ask me all those damn questions? Are you trying to make trouble between us?

HATTIE — [*Controlling herself — quietly*] No, Jim.

JIM — [*After a pause — contritely*] I'm sorry, Hattie. I'm kind of on edge today. [*He sinks down on his chair — then goes on as if something forced him to speak*] After that we got to living housed in. Ella didn't want to see nobody, she said just the two of us was enough. I was happy then — and I really guess she was happy too — in a way — for a while. [*Again a pause*] But she never did get to wanting to go out any place again. She got to saying she felt she'd be sure to run into someone she knew — from over here. So I moved us out to the country where no tourist ever comes — but it didn't make any difference to her. She got to avoiding the French folks the same as if they were Americans and I couldn't get it out of her mind. She lived in the house and got paler and paler, and more and more nervous and scarey, always imagining things — until I got to imagining things, too. I got to feeling blue. Got to sneering at myself that I wasn't any better than a quitter because I sneaked away right after getting married, didn't face nothing, gave up trying to become a Member of the Bar — and I got to suspecting Ella must feel that way about me too — that I wasn't a *real man!*

HATTIE — [*Indignantly*] She couldn't!

JIM — [*With hostility*] You don't need to tell me! All this was only in my own mind. We never quarreled a single bit. We never said a harsh word. We were as close to each other as could be. We were all there was in the world to each other. We were alone together! [*A pause*] Well, one day I got so I couldn't stand it. I could see she couldn't stand it. So I just up and said: Ella, we've got to have a plain talk, look everything straight in the face, hide nothing, come out with the exact truth of the way we feel.

HATTIE — And you decided to come back!

JIM — Yes. We decided the reason we felt sort of ashamed was we'd acted like cowards. We'd run away from the thing — and taken it with us. We decided to come back and face it and live it down in ourselves, and prove to ourselves we were strong in our love — and then, and that way only, by being brave we'd free ourselves, and gain confidence, and be really free inside and able then to go anywhere and live in peace and equality with ourselves and the world without any guilty uncomfortable feeling coming up to rile us. [*He has talked himself now into a state of happy confidence.*]

HATTIE — [*Bending over and kissing him*] Good for you! I admire you so much, Jim! I admire both of you! And are you going to begin studying right away and get admitted to the Bar?

JIM — You bet I am!

HATTIE — You must, Jim! Our race needs men like you to come to the front and help — [*As voices are heard approaching she stops, stiffens, and her face grows cold.*]

JIM — [*Noticing this — warningly*] Remember Ella's been sick! [*Losing control — threateningly*] You be nice to her, you hear! [MRS. HARRIS *enters, showing* ELLA *the way. The colored woman is plainly worried and perplexed.* ELLA *is pale, with a strange, haunted expression in her eyes. She runs to* JIM *as to a refuge, clutching his hands in both of hers, looking from* MRS. HARRIS *to* HATTIE *with a frightened defiance.*]

MRS. H. — Dere he is, child, big's life! She was afraid we'd done kidnapped you away, Jim.

JIM — [*Patting her hand*] This place ought

to be familiar, Ella. Don't you remember playing here with us sometimes as a kid?

ELLA — [*Queerly — with a frown of effort*] I remember playing marbles one night — but that was on the street.

JIM — Don't you remember Hattie?

HATTIE — [*Coming forward with a forced smile*] It was a long time ago — but I remember Ella. [*She holds out her hand.*]

ELLA — [*Taking it—looking at* HATTIE *with the same queer defiance*] I remember. But you've changed so much.

HATTIE — [*Stirred to hostility by* ELLA'S *manner — condescendingly*] Yes, I've grown older, naturally. [*Then in a tone which, as if in spite of herself, becomes bragging*] I've worked so hard. First I went away to college, you know — then I took up postgraduate study — when suddenly I decided I'd accomplish more good if I gave up learning and took up teaching. [*She suddenly checks herself, ashamed, and stung by* ELLA'S *indifference*] But this sounds like stupid boasting. I don't mean that. I was only explaining —

ELLA — [*Indifferently*] I didn't know you'd been to school so long. [*A pause*] Where are you teaching? In a colored school, I suppose. [*There is an indifferent superiority in her words that is maddening to* HATTIE.]

HATTIE — [*Controlling herself*] Yes. A private school endowed by some wealthy members of our race.

ELLA — [*Suddenly—even eagerly*] Then you must have taken lots of examinations and managed to pass them, didn't you?

HATTIE — [*Biting her lips*] I always passed with honors!

ELLA — Yes, we both graduated from the same High School, didn't we? That was dead easy for me. Why I hardly even looked at a book. But Jim says it was awfully hard for him. He failed one year, remember? [*She turns and smiles at* JIM *— a tolerant, superior smile but one full of genuine love.* HATTIE *is outraged, but* JIM *smiles.*]

JIM — Yes, it was hard for me, Honey.

ELLA — And the law school examinations Jim hardly ever could pass at all. Could you? [*She laughs lovingly.*]

HATTIE — [*Harshly*] Yes, he could! He can! He'll pass them now — if you'll give him a chance!

JIM — [*Angrily*] Hattie!

MRS. H. — Hold yo' fool tongue!

HATTIE — [*Suddenly*] I'm sorry. [ELLA *has shrunk back against* JIM. *She regards* HATTIE *with a sort of wondering hatred. Then she looks away about the room. Suddenly her eyes fasten on the primitive mask and she gives a stifled scream.*]

JIM — What's the matter, Honey?

ELLA — [*Pointing*] That! For God's sake, what is it?

HATTIE — [*Scornfully*] It's a Congo mask. [*She goes and picks it up*] I'll take it away if you wish. I thought you'd like it. It was my wedding present to Jim.

ELLA — What is it?

HATTIE — It's a mask which used to be worn in religious ceremonies by my people in Africa. But, aside from that, it's beautifully made, a work of Art by a real artist — as real in his way as your

Michael Angelo. [*Forces* ELLA *to take it*] Here. Just notice the workmanship.

ELLA — [*Defiantly*] I'm not scared of it if you're not. [*Looking at it with disgust*] Beautiful? Well, some people certainly have queer notions! It looks ugly to me and stupid — like a kid's game — making faces! [*She slaps it contemptuously*] Pooh! You needn't look hard at me. I'll give you the laugh. [*She goes to put it back on the stand.*]

JIM — Maybe, if it disturbs you, we better put it in some other room.

ELLA — [*Defiantly aggressive*] No. I want it here where I can give it the laugh! [*She sets it there again — then turns suddenly on* HATTIE *with aggressive determination*] Jim's not going to take any more examinations! I won't let him!

HATTIE — [*Bursting forth*] Jim! Do you hear that? There's white justice! — their fear for their superiority! —

ELLA — [*With a terrified pleading*] Make her go away, Jim!

JIM — [*Losing control — furiously to his sister*] Either you leave here — or we will!

MRS. H. — [*Weeping — throws her arms around* HATTIE] Let's go, chile! Let's go!

HATTIE — [*Calmly now*] Yes, Ma. All right. [*They go through the portières. As soon as they are gone,* JIM *suddenly collapses into a chair and hides his head in his hands.* ELLA *stands beside him for a moment. She stares distractedly about her, at the portrait, at the mask, at the furniture, at* JIM. *She seems fighting to escape from some weight on her mind. She throws this off and, completely her* old *self for the moment, kneels by* JIM *and pats his shoulder.*]

ELLA — [*With kindness and love*] Don't, Jim! Don't cry, please! You don't suppose I really meant that about the examinations, do you? Why, of course, I didn't mean a word! I couldn't mean it! I want you to take the examinations! I want you to pass! I want you to be a lawyer! I want you to be the best lawyer in the country! I want you to show 'em — all the dirty sneaking, gossiping liars that talk behind our backs — what a man I married. I want the whole world to know you're the whitest of the white! I want you to climb and climb — and step on 'em, stamp right on their mean faces! I love you, Jim. You know that!

JIM — [*Calm again — happily*] I hope so, Honey — and I'll make myself worthy.

HATTIE — [*Appears in the doorway — quietly*] We're going now, Jim.

ELLA — No. Don't go.

HATTIE — We were going to anyway. This is your house — Mother's gift to you, Jim.

JIM — [*Astonished*] But I can't accept — Where are you going?

HATTIE — We've got a nice flat in the Bronx — [*With bitter pride*] in the heart of the Black Belt — the Congo — among our own people!

JIM — [*Angrily*] You're crazy — I'll see Ma — [*He goes out.* HATTIE *and* ELLA *stare at each other with scorn and hatred for a moment, then* HATTIE *goes.* ELLA *remains kneeling for a moment by the chair, her eyes dazed and strange as she looks about her. Then she gets to her feet and stands before the portrait of* JIM's *father — with a sneer.*]

ELLA — It's his Old Man — all dolled up like a circus horse! Well, they can't help it. It's in the blood, I suppose. They're ignorant, that's all there is to it. [*She moves to the mask — forcing a mocking tone*] Hello, sport! Who d'you think you're scaring. Not me! I'll give you the laugh. He won't pass, you wait and see. Not in a thousand years! [*She goes to the window and looks down at the street and mutters*] All black! Every one of them! [*Then with sudden excitement*] No, there's one. Why, it's Shorty! [*She throws the window open and calls*] Shorty! Shorty! Hello, Shorty! [*She leans out and waves — then stops, remains there for a moment looking down, then comes back into the room suddenly as if she wanted to hide — her whole face in an anguish*] Say! Say! I wonder? — No, he didn't hear you. Yes, he did too! He must have! I yelled so loud you could hear me in Jersey! No, what are you talking about? How would he hear with all the kids yelling down there? He never heard a word, I tell you! He did too! He didn't want to hear you! He didn't want to let anyone know he knew you! Why don't you acknowledge it? What are you lying about? I'm not! Why shouldn't he? Where does he come in to — for God's sake, who is Shorty anyway? A pimp! Yes, and a dope-peddler, too! D'you mean to say he'd have the nerve to hear me call him and then deliberately —? Yes, I mean to say it! I do say it! And it's true, and you know it, and you might as well be honest for a change and admit it! He heard you but he didn't want to hear you! He doesn't want to know you any more. No, not even him! He's afraid it'd get him in wrong with the old gang. Why? You know well enough! Because you married a — a a — well, I won't say it, but you know without my mentioning names! [ELLA *springs to her feet in horror and shakes off her obsession with a frantic effort*] Stop! [*Then whimpering like a frightened child*] Jim! Jim! Jim! Where are you? I want you, Jim! [*She runs out of the room as*

THE CURTAIN FALLS

Scene 2

The same. Six months later. It is evening. The walls of the room appear shrunken in, the ceiling lowered, so that the furniture, the portrait, the mask look unnaturally large and domineering. JIM *is seated at the table studying, law books piled by his elbows. He is keeping his attention concentrated only by a driving physical effort which gives his face the expression of a runner's near the tape. His forehead shines with perspiration. He mutters one sentence from Blackstone over and over again, tapping his forehead with his fist in time to the rhythm he gives the stale words. But, in spite of himself, his attention wanders, his eyes have an uneasy hunted look, he starts at every sound in the house or from the street. Finally, he remains rigid, Blackstone forgotten, his eyes fixed on the portières with tense grief. Then he groans, slams the book shut, goes to the window and throws it open and sinks down beside it, his arms on the sill, his head resting wearily on his arms, staring out into* the night, the pale glare from the arc-lamp on the corner throwing his face into relief. The portières on the right are parted and HATTIE *comes in.*

HATTIE — [*Not seeing him at the table*] Jim! [*Discovering him*] Oh, there you are. What're you doing?

JIM — [*Turning to her*] Resting. Cooling my head. [*Forcing a smile*] These law books certainly are a sweating proposition! [*Then, anxiously*] How is she?

HATTIE — She's asleep now. I felt it was safe to leave her for a minute. [*After a pause*] What did the doctor tell you, Jim?

JIM — The same old thing. She must have rest, he says, her mind needs rest — [*Bitterly*] But he can't tell me any prescription for that rest — leastways not any that'd work.

HATTIE — [*After a pause*] I think you ought to leave her, Jim — or let her leave you — for a while, anyway.

JIM — [*Angrily*] You're like the doctor. Everything's so simple and easy. Do this and that happens. Only it don't. Life isn't simple like that — not in this case, anyway — no, it isn't simple a bit. [*After a pause*] I can't leave her. She can't leave me. And there's a million little reasons combining to make one big reason why we can't. [*A pause*] For her sake — if it'd do her good — I'd go — I'd leave — I'd do anything — because I love her. I'd kill myself even — jump out of this window this second — I've thought it over, too — but that'd only make matters worse for her. I'm all she's got in the world! Yes, that isn't bragging or fooling myself. I know that for a fact! Don't you know that's true? [*There is a pleading for the certainty he claims.*]

HATTIE — Yes, I know she loves you, Jim. I know that now.

JIM — [*Simply*] Then we've got to stick together to the end, haven't we, whatever comes — and hope and pray for the best. [*A pause — then hopefully*] I think maybe this is the crisis in her mind. Once she settles this in herself, she's won to the other side. And me — once I become a Member of the Bar — then I win, too! We're both free — by our own fighting down our own weakness! We're both really, truly free! Then we can be happy with ourselves here or anywhere. She'll be proud then! Yes, she's told me again and again she'll be actually proud!

HATTIE — [*Turning away to conceal her emotion*] Yes, I'm sure — but you mustn't study too hard, Jim, You mustn't study too awfully hard!

JIM — [*Gets up and goes to the table and sits down wearily*] Yes, I know. Oh, I'll pass easily. I haven't got any scarey feeling about that any more. And I'm doing two years' work in one here alone. That's better than schools, eh?

HATTIE — [*Doubtfully*] It's wonderful, Jim.

JIM — [*His spirit evaporating*] If I can only hold out! It's hard! I'm worn out. I don't sleep. I get to thinking and thinking. My head aches and burns like fire with thinking. Round and round my thoughts go chasing like crazy chickens hopping and flapping before the wind. It gets me crazy mad — 'cause I can't stop!

HATTIE — [*Watching him for a while and seeming to force herself to speak*] The doctor didn't tell you all, Jim.

JIM — [*Dully*] What's that?

HATTIE — He told me you're liable to break down too, if you don't take care of yourself.

JIM — [*Abjectly weary*] Let 'er come! I don't care what happens to me. Maybe if I get sick she'll get well. There's only so much bad luck allowed to one family, maybe. [*He forces a wan smile.*]

HATTIE — [*Hastily*] Don't give in to that idea, for the Lord's sake!

JIM — I'm tired — and blue — that's all.

HATTIE — [*After another long pause*] I've got to tell you something else, Jim.

JIM — [*Dully*] What?

HATTIE — The doctor said Ella's liable to be sick like this a very long time.

JIM — He told me that too — that it'd be a long time before she got back her normal strength. Well, I suppose that's got to be expected.

HATTIE — [*Slowly*] He didn't mean convalescing — what he told me. [*A long pause.*]

JIM — [*Evasively*] I'm going to get other doctors in to see Ella — specialists. This one's a damn fool.

HATTIE — Be sensible, Jim. You'll have to face the truth — sooner or later.

JIM — [*Irritably*] I know the truth about Ella better'n any doctor.

HATTIE — [*Persuasively*] She'd get better so much sooner if you'd send her away to some nice sanitarium —

JIM — No! She'd die of shame there!

HATTIE — At least until after you've taken your examinations —

JIM — To hell with me!

HATTIE — Six months. That wouldn't be long to be parted.

JIM — What are you trying to do — separate us? [*He gets to his feet — furiously*] Go on out! Go on out!

HATTIE — [*Calmly*] No, I won't. [*Sharply*] There's something that's got to be said to you and I'm the only one with the courage — [*Intensely*] Tell me, Jim, have you heard her raving when she's out of her mind?

JIM — [*With a shudder*] No!

HATTIE — You're lying, Jim. You must have — if you don't stop your ears — and the doctor says she may develop a violent mania, dangerous for you — get worse and worse until — Jim, you'll go crazy too — living this way. Today she raved on about "Black! Black!" and cried because she said her skin was turning black — that you had poisoned her —

JIM — [*In anguish*] That's only when she's out of her mind.

HATTIE — And then she suddenly called me a dirty nigger.

JIM — No! She never said that ever! She never would!

HATTIE — She did — and kept on and on! [*A tense pause*] She'll be saying that to you soon.

JIM — [*Torturedly*] She don't mean it! She isn't responsible for what she's saying!

HATTIE — I know she isn't — yet she is just the same. It's deep down in her or it wouldn't come out.

JIM — Deep down in her people — not deep in her.

HATTIE — I can't make such distinctions. The race in me, deep in me, can't stand it. I can't play nurse to her any more, Jim, — not even for your sake. I'm afraid — afraid of myself — afraid sometime I'll kill her dead to set you free! [*She loses control and begins to cry.*]

JIM — [*After a long pause — somberly*] Yes, I guess you'd better stay away from here. Good-by.

HATTIE — Who'll you get to nurse her, Jim, — a white woman?

JIM — Ella'd die of shame. No, I'll nurse her myself.

HATTIE — And give up your studies?

JIM — I can do both.

HATTIE — You can't. You'll get sick yourself! Why, you look terrible even as it is — and it's only beginning!

JIM — I can do anything for her! I'm all she's got in the world! I've got to prove I can be all to her! I've got to prove worthy! I've got to prove she can be proud of me! I've got to prove I'm the whitest of the white!

HATTIE — [*Stung by this last — with rebellious bitterness*] Is that the ambition she's given you? Oh, you soft, weak-minded fool, you traitor to your race! And the thanks you'll get — to be called a dirty nigger — to hear her cursing you because she can never have a child because it'll be born black —!

JIM — [*In a frenzy*] Stop!

HATTIE — I'll say what must be said even though you kill me, Jim. Send her to an asylum before you both have to be sent to one together.

JIM — [*With a sudden wild laugh*] Do you think you're threatening me with something dreadful now? Why, I'd like that. Sure. I'd like that! Maybe she'd like it better, too. Maybe we'd both find it all simple then — like you think it is now. Yes. [*He laughs again.*]

HATTIE — [*Frightenedly*] Jim!

JIM — Together! You can't scare me even with hell fire if you say she and I go together. It's heaven then for me! [*With sudden savagery*] You go out of here! All you've ever been aiming to do is to separate us so we can't be together!

HATTIE — I've done what I did for your own good.

JIM — I have no own good. I only got a good together with her. I'm all she's got in the world! Let her call me nigger! Let her call me the whitest of the white! I'm all she's got in the world, ain't I? She's all I've got! You with your fool talk of the black race and the white race! Where does the human race get a chance to come in? I suppose that's simple for you. You lock it up in asylums and throw away the key! [*With fresh violence*] Go along! There isn't going to be no more people coming in here to separate — excepting the doctor. I'm going to lock the door and it's going to stay locked, you hear? Go along, now!

HATTIE — [*Confusedly*] Jim!

JIM — [*Pushes her out gently and slams the door after her — vaguely*] Go along! I got to study. I got to nurse Ella, too. Oh, I can do it! I can do anything for her! [*He sits down at the table, and opening the book, begins again to recite the line from Blackstone in a meaningless rhythm, tapping his forehead with his fist.*]

ELLA *enters noiselessly through the portières. She wears a red dressing gown over her nightdress but is in her bare feet. She has a carving knife in her right hand. Her eyes fasten on* JIM *with a murderous mania. She creeps up behind him. Suddenly he senses something and turns. As he sees her he gives a cry, jumping up and catching her wrist. She stands fixed, her eyes growing bewildered and frightened.*]

JIM — [*Aghast*] Ella! For God's sake! Do you want to murder me? [*She does not answer. He shakes her.*]

ELLA — [*Whimperingly*] They kept calling me names as I was walking along — I can't tell you what, Jim — and then I grabbed a knife —

JIM — Yes! See! This! [*She looks at it frightenedly.*]

ELLA — Where did I —? I was having a nightmare — Where did they go — I mean, how did I get here? [*With sudden terrified pleading — like a little girl*] O Jim — don't ever leave me alone! I have such terrible dreams, Jim — promise you'll never go away!

JIM — I promise, Honey.

ELLA — [*Her manner becoming more and more childishly silly*] I'll be a little girl — and you'll be old Uncle Jim who's been with us for years and years — Will you play that?

JIM — Yes, Honey. Now you better go back to bed.

ELLA — [*Like a child*] Yes, Uncle Jim. [*She turns to go. He pretends to be occupied by his book. She looks at him for a second — then suddenly asks in her natural woman's voice*] Are you studying hard, Jim?

JIM — Yes, Honey. Go to bed now. You need to rest, you know.

ELLA — [*Stands looking at him, fighting with herself. A startling transformation comes over her face. It grows mean, vicious, full of jealous hatred. She cannot contain herself but breaks out harshly with a cruel, venomous grin*] You dirty nigger!

JIM — [*Starting as if he'd been shot*] Ella! For the good Lord's sake!

ELLA — [*Coming out of her insane mood for a moment, aware of something terrible, frightened*] Jim! Jim! Why are you looking at me like that?

JIM — What did you say to me just then?

ELLA — [*Gropingly*] Why, I — I said — I remember saying, are you studying hard, Jim? Why? You're not mad at that, are you?

JIM — No, Honey. What made you think I was mad? Go to bed now.

ELLA — [*Obediently*] Yes, Jim. [*She passes behind the portières.* JIM *stares before him. Suddenly her head is thrust out at the side of the portières. Her face is again that of a vindictive maniac*] Nigger! [*The face disappears — she can be heard running away, laughing with cruel satisfaction.* JIM *bows his head on his outstretched arms but he is too stricken for tears.*]

CURTAIN

Scene 3

The same, six months later. The sun has just gone down. The spring twilight sheds a vague, gray light about the room picking out the Congo mask on the stand by the window. The walls have shrunken in still more, the ceiling now barely clears the people's heads, the furniture and the characters appear enormously magnified. Law books are stacked in two great piles on each side of the table. ELLA *comes in from the right, the carving-knife in her hand. She is pitifully thin, her face is wasted, but her eyes glow with a mad energy, her movements are abrupt and spring-like. She looks stealthily about the room, then advances and stands before the mask, her arms akimbo, her attitude one of crazy mockery, fear and bravado. She is dressed in the red dressing-gown, grown dirty and ragged now, and is in her bare feet.*

ELLA — I'll give you the laugh, wait and see! [*Then in a confidential tone*] He thought I was asleep! He called, Ella, Ella — but I kept my eyes shut, I pretended to snore. I fooled him good. [*She gives a little horse laugh*] This is the first time he's dared to leave me alone for months and months. I've been wanting to talk to you every day but this is the only chance — [*With sudden violence — flourishing her knife*] What're you grinning about, you dirty nigger, you? How dare you grin at me? I guess you forget what you are! That's always the way. Be kind to you, treat you decent, and in a second you've got a swelled head, you think you're somebody, you're all over the place putting on airs, why, it's got so I can't even walk down the street without seeing niggers, niggers everywhere. Hanging around, grinning, grinning — going to school — pretending they're white — taking examinations — [*She stops, arrested by the word, then suddenly*] That's where he's gone — down to the mailbox — to see if there's a letter from the Board — telling him — But why is he so long? [*She calls pitifully*] Jim! [*Then in a terrified whimper*] Maybe he's passed! Maybe he's passed! [*In a frenzy*] No! No! He can't! I'd kill him! I'd kill myself! [*Threatening the Congo mask*] It's you who're to blame for this! Yes, you! Oh, I'm on to you! [*Then appealingly*] But why d'you want to do this to us? What have I ever done wrong to you? What have you got against me? I married you, didn't I? Why don't you let Jim alone? Why don't you let him be happy as he is — with me? Why don't you let me be happy? He's white, isn't he — the whitest man that ever lived? Where do you come in to interfere? Black! Black! Black as dirt! You've poisoned me! I can't wash myself clean! Oh, I hate you! I hate you! Why don't you let Jim and I be happy? [*She sinks down in his chair, her arms outstretched on the table. The door from the hall is slowly opened and* JIM *appears. His bloodshot, sleepless eyes stare from deep hollows. His expression is one of crushed numbness. He holds an open letter in his hand.*]

JIM — [*Seeing* ELLA — *in an absolutely dead voice*] Honey — I thought you were asleep.

ELLA — [*Starts and wheels about in her chair*] What's that? You got — you got a letter —?

JIM — [*Turning to close the door after him*] From the Board of Examiners for admission to the Bar, State of New York — God's country! [*He finishes up with a chuckle of ironic self-pity so spent as to be barely audible.*]

ELLA — [*Writhing out of her chair like some fierce animal, the knife held behind her — with fear and hatred*] You didn't — you didn't — you didn't pass, did you?

JIM — [*Looking at her wildly*] Pass? Pass? [*He begins to chuckle and laugh between* sentences and phrases, rich, Negro laughter, but heartbreaking in its mocking grief] Good Lord, child, how come you can ever imagine such a crazy idea? Pass? Me? Jim Crow Harris? Nigger Jim Harris — become a full-fledged Member of the Bar! Why the mere notion of it is enough to kill you with laughing! It'd be against all natural laws, all human right and justice. It'd be miraculous, there'd be earthquakes and catastrophes, the seven Plagues'd come again and locusts'd devour all the money in the banks, the second Flood'd come roaring and Noah'd fall overboard, the sun'd drop out of the sky like a ripe fig, and the Devil'd perform miracles, and God'd be tipped head first right out of the Judgment seat! [*He laughs, maudlinly uproarious.*]

ELLA — [*Her face beginning to relax, to light up*] Then you — you didn't pass?

JIM — [*Spent — giggling and gasping idiotically*] Well, I should say not! I should certainly say not!

ELLA — [*With a cry of joy, pushes all the lawbooks crashing to the floor — then with childish happiness she grabs* JIM *by both hands and dances up and down*] Oh Jim, I knew it! I knew you couldn't! Oh, I'm so glad, Jim! I'm so happy! You're still my old Jim — and I'm so glad! [*He looks at her dazedly, a fierce rage slowly gathering on his face. She dances away from him. His eyes follow her. His hands clench. She stands in front of the mask — triumphantly*] There! What did I tell you? I told you I'd give you the laugh! [*She begins to laugh with wild unrestraint, grabs the mask from its place, sets it in the middle of the table and plunging the knife down through it pins it to the table*] There! Who's got the laugh now?

JIM — [*His eyes bulging — hoarsely*] You devil! You white devil woman! [*In a terrible roar, raising his fists above her head*] You devil!

ELLA — [*Looking up at him with a bewildered cry of terror*] Jim! [*Her appeal recalls him to himself. He lets his arms slowly drop to his sides, bowing his head.* ELLA *points tremblingly to the mask*] It's all right, Jim! It's dead. The devil's dead. See! It couldn't live — unless you passed. If you'd passed it would have lived in you. Then I'd have had to kill you, Jim, don't you see — or it would have killed me. But now I've killed it. [*She pats his hand*] So you needn't ever be afraid any more, Jim.

JIM — [*Dully*] I've got to sit down, Honey. I'm tired. I haven't had much chance for sleep in so long — [*He slumps down in the chair by the table.*]

ELLA — [*Sits down on the floor beside him and holds his hand. Her face is gradually regaining an expression that is happy, childlike and pretty*] I know, Jim! That was my fault. I wouldn't let you sleep. I couldn't let you. I kept thinking if he sleeps good then he'll be sure to study good and then he'll pass and the devil'll win!

JIM — [*With a groan*] Don't, Honey!

ELLA — [*With a childish grin*] That was why I carried that knife around — [*She frowns — puzzled*] — one reason — to keep you from studying and sleeping by scaring you.

JIM — I wasn't scared of being killed. I

was scared of what they'd do to you after.

ELLA — [*After a pause — like a child*] Will God forgive me, Jim?

JIM — Maybe He can forgive what you've done to me; and maybe He can forgive what I've done to you; but I don't see how He's going to forgive — Himself.

ELLA — I prayed and prayed. When you were away taking the examinations and I was alone with the nurse, I closed my eyes and pretended to be asleep but I was praying with all my might: O, God, don't let Jim pass!

JIM — [*With a sob*] Don't, Honey, don't! For the good Lord's sake! You're hurting me!

ELLA — [*Frightenedly*] How, Jim? Where? [*Then after a pause — suddenly*] I'm sick, Jim. I don't think I'll live long.

JIM — [*Simply*] Then I won't either. Somewhere yonder maybe — together — our luck'll change. But I wanted — here and now — before you — we — I wanted to prove to you — to myself — to become a full-fledged Member — so you could be proud — [*He stops. Words fail and he is beyond tears.*]

ELLA — [*Brightly*] Well, it's all over, Jim. Everything'll be all right now. [*Chattering along*] I'll be just your little girl, Jim — and you'll be my little boy — just as we used to be, remember, when we were beaux; and I'll put shoe blacking on my face and pretend I'm black and you can put chalk on your face and pretend you're white just as we used to do — and we can play marbles — Only you mustn't all the time be a boy. Sometimes you must be my old kind Uncle Jim who's been with us for years and years. Will you, Jim?

JIM — [*With utter resignation*] Yes, Honey.

ELLA — And you'll never, never, never, never leave me, Jim?

JIM — Never, Honey.

ELLA — 'Cause you're all I've got in the world — and I love you, Jim. [*She kisses his hand as a child might, tenderly and gratefully.*]

JIM — [*Suddenly throws himself on his knees and raises his shining eyes, his transfigured face*] Forgive me, God — and make me worthy! Now I see Your Light again! Now I hear Your Voice! [*He begins to weep in an ecstasy of religious humility*] Forgive me, God, for blaspheming You! Let this fire of burning suffering purify me of selfishness and make me worthy of the child You send me for the woman You take away!

ELLA — [*Jumping to her feet — excitedly*] Don't cry, Jim! You mustn't cry! I've got only a little time left and I want to play. Don't be old Uncle Jim now. Be my little boy Jim. Pretend you're Painty Face and I'm Jim Crow. Come and play!

JIM — [*Still deeply exalted*] Honey, Honey, I'll play right up to the gates of Heaven with you! [*She tugs at one of his hands, laughingly trying to pull him up from his knees as*

THE CURTAIN FALLS

THE OVERCOAT

By Sally Benson

It had been noisy and crowded at the Milligan's and Mrs. Bishop had eaten too many little sandwiches and too many iced cakes, so that now, out in the street, the air felt good to her, even if it was damp and cold. At the entrance of the apartment house, she took out her change purse and looked through it and found that by counting the pennies, too, she had just eighty-seven cents, which wasn't enough for a taxi from Tenth Street to Seventy-Third. It was horrid never having enough money in your purse, she thought. Playing bridge, when she lost, she often had to give I.O.U.'s and it was faintly embarrassing, although she always managed to make them good. She resented Lila Hardy who could say, "Can anyone change a ten?" and who could take ten dollars from her smart bag while the others scurried for change.

She decided it was too late to take a bus and that she might as well walk over to the subway, although the air down there would probably make her head ache. It was drizzling a little and the sidewalks were wet. And as she stood on the corner waiting for the traffic lights to change, she felt horribly sorry for herself. She remembered as a young girl, she had always assumed she would have lots of money when she was older. She had planned what to do with it — what clothes to buy and what upholstery she would have in her car. Of course, everybody nowadays talked poor and that was a comfort. But it was one thing to have lost your money and quite another never to have had any. It was absurd, though, to go around with less than a dollar in your purse. Suppose something happened? She was a little vague as to what might happen, but the idea fed her resentment.

Everything for the house, like food and things, she charged. Years ago, Robert had worked out some sort of budget for her but it had been impossible to keep their expenses under the right headings, so they had long ago abandoned it. And yet Robert always seemed to have money. That is, when she came to him for five or ten dollars, he managed to give it to her. Men were like that, she thought. They managed to keep money in their pockets but they had no idea you ever needed any. Well, one thing was sure, she would insist on having an allowance. Then she would know where she stood. When she decided this, she began to walk more briskly and everything seemed simpler.

SALLY BENSON'S *stories are known to a large reading public. "The Overcoat" is generally regarded as one of her very best and was reprinted in O'Brien's annual collection for 1935.* (November, 1934)

The air in the subway was worse than usual and she stood on the local side waiting for a train. People who took the expresses seemed to push so and she felt tired and wanted to sit down. When the train came, she took a seat near the door and, although inwardly she was seething with rebellion, her face took on the vacuous look of other faces in the subway. At Eighteenth Street, a great many people got on and she found her vision blocked by a man who had come in and was hanging to the strap in front of her. He was tall and thin and his overcoat which hung loosely on him and swayed with the motion of the train smelled unpleasantly of damp wool. The buttons of the overcoat were of imitation leather and the button directly in front of Mrs. Bishop's eyes evidently had come off and been sewed back on again with black thread, which didn't match the coat at all.

It was what is known as a swagger coat but there was nothing very swagger about it now. The sleeve that she could see was almost threadbare around the cuff and a small shred from the lining hung down over the man's hand. She found herself looking intently at his hand. It was long and pallid and not too clean. The nails were very short as though they had been bitten and there was a discolored callous on his second finger where he probably held his pencil. Mrs. Bishop, who prided herself on her powers of observation, put him in the white collar class. He most likely, she thought, was the father of a large family and had a hard time sending them all through school. He undoubtedly never spent money on himself. That would account for the shabbiness of his overcoat. And he was probably horribly afraid of losing his job. Mrs. Bishop couldn't decide whether to make his wife a fat slattern or to have her an invalid.

She grew warm with sympathy for the man. Every now and then he gave a slight cough, and that increased her interest and her sadness. It was a soft, pleasant sadness and made her feel resigned to life. She decided that she would smile at him when she got off. It would be the sort of smile that would make him feel better, as it would be very obvious that she understood and was sorry.

But by the time the train reached Seventy-Second Street, the closeness of the air and the confusion of her own worries had made her feelings less poignant, so that her smile, when she gave it, lacked something. The man looked away embarrassed.

Her apartment was too hot and the smell of broiling chops sickened her after the enormous tea she had eaten. She could see Maude, her maid, setting the table in the dining-room for dinner. Mrs. Bishop had bought smart little uniforms for her, but there was nothing smart about Maude and the uniforms never looked right.

Robert was lying on the living-room couch, the evening newspaper over his face to shield his eyes. He had changed his shoes, and the gray felt slippers he wore were too short for him and showed the imprint of his toes, and looked depressing. Years ago, when they were first married, he used to dress for dinner sometimes. He would shake up a cocktail for her and things were quite gay and almost the way she had imagined they would be. Mrs. Bishop didn't believe in letting yourself go and it seemed to her that Robert let himself go out of sheer perversity. She hated him as he lay there, resignation in every line of his body. She envied Lila Hardy her husband who drank but who, at least, was somebody. And she felt like tearing the newspaper from his face because her anger and disgust were more than she could bear.

For a minute she stood in the doorway trying to control herself and then she walked over to a window and opened it roughly. "Goodness," she said. "Can't we ever have any air in here?"

Robert gave a slight start and sat up. "Hello, Mollie," he said. "You home?"

"Yes, I'm home," she answered. "I came home in the subway."

Her voice was reproachful. She sat down in the chair facing him and spoke more quietly so that Maude couldn't hear what she was saying. "Really, Robert," she said, "it was dreadful. I came out from the tea in all that drizzle and couldn't even take a taxi home. I had just exactly eighty-seven cents!"

"Say," he said. "That's a shame. Here." He reached in his pocket and took out a small roll of crumpled bills. "Here," he repeated. And handed her one. She saw that it was five dollars.

Mrs. Bishop shook her head. "No, Robert," she told him. "That isn't the point. The point is that I've really got to have some sort of allowance. It isn't fair to me. I never have any money! Never! It's got so it's positively embarrassing!"

Mr. Bishop fingered the five dollar bill thoughtfully. "I see," he said. "You want an allowance. Don't I give you money every time you ask for it?"

"Well, yes," Mrs. Bishop admitted. "But it isn't like my own. An allowance would be more like my own."

"Now, Mollie," he reasoned. "If you had an allowance, it would probably be gone by the tenth of the month."

"Don't treat me like a child," she said. "I just won't be humiliated any more."

Mr. Bishop sat turning the five dollar bill over and over in his hand. "How much do you think you should have?"

"Fifty dollars a month," she told him. And her voice was harsh. "That's the least I can get along on. Why, Lila Hardy would laugh at fifty dollars a month."

"Fifty dollars a month," Mr. Bishop repeated. He ran his fingers through his hair. "I've had a lot of things to attend to this month. But, well, maybe if you would be willing to wait until the first of next month, I might manage."

"Oh, next month will be perfectly all right," she said, feeling it wiser not to press her victory. "But don't forget all about it. Because I shan't."

As she walked toward the closet to put away her wraps, she caught sight of Robert's overcoat on the chair near the door. He had tossed it carelessly across the back of the chair as he came in. One sleeve was hanging down and the vibration of her feet on the floor had made it swing gently back and forth. She saw that the cuff was badly worn and a bit of the lining showed. It looked dreadfully like the sleeve of the overcoat she had seen in the subway. And, suddenly, looking at it, she had a horrible sinking feeling, as though she were falling in a dream.

THE BALLAD OF THE GALLOWS-BIRD

By Edwin Markham

I LAY in wait till he reacht the rock
    And then I dirked him dead,
And left a blood-drip on the road,
    A scribble of rusty red.

For a hundred sleepless years the feud
    Had leaped from sire to son,
The blood-lust burning hot in our hearts,
    And now the war was won.

No more should I be forced to see
    That carcass glower and gloat —
Nor see the snake in his eye, nor hear
    The jackal in his throat.

So as I hurled him into death
    My glad hate gave a yell;
For I knew his deeds had dug his name
    In the iron Book of Hell.

II

And now on the old abandoned road
    Where many a man had bled,
I was stamping out the new blood-marks,
    The scribble of rusty red,
When a horde of men stormed down the glen,
    And doom was in their tread.

With mongrel howls and tiger scowls,
    They beat me to my knees:
They spikt on high a gallows-beam
    Between two blasted trees.
There came a crash of curses, then
    A rope . . . a wrenching twist . . .
And I was floating away, away,
    Into a world of mist.

Ages I seemed to swirl and swirl,
    Like driftwood on a sea;
And then I came to life again,
    And all was well with me!

I had seen the lynchers crowd the road,
    Had heard their yells condemn.
But now I had slipt from the strangling rope:
    I had outwitted them!

'Twas joy to see the dark boughs shake
    Against the evening red;
To see the birds go, one by one,
    To their high nests overhead;
To sense the old familiar earth
    And know I was not dead.

To drink the air was wonderful,
    To smell the ground was good;

EDWIN MARKHAM, *who died in 1940 and who is best remembered for his* The Man With the Hoe, *submitted "The Ballad of the Gallows-Bird" to many other magazines before he sent it to this one, which was delighted to print it and hailed it as a milestone in ballad-writing.* (August, 1926)

And it was comforting to hear
  The nightjar in the wood.

III

'Twas joy to feel the firm old earth,
  Save that I knew I must
Trample and hide from the eyes of men
  That scribble of bloody rust.
But I could not stamp the red marks out,
  The indictment in the dust.

And then in the deep of my brain I heard
A loud cry: "You are a gallows-bird,
  And you must flee from men!"
Yes, I knew I would swing on the hempen
    string,
  Be strung to the beam again,
    Unless I fled into unknown lands
From the blood of the murder-glen.

Then suddenly I saw my dead
  Stretched out across the road.
I knew I must rid the world of him;
So I lifted the body, gray and grim,
  To carry away the load.

And I said I would go by the way of the
    sea,
  By a lone road winding far;
Yet a road that would reach the friendly
    shore
  Before the morning star.
For down in the sea you can hide your
    dead,
  Where millions of dead men are. . . .

And then a thought of her at home
  Flasht on my troubled brain:
I saw her face, her anxious face,
  Pressed to the window-pane.

I saw the supper table spread,
  My old chair ready and warm:
I heard the steaming kettle sing,
  Glad of the rising storm.

Yet on I strode: I dared not turn,
  Nor any pleasure win
Till I had reached the all-welcoming sea
  And flung the body in.

IV

So into the night I carried my load
  With slow unsteady tramp;
While over the hell-black clouds a moon
  Was holding a ghostly lamp.

On, on I strode to the brink of voids,
  Where suddenly I came
On a mighty gateway in a wall,
  Which must have had old fame.
Carved on the cross-bar overhead,
There gloomed a word could not be
    read —
  A half-obliterate name.
The gate's vast shadow on the night
  Lookt like a gallows-frame.

Like some huge cromlech rose the shafts,
  Prodigious in their girth —
Rose ruined by the winds and rains
  Of ages old as earth;
And high on the pillars were cryptic
    words
  In crumbling letters held —
Words chiseled there by unknown powers
  Of mystery and eld.

The seven that had eluded Time,
  I read from a rocky shelf:

"Be hard!" .... Then thundered the
   final five:
"Each man is for himself!"

When the clouds rolled back, I chilled as
      one
   Whose body is bled white;
For out on the voids a Monster Man
   Stood brooding bane and blight.
Lifting aloft his massive form,
   Like some sky-filling thunder-storm,
He leaned over hollow and hight,
And shook contagion from his hands,
   And from his charnel breath
Blew down upon a hundred lands
   The slow black snow of death.

Were the voids upbreathing this Monster
      Shape
   As the soul of all below?
How strange that under the awful form,
   Under the cold black snow,
Thousands were dancing in reckless whirls
   As if they did not know —
Their crackling laughters breaking the
      night
   As they flickered to and fro!

V

I saw, yet I dared the roads ahead:
   Strangely they did entice.
I swung down canyons that seemed to be
   A ruined paradise;
Yet Something trying to hold me back
   Plucked at my garment thrice.

But I heeded not the cryptic sign;
   For I felt my spirit leap,
As I heard far voices calling me,
   Like music heard in sleep —

Far voices calling, calling me
   To join them in the deep.

And then there came a burst of jeers,
   Of wranglings, curses, groans;
As if huge Powers in monstrous mills
   Were grinding stones on stones.

Yet over it all my own made call;
   So on I carried my pack —
On, on I trampt, although I saw,
   In the grime of the trodden track,
Thousands of footprints going down,
   But saw none coming back.

And searching the marks in the dust, J
      found
   No footprint of a child;
Nor ever heard on that lonesome road
   Young laughter light and wild.

Night deepened, and a strange wind
      stirred
   The boughs with mournful gust;
And in some lonely wood I heard
   An owl forebode the dust.

VI

Oh, weary it was to carry my dead,
   Although my back was strong;
So to lighten the load on the winding
      road,
   I chanted a tavern song
We had roared aloud in our college crowd,
   When nights were never too long.

But the burden sagged and my footsteps
      dragged,
   Till high on a lonely dune,

I flung the accursed body down
  Beside a salt lagoon.
I flung it down on a haggard cliff,
  Under a haggard moon.

A moment I drew my breath with might,
Then into the husht and spectral night,
  I carried my dead away.
But out of the ground there came a sound,
  A voice that seemed to say:
"On, on, for a man must carry his dead,
  And carry till Judgment Day!"

VII

The gulfs were hungry and the roads
  Were scorcht with ancient thirst;
And the starving trees reacht out their
    boughs,
  Like leprous arms accurst.
At dawn some crumbling castle walls
  Upon my vision burst.

And there I stoopt with parching lips
  To drink from a sluggish moat;
And I saw my face in the watery glass,
  Like a dead man's face afloat;
And I saw a streak below my chin,
  A black bruise round my throat!

And then I knew, as never before,
  My going must be fleet;
So tightening my arm around my dead,
  I started to my feet.

Breathless, I fled toward the lower voids,
  Scoopt out in grim ravines,
With bottomless tarns and pitchy pools
  Spotted with sulphurous greens.

Strange crowds were scattered along the
    way,
  Each drifting to his own,
Wild fancies flashing from their brains
  With jeer and laugh and groan.

I saw nine beggars under a cliff:
  Each on his separate stone,
Stood boasting of his kingly realm
  And of his golden throne!

And under other cliffs were crowds
  Babbling with loud ha-hahs.
From a shelving rock a reasoner cried:
  "The God-fear has no cause:
The 'black coats' try to set you quaking,
But evil is only good in the making.
  Sin? We have pulled her claws:

"Their Jah has no avenging rod:
Great Nature is the only God —
  Her laws the only laws."
A listening host stood under his spell,
  And gapt their long applause.

At last he cried: "Behold — 'tis day!
Light has dispelled the fears.
You need no battling soul, I say:
We all are going the upward way —
  Up to the Higher Spheres!"

Another reasoner from a rock
  Shouted the name Voltaire,
And cried: "There is no other world,
  There is no Over There."

His logic flasht with light: I knew
  The truth of every thrust:
I knew that the dead are *dead*, that men
  Rise never from the dust.

VIII

I shifted my load and kept the road
  Till the noise of the babblers thinned,
Till I saw dead boughs of the devil-trees
  Laugh white in the iron wind,
As if the gaunt and naked ribs
  Of huge Behemoth grinned.

And roots, like serpents stabbed with pain,
  Upsprang without a sound,
Writhed in the red air terribly,
  And plunged into the ground.

And then I came to shattered shapes
  On roads they did not know:
They could not see their way, nor name
  The place they had to go.
For all were blind, and with blind hands
  They searcht the empty air,
As if to find a friendly door,
  A door that was not there.

Never had men on earth before
  Such tortured starving lips:
Had they battled, bare-breasted, with demon seas,
  On doomed and desperate ships?

I could almost hear a silent cry
  In their scared mouths gaping wide.
And I shouted: "What Thing has sent you here?"
And the oldest shape replied:
"Seeking, seeking, we came this way:
  We know not why we came:
We know not why we took this road,
  Nor where to put the blame.

"Ever we sought our happiness,
  A frail, sea-going band.
We ventured every wind that blew
  Toward rock or reef or sand;
Till we all went down on a floating wreck,
  A wreck we took for land!"

IX

Far down in a craggy gorge below,
  Where the broad highway gropes,
A shaggy man was rolling huge stones
  Up the steep mountain slopes,
To build him a tomb, a tomb that now
  Was the goal of all his hopes.

Time-eaten was his parchment face,
  Blood-rusted was his beard;
And battling with his boulder, he
Clutcht at the ground with foot and knee,
  And slowly the stone upreared.
And man and boulder seemed one beast
In a silent battle that never ceast —
  A battle fierce and weird.

I lookt, I quaked: he was a man
  That I had known of old,
The man I dirked that night in Nome,
  Over the cards and gold.
I long had thought him in his shroud
  Under the graveyard mold.

He saw me. Starting up, all hate,
  He let the boulder plunge —
Go whirling to the nether deeps
In ever glad and greatening leaps.
  Then with a lion lunge
And bursts of hot carnivorous breath,
He sprang at me with curdling yell. . . .

I suddenly heard my burial knell,
　I felt the strangle of death!

In a crash of dread I turned and fled
　From Death's descending will;
For who can fight a man once dead,
　Whom daggers cannot kill?

And then by the barren river shore,
　The dead man on my back
Upstarted alive, his hate aflame;
　And gliding to the ground, he came
With curses on my track!

My murdered men now came abreast,
　Their cries a panther blast;
And I was fleeing down the voids,
　Death-dreading and aghast.
I heard their breaths behind me strive,
　Their dead feet coming fast.

I sped by a chain of river pools:
　Before me rusht the moon;
And I caught the gleam of her baleful eye
　In many a dark lagoon.
And high on the ridges I saw the stooped
　And tortured tamaracks,
Fleeing like witches down the gale
　With burdens on *their* backs.

A twisted, blasted, ominous oak,
　Curst by some ancient ban,
Reacht out its naked and knotted arms
　To seize me as I ran.

Wild terrors winged my canyon flight;
　My foes were left behind,
Fading away until they seemed
　Mere phantoms of the mind.

X

That night I walked a roaring town,
Where all were pleasuring, king and
　　clown.
　Spewed out of every den,
The scarlet girls, in whispering skirts,
　Were picking up the men,
With laugh of twisted mirthless mouth
　And leer of loveless eyes.
One offered to me her painted lips,
　The kiss that money buys;
And made the secret Cyprian sign,
　The signal lewd and bold,
　Which even in Sodom was old.

One skinny hag, a wreck of wrecks,
A harlot withered out of sex,
　Was squat upon the ground,
　Her fingers twitching at her skirts
　In never-ceasing round.
Now staggering to her worn-out feet,
　She blinkt a watery eye
And pointed with a shaking hand
　And piped a quavering cry:

"Once I was young and happy as they:
My head was high, my gowns were gay.
Gallants came riding in golden coats,
With jewels at their ruffled throats.
(Ha, still they're fastened to my chain:
I keep them riding in my brain!)
Whew, but these fools, these nibbling
　　mice,
Take anything that has the price!
　Ho, ho, but I came high —
　Not every passer-by!
Once I had silk-embroidered beds . . .
　Now with the dogs I lie,
And all men turn away their heads.
　Not even a hooted slave

Will take me now, for whom a king
  One time a kingdom gave!"

XI

At this, she ogled with horrid eyes,
  And I fled from the bag of bones.
At times I passed enormous cirques,
  Heapt with gigantic stones,
Where beast-men labored in the night
  With mutterings and huge groans,
Building (for whom?) vast citadels
  And palaces and thrones.
A grim host heaved at mighty boulders,
  Or carried them high on bleeding
    shoulders.
Some with terrific might
Battered the cliffs; while an awful storm
  Of curses tore the night.

And then I came to a Babel tower,
  Half-builded in the sky;
And some one from its misty top
  Sent down a warning cry.

I lookt, and high on the soaring peak
  A shape I seemed to see
Lean out from the fading tower, and
    wave
  A phantom hand to me.

Then from the cast-off boulders heaped
  About the monstrous base,
A chained shape lifted in agony
  A charred distorted face.

Heaving his body slowly up,
  He shook his shattered hands,
And strove with stammering lips to speak
  Some language of dead lands.

Fear quickened my feet; but as I swung
  Into the gulfs ahead,
I still could hear those ruined lips
  Cry to me as I fled.

XII

At dawn I passed a tottering shape,
  Bent with a load of earth,
A shape the lust of a dragon-man
  Might gender into birth.

"Caliban, where do you go?" I cried,
  And the bent shape answered me:
"I go to pay an incredible debt:
  I am doomed to fill the sea.

"The last load must be carried down,
  The debt must all be paid:
All mountains, all must melt before
  The pecking of one spade.

"Tell me if when the ages end
  The task will all be done?
Can I survive the trampling years —
  Can I outlast the sun?"

I answered not, but fled aghast
  From the horror of the hill —
Fled deeper, deeper into the voids
  Curst by an Evil Will,
By a Power that seemed to be grinding
    men
  In some prodigious mill.

XIII

Now I heard wild uproar in the rocks.
  I lookt: a host of shapes
Came up from a pit, like blackamoors
  With visages of apes.

And soon each one of the mongrel crowd
    Was shouting from his stall:
"I am the lord of the Higher Spheres:
    I have the key to all!"

And now I strode to a turn in the road,
    Where I peered into mammoth caves,
    Dusty as ancient graves,
Where monster man-bats clung to the walls
    With skinny hands that seemed
Long vulture-talons; while their heads
    Hung downward as they dreamed.

But one awoke and lookt at me
    With staring owl-like eyes,
    And screecht, "I am all wise!"
Whereat the caverns from end to end,
    Chimed hoarsely, "Wise, all wise" —
A chorus that slowly died away
    Till slumber husht their cries.

Then I past great heaps of human bones;
    But as I swung along,
I heard come out from under the bones
    Snatches of obscene song,
Mixt with wild curses at some God
    Who seemed to have done them wrong.

XIV

I had reacht the floor of the last abyss,
    Where some one, in his flight,
    Had raised a giant wayside cross,
    Which once had stood upright.
It is now a winter-ruined wreck,
    Where wild birds roost at night,
Lightnings have shattered it with fire,
    Storms blackened it with blight.

Here, too, at the end of the canyon roads,
    A cliff soars huge and high,
    A cliff that has for ages dared
    The terrors of the sky.
And on its mighty front defaced
    By the slow tooth of Time,
I read this ancient warning traced
    (By whom?) in earth's mysterious prime:
    "*O traveler, at last you tread
    The second death. O comrade, know
    You must not any farther go:
    Dare not the awful dust ahead,
    Where sleep the inframundane dead!*"

Yet I dared the fate that lay in wait,
    Defied the ancient ban:
Now I was free of the Thing Accurst:
    I was the superman!
So I shouted to the void ahead:
    "You have waited ages for this:
Do you not feel me drawing near —
    Feel me, O last abyss?"

I knew I was lord of that land abhorred
    Where nightmares breed their spells,
Where buzzards swing in the brazen sky,
    Over deserts and dead wells.

A viper with ever-moving heads,
    Red scorpions spitting scorns,
Tarantulas with shaggy thighs,
    Reptiles with waving horns,
Were crawling among the carrion flowers
    And cacti thick with thorns.

And here were shapes — half man, half beast —
    Who glared from dune and den,
Or lunged as swine upon all fours,
    Or bellied in the fen.

A beast is hid in the human, they say:
  Had the hidden pusht outward then —
Had the beast pusht out in these fearsome
    shapes,
  In these grunting hogs, in these grinning
    apes —
Monsters that once were men?

From their giant jaws shot yellow tusks,
  Like roots that cleave a cliff,
And grisly manes from their shoulders
    sprang,
  Bristling and iron stiff.
And some were crunching at naked bones,
  Cramming their hungry maws;
And as they ate I heard the grind
  Of crocodilian jaws.

One shape sat humpt by a heap of gold,
  At a cavern mouth alone.
He was watching, watching his golden
    hoard,
  A beast-man turned to stone —
All dead but the eyes, his lips beyond
  The comfort of a groan.

XV

Now far behind me soared the cliffs
  With naked precipice;
And on before was the shattered floor
  Of some unknown abyss.

Onward I strode, the hot air baked
  The tongue within my head,
In vain I searcht for water-pools
  In a dried-up river bed.

Gasping, I thought of that day in youth
  When I stretcht by a river brink,
And the green frogs leapt from the mossy
    rocks,
  And peered to see me drink,
While I beheld at the water's edge
  The cool bright bubbles wink.
And over me swung a wind-toucht bough,
  Where there were nest and song;
And an April flower came circling down
  And lightly sailed along.

Then I dreamed of the time when I
    forded streams
  On my horse's splashing hoofs,
Feeling a cool delicious air
  Come down from leafy roofs.

I remembered too that ocean cliff,
  Cooled by a thousand waves,
Wild tides that crasht on the windy shores
  And thundered in the caves. . . .

Then the sand's breath came like a fur-
    nace flame;
  The cool bright waters fled;
The frightful thirst was back, the blood
  Was pounding in my head.
And now I rose on a plain of tombs,
  A kingdom of the dead.

Yes, I was tramping the desert roads
  Of cities gone to dust;
For here were watered gardens once,
  And winds with fragrant gust.
It seemed that the ashes under my feet
  Still pulsed with the ancient lust.

The sands reacht out to the brazen sky,
  A sea of silent waves;
For all the plain, from rim to rim,
  Was husht with ancient graves.

Ages the graves had been empty mouths
  Gaping against the sky —

Graves damned with a death that has no
   name,
 A death that cannot die.

It was a pulseless, shrouded world,
   Save for one thing of dread:
I saw in a hollow skull a snake
   Lie coiled with flattened head,
With lidless, cold, inscrutable eyes —
   The living in the dead.

The sense of ruined Babylons
   Lay on these somber lands.
Up from old graves the skeletons
   Lifted imploring hands;
While slow years crumbled them, and
   blew
 Their ashes to the sands.

XVI

The mesquites watching the road were
   husht
   And white with alkali;
But soon the ghosts of little winds
   Began to whisper by,
And slowly the boughs began to stir
   With the world's primeval sigh.
Now rumors ran in the rusty sage,
   While one tall thistle-stalk
Leaned to a comrade by the road
   As if in hurried talk.

Then lightnings darted their serpent
   tongues
   From caverns in the cloud;
Black thunders tramped the shaking
   world:
   Mad torrents bellowed loud.
Wild terrors leaped on my heart: I felt
   The mold upon the shroud!

For heaven on heaven cracked overhead:
   I saw far lightnings smite
Canyon and crag with bolts of red
   Insufferable light.

A bearded comet passed: it seemed
   A specter in the gloom,
And craggy-throated Tempest blew
   The trumpets of the doom.

A whirlwind as a monster worm
   Twisted and bellied by,
Sucking dead cities up to spew
   Their ashes on the sky.

And the dead leapt out of a million graves,
   Rusht from their narrow rooms.
The dead went dancing with the dead
   Upon the plain of tombs.

Then high on a whirlwind's shining top,
   High on its giddying gyre,
I saw a host of warriors ride,
   Harnessed in awful fire.

Was it a host of seraphs rode
   High over peak and plain,
Shining in splendid zones of light
   Like rainbows after rain?
Were they watchers out on a mercy quest
   To ease the souls in pain?
Or were they only fever-forms
   Whirled in my crazing brain?

XVII

I was there in a terror and wonder world:
   Was it builded all of dream?
If so, it was more strangely real
   Than all the things that seem
So true, so tried, so undenied
   In life's familiar scheme. . . .

And then I thought of her at home —
   How long she had to wait,
Her life now curdled to one hope,
   The click of the garden gate.

I could almost see her call my hound
   And stroke his shining fur,
And tell him to go and search the roads
   And bring me home to her.

So with sharp longing in my heart
   To see her face again,
I turned to climb from the awful void,
   The void that swallows men.
I would steal at night to our hidden home
   High up in the mountain glen.

And I wondered how her face would shine
   When she saw me home once more.
Ah, would she look as when first she came
   Laughing into the door,
With the rain still flashing on her hair
   And on the rose she wore?

So I turned and trampt the roaring roads
   Till night was at her noon,
And slowly out of the crags came up
   A blind and bloody moon.

And then a new day reddened the East,
   Then reddened on the West;
And yet my wild thoughts drove me on
   Toward her and life's one rest.

XVIII

For I hated all in the world beside:
   My heart was dead as stone,
And I knew that I was a wolf in the world —
   Alone, alone, alone.

And I knew though I mixed with a world of men,
   I still should be alone.

So I wandered, wandered many trails,
   Until one night of dread
I was back on the old abandoned road
   Where I had struck him dead
And left the blood-drip in the dust,
   The scribble of rusty red.

That ruined bridge, that jutting cliff,
   That blasted sycamore —
The very rocks of the roads — their old
   Familiar likeness wore.
And yet they were toucht with a spectral air
   I had never seen before.

Yet on I strode through the ghostly night;
   My heart was wild and hot;
One turn in the road, and I would see
   The roof of our lighted cot!
One turn, and I would be with her —
   And all the roads forgot!

But as I panted the last long mile,
   A-stumble and agape,
I suddenly came on a gallows-beam,
   Where swung a strangled shape —
Two blasted trees with a beam across,
   Where swung a dangling shape!

Naked and lone the gallows loomed —
   Its black on the black of night.
Then sudden lightnings lit the sky
   A swift and terrible white;
And the gallows leaped with its ghastly load
   Against the shaking light.

And high on the gallows-beam I saw
   Two ravens making mirth;
While the huge frame of the gallows flung
   A shadow on the earth.

It was the ghost of a gallows-tree
   Loomed with its awful load:
It was the ghost of a gallows flung
   Its shadow on the road.

And there in the shadow lay my hound,
   Watching the gallows-tree,
But why did he suddenly startle up,
   Whimper and run from me?
I curst the beast that ever such
   Ingratitude should be.

XIX

And now my nearing steps disturbed
   The ravens at their feast,
There where the dead man swung in the wind
   With sound that never ceast.
For they drew their heads from out his brain
   (Still did the swung rope creak)
And little crumbs of carrion
   Clung to each happy beak.

And now they whetted their beaks with care
   Upon the gallows-beam,
Then slowly turned their knowing eyes
   Upon me with a gleam.

A sudden gust, and the strangled shape,
   That humped and dangling thing,
Wheeled round its face, with holes for eyes. . . .
   'Twas *I* that hung against the skies:
   'Twas I on the rope a-swing!

It was my own, *own* body I saw
   A-swing in the spectral night:
It was my own, own body I saw
   Fade slowly from my sight.
And with it faded the hills of home
   And all my life's delight!

Then a sudden shout crasht into my brain,
   The truth on my spirit fell. . . .
God of my soul! I was *dead* . . . and *damned*. . . .
   And trampt the roads of hell!

ONE NIGHT AT CONEY

By Robert M. Coates

He said: it was one night at Coney Island last summer, and it was one of those things that leave you wondering. There are times, you know, when events around you take on a strange force and direction, as if they had been aimed at you, and at you alone. You are wandering with the crowd and in the crowd; suddenly you observe a gesture, you overhear a meaningful phrase: some little drama has its course before your eyes, and it seems that you, and in the whole crowd no one but you, have been singled out to witness it.

Even more, there seems to be a duty involved, an obligation laid on you. The actors are all strangers and all oblivious to you, yet you understand their problems and their emotions as intimately as might a participant, and the whole action revolves around you as if you were its center. As if some rôle had been left open for you — the rôle, perhaps, that would decide the issue — if you would but assume it.

But before you can determine what that rôle may be, the episode is over, the incident is ended, the actors scattered again in the crowd. You are left wondering.

I was down there alone, that evening. It was hot, I remember, but there was a kind of seaside freshness in the air, and the noise and the lights and the music — even the fat rank smells that filtered over everything — gave an effect of happy-go-lucky companionableness to the crowds. People bunched in front of sideshows, turning friendly faces up towards the exhorting barkers, then — dislodged one by one by the massed pressures behind them — let themselves be carried on again, unprotesting and unresisting, towards whatever might lie beyond. There was no hurrying, no purposeful striding this way or that, but only an easy-flowing merging of all impulses into one. I went drifting down the Bowery to its end at Steeplechase Park, and was about to turn back again when I saw a small group of people standing on the sidewalk across the street. Two boys were dancing for pennies, to the tune of the Steeplechase band inside the park; it was they whom the crowd was watching.

They were doing the Lindy Hop, if you know the dance: the main thing about it is that at every second measure the two dancers separate, though still keeping step, dance four beats apart and then

ROBERT M. COATES *is one of the abler novelists and short story writers of our time. This story is one of his most successful, and after ten years is still being discussed.* (May, 1934)

come together, then separate again, and so on. It's a dance of strict timing, and this, and the mutual retreating and advancing, give it an oddly formal character, in spite of its jazz beat and its rapid movement.

The two boys were dancing as if they had always danced together. One, and the older — he may have been sixteen or eighteen — was a mulatto; he wore a sweatshirt and dirty white canvas pants, but he moved with a grace and ease that had a foreign and slightly unpleasant flavor. He danced like a Latin bravo, with a kind of sinister condescension; he danced too well, and his partner — a white boy, he was, and younger — followed like a girl, with a girl's unhindering docility.

There was something vaguely disquieting about it all. There's no harm, surely, life being what it is, in two lads dancing to the tune of a brass band while a crowd watches, but if the dance becomes an end in itself — if the one shows too bold a dominance and the other a too practiced subservience — you begin thinking of the sexual margins that surround their actions, and the terrible ruthlessness of vice, that fastens itself most securely on the young.

II

I watched for a moment, and then my attention was attracted — by I don't know what: by a sort of aura of excitement that surrounded him, I imagine — to a man standing beside me. He was a tallish fellow, thin-bodied, but with an abnormally round soft face and a wide mouth, and he had on a raincoat cut like a trench coat, deliberately shabby and disreputable-looking, and a soft felt hat very floppy in the brim, with the crown tucked in all around, the way boys at college used to do a dozen or so years ago. Only his was tucked in too deeply, which gave it a kind of comic pancake look, above that soft broad face of his.

I knew what he was, of course; there's a softness about the eyes and a certain sugariness about the mouth that gives them all away. Just now he was in a sort of quiet frenzy, all by himself, as he watched the dancing boys. Here in the rough-and-tumble of Coney he had stumbled on a spectacle that suited his own peculiar passions, and there was something horrible about the relishing way he welcomed it. His delight was past concealment; it greased his face and glistened in his eyes, it set his lips twitching and his whole body rocking convulsively. He couldn't stand still: he wanted to be right in among them, and all the while he was glancing slyly about, as if he half hoped that the orgy would become general. Suddenly, as if he could no longer contain himself, he turned and spoke to a young fellow on the other side of him.

This was a young Italian of a type Coney Island is full of — hatless, slick-haired and sharp-featured, white-sweatered and brown as mahogany — and he started and his eyes took a covert slant when he saw who it was that he had to do with. I couldn't hear what was said, but the Italian nodded and answered, and then listened, and then I saw a fixed smooth grin come over his face and saw his hand behind his back making beckoning gestures to two other lads, twins of his as to clothes and slickness, who began moving slowly towards him.

And then in a pause in the music I heard the tall man speaking. He was saying — and his voice wasn't high, but it had that fluty note that you'd know the whole world over: "Let's do things together," he said. "Let's wander down to Feldman's, maybe, and sip a beer."

I knew what was going to happen before he did. He was still standing there, his face all cajolery and eagerness, but I saw the other's grin thin a little, and I remember how, as I watched them, suddenly everything else — the heat, and the distant tumbling of the surf, the clatter of roller coasters, the brassy persistence of the band — all became separate items, distinct and unconnected, against this central silence.

Then they all fused. Without a word of warning, with the same hard smile still flattening his mouth — "Sure, I'll do things with you!" the Italian had said, and chopped a vicious short right, flush to the fairy's face.

It missed the jaw, landing high on his cheek; it staggered him; he didn't go down, but in the moment of impact it was almost as if the blow had shaken his eyes loose from his head: they went instantly round, fixed, popping with terror. Then — with the panic alacrity of a rabbit, of any animal to whom flight is the one protection — he ran. I remember the curious effect his fright and his flight had on me, how almost sickeningly they revealed the terrible aloneness of the man: nowhere, not even in the thickest crowd, could he find a comrade, nowhere could he make a stand.

That is all you usually see, as you pass in a crowd. You hear a phrase, you observe a gesture, and then — before the phrase can be completed or the final significance of the gesture be made clear — you are swept on again, as the crowd carries you. The outcome remains a mystery.

So I watched that flat hat of his going bobbing through the crowds on the Bowery, and the three white sweaters dodging after it — watched, without moving to follow them, until at last I lost sight of them all. I loitered a few minutes more, till the music stopped and the boys stopped dancing and my own little crowd dispersed. Then, slowly, I started back up the Bowery again, having nowhere much else to go. I'd gone only a block or two before I saw him again.

III

I had come to one of those sideshows in which motorcycle riders perform in a saucer track. It was a high, ungainly structure, all braces and beams outside to stay the bowl-shaped track, with a kind of rim around the upper edge where the spectators stood. A show was going on at the time: you could hear the rattle of the exhausts, and the recurrent rumble and creak of the tires on the wooden planking as the machines spun around. Then the motor-sound slackened to an uneven popping, and I heard a voice shouting something unintelligible inside. The show was over, and the spectators began edging their way around the platform and down the stairs to the street.

One figure remained still standing there. It was the fairy. There was a huge arc light mounted on a pole in the center of the track and almost level with its top, and the light from it poured up out of the bowl like the glare from the crater of a volcano. Against it, his figure stood out with a sharpness of silhouette that was somehow symbolical: up there, in that brilliant isolation, his little flat hat and the drooping lines of his raincoat, his gangling uncertain legs, seemed to distinguish and define him, like a uniform. They seemed the very outline of all his kind.

By now, the riders had wheeled their machines out on the platform in front and were racing their motors to attract a crowd; the barker was beginning his chant. He still stood there, leaning as if absorbed on the inner railing, and staring down at the empty track. I couldn't help but feel sorry for him, marooned as he was up there. Whatever the impulse that had driven him up there for refuge, it had been a bad one: in the whole of the island he could hardly have found a more conspicuous position than the one he was left in now.

Down in a little alley at one side of the track the three boys were waiting for him. They watched him for a minute, then one of them scuffed a stone loose in the ground, picked it up and threw it. It didn't hit him, but it struck the planking and went bouncing along the platform; at the sound the barker, the ticket sellers, everyone out front looked up inquiringly. Then one of them ran quickly up the stairs. They were too far away for me to hear what was said, of course; I only saw the carnival man, burly and competent, advancing on the fairy, and the fairy making gestures of protest and remonstrance. He even put his hand to his pocket, as if to pay for another performance, but the carnival man — he knew there was something in the wind, I suppose — would have none of that. So, slowly, with the other following implacably behind him and the crowd below watching curiously, the fairy made his way back around the rim of the track and began his descent to the street. The three boys moved forward to meet him.

And there, of course, clearly and unmistakably, was the moment for me to intervene. There was the pause that I recognized, when — the stage in readiness, the action halted, the actors as yet irresolute and undecided — everything seemed to wait for me to assume my rôle in the drama. But what was the rôle, and why should it devolve on me? Here was a man whom I did not know and for whom I had no sympathy whatever, being driven ignobly from hiding to face his pursuers; here were his pursuers, as vicious in their unrelenting cruelty perhaps as he, waiting to fall upon him: and all strangers and all oblivious to me, and yet I stood watching them, knowing their several aims and their meanings, knowing that I alone, among all the crowd that witnessed the incident, had seen its beginnings and could judge its causes — knowing that I, by the weight of my presence now, if I would, might decide the issue between them. But why had I been the one selected? What was expected of me? What was I to do?

What I did, of course, was to go my

way — leaving him to twist and turn as he might, and they to follow him, towards whatever dark alley they might corner him in at last. I knew what would happen to him there.

Or even, in this case, in no darkness, but in the crowded street itself. His fault was such that they, and they alone, would have righteousness on their side. There is a convention in such matters, even the cop on the beat will usually acquiesce in the right of every man to beat up the fairy who accosts him. They might come upon him anywhere, in the midst of the crowd or under a lonely street lamp: no one would bother them, no one would interfere. There would be no one now that he could turn to for aid.

IV

Half an hour afterward I was up in the subway terminal, waiting for a train to take me home, and there I saw him again. He was sitting on a bench, down towards the end of the platform, and I almost stumbled over him before I noticed him, for he was sitting huddled pretty much in a heap, in the darkest corner he could find. When the train came in and he got aboard it, I could understand why.

They had worked on him, there was no doubt of that. One sleeve of his raincoat was ripped half off at the shoulder, and the belt, torn loose from its buckle, was dangling down his back. He had been down in the mud too, apparently, for one trouser leg was streaked with dirt, and his hands were grimy with it. His face was a mess: there was dried blood from his nose caking his upper lip, and one side of his mouth, and the fleshy part of his jaw, had that pulped puffed look that you get not from one blow but from a hammering succession of them. One of his eyes looked pretty bad.

Oddly enough, though, he still had his little flat hat, and it sat on his battered face as incongruously as ever.

He sat in the forwardmost corner of the car, very much to himself. People came aboard, one by one, while the train waited in the station; each one glanced at him with that quick noncommittal stare of the New Yorker, then looked strictly away again. He paid little attention. Once he looked up, and for an instant his eye met mine; then it moved on, roving over the other passengers. He hadn't recognized me. His gaze held no reproach.

Then, with a curious kind of weariness, like an old man making himself comfortable one step at a time, he propped his elbows on his knees, leaned slowly forward, and brought his head down to rest on his hands. He rode that way almost all the way into town.

And all the way I had been sitting and watching him, and wondering; and then suddenly I remembered. It had been long ago, when I was a freshman at college, and it happened at Savin Rock, a summer resort near New Haven. It was an evening in spring and I had been down there, and then I was sitting at the end of the seat in an open trolley car, waiting for it to start. And then, and just as the trolley started, I saw a man running toward me, a man pursued by a crowd of yelling boys. His hat was gone and his coat was flying, he was panting and sobbing — and I remembered the curious consternation that overcame me when I saw that the man, this full-grown man, was actually crying, that his face was streaming with tears.

I was younger then, and full of innocence, and I had not the slightest idea what the man had done or why the others pursued him. But he ran alongside the car, scrambling and clutching for a foothold as it gathered speed, and now I remembered that on a sudden impulse I had put down my hand and seized him, and hauled him safely onto the running board and into the car.

Now I remembered that I had given that other one my hand.

LITANY

By Charles Angoff

When the sun rises on another day
  Of broken hopes, vain yearnings, and futile waiting,
And hearts get a little colder
And love more distant than the most distant star
And even sleep begins to lose its small solace —
O Lord, remember us.

When the vast unreason of the immemorial sequence,
Strife and peace and more strife,
Engulfs us with such calm and mocking disregard,
And all dreams and aspirations
Lose their ultimate comfort —
O Lord, remember us.

When the smiles of children, the final support,
Recede and join the independent throng,
Leaving us with the one certainty
That they too will soon
Wait for answers that never come —
O Lord, remember us.

When death comes with false friendliness,
Bringing an end to nothing
And no future intimations
Save the repetition of this life
But on the scale of a worm —
O Lord, remember us.

(April, 1943)

CRUSADE FOR AIR POWER

By Major Alexander P. de Seversky

Wanted: Audacity

AT the outset of the war, the Allies found themselves stymied. Germany had out-thought and out-planned and out-visualized them in its employment of Air Power. Now these Allies are making super-human efforts to imitate the Germans and catch up with Nazi equipment and strategy. If they persist in such efforts, they will remain stymied. Imitation is the most hopeless form of warfare, especially in the air where the tempo is breath-taking and the dynamics streamlined. People who cannot conceive and plan beyond what they see with their eyes and feel with their hands have no place in the formulation of a modern defense system. Their best attainments will be built on the tactics of today, and therefore useless in the actual combat of tomorrow.

The present German utilization of Air Power was conceived nearly five years ago. The conception went far beyond the mechanical performance of that time, assuming progress which was not visible to the naked eye. The whole idea seemed far-fetched to the rest of the world. But the Germans had the courage of their imagination, and their scheme was realistic when the moment arrived for its actual use. It is apparent that the machinery of German national defense, especially in relation to Air Power, is geared for execution of bold plans far beyond the routine of military textbooks and business slogans.

The hope of our national defense lies in the same sort of audacity in thinking and planning. We must plan our Air Power beyond the limits of the present range of operations and gear our aviation industries for the production of tomorrow's equipment. By merely continuing to build more warships, more guns, more aircraft of the current models, we are inviting disappointment if not disaster. We must unshackle our national imagination — potentially the most robust in the world — and work up confidence in our visions. *(August, 1940)*

MAJOR ALEXANDER P. DE SEVERSKY, *whose air-power crusade has had a profound effect on American strategic thought, first presented his views to the general public through this magazine. His ideas at the time were startling to the point of being sensational. Since then, most of them have been accepted even by many old-line military commentators. The excerpts reprinted here are drawn from the author's many articles in the pages of this magazine, beginning with August, 1940; in each case the issue is indicated at the end of the excerpt. This is part of the material on which Walt Disney based his remarkable motion picture,* Victory Through Air Power.

LINDBERGH WRONG ON BRITAIN

ALL sentiment aside, there seems to me no valid excuse for a defeatist attitude in relation to Britain's prospects in the war. I am convinced not merely that it has a chance of winning but that, given the full material backing of the United States, it has only a minor chance of not winning. In offering this broad summation I am speaking, of course, not only of England but of the British Empire.

I base my judgment first of all on the fact that this conflict is developing primarily into an air war, with victory ultimately on the side of the superior Air Power. The British Empire plus the United States add up to an aviation potential decisively outweighing Germany's, even with a conquered Europe in tow.

Lindbergh was correct when he said that Germany now has a strategic advantage because its air bases surround the British Isles in a semicircle from Narvik to the Bay of Biscay. But he failed to note that this condition is by no means eternal. If Germany were simply fighting the British Isles, his conclusion might possibly hold. But Germany is fighting the British Empire and, in terms of production, also America. In the same sense that Germany today surrounds England, *the Empire and its allies surround Germany and the conquered area under its tutelage.*

The range of striking air forces is being quickly enlarged, and with every increase the strategic relation between Europe and Britain tends to be reversed. We come ever closer to the day when Germany, all of Europe, will be the center of a circle of hostile Air Power. Recent British entrenchment in North Africa, for example, foreshadows that encirclement. In the long run — and admittedly it may be a long and costly run — it will be easier for the British to obtain control of the air over Europe than for Europe to assume control of the skies above the British Empire. The direct attack on Germany's vital centers will be undertaken from far-flung bases; not alone from Africa and perhaps the Near East but inevitably, in time, from Canada and even India. To cope with this, Hitler would have to dominate the skies over virtually the entire globe.

Colonel Lindbergh has pictured England as a concentrated target, in the center of Germany's scattered bases. By his own logic, we must visualize Europe as comparatively a concentrated target surrounded by hostile Air Power operating from widely scattered encircling bases. Once we admit the possibility of superior Anglo-American Air Power, we must also admit the likelihood that the European target may be hammered into submission.

(*May, 1941*)

AID TO BRITAIN

CAN we prepare for our own defense if we "deplete" our forces and "strip" our aviation for Britain? My answer is that the very process of building for Britain — or, for that matter, for anyone else — serves to fortify our own strength.

I agree completely with Secretary of War Stimson's statement, in his letter to the Foreign Relations Committee, that it is not the number of planes on hand that counts in measuring national security — but the capacity for producing planes. Certainly we need an adequate number of all types of aircraft to keep our personnel in combat trim. Beyond that, our accretion of power must be judged by the expansion of our production facilities, the development of contingents of skilled labor in the defense industries, our intensive experience in building, handling and maintaining large masses of airplanes.

These are things which we cannot ship to England or anywhere else. They stay with us as a permanent fortification of our country. They are the immediate dividends on the investment of effort and materials in provisioning Britain. Our over-all task of preparing for the future air war is at this stage a matter of audacious designing, experimenting, planning. None of that, of course, is handicapped by the mass production for Britain; on the contrary, that production serves as a proving ground for creative aeronautical effort. In the act of equipping the British we shall be laying the foundation for our own air supremacy.

(May, 1941)

When USA Is Bombed

IT will matter nothing that the armadas of bombers, thousands of them perhaps, will travel ten hours or more before reaching American objectives. They will be crossing at substratospheric altitudes, perhaps with relief crews, under ideal conditions of comfort. On arrival at their destinations, the crews will be as fresh and rested as if they had stepped out of their own homes after breakfast. In modern planes, after all, what is the difference between flying for three hours to the interior of Germany or Italy, and flying ten hours across the ocean to the interior of the United States? Of all the elements involved in the undertaking, the period of approach is the least risky and the least exhausting. Once over enemy territory, whether the bomber is above the Ruhr or Pennsylvania, the Midlands or Chicago, London or New York, makes not the slightest difference technically. The procedure after arrival is identical — and the disastrous consequences of the visit are identical.

It is a curious truth, though not yet widely understood, that the more industrialized a country is, the more vulnerable it is to destruction from overhead. American industries, grouped in thick-sown concentrations dependent on centralized sources of power, make ideal targets for air attacks. The tremendous expanse of our country may give us a feeling of hugeness, but the vital centers are few and extremely exposed.

I contend that those who deny the practical possibility of an eventual air attack on America are lulling the American people into a false sense of safety as dangerous as the "Maginot Line mentality" that cost France its independence.

(May, 1941)

The Twilight of Sea Power

OUR great two-ocean multi-billion-dollar Navy, now in construction, should be completed five or six years from now — just in time to have all of its battleships scrapped. The smaller and swifter units and the undersea craft may continue their auxiliary tasks under the shielding wings of Air Power; the rest will be consigned to the museums of outlived weapons along with the bow and arrow and the blunderbuss. As a primary, self-sufficient branch of national defense, fleets will be finished. References to naval might as our "outer defense" or "first line of defense" will seem echoes of a far-off past. The complacency with which we once relied on such slogans will seem as tragic and incredible to Americans as reliance on Maginot Lines must now seem to Frenchmen.

To those who have not caught up with the revolution in war strategy brought about by the advent of Air Power, this may sound like exaggeration; to naval diehards it will sound like blasphemy. Yet a little patient consideration of facts already in high relief on the landscape of the present war will reveal that I am merely setting down the inescapable conclusion we must draw from recent experience. As we approach the end of the second year of the Second World War, it is startlingly clear that the navies of all nations have already and irretrievably lost their function of strategic *offensive* action. They still play a *defensive* rôle — against other navies — but only in waters as yet beyond the reach of aviation. As that reach is extended — with the rapid enlargement of Air Power range — the margin of defensive usefulness shrinks, and it is quite possible to foresee the inevitable vanishing point.

The lessons of the war now in progress cannot be shouted down by rhetoric invoking the glories of naval history. It is a matter of sense, not of sentiment. The towering fact is that fleets can no longer approach hostile shores which are guarded by first-class aviation forces. For centuries the chief job of navies was to carry war to the enemy: to attack the outer ramparts of a country, its coastlines and harbors and fortresses. Now that job has been taken over almost entirely by Air Power.

The grip of clichés on the mind of man is not easy to break. In England, as in our own country, the notion that "the country's chief defense is its navy" has acquired the force of a commandment handed down from Mt. Sinai. Doubtless it is being repeated through sheer habit in the British Isles now, even while Air Power is so strikingly their main reliance at this juncture. But we need only imagine the RAF out of commission — not a ship could then reach England, for all that the Admiralty could do. The approaches would be as Nazi-dominated from the air as the Skagerrak and Kattegat Straits. Not a battleship could survive under the roof of enemy aviation long enough to interfere with German plans for invasion or for unhampered annihilation of England without benefit of invasion.

The type of strategic thinking which continues, through inertia, to rest on the old assumptions of Sea Power — though they belong to an epoch that is coming quickly to an end — constitutes a brake on the full growth of the new "first line of defense," Air Power. Minds that have not caught up with this reality are incapable of grappling with the problems of national defense in the real modern world. No matter how brilliant their strategy, it is earthbound at a time when war has soared into a new dimension.

Modern military aviation, having clipped Sea Power of its offensive functions, leaves it strategically crippled. This represents a fateful milestone in the history of war-making and therefore a turning point in the power relations of the major nations. The implications of the event add up to a fundamental change in the history of the immediate future.

(*June, 1941*)

For an Autonomous Air Force

In the higher reaches of our military service the idea of an independent Air Force has never been regarded as a matter for discussion. It has simply been treated as insubordination and squelched by main force. The martyrdom of General William Mitchell was accomplished publicly and demonstratively in order to warn other "rebels." The intimidation has in large measure been successful. Nevertheless, there are other "General Mitchells" today, kept down, "exiled" to distant posts, or forced out because they demand the emancipation of Air Power. The American people should understand that the heat on both sides of the controversy is not artificial. This is not a dispute over division of authority but a basic question of organization that goes straight to the heart of our defense program.

It is no accident that complacent or shortsighted men, aeronautically speaking, have tended to reach the top. The set-up makes it almost inevitable. The officer, convinced of the paramount rôle of Air Power, who defends his views, steps on tender political toes. There are too many old-fashioned admirals and generals in the path, whose distrust of the aviation "intruder" must be placated. Only an officer with a happy talent for handshaking and backslapping normally rises to high authority; and that sort of political-minded personality rarely goes with military and aviation genius. Nor is his job to be envied: he is caught between the realities of Air Power and the pressure of aviation personnel for better equipment, on one side, and the orthodoxies of the older services on the other.

True Air Power must function in its own element — the "air ocean" that envelops the globe. It is a single and continuous element, calling for a single and continuous Air Command. Before we can hope to achieve freedom of the seas, under the new conditions, we must achieve freedom of the skies; and for that we need a single agency vested with the full job. To divide aviation into two artificial portions, Army aviation and Navy aviation, as we are now doing, is to court disaster. It violates the first principle of military science. Just suppose we had two Navies, as we now have two aviations — a Navy under the command of the Army and another under the command of the Marines! Arbitrarily splitting the skies into two segments is no less ludicrous. Each of the segments, in turn, is limited in its growth by the needs of the particular service to which it is indentured. No matter how efficient it becomes, it cannot escape the limitations of the special mentality and strategy of that service. Aircraft employed in common tactical action with the Army or the Navy should, of course, be under their direct command, like their other weapons. But that has nothing to do with true Air Power, whose job is to maintain freedom of the skies beyond the reach of the older services.

(*July, 1941*)

After Pearl Harbor

AMERICAN losses in the first weeks of the Pacific Ocean war, tragic as they were, may yet prove a blessing in disguise in the broader pattern of events. As the lessons of those weeks are assimilated, they may add up to a providential warning against complacent reliance on old-fashioned formulas of Sea Power — a warning to bring not only our equipment but *our thinking* into line with the new aviation epoch.

Public opinion in our country, as reflected in press and radio comment, already shows a keen awareness of those lessons. No matter how many surface ships and troops were involved in the actions, the dominance of the aerial factor was too clear to be missed. The disaster at Pearl Harbor amounted to an *aerial* defeat, underscoring naval impotence. Enemy landings on the Philippine Islands were made under cover of strong air forces and such toll as we took of Japanese transports must be credited primarily to our aviation on the islands. The most conspicuous American item on the credit side, the sinking of the battleship *Haruna*, was obtained by our airplanes. The destruction of two of the most modern British dreadnaughts, the *Prince of Wales* and the *Repulse* — ships built especially to withstand assault from the skies — was likewise accomplished by airplanes.

America has been as shocked by the easy victory of Japanese Air Power over proud first-line ships of the American and the British Navies as France was by the way Hitler ignored its Maginot Line. The parallel is a true one. In both cases surface obstacles, two-dimensional defenses, proved useless against a third-dimensional menace from overhead. The Maginot Line is a fixed fortification, battleships are mobile fortifications — but both of them are earthbound and impotent against the soaring threat of modern Air Power. Whether such barriers survive depends not at all on their own strength. It depends on whether a nation can protect them with Air Power superior to the enemy's.

Fortunately, the shock of our disasters comes at the very start of our war, and not, as in France, at the end of their war. Our geographical position, and the fact that Japan, too, has not yet exploited the full possibilities of aviation, gives us the time to revise our strategy and to forge the new weapons to match it. Provided we start now, we shall be starting from scratch in the race for supremacy so far as the genuine long-range, hard-hitting, specialized aviation of tomorrow is concerned.

(*February, 1942*)

Strategy and Leadership

WHAT is called for is an all-out *aerial strategy*. Not merely aviation as a supplement to old-fashioned surface strategy — but the plans and the equipment, the creative imagination and the audacious leadership, looking toward the elimination of the enemy's Air Power and the enforcement of full mastery of the skies. Everything else is secondary and follow-up procedure, simply the exploitation of air ascendancy on the surface.

Those who do not grasp this new reality are disqualified by definition to lead a modern war. No matter how brilliant they may be, they remain brilliant soldiers and sailors, not airmen attuned to the tempo, the space-relations, the grand scale of aerial warfare.

Real aerial strategy — the only guarantee of victory — calls for minds freed from old military illusions. It calls for men as thoroughly "sold" on Air Power as a good admiral is "sold" on Sea Power — as convinced of its decisive rôle and its potentialities for growth as Air Marshal Göring is convinced of it. Men steeped in the tradition and techniques of mile-by-mile conquest of territory, able and intelligent though they be, live in a different military world from modern airmen. They talk a different strategic language. They can never quite comprehend what we mean when we reject mile-by-mile tactics and speak in terms of the control of total areas by throwing a solid and impregnable roof of aerial force over them. Only airmen can grasp the idea of combat purely in latitude and longitude, ignoring the contours of the land far below or whether it is a dry or a wet surface. They think in three-dimensional terms in their own sphere as naturally as a general or an admiral thinks in two-dimensional surface relations.

Let us not fool ourselves into believing that an older breed of military mind can be reformed and adjusted to the new aerial facts. The most that can be expected is that these older strategists will learn some lessons, will make concessions to the new weapons, and will try to catch up with the enemy. But that is not enough for victory. *A totally new strategy can never be put into effect successfully by those who created the old one which proved fallacious or inadequate.* Military conceptions are not put on and taken off like different cloaks for different climates. Strategy is the expression of a man's mind, the embodiment of his military philosophy and convictions. A new strategy, a new approach to the problem of achieving victory under totally different conditions, implies a new type of mind. Fortunately we have in America scores of brilliant military aviation men, chafing under the present set-up, eager to give all they have to the cause of victory, fully capable of developing a true aerial strategy, and willing to assume responsibility.

(*February, 1942*)

"Stunt" Raids

THE talk of "token" bombings and "stunt" or "suicide" raids may be safely discounted. Strategically, such attacks make no sense; they cannot possibly do enough damage to justify the risk and the investment of equipment. Psychologically, they would be self-defeating, because they would do wonders in stirring up American fighting spirit and unifying the nation. Why should Hitler and the Mikado take the trouble to rouse a sleeping nation?

What the Axis fears most, in relation

to the United States, is our launching of a vigorous program of construction on long-range aircraft, planned to strike the enemy at his heart in his own citadel of power. Every stirring of American intelligence in this connection alarms the fascist allies by raising the threat of offensive initiative against them. They want us to remain committed, as long as possible, *exclusively* to a mile-by-mile strategy based on surface lines of communication, sprawled around the entire planet. The more firmly we adhere to "classic" pre-aviation strategic ideas, the more secure Germany and Japan feel in their superiority of position. Operating as they do on interior lines, while we fight on exterior lines, they have a clear tactical advantage which would be cancelled out by a direct aerial strategy on our part.

The Axis knows that sooner or later Americans will awaken to this fact, and will recognize the necessity for direct, long-range aerial warfare. It can only hope to postpone that moment of awakening. I can give no guarantees in this matter, particularly since Germany has made egregious strategic blunders in the past — in the attack on Russia without adequate preparation, for instance. But it seems to me incredible that Hitler should offer us a sample or preview of his long-range bombardment. That, he must know, is the one thing best calculated to break down the prejudice and orthodoxy which now prevent clear thinking and vigorous action here on genuine air power.

When the bombing comes, there is every reason to expect, it will be the real thing. It will be an all-out and continuous aerial attack in full force, carefully prepared to achieve its objective swiftly and completely. With its experience in the Battle of Britain as a warning, Germany this time will not rely on makeshift equipment or mere numerical superiority, but will come geared to force a clear-cut decision in the air.

(*April, 1942*)

BALLYHOO VS. FACTS

WHATEVER reverses we may suffer on the fields of battle, we continue to be magnificently victorious in our publicity, advertising and after-dinner oratory. True, our fighter planes may be outclassed in combat by British, German and even Jap fighters. But gleaming pursuits, doctored by commercial artists, zoom through picturesque skies to do superman feats in full-page newspaper ads and double-spreads in the magazines.

Before me is an all-out advertisement by an oil company. Streamlined drawings and typography tell the American people that "OUR PILOTS FLY FASTER . . . FLY HIGHER . . . FLY FARTHER . . . *than Axis planes* . . . because of 100-Octane Aviation Gasoline."

Now it happens that all major nations, including Germany, use 100-octane fuel. But skip that. More significant is the fact that our pilots *don't* fly faster; the best German and British pursuits thus far have outflown ours; only in the bomber class, where speed is not the paramount consideration, have we measured up. We *don't* fly higher; on the contrary, our main fighters, the P-40 (Kittyhawk and Tomahawk) and P-39 (Airacobra) are stymied by engine shortcomings above the critical altitude of sixteen thousand feet, though British and Axis planes function above thirty thousand feet. And, finally, we don't fly farther; the best British bombers could easily out-distance American bombers with equally useful loads; Jap pursuits have utilized emergency ranges that left us sadly in the lurch.

It must be assumed that national advertising which makes such extreme claims for the most important weapon of the war has at least the tacit consent of our military authorities. Whom are we fooling with these silly and mischievous boasts? Such make-believe merely explodes in our faces in the only test that counts in wartime — the test of actual combat.

The glory of our gallant pilots is that they are doing superb work *despite* inferior equipment. The records of our Colin Kellys and "Butch" O'Hares and hundreds of others, living and dead, are doubly brilliant in the eyes of those Americans fully aware of the equipment handicaps with which they started. We do these heroes and the whole of our peerless aviation personnel a great injustice by blurring that fact. And sentiment aside, we compromise our whole war effort by confusing the issue of technical quality in aerial warfare, by tolerating the *ersatz* superiority of commercial and political braggadocio in place of true superiority.

The tendency to overpraise existing or projected planes acts as a soporific. What we need, instead, is a strong stimulant. What we require from American public opinion is not easy applause but tough challenge.

(*September, 1942*)

Is Our Army Too Large?

THE kind of military weapons and services a nation builds should provide an index to the kind of war it is gearing to fight.

The astronomical figures set up as goals by all our services may consequently be accepted as an indication that America is determined to fight every variety of war simultaneously: a 1917 trench-and-bayonet war, a sea-power war, and ultimately even two Air-Power wars — one naval, the other land. At the same time, it proposes to fight an ultra-modern and streamlined technological war, expressed in the language of modern production and the most advanced weapons.

The fact that we are trying to pile up maximum amounts of everything new and old betrays the absence of expert guidance. The expert knows precisely what he needs to build his edifice, as it were, and doesn't accumulate immense amounts of every conceivable building material. It is an old and true military principle that no nation can be equally strong on land, at sea and in the air. Prodigal America may have ignored this principle in the past; it can ignore it no longer, as the cumulative shortages are proving.

To carry out in full any such concurrent preparations in all directions as we are now seeking, we would need a population of at least one billion and national resources larger than the entire world possesses. In this day and age, it is not merely proper but necessary to raise the question of how large an army a country requires for its actual fighting needs. The science of war-making has long passed the stage where sheer weight of flesh and muscle decides the outcome.

If there is one thing that this war has proved beyond doubt it is that the decision will not be scored by sheer volume of men and metal but by superior weapons and superior strategy. Whenever we sacrifice quality for bulk, brainpower for manpower, we are playing into the hands of the enemy. In the final analysis, America's principal assets are its natural resources and productive genius. Insofar as we weaken or handicap these assets, we are unwittingly undermining our own strength. (*November, 1942*)

TRUE AIR STRATEGY STILL TO COME

BECAUSE a number of books on aviation have become best sellers and because reports from the fronts are more outspoken than formerly in acknowledging the importance of aircraft, too many Americans are under the delusion that "Air Power" has been "recognized" and that it is now merely a question of adequate production. They are under the impression that the basic ideas of the advocates of true Air Power have been accepted and put into practice. It seems to me desirable, therefore, to make it clear that those ideas are still treated as heresy on the upper levels of American war leadership.

We do have more and better aircraft, of course, though in general they are still below the British and German standards of military quality. But the improved planes thus far exhibited in combat were basically designed as auxiliaries of the Army and Navy and still carry that original curse. Wrongly conceived in the first place, they do not represent Air Power in the sense that General Billy Mitchell and his followers have used the term. Our aviation has not been planned for the strategic job of taking command of the air over enemy territory and carrying the war to the enemy's heart.

Many of our ablest air officers have been assigned to important overseas commands. For the first time, an air officer has been made a full general. But if the public should thereby be lulled into the belief that there has been a genuine change in Air-Power organization — or a genuine approach to Air-Power strategy — these things may do more harm than good.

Airmen take an ever larger part in the planning, but only as specialized consultants. They cannot assert themselves and fight for their conception of how the war should be conducted as top generals and admirals can. There is no aviation "opposite number" for Colonel Knox or Mr. Stimson, for General Marshall or Admiral King.

America is still without the kind of autonomous Air-Power system which Britain has in its Royal Air Force. We still have no semblance of real *unity of command in the air*. Army aviation, Navy aviation, Marine Corps aviation operate in the selfsame skies in a maze of overlapping authority. Disputes over aerial jurisdiction have not been ended. The

CRUSADE FOR AIR POWER

Army and the Navy are competing for control over land-based aviation.

This chaos in the air is not accidental. It cannot be cleared up by "good will" and "co-operation" between the services. It is the result — the inevitable result — of mistaken strategic ideas. Everywhere the war is resolving into a struggle for superiority in the skies. But military organization and leadership have not been reformed to meet this new situation. They remain in line with the assumption that this is a surface war.

(May, 1943)

"*German soldiers will never leave Russian soil!*"

(April, 1941)

TALES FROM OKLAHOMA

By George Milburn

Iron Filigree

Vince Blanc wasn't any ordinary blacksmith. He was more than a horseshoer. He seemed to get a lot of pleasure out of working with iron. He made a wrought-iron sign to hang in front of his blacksmith shop — a big stallion rampant on a huge horseshoe, with "Blanc's Blacksmith Shop" spelled out in iron block letters six inches high.

Vince was a scrawny little Frenchman with a sallow complexion. He had a little tuft of hair growing out from his lower lip. He walked to and from work naked to the waist. He was so stooped and thin no one would have taken him for a blacksmith.

Vince got the contract to build the steel cells for the new county jail. He lost money on the job, because he had to underbid the jail contractor in Cincinnati, but the work he did on these steel cages made the county jail a show place for years. He decorated one of the cages with lacey, wrought-iron scroll work. He wanted to finish them all that way, but the county commissioners were in a hurry for the job.

Vince's wife, Martha Blanc, was a fat woman. He was a Catholic, but she had been converted to the Campbellite faith. Every Sunday morning Vince would hitch up the surrey for Martha and she would drive around to get the two neighboring families, the Stufflebeans and the Riggses, to take them to church. Mrs. Blanc had a wide reputation for being neighborly.

The meals at the Blanc's never varied. Month in and month out they ate fried steak, bakery bread, flour gravy and drank boiled black coffee. Steak for breakfast, steak for dinner, steak for supper. Every day at eleven o'clock the neighbors would hear Mrs. Blanc pounding the steak for Vince's dinner. In about an hour he would come along, his bare back covered with coal dust, carrying two pounds of steak for the evening meal and the next day's breakfast. Mrs. Blanc always said that Vince was puny anyway and that he needed meat to give him strength.

As he grew thinner and more wizened his wife prospered in flesh. The blacksmith business wasn't so much any more,

---

GEORGE MILBURN'S *sketches of life in Oklahoma were first printed in this magazine and instantly aroused attention for their high literary merit as well as for their remarkable portrayal of Middle-Western life. After a lapse of about fifteen years they retain their power. The publication date of each sketch is given at its end.*

since automobiles came in, and Vince always refused to put in a line of automobile repairs. The horseshoeing and wheelwright work scarcely paid. But the Blancs had been frugal, and they had a comfortable sum drawing interest at the First National Bank.

One afternoon Vince came home complaining about his side. He was dead the next morning when Martha tried to awaken him. At that time Mrs. Blanc had grown so large that she rubbed against the door jambs when she went from one room to another. Soon she took to her bed too.

The Blancs had no known relatives. Both had been Orphans' Home children and they had grown up together alone. But it was just as well, because the Stufflebeans and the Riggses, to whom Mrs. Blanc had been such a good neighbor, attended to her and did the housework.

When Martha Blanc got down in her bed and couldn't get up she and the Stufflebeans and the Riggses were the closest friends in the world. But her illness made her cross and pettish. Sometimes she would favor one family and then the other. One day she wouldn't permit anyone but Mrs. Riggs to enter the bedroom and the next day she wouldn't eat any food except that which had been prepared by Mrs. Stufflebean. Instead of making the two families lose patience with her, Mrs. Blanc's petulance began to make them distrust each other, and slowly this feeling turned to hatred. When the two families began to speculate on whom Mrs. Blanc was going to favor in her will the enmity burst forth in all its bitterness.

On days when the Riggses were in the sick woman's favor they would run down the Stufflebeans to her for all they were worth. And when the Stufflebeans attained the privacy of the sickroom they would revile the Riggses.

All this time, instead of making her thin, Mrs. Blanc's strange malady caused her to grow larger and larger. It took the combined forces of one family to lift her while they changed the bedclothing.

Martha Blanc died one night. The next morning the Riggses and the Stufflebeans were out in the Blanc kitchen blackguarding one another. Up in the front part of the house the carpenters were hammering with cold chisels, trying to cut off the wrought iron hinges Vince Blanc had put on his front door. They had to get the door off before they could bring in Mrs. Blanc's great coffin.

Out in the front yard Earl Abernathy, the leading town mortician, and Ed Luckenbill, from the Green Front Furniture Store, were arguing about whose coffin was going to be used for the ceremony. The Riggses had gone to Abernathy's Funeral Home and made funeral arrangements a month before Mrs. Blanc died. Earl Abernathy had ordered a special-built coffin. Two weeks later the Stufflebeans had gone to the Green Front Furniture Store and given Ed Luckenbill Mrs. Blanc's measurements, so that he could have a coffin made for her.

For a while it looked as if there would have to be two funerals for the great sheeted pile that had been Martha Blanc. Then Earl Abernathy thought to go in and take the cadaver's measurements. He found that the Riggses had ordered the coffin from him two weeks too early. It was far too small.

Martha Blanc left her money to the county, specifying that it be used to finish the iron scroll work on the cells in the county jail.

(*November, 1929*)

II
Yellow Paint

When news that the armistice had been signed reached our town Mayor Esterbrook proclaimed a special holiday. All the merchants signed an agreement to close their stores, the firebell rang all day long and there was a celebration. Fords drove up and down Broadway tooting their horns and a bunch of men who had been exempt from the draft got up on the roofs of the three-story buildings on the west side of Broadway and began to shoot off firearms. Birdshot hailed down on the shingle roof of the Kentucky Colonel Hotel that whole afternoon.

Along toward night some of the farmers who had come to town that day without knowing that it was going to be a holiday began to want to get their goods and get back home. But all the stores were closed, and it looked as if they would have to drive back home and come back to town the next day to do their buying.

Some of the farmers had come long distances, seven, ten and fifteen miles. Some of them were out of food at home. Four or five of these went down to Old Man Farnum's house and asked him if he wouldn't open his store so that they could get some of the things they had to have, like kerosene and dry salt meat and compound lard and coffee.

Old Man Farnum called himself "The Square Deal Merchant" and he ran a general merchandise store on the east side of Broadway which he called "The Old Ironclad." He called it that because its framework was covered with galvanized sheet-iron pressed in imitation of imitation cut-stone concrete blocks.

Old Man Farnum had a wide reputation for honesty, but he had some queer ways. He never would advertise in the *Weekly Recorder*, always saying that a satisfied customer was the best advertisement. He never carried any fancy groceries like most of the other stores in town, but only staples.

In the general merchandise part of his store, however, he allowed his fancy to wander and he would sometimes stock things he knew, in reason, he couldn't sell. He seemed to buy such things because they were what he would have liked when he was a child. Once he got two dozen tambourines. He kept them on his shelves for years. Another time he got a lot of little bisque shepherdesses which he finally gave away as premiums.

He was very proud, and even though he had gray hair he walked very straight and he would not stand for anyone calling him Old Man to his face. Once he ordered a farmer out of his store for calling him Grandpap.

Well, Old Man Farnum told the farmers who came to him that he absolutely couldn't sell them any goods that day, because he had signed an agreement to close up. He saw the fix they were in, though, and they persuaded him so earnestly that he finally agreed to accommodate them by opening up the back end of his store.

Ellis Grice, the United States marshal in our town, came up the back alley just as Old Man Farnum was helping a farmer put some goods in his wagon. Ellis was an old outlaw hunter. He claimed to have been the man who captured Cherokee Bill, and Mrs. Grice boasted that she sewed the hood they hanged Cherokee Bill in.

Ellis came over to where some men were sitting in front of the De Luxe Barber Shop talking about how sorry they were they hadn't been in the war and about how glad they were it was over.

"Old Man Farnum has opened up his store and is selling goods out the back door," Ellis said.

"And it Armistice Day, too!" someone said.

"That old man ain't got no respect for nothing."

"He ought to have someone go tell him the kind of a dirty slacker he is," Hart Summers said.

"They ought to paint his storefront yellow," said Clarence Everts, a boy who had been in the last draft, but who hadn't been called.

"If someone will paint it, I'll pay for the paint," said Ellis Grice.

The next morning Old Man Farnum got down to his store at daylight, as was his custom. When he opened the front doors he felt the wet paint on his hand. He struck a match and then he could see that the whole front of his store, glass windows and all, was covered with a heavy coat of yellow paint.

Old Man Farnum set to work with rags and kerosene to clean the paint off before anybody else got up and about. But the more kerosene he would put on the more the paint would run, and by broad day the windows were still smeared with yellow, and the paint-kerosene mixture was running across the sidewalk in little rivulets. Finally the old man hired a couple of Negro boys to help him and by noon they got nearly all the paint cleaned off.

The old man's pride was deeply wounded. One of his sons, Newton, a gawky, six-foot boy who used to clerk in the store, had died of influenza in training camp. His other son, Harry, later turned up at the United States Veterans' Hospital in Muskogee with his arms and the lower half of his face blown off.

Old Man Farnum was cut up pretty badly to think that they had painted his storefront yellow just as they had painted Norden's grocery and Fraunhoffer's bakery and Oberchain's butcher shop earlier in the war. He began to look for sympathy among the farmers who were his customers, explaining to them the circumstances over and over again. But most of them were men who didn't want to take issue with general opinion, so they would listen, shaking their heads and making little clicks with their tongues and not saying anything. When two of the farmers for whom the old man had opened the back of his store that afternoon of the first Armistice Day started trading at another store to escape his explanations, Old Man Farnum's hurt changed to slow-burning anger.

A day or two after the painting news had come that the first Armistice Day had been a fake, and that the armistice had not been signed that day at all. Old Man Farnum used to stand for hours in the front part of "The Ironclad" with his hands pressed firmly down on a counter, gazing out of the front window. His face would set in hard, grim lines and his jaw muscles would twitch.

He stopped explaining to people after a few months. His trade had drifted away until only a few old customers and some sympathetic German farmers were left.

Ellis Grice, the United States marshal, used to walk past "The Ironclad" two or three times a day. He had to go past in order to get to the Justice of the Peace's offices next door.

One day it got to Old Man Farnum that Ellis had bought the yellow paint used to paint his storefront. Milan Decker, a boy who worked at the Minnetonka Lumber Company, where the paint was bought, was going with a German farmer's daughter named Margarete Bieberdorf. Margarete told her father, and Bieberdorf came in and told Old Man Farnum.

The old storekeeper waited all that day for Ellis, but Ellis did not come past. The next morning about nine o'clock, however, Ellis came hurrying by with a kind of pacing step he had.

"Good morning, Captain Nightrider," said Old Man Farnum with his softest drawl. He stepped out of his store door and blocked Ellis' way.

"Howdy, Mr. Farnum, howdy," said Ellis. He tried to walk around.

"Wait a minute, Captain Nightrider. I owe you for a little painting job you did for me here last fall."

"Why, Mr. Farnum —" began Ellis, but he never finished that sentence.

Old Man Farnum brought up the soda-water bottle he had been gripping in his right hand, and he bashed Ellis across the face with it. The bottle shattered and the lower half of it tinkled on the cement sidewalk. Ellis' face spouted blood. His nose bulged curiously.

Old Man Farnum looked at him for a minute. Then he tossed the bloody bottle neck he was holding into the street and went back into his store.

Ellis Grice, the old outlaw hunter, stood there with his face a bloody blur. He began to weep, saying, "I never done it, Mr. Farnum! I never done it! Anyone who says I done it is a goddam liar, Mr. Farnum."

Finally he turned around, still weeping, and went off down the street to Doc Boyd's office, sobbing over and over, "Anybody will tell you I never done it, Mr. Farnum!"

It took Doc Boyd quite a while to get the glass picked out of Ellis' face, and his nose never did get set straight again.

(*December, 1929*)

III

THOSE SEAGRAVE BOYS

THE Seagrave place was out in the sand hills, ten miles from town. The house was entirely surrounded by a big apricot orchard. Even in winter there was a heady, luscious odor about, and in the spring and summer for miles along the road you could tell you were approaching Old Man Seagrave's. The roads were almost impassable in bad weather, but they never kept the Seagrave homestead from being a haven for everyone in that part of the State who appreciated good liquor. Old Man Seagrave made the best apricot brandy in the county.

Old Man Seagrave himself was so kind and gentle that it seemed strange he should have fathered such an ornery lot of boys. Those Seagrave boys, Ote, Elzy, Rafe and Bert, were the terror of all that hill country west of town. There wasn't anything they wouldn't do. The old man, though, was the most hospitable, genial soul a person could wish for.

He didn't compete with bootleggers. He charged ten dollars a gallon for brandy that would have brought fifteen dollars a quart in Tulsa. Old Man Seagrave sold only to people he liked, and he liked everyone who liked his liquor. If he liked you well enough he would ask you in the parlor to drink with him. No one ever paid anything for a drink taken in the Seagrave parlor.

The old man would sit back with his stockinged feet up on the nickel-plated guard of the base-burner that towered in the center of the room. He would pour a drink and sniff the bouquet. He would turn the little tumbler of brandy so that when it caught the light it would be a sparkling lump of topaz there in his hand. The old man's talk was as easy and mellow as his liquor.

One night his youngest boy, Bert, said: "Pa, if you wasn't so damn chinchy you'd let me get a speed car, and then I'd show you how to make some real jack. I was talking to a guy down to town last Saturday night and he said they was paying $20 a quart in Telsy for plain old corn colored with iodeen and with a fancy label slapped on it. You ought to let me make you some real jack."

"No, Bert, son, I ain't honin' for no more money than what I got. I got friends in Telsy right now that drives all the way down here to buy my brandy. Forty-five mile. Beside, they's a lot of them Telsy millionaires that don't *know* good liquor. I'd a dang sight ruther give my brandy to my friends than to sell it to some rich man. Not when he cain't tell the difference between my brandy and that pizen they're selling now."

"Ah, you're a goddam old fool," Bert said.

"Well, I reckon I am, son, but Paul says, 'Let ye become a fool so as ye may be wise.'"

Old Man Seagrave liked to support his statements with Scripture. He would be talking about some liquor other than his own, and he would say: "It just grieves me, and I sure hate to say it, but all the young folks are going to Hell, putting this rot-gut and pizen that they're selling now in their stomachs. It was hitting at the way people are drinking nowadays in Corinthians where it says, 'Ye are God's temple and if any man defile the temple of God, him God shall destroy.'

"The Good Book foreseen a lot of things like that. These here folks that go around defiling their bodies with this rot-gut corn whiskey are the accursed of God. Now, this here brandy of mine ain't never defiled no one. It's good for your bowels and it tones up your system.

Paul says, 'Take a little wine for your stomach's sake,' but Paul never had tasted none of my brandy. I been drinking this brandy for thirty year. I ain't never had a sick day in my life and I'm away past sixty.

"When I first come out here part of this orchard was already here. That was before the railroad come through. The orchard was in peaches then, planted by the Indians. A Creek by the name of Wakochee. The Creeks was a civilized people, but the orchard was all run down. I ordered me some apricot slips from Missoury, and they sent them acrost by stage. Since then I been making my own grafts. I been working with this orchard for a long time now."

Old Man Seagrave would drink and talk on like that. He was comfortably fixed. He didn't have a grudge against anyone in the world. When one of his boys got in a scrape he would hitch up the buckboard and drive over to the county J. P. court to pay the fine. He paid the sheriff fifty dollars a month protection money.

One year Jap Strakey, a younger, more enterprising man, was elected sheriff. Jap raised Old Man Seagrave's assessment to $100 a month. That was more than the old man could afford to pay, so he stopped distilling. He pensioned the two old jennets he had used to drive around the big vat, crushing the apricots.

There were about five hundred gallons of brandy aging in Seagrave's cellar. He put the oldest of it in gallon jugs and the rest in five- and ten-gallon kegs. He buried it all over those hills, on other farmers' land. He had crude maps of his caches, and when anyone came to get liquor the old man would sell the directions to where a gallon jug was buried for $10 and to where a five-gallon keg was lying for $50. The brandy in the ten-gallon kegs hadn't aged enough to suit the old man, and he wouldn't sell any of it. Old Man Seagrave concealed all of the brandy so well very little of it was found by accident. People are still digging up those hills, searching for ten-gallon kegs.

The new sheriff didn't make more than one or two liquor raids on the Seagrave place, but he did begin to bear down on the Seagrave boys. He managed to give the old man plenty of trouble that way.

One night Lawyer Weatherby sat in the Seagrave parlor drinking the last of the 1899 brandy with Old Man Seagrave. The old man was talking easily. It was almost like old times.

Two days before his oldest boy, Ote, had been sentenced to the electric chair for killing his sweetheart. He had split her head in two with a cotton hoe. At that moment a sheriff's posse was searching for Elzy, the second boy. On a Sunday night he had gone to a Holy Roller arbor over at Records' Grove. He was drunk. While the others were shouting and jumping, Elzy had dragged a sixteen-year-old girl from the ecstatic crowd and assaulted her. The old man was talking about Elzy.

"You know, Judge, what grieves me most about Elzy was that they say he got drunk on a female tonic. Now you know I never raised Elzy like that, Judge. It's stuff like that that makes a man mean. My brandy never made nobody mean, and it grieves me to think that Elzy went and drunk stuff like that when he could a-got my brandy at home."

Rafe, the third son, came in the room. He said, "Pa, give me twenty bucks."

"Twenty bucks, son?"

"You heerd me. Your head ain't no sack."

"What do you want twenty dollars for, Rafe? I just gave you ten dollars last night."

"Lissen here, you goddam old simp! Are you goin' to jar loose with that jack, or am I goin' to have to bust you one to get it?"

The old man got out a leather pouch and took out some bills. He gave Rafe three old fives, four new ones and some silver. Rafe took the money and went out. The old man started talking about his other boys again as though nothing had happened.

"Now, you take Bert. Bert's my baby. Bert didn't mean no harm, but they've got him up over there in the county jail now, and they's talk of lynching him going around. Now, what did Bert do to have folks talk about him like that? He went over here to Wimberly's to a square dance here last Saturday night, it's a week ago. That oldest Wimberly boy had him on a celluloid collar. All Bert done was to stick a match against it. He didn't know the danged collar was going to burn that boy's neck and face like it done.

"I tell you, Judge, if anybody had worked hard bringing up a passel of boys, learning them to fear God and drink pure liquor instead of this rot-gut like some of them is selling nowadays, I reckon they'd understand about them boys of mine. Them boys ain't mean boys, Judge. They're just playful."

(July, 1930)

"*I wonder how one goes about setting up a decadent democracy?*"

(April, 1943)

STEPHEN A. DOUGLAS

By Edgar Lee Masters

Douglas was born at Brandon, Vermont, on April 23 (Shakespeare's birthday), 1813, and died at Chicago in June of 1861. Into these forty-eight years he compressed greater and more important activity than any American statesman since the days of the Revolution.

He was well blooded and descended. His father was a successful physician, whose mother, born of the Arnold family, was sprung from that Governor Arnold who was identified with Roger Williams in the founding of Rhode Island. But in Douglas, the statesman, there was no drop of dissenting or doctrinaire blood. He was all clear vision, forthrightness, of immense practical sense, upright, courageous to the last degree, truthful, and filled with contempt for the reformer, the pharisee and the moralistic impostor. But he was like an animal born into an environment which is hostile to its existence. Despite his great successes, his preëminent fame, he was gradually carried into the stormy waters which began to flow about the United States in the second decade of the Nineteenth Century, when, Jefferson having put down Federalism, a barrel was thrown to the whale by the revivalistic cry of Negro emancipation. These waters, beaten into fury by the capitalism of the time, and later, were too much for Douglas' great strength. He battled with them manfully and with success for a time. Then they overwhelmed his career and cut short his life.

The weird dreams, the loose metaphysics, the radicalism which made such a variety of religious faith from 1820 to 1860 were no part of Douglas' ontogeny. He knew about them to despise them; he breathed them in but they entered to no extent into his composition. These things might be fruitful in suggestion to Emerson, and form the substance of Whitman's chants. They went over the head of Douglas. And thus it came to pass that he has been written down as lacking in spirituality, when in fact he was a statesman of Nietzschean quality, who subordinated the current morality to practical, hard programmes. But all the while he was immensely devoted to America in efforts to make it great and

---

EDGAR LEE MASTERS' *eminence in American literature rests not alone upon his* Spoon River Anthology *and other books of verse, but also upon his trenchant political essays, especially those dealing with characters underestimated in orthodox histories and biographies. His article on Senator Douglas is an excellent example of his prose writings.* (January, 1931)

enlightened. He became the leader of the New America of his time. But it was a New America that was captured by Anglophiles of the type of Hay, Roosevelt, Lodge and the like. Imperialism snuffed out the Douglas idea.

Douglas was a little man. As a boy he was delicate, with a very large head. He was precocious and quick-witted, with a vast memory. In maturity he became stout and rugged, and his great swelling voice seemed to be too powerful to come from so small a body. Men are still living who heard him roll out his great periods in defense of popular sovereignty from the stumps of Illinois, where, because of his small stature and his intrepid forensic courage, he was known as the Little Giant.

When Douglas was three months old his father, Dr. Douglas, died suddenly, leaving Sarah Fisk Douglas, the widow, to make her way the best she could. Accordingly, she went to live with a bachelor brother on a farm near Brandon. And there Douglas, until he was fifteen, lived the life of a farmer boy of the time. He had been led to believe that this uncle would educate him, but the bachelor married, and an heir was born to him, and thus Douglas suffered his first bitter disappointment. But he met it manfully. He now trudged off to Middlebury, Vt. where he learned the cabinet making trade. He worked there two years, and left off only because he was not strong enough to pursue it. When he became famous and powerful he was not wont to mention his life as a farm boy, or as a cabinet maker. In the days when aspirants for office tricked the imaginations of the populaces by referring to the hardships of their youth, Douglas scorned this device. Once in the debates with Lincoln he referred to the fact that while Lincoln was making rails in Sangamon county, Illinois, he was making cabinets in Morgan county. But he never ran for the Senate as the cabinet maker candidate. When he ran for President he presented his principles and his achievements as a Senator as recommendations for votes.

Having earned enough money now for a term of schooling, he attended the academy at Brandon for a year. Then his mother married again; and Douglas went with her to her new home — near Canandaigua, N. Y. He was now fifteen. He entered the academy at Canandaigua, where he pursued legal and classical studies. His gifts and his amiable disposition made him a great favorite with his fellow students. Already he showed a lively interest in politics, and became a leader of the student bodies. It was now 1828. The immortal amœba known as Hamiltonism, though cut into a thousand pieces by Jefferson, had grown together as the National Republican party, led by John Quincy Adams, who strove to affix false characters upon the personality and the career of Jackson. Douglas at Canandaigua resented this with fervor; and in the debating clubs he showed up the political heredity of Adams. Later, when the National Republicans changed their name to the Whigs, claiming that they were bent upon resisting the Tory despotism of Jackson, Douglas was in full-fledged power to expose the dishonesty of that spurious pretense.

During his four years at Canandaigua he was in frequent debates on political subjects. The readiness of his speech, his gift for words, his quick retorts and his great memory for historical and political information made him marked. From the first he allied himself with the Jeffersonian faith of little government and much liberty, State sovereignty and strict construction of the Constitution. His mind had one birth; but it was a rich one, and carried in itself the possibilities of great development. He lived to see the capitalism of railroads arise; and he had more to do with railroad building as Senator than any other statesman. But in dealing with these new phases of the American unfolding he was a Jeffersonian, and he remained such to the end of his life.

In June, 1833, he left New York for Illinois. He often confessed to the mental liberalization which the prairies brought to his mind. In Vermont his vision was hemmed in by hills and mountains. In Illinois he could use his far-sightedness to the full. And his was a far-sighted mind. On the way west he became gravely ill at Cleveland, and almost died. But, recovering, he went on, reaching Jacksonville, Ill., in November of 1833, with thirty-seven cents in his pocket. There was no work for him in Jacksonville; so he walked sixteen miles to Winchester, where he tried to get a school to teach. He failed. But on the second morning of his stay he got employment as the clerk of an auction, where for three days' work he earned six dollars. What was better, he won the admiration of the people with his comments on politics. It was a Jackson neighborhood. The people became interested in his behalf. They got a school for him to teach, consisting of forty pupils, and thus he was launched. A lawyer lent him law books, and he studied for nearly a year while teaching school. The next year, before he was twenty-one, he was licensed to practice law. He then went to Jacksonville and opened a law office.

II

Chicago, at this time, had been incorporated as a town less than a year. It was filling up with New Englanders, with National Republicans and Whigs, with real estate crooks, and with moral impostors. In twenty years the Germans were to come there; and also to points along the Mississippi river, and into Northern Illinois. But for long the State was to be Democratic. Great floods of Irish came to build the Illinois and Michigan Canal. Two-thirds of the people of the State, measuring from the north southward, were of the old stocks of Tennessee, Kentucky and Virginia. These were to be Douglas' friends always, saving that Abraham Lincoln from Kentucky, who deserted his father's Jacksonian adherence for a devotion to the Whig Henry Clay, was never to be Douglas' friend; indeed, was to be his enemy from 1837 onward.

But in Jacksonville Douglas was among his own kind of people. This was largely true, too, when he was in Springfield. After he went to Chicago his unfailing good manners, his integrity of mind, his great ability made and kept him friends.

But here and there in Illinois, in the making of another age, in the breaking up of old alliances, he encountered enemies and obstacles at last. There was Trumbull, the Connecticut Democrat, who turned against him; and John M. Palmer, another Democrat who left him for Lincoln, as later he left Bryan for the gold democracy. It is not difficult, in reading history, to see how the renegade emerges, and how he is always of the same spirit. One can almost spot him by the look out of his eyes. What passes for independence of spirit turns out to be a manifestation of envy, or mere sulkiness and stubbornness of disposition.

At Jacksonville it was soon known that Douglas knew the history of his country. His oratorical ability was early recognized from his emphatic defeat of a local leader of maturity and experience in a debate. In no time he was the leader of the Jackson democracy of Jacksonville and its county and neighborhood. Within a year of his coming he was made public prosecutor of the first judicial circuit. He served in this office for two years, with great success and credit. In 1836 he was nominated for the Legislature, and elected. He took his seat as the youngest member of that body in December, 1836.

As a legislator he showed great judgment. He was against all public improvements, internal improvements as they were called, that the State could not pay for. He was against the United States Bank and for the sub-treasury. He was against the tariff. He advocated a railroad for the entire length of Illinois, north to south. He abolished divorce by the Legislature, and substituted for it divorce by the courts. He brought about the convention system in Illinois for the nomination of candidates for office. He was one of the most influential men in the removal of the capital from Vandalia to Springfield, which was brought about by great corruption and log rolling, all of which he opposed. Meanwhile, President Van Buren made him register of the land office at Springfield, and he began to be prosperous. In 1838, at twenty-five, he was nominated for Congress in the Springfield district, which had been running a Whig majority of about 3,000 votes. More than 36,000 votes were cast at the election. Douglas was counted out by a majority of five. He declared that he had been defrauded of the election, but after consideration he abided by the count.

When he was twenty-eight he was appointed secretary of state for Illinois. This office he held but a month when he was appointed to one of the justiceships of the Supreme Court of Illinois — at twenty-eight. Illinois was a provincial State at the time, but no less it was rich in able middle-weights, who gasped and writhed with envy to see this Vermonter, whom they expected to assume Eastern airs among them, go about with such democratic amiability, and take all the plums away from them. Among these was Lincoln, whose melancholy, so much in evidence in bronze, was due as much to political disappointment as to viscera collapsed from sedentary life. In December of 1842, when Douglas was under the constitutional age to serve as Senator, he received fifty-one votes in the Legislature for that office, when the successful candidate received fifty-six votes. The next year, he was elected to Congress. There he met the object of his boyish dislike, the venerable John Quincy Adams, who took pains to record in his diary many bitter comments on Douglas and his activities.

Douglas was reëlected to Congress. In his second term he was made chairman of the House Committee on Territories, and became the builder of the West. He distrusted and disliked England, true to the Jeffersonian faith and its insight. At the time we were in controversy with England about Oregon. Douglas tried to have the whole Louisiana Territory north and west of Missouri made into an organic entity under the Constitution. In this he failed. He was against internal improvements save as they related to definite Federal purposes under the Constitution. He was a railroad builder; but his plan was to give land to the States, not to the railroads. Let the States then make their own terms with the railroads for their building.

When Lincoln became President the public land was given outright to the railroads, millions of acres of it; and what was not given to them they stole in equal proportions. In 1843 Douglas tried to organize the Great Western Railway Company, by granting lands to the State of Illinois. In 1851 this came to pass, when he was in the Senate. The railroad promoters then tried to circumvent his policy and plan. They got the Legislature of Illinois to deed the lands granted the State to the railroad. But Douglas trumped their trick. He compelled the promoters to deed the lands back to the State. It was done and the Illinois Central was built.

While Douglas was in the House the Oregon question was making trouble. He declared in a speech that he would take Oregon by force, if necessary, and that he would blot out "the lines on the map which now mark our territorial boundaries on this continent, and make the area as broad as the continent itself." He proposed a joint resolution in 1845 for the annexation of Texas, claiming that Texas became the property of the United States by the Louisiana Purchase of 1803, and that the retrocession of Texas to Spain in 1819 was void.

III

In 1846, when Douglas was thirty-three years of age, he was elected by the Illinois Legislature United States Senator for the six years beginning March 4, 1847. At about this time he was married to Martha Martin, the daughter of a wealthy planter of North Carolina. He was now making money in land speculation in Chicago. Amid so many diverse activities he seemed to have time for everything that entered his active mind. He gave freely out of his wealth to charity; he was hospitable. He was interested in education, and he gave land to found a university in Chicago. It was called the Chicago University. The cornerstone of its main building was laid in 1856, and after many years it became the present University of Chicago.

The day that Douglas took his seat as a Senator he was appointed chairman of the Senate Committee on Territories. So that what he had done for the West and for the new Commonwealths in the House, he now carried forward in the Senate. He framed or reported all the bills by which Utah, New Mexico, Washington, Kansas, Nebraska, Oregon and Minnesota became Territories; and those by which Texas, Iowa, Florida, California, Wisconsin, Oregon and Minnesota became States. The Constitution merely reads that new States may be admitted into the Union, and that the general government shall guarantee to each a republican form of government. Hence Douglas would not have cared, legally speaking, whether Utah came into the Union with polygamy or not; just as he said to audiences all over Illinois that he did not care whether Kansas voted slavery up or down when she knocked for admission. But it is clear that this sort of unmoral indifference, this kind of political libertarianism laid him open to violent and successful attack from the lofty-minded Sumners, and from the temperance and religious fanatics like Ichabod Codding, who organized the Republican party in Illinois in 1854.

Douglas saw in all attempts to regulate Territories and States in their domestic institutions, in their police powers, that tyranny which John Stuart Mill pointed out in his "Essay on Liberty." Writing of the Mormons Mill said:

> When they have left the country to which their doctrines were unacceptable, and established themselves in a remote corner of the earth, which they have been the first to render habitable to human beings, it is difficult to see on what principles but those of tyranny they can be prevented from living there under what laws they please, provided they commit no aggression on other nations and allow perfect freedom of departure to those who are dissatisfied with their ways.

At this point we are able to see that Douglas was the greatest advocate of liberty of his time, in American politics, and how there has been no American statesman since his day worthy to be classed with him. In those years from 1851 to 1861 he stood as a redoubtable tower of strength in the protection of liberty and common sense for all the States and all the people, around whom all the forces of slave-morality, and moral charlatanism swarmed and hooted, while they cast stones and firebrands. He was like Dithyrambus who fought at the pass of Thermopylæ, the Persians being the intermeddlers, the temperance fanatics, the agitators for this or the other interference in business not their own. For the great principle of local self-government he fought and worsted mobs. In the Senate he cowed and put down Golden Rule Chase and Higher Law Seward, and the precious snob and corruptionist Sumner.

He never tried with any audience to win favor by using the Bible. He never spoke of God save as Nature, and as law. When Lincoln in the debates brought out his doctrine of a "house divided against itself" Douglas did not retort with something from the Bible, as he might have done. Instead, he proved that Lincoln's mind was divided against itself, and that Lincoln's argument for Negro equality in one breath, and his argument for white supremacy in the next were irreconcilable arguments and positions, and that Lincoln's mind could not stand upon them. Douglas in the debates showed that there was no difference between reducing all the States and Territories to one level on the subject of the Negro, whether by that reduction he was kept a slave or made a free man, and the making of the whole land subject to the prohibition of drink by Congressional action. To make Nebraska free or slave by Congressional fiat was the same thing as to make Iowa without drink because Maine was, and by the like fiat.

He pointed out that that would be despotism. He proved that the two things were exactly alike, and by doing so showed his far-sightedness as well as his fundamental philosophy. If Congress could refuse admission to Kansas because she had adopted a slave constitution, it could keep out Utah because of polygamy, and it could keep out Arizona because it stood for the recall of judges, as Taft actually did so. A principle once violated leads to any absurdity. But what about the morality of slavery and drink?

Douglas maintained that morals were for individuals to decide for themselves. He held that there is a limit to the legitimate interference of collective opinion with individual independence. He insisted upon people minding their own business. In this advocacy he incurred the Christian forces of the time, which were interested in saving souls, in making everyone act in every way exactly as they ought, exactly as they ought being first determined by the Christian community. Douglas knew that uniformity among the States was death to initiative and progress, that when people stop growing then they cease to be individual.

Lincoln did not value these truths or understand them. As a Whig, as an offshoot of Federalism, Centralism, he believed in making all the States free; and he said that they would become all free or all slave, in extricating themselves from the contradiction of being part slave and part free. There was no chance in the world of their becoming all slave; there was a chance of their becoming all free by natural and peaceful processes; just as Virginia was on the road to emancipation when Garrison began to assail the South, and turned Virginia in self-defense to postpone emancipation. It was because of the fact that America fell into the control of agitators and moralists, as well as hungry office-seekers, and those who wanted to centralize the government for plunder and power, that the war came on in 1861.

In the perspective of time Douglas appears as the one conspicuous man in America who had any sense as the mists of sectionalism began to deepen into the clouds of war. A country never needed strong men with thinking minds to a greater degree than America needed them in 1861, and in the years just before. America needed them in vain. They were not in America to be had. If Douglas had had the support of Jefferson Davis the country would have been saved the war. At the time nearly everyone was insane, both North and South. Certainly in the North every politician was insane but Douglas. As to the South, the insanity there can be manifested by considering the rift between Davis and Douglas.

Douglas from 1850 had stood upon the

principle of territorial control of slavery; and upon that principle he had reported and brought to passage the Kansas-Nebraska legislation of 1854. But in 1857 the Supreme Court held that an owner could take his slaves into a Territory, and that they were not emancipated, even though that Territory were free in virtue of a Federal law itself, not to say a territorial law. Davis then took the ground that the Constitution carried slavery into a Territory against the will of the inhabitants thereof. Douglas would not take that ground. He subscribed to the philosophy that the Supreme Court had laid down: that an owner could take his slaves into a Territory; but whether he could keep them there in slavery, Douglas argued, depended upon police regulations of the Territory.

The insanity of the Southern leaders can be better appreciated when it is considered that all this dialectic was with respect to Kansas and Nebraska, where slavery would never have gone, and would never have lived, if it had gone. The climate and the agricultural needs were both against slavery — Nature's God. This was the fight then. And because Douglas would not accede to the Davis doctrine, purely abstract in the situation, Davis drew away, and carried with him the South. That elected Lincoln. Except for this puerile defection Douglas would have beaten Lincoln by nearly 1,000,000 votes.

What led up to this crisis of interpretation respecting Territories must be briefly summarized in order to understand Douglas' career. First, there was the Old Northwest, out of which the States of Ohio, Michigan, Illinois, Indiana, Wisconsin were carved. This belonged to Virginia. While the United States were operating under the Articles of Confederation Virginia ceded this Territory to the United States. But a condition of the cession, the deed, was that slavery should not exist in the Territory. The cession was accepted on that condition. No Congress of the Articles, no Congress of the Constitution abolished slavery there. It was all a matter of compact, of treaty so to speak, of which Virginia was the author. Thus that clause in the Constitution which gave Congress the power to "make needful rules and regulations" with respect to the Territory and other property of the United States was not meant to enable Congress to abolish slavery where it was forbidden to come by the terms of a cession, but to enable Congress to make rules and regulations for the sale of the lands of the Territory to settlers.

IV

Nevertheless Webster, in 1850, argued not only that the clause in question gave Congress imperial power over its Territories, not only the Old Northwest, but also the Louisiana and Mexican Territories; but also that Congress under the Constitution had exercised that power over the Old Northwest. Congress never exercised imperial power over the Old Northwest. It treated the land with strict regard to the terms of the Virginia cession. And thus Webster was logically in error; he was historically at fault.

Then, in 1860, Lincoln took Webster's

speech of 1860 and paralleled its historical points and its legal argumentations in his Cooper Institute speech, which dealt with Kansas and Nebraska, Territories carved out of the Louisiana Purchase. In other words, Congress had all power over Kansas and Nebraska, because it had had all power over the Old Northwest; and besides all this, the power had been exercised by the Fathers, who had thus bequeathed a sacred precedent. Lincoln, too, was wrong, as Webster was. And it may be mentioned in passing that Lincoln utterly ignored the settled, fundamental, and plainly written rule that the Constitution is a grant of power to Congress, which gives Congress no power not written. Lincoln's thesis for the Cooper Institute speech was that nothing in the Constitution forbade the Federal government from prohibiting slavery in the Territories. His whole speech rested upon that obvious sophism.

In 1820 came the Missouri Compromise, so called. Missouri was carved out of the Louisiana Purchase of 1803, which was sixteen years after the acquisition of the Old Northwest, and as many after the adoption of the Constitution. The Missouri Compromise divided the Louisiana Purchase by a line drawn west from the Mississippi river at latitude 36° 30', north of which slavery was forbidden; south of which it was permitted. In point of fact, Missouri was not admitted to the Union under that compromise. The North, having forced the South to accede to the drawing of the sectional line, fought the admission of Missouri to wring other concessions. But that need not concern us here. Kansas and Nebraska lay north of 36° 30'; so when Douglas came to organize them into Territories the fraudulently imposed compromise rose up to perplex him.

As a result of the war with Mexico the United States had acquired Utah, New Mexico and California, as the whole West was called, excluding the Louisiana Purchase. In 1850 Webster and Clay were in the Senate, and Douglas was there, too, not less influential or able or active than they in the settlement of the questions respecting new Territories to be carved from the Mexican grants. Now, the Mexican grants and the Louisiana Purchase overlapped at different places; so that when Webster and Clay and Douglas put together the bill for the organization of New Mexico and Utah, by which slavery was neither legislated into those Territories nor forbidden in them, a repeal by implication of the Missouri Compromise resulted. Utah was wholly north of 36° 30'. True, Utah was far west of the western boundary of the Louisiana Purchase; but essentially that made no difference. There were portions of Colorado and Kansas where the Compromise of 1850 and the Missouri Compromise positively conflicted, so that the strict legal rule of repeal took hold.

With the laws so made and abided in by everyone — by Whigs and Democrats alike, by the platforms of both parties in 1852, confirming and praising the work of Webster and Clay and Douglas with respect to Utah and New Mexico and California — with all this as background, Douglas took hold of the task of organizing Nebraska and Kansas. This was in 1854, three years before the Dred Scott decision, which invalidated the Missouri Compromise by announcing the doctrine that the Constitution recognized slavery, that the Constitution was over every foot of American soil, and that slavery went into every Territory under the protection and by force of the Constitution.

In 1852 Lincoln was campaigning in the Springfield district for the Whig nominee for President. He was lauding the Compromise of 1850, and Clay who was one of its authors. In a few years he traduced Douglas in the most villainous manner for bringing about a repeal of the Missouri Compromise by his Kansas-Nebraska bill; when in point of fact the Missouri Compromise had been repealed by the Compromise of 1850, by Webster and Clay, Lincoln's idols. If ever a man was lied off the scene of life, it was Douglas. In speeches before the debates with Douglas, and in those debates, Lincoln, with expressions of great moral fervor, denounced Douglas for repealing the Missouri Compromise when framing the Kansas Nebraska bill. All over America was blown the lie that Douglas had so dealt with Kansas-Nebraska in obedience to the Southern slavocracy, and to advance his chances for the Presidency. Beveridge in his biography of Lincoln, proved that this was untrue, that it was a gross libel. Historians and research workers have brought to light indisputable facts to prove that Douglas, in all this Kansas-Nebraska matter, was acting true to an old form; that he was concerned primarily and chiefly with a transcontinental railroad.

One could not be built through territory unorganized and unpoliced. There was rivalry between the North and the South as to which section should get the eastern terminus of such a railroad. Memphis wanted it to connect with Charleston on the coast. New Orleans wanted it. Chicago wanted it. Douglas was a Chicago man, and devoted to that city. He had to make concessions to get the railroad for the North. He first framed the Kansas-Nebraska bill to read that those Territories should do as they pleased on the matter of slavery; and that they could come into the Union with or without slavery, as their people should decide. That was the doctrine of Webster and Clay with reference to Utah and New Mexico. Then Senator Dixon of Kentucky, as the price of his friendship to the bill, wanted it to contain express words to the effect that the Compromise of 1850 had repealed the Missouri Compromise of 1820. Douglas had first drawn the bill to read that the Missouri Compromise, being inconsistent with the "principle of non-intervention by Congress with slavery in the States and Territories, . . . as recognized by the legislation of 1850, . . . is hereby declared inoperative and void." To please Senator Dixon, Douglas struck out the word "inoperative," and inserted the words, "inconsistent with," and "null and void." Is there any real difference between these phrasings? There is none.

What States voted in the Senate for this Kansas-Nebraska bill? Two-thirds voted for it. They were New Hampshire, New Jersey, Pennsylvania, Illinois, Indiana, Michigan, Iowa, Delaware, Virginia, North Carolina, South Carolina, Georgia, Florida, Mississippi, Missouri,

Arkansas, Kentucky, Alabama, Louisiana and California. In the House the bill carried by a vote of 113 yeas to 100 nays.

The Senators who had to swallow defeat were Sumner of Massachusetts, Chase of Ohio, and Seward of New York. The States in the Senate which had voted for the Compromise of 1850 were twenty, and those which had voted against it six, with two divided, and two not voting. Seward was in the Senate in 1850, but he voted neither one way nor the other, though it would have been convenient for him to have taken a stand. He dodged. And now these men of great moral principle, who had been on every side of every question like Dryden's Zimri; who had been anti-Masonics, Knownothings, Free-soilers, and Whigs, and what not; and who all their lives had preached the moralities, but had flitted this way and that in the pursuit of money and reputation — these men plotted to destroy the faithless and satanic Douglas, for the un-Christian and iniquitous Kansas-Nebraska bill!

V

Douglas, ever since the deaths of Webster and Clay in 1852 and of Calhoun in 1850, had been the master mind of the Senate, as well as the undisputed leader of the Democratic party. As chairman of the Committee on Territories he had had charge of the most important legislation of the time. He had out-argued Seward and Chase and Sumner, and routed them over and over again, until they were wary of engaging in debate with him. He knew more than they did. He was readier with his knowledge. His mind worked with finer accuracy; and as he was of clearer integrity than they were, he drove his thought through their obscurantism with tal effect.

His mind was realistic and honest. He was not trying to apply Hebraic Puritanism out of the Bible to questions of legislation. He boldly proclaimed everywhere that morals belonged to the individual life, and laws to the sphere of the state. Yet now there was a chance to confuse the two spheres of morals and the state, to make them one under God's dispensation! Though compelled to bend to Douglas' supremacy in the Senate, Sumner and Chase saw that there was a body before which they could worst Douglas. That body was the mob. How then could the mob be set after Douglas?

On January 24, 1854, Douglas moved in the Senate that the Kansas-Nebraska bill be taken up. Chase and Sumner requested delay in order to give them time to examine the bill. They were lying. On January 19th they had issued their "Appeal of the Independent Democrats in Congress to the People of the United States," based upon an examination of the bill; and by the time it came on for consideration the Appeal had been printed in the Abolition organ, the *National Era*, in the New York *Times*, and the New York *Tribune*. The mob had been aroused. But not by independent Democrats. Neither Chase nor Sumner was an independent Democrat. The four members of the House who signed the Appeal were all Abolitionists, one of them being Joshua R. Giddings of Ohio, one of the violent fanatics of the time. Naturally, as the Appeal originated in false pretense, so was it chock full of mendacity and pious malice. It charged that the Kansas-Nebraska bill was the result of a plot on the part of the slavocracy, a falsity that Lincoln afterward circulated all over Illinois in his campaign to destroy Douglas. It misstated the history of the Old Northwest, of the Missouri Compromise, and that of 1850. Finally it said: "We implore Christians and Christian ministers to interpose. Their divine religion requires them to behold in every man a brother, and to labor for the advancement of the human race." This "enormous crime" must be put down!

And so it was that the Holy Bible was set after the unprincipled Douglas by Golden Rule Chase and by Higher Law Seward. So it was that Lincoln concocted the "house divided against itself" speech. When Douglas answered him, Lincoln slyly retorted that Douglas' quarrel was with the Saviour, not with himself, Lincoln. Although, when the bill came up in the Senate Douglas poured his invective and his analysis over the cowering heads of Sumner and Seward and Chase, and carried the day, yet the mob had been evoked from the purlieus of America. Douglas was hanged in effigy all the way from New York to Chicago. He was denounced as Benedict Arnold Douglas; and in Chicago, where he tried to tell an audience what the bill was, what had brought it about, and what it meant and did not mean, he was hooted down by the Bible fanatics, and by political charlatans, by the ignorant and the violent.

In 1858 Douglas came up for reëlection to the Senate, and Lincoln was his opponent. The famous debates ensued during the Summer of 1858. Lincoln reiterated the mendacities of the Appeal; he used the Bible to the full. He assumed high moral ground, and with venomous satire he pointed to Douglas as a sort of spoiled darling of the slavocracy, whose evil life of unprincipled expediency had won him fame and riches. While he, humble Abraham Lincoln, had remained poor and lowly in the paths of the good and the honorable life! He charged Douglas with being in a conspiracy to bring about the Dred Scott decision of 1857; when Douglas would have been a fool to have done such a thing, with the Kansas-Nebraska bill of 1854 on his hands.

Douglas showed that the Dred Scott decision was a moot case concocted by Abolitionists; that Dred Scott's owners were a Mrs. Chaffee, and her husband, an Abolitionist member of Congress from Massachusetts; that the lawyers on both sides were Abolitionists. In the face of all this Lincoln persisted to the last debate in charging Douglas with conspiracy to get the Supreme Court to decide the Dred Scott case for the slavocracy. Obstinacy in repeating this false charge did not win the point for Lincoln. It only threw upon Douglas the extra labor of recapitulating the facts whenever Lincoln made the charge.

A similar task rested upon Douglas with reference to the Missouri Compromise and the Compromise of 1850, which Lincoln garbled, and which Douglas had to ungarble. All that Lincoln said in these debates was favorable to an undoing of all these compromises, though in 1852 he had committed himself with enthusiasm to the Compromise of 1850. Was it better to repeal the Kansas and Nebraska bill, and enact a law that slavery could not go into those Territories? Or was it better to let Kansas and Nebraska settle slavery for themselves, considering that according to the high authority of Webster, and the higher authority of physical facts, slavery would never find a hospitable ground in those Territories, even under the rule of non-intervention by Congress? Was it better to unchain the Bible and the mob until there was war which cost the country 700,000 lives, and at the least in principal and interest $22,000,000,000; or was it better to let the gradual processes of time end the slavery matter, under the Presidency of a rationalist like Douglas, and under Presidents with similar reactions to the question? All the histories, school and others, have been written in favor of war and the Lincoln philosophy. But that does not settle the matter, because the indubitable facts remain for human reason and intelligence to exercise themselves upon.

At Alton on October 15, 1858, Douglas in the last debate with Lincoln fervently appealed to the best judgment of America to enforce the policy that would keep every State in attention to its own business, without intermeddling with the business of the other States, on the slavery question, and prophetically on the liquor question too. "Why can we not thus have peace?" he asked. "Why should we thus allow a sectional party to agitate this country, to array the North against South, and convert us into enemies instead of friends, merely that a few ambitious men may ride into power on a sectional hobby?" In truth a sectional party had now for four years been rending the country. The Republican party was organized a few months after Chase and Sumner issued the Appeal.

VI

When the War broke over the land Douglas went to Illinois in order to hold that State in line for the Union. His speeches at Chicago and at Springfield have been described by those who heard them as the most moving and powerful of his whole life. He was not thinking, probably, that he would soon be dead, and that worldly prudence need not be consulted. If he did have regard to his future career, then he reflected that in 1864 he would be striving for reëlection to the Senate; or that he might be running for President again; and in that case how should he come before the people? As a man who was favorable to Secession, or as one who stood for the Union? Therefore, was his stand for the Union dictated by other than considerations of expediency?

His numerous detractors said that he was only trying to hold on to his career by pretending to stand for the Union in June of 1861, when in his heart he was really for Secession. Like men before him and since, his character had been so calumniated that every thing he did was, in these days of his decline, suspected. Yet one fact stands out. In the Fall of 1860 he answered a heckler in Virginia by saying that he was against disunion, and that the election of a Republican President would not justify Secession. Virginia in the election gave him but 16,290 votes, while the combined vote of Breckenridge and Bell was 149,004. Despite this great evidence of his courage and his good faith, his old enemies, Sumner in chief, spoke of his services in the Senate in February of 1861, and in Illinois in June, with skeptical contempt. He should be watched; for he was still the sagacious casuist in his familiar rôle of satanic duplicity!

In that month of February, 1861, when the Southern States had a *de facto* and a *de jure* government, the question was what was to be done about it? Some of the questions were not new. In 1832 Jackson thought of blockading the port of Charleston to put down Nullification. Webster showed that this could not be done, except by pure usurpation on Jackson's part. In 1832 there were Federal marshals and judges in South Carolina to whose assistance the military might by some legal theory have been sent. In 1861 there were no Federal officers in the South to act and to be assisted by Federal power.

Douglas pointed all this out in a speech in the Senate of great eloquence. He followed Webster in proving that Lincoln could no more blockade the Southern ports than Jackson could have done it — not without usurpation. Douglas still, as always, was for the law, for the Constitution. Before him sat those who were for neither: Golden Rule Chase, and Higher Law Seward, and the Anglophile Sumner, all with cool arrogance and supercilious contempt written on their faces. Sumner in his habitual spats, clothed in New England self-sufficiency, eyed Douglas with a patronizing smile.

None of these gentry need trouble themselves now to answer him. He was down; and the Appeal had destroyed him and his party. The tariff was soon to take the government, which for so long the Democrats had fought. The national bank was soon to be resurrected by the grace of Golden Rule Chase. In the far distance were Prohibition, bureaucracy, the trusts, imperialism, and the loftiness of a Christian Republic free of slavery, polygamy and drink!

History was to be written as monopolists and Christians wanted it written. Lincoln was to become the colossal hero whose powerful logic, and deep spirituality put down the crafty Douglas; and then won the War and abolished slavery. The strength of the legend still prospers Lincoln, and to make it more exciting in the relation it always carried Douglas' name as a footnote, to say that he was the man with whom Lincoln debated in 1858, and routed with mastering ability and clearer hold on God's truth. But for those who have the time and the power to follow up the footnote it will be seen that Douglas was superior to Lincoln in genius, in strength of mind, and in moral character.

There was nothing now for Douglas to do but to die. The fitting time had come. And he did die with strength and with dignity. Perhaps in so making his exit from the world he balanced all scores in his last conscious thoughts about the mad scenes through which he had walked to the best of his vision.

THE VIRGINIANS ARE COMING AGAIN

By Vachel Lindsay

BABBITT, your tribe is passing away.
This is the end of your infamous day.
The Virginians are coming again.

With your neat little safety-vault boxes,
With your faces like geese and foxes,
You,
Short-legged, short-armed, short-minded men,
Your short-sighted days are over,
Your habits of strutting through clover,
Your movie-thugs, killing off souls and dreams,
Your magazines, drying up healing streams,
Your newspapers, blasting truth and splendor,
Your shysters, ruining progress and glory, —
Babbitt, your story is passing away.
The Virginians are coming again.

All set for the victory, calling the raid,
I see them, the next generation,
Gentlemen, hard-riding, long-legged men,
With horse-whip, dog-whip, gauntlet and braid,
Mutineers, musketeers,
In command
Unafraid:
Great-grandsons of Tidewater, and the bark-cabins,
Bards of the Blue Ridge, in buckskin and boots,
Up from the proudest war-path we have known —
The Virginians are coming again.

The sons of ward-heelers
Threw out the ward-heelers,

VACHEL LINDSAY, *who died in 1931, was the author of* The Congo and Other Poems, General William Booth Enters into Heaven *and* The Chinese Nightingale, *all major events in contemporary American culture.* (July, 1928)

THE VIRGINIANS ARE COMING AGAIN

The sons of bartenders
Threw out the bartenders,
And made our streets trick-boxes all in a day,
Kicked out the old pests in a virtuous way.
The new tribe sold kerosene, gasoline, paraffine.
Babbitt sold Judas. Babbitt sold Christ.
Babbitt sold everything under the sun.
The Moon-Proud consider a trader a hog.
The Moon-Proud are coming again.

Bartenders were gnomes,
Pitiful tyrants, hairy baboons.
But you are no better with saxophone tunes,
Phonograph tunes, radio tunes,
Water-power tunes, gasoline tunes, dynamo tunes,
And pitiful souls like your pitiful tunes,
And crawling old insolence blocking the road;
So, Babbitt, your racket is passing away.
Your sons will be changelings, and burn down your world.
Fire-eaters, troubadours, conquistadors!
Your sons will be born, refusing your load,
Thin-skinned scholars, hard-riding men,
Poets unharnessed, the moon their abode,
With the statesman's code, the gentlemen's code,
With Jefferson's code, Washington's code,
With Powhatan's code!
From your own loins, for your fearful defeat
The Virginians are coming again.

Our first Virginians were peasants' children
But the power of Powhatan reddened their blood,
Up from the sod came splendor and flood.
Eating the maize made them more than men,
Potomac fountains made gods of men.

In your tottering age, not so long from you now,
The terror will blast, the armies will whirl,
Cavalier boy beside Cavalier girl,
In the glory of pride, not the pride of the rich,
In the glory of statesmanship, not of the ditch.
The old grand manner, lost no longer:
Exquisite art born with heart-bleeding song

Will make you die horribly, raving at wrong.
You will not know your sons who are true to this soil;
For Babbitt could never count much beyond ten,
For Babbitt could never quite comprehend men.
You will die in your shame, understanding not day.
Out of your loins, to your utmost confusion
The Virginians are coming again.

Do you think boys and girls that I pass on the street,
More strong than their fathers, more fair than their fathers,
More clean than their fathers, more wild than their fathers,
More in love than their fathers, deep in thought not their fathers',
Are meat for your schemes diabolically neat?
Do you think that all youth is but grist to your mill
And what you dare plan for them, boys will fulfill?
The next generation is free. You are gone.
Out of your loins, to your utmost confusion
The Virginians are coming again.

Rouse the reader to read it right.
Find a good hill by the full-moon light,
Gather the boys and chant all night:
"*The Virginians are coming again!*"

Put in rhetoric, whisper and hint,
Put in shadow, murmur and glint;
Jingle and jangle this song like a spur.
Sweep over each tottering bridge with a whirr,
Clearer and faster up Main Street and pike.
Till sparks flare up from the flints that strike.
Leap metrical ditches with bridle let loose.
This song is a war, with an iron-shod use.
Let no musician, with blotter and pad
Set down his pot-hooks to make the song sad.
Find
Your own rhythms
When Robert E. Lee
Gallops once more to the plain from the sea.
Give the rebel yell every river they gain.
Hear Lee's light cavalry rhyme with rain.
In the star-proud, natural fury of men
The Virginians are coming again!

TRIAL BY JURY

By James M. Cain

CHARACTERS:
MR. GAIL, *foreman*.
MESSRS. HAGAR, BASSETT, ZIEGLER, FUNK, REDDICK, PETRY, LEE, DYER, PENNELL, MOON, *and* WEMPLE, *members of the jury empaneled to hear the case of the State vs. Summers.*

The scene is a jury room, late in the afternoon. The jurors have just filed in. They break ranks and take to the chairs with which the place is provided, some sitting solemnly apart, others hooking their heels on the edge of the table which stands in the middle of the room, and still others camping within range of the cuspidor.

MR. GAIL — Well men, le's git at it. What I mean, le's git a verdick quick, so's we can git out in time for supper.

MR. DYER ⎫ You said it!
MR. LEE ⎬ That suits me!
MR. REDDICK ⎭ You're tooting!

MR. BASSETT — 'Cepting only that State's attorney tooken away all my appetite for supper.

MR. REDDICK — Me too. I never seen such a looking sight in my life.

MR. BASSETT — "For the honor of our fair State, gentlemen, for the honor of your State and my State, I ask you to return a verdict of murder in the first degre-e-e-e-e!" And then all that whooping and hollering wasn't enough for him. Oh, no! He had to spit all over you.

MR. GAIL — The spit, it wasn't so good, but what we got to talk about now is the verdick.

MR. WEMPLE — Yeah, the verdick.

MR. GAIL — What we going to do?

MR. PENNELL — I kind of feel like we ought to hear what Mr. Petry thinks about it.

MR. PETRY — This is a hard case. This is an exceptional hard case.

MR. WEMPLE — This is the balled-uppest case I ever hear tell of in my life.

MR. MOON — How come that fellow to git killt?

MR. WEMPLE — What's the matter? Was you deef you couldn't hear what them people was saying out there?

MR. MOON — I heared what they said, but seems like I can't quite git the hang of it.

MR. WEMPLE — Hunh!

MR. MOON — Yes sir. Scuse me, sir.

MR. WEMPLE — Scuse you? Say, fellow, what ails you, anyhow?

JAMES M. CAIN, *whose* The Postman Always Rings Twice *made his name a household word among lovers of hard-boiled fiction, contributed frequently to this magazine. His present sketch deals with the Ku Klux Klan hysteria of sixteen years ago, and it describes one aspect of that unhappy phase of American history powerfully.* (January, 1928)

Mr. Moon — Yes sir. I ain't quite got it straight yet, like of that.

Mr. Wemple — Well, for the love of Mike quit looking like the police was after you every time I look at you. . . . Which is the part you don't understand?

Mr. Moon — About the singing.

Mr. Wemple — Why, there wasn't nothing to that. That there was to fill him with the holy fire.

Mr. Moon — Oh yeah. Thank you, sir, Mr. Wemple. Oh yeah. The holy fire.

Mr. Petry — I expect you better explain how it was, Mr. Wemple. Anyway, as good as you can. 'Cause this man don't act like he was so bright nohow, and maybe it wouldn't hurt the rest of us none if we was to kind of go over it once more, just to git it all straight.

Mr. Pennell — If Mr. Petry, he feels like he's got to hear it oncet more, then I reckon we all better hear it.

Mr. Wemple — Well, the way I git it, this here Summers, what they got on trial, he wouldn't never go to church.

Mr. Funk — 'Cepting only he's a Disciples of Christ and there ain't no Disciples church nowhere around here.

Mr. Wemple — Well, one thing at a time. Whatever the hell he's a Disciples of, he wouldn't never go to church. So the Ku Klux got it in their head to go out to his place and try to bring him around.

Mr. Funk — It wasn't no such thing. They was sore at him 'cause he went to work and boughten hisself a disc harrow offen the mail-order house 'stead of down at the store.

Mr. Wemple — Well then, damn it to hell, you know so much about it, suppose *you* tell it!

Mr. Reddick
Mr. Bassett } Let the man talk!
Mr. Ziegler

Mr. Funk — All right. But why don't he tell it right?

Mr. Wemple — I'm trying to tell what them witnesses said. After we git that all straight, why then maybe we can figure the fine points on how much they was lying.

Mr. Petry — I think Mr. Wemple's telling it the way most of us heard it.

Mr. Wemple — So they went out to his place, this here Beekman what got killt and five other of them, all dressed up in them nightgowns.

Mr. Ziegler — And got it in the neck.

Mr. Wemple — In the neck and the funny-bone and the seat of the pants and a couple of other places where maybe they're picking the shot out yet. 'Cause this here Summers, he ain't only boughten hisself a disc harrow offen the mail-order house, but a 12-gauge, single-barrel, six-shot pump-gun too. And when they commence bearing down on the close harmony, what he done to them was a plenty.

Mr. Lee — I swear I never heared the beat of that in all my life. Idea of going to a man's house three o'clock in the morning and commence singing right on his front stoop!

Mr. Dyer — And "Nearer My God to Thee"!

Mr. Reddick — They was a hell of a sight nearer than they figured on.

Mr. Wemple — And Beekman, he got it

in about all the places there was, and in the middle of the stummick too, and he bled to death. So he come about as near as he's going to git. So that's how come he got killt.

Mr. Petry (*To* Mr. Moon) — Do you understand now?

Mr. Moon — Oh yeah, oh yeah. Anyways, a whole lot better. Thank you sir. Thank you, Mr. Wemple.

Mr. Gail — Well men, what are we going to do?

Mr. Wemple — That there is a question. . . . Mind, I ain't afraid of the Ku Klux. If this here Beekman was in it, and this here Summers what killed him had the right on his side, I'd turn Summers loose just as quick as I would anybody.

Mr. Gail
Mr. Hagar
Mr. Lee
Mr. Dyer } Me too! I ain't afraid of
Mr. Ziegler   no Ku Klux!
Mr. Reddick
Mr. Funk
Mr. Pennell

Mr. Petry — Mr. Wemple, I don't believe there's a man in this room that's afraid to do his duty on account of the Ku Klux. Unless —

Mr. Moon — I ain't afraid of the Ku Klux. Not me.

Mr. Petry — Then I think that's one thing we don't have to worry about. All the same, I think it wouldn't hurt none if all of us was to remember that what goes on in this room ain't to be told outside.

Mr. Wemple — That's understood. Or dam' sight better had be. But what I started to say, we got to be sure this here Summers had the right on his side.

Mr. Hagar — Look to me like he did all right.

Mr. Funk — What I say, when them Ku Klux goes to take a fellow out, why don't they take him out or else stay home?

Mr. Bassett — That's me. I never see such a mess-around-all-the-time-and-then-never-do-nothing bunch in all my life.

Mr. Ziegler — And all this "Come to Jesus."

Mr. Hagar — And "Sweet Adeline."

Mr. Reddick — What's the good of that? Everybody knows what they was there for. Then why the hell don't they up and do it thouten all this fooling around?

Mr. Funk — All the time making out they don't never do nothing 'cepting the preacher told them to do it.

Mr. Dyer — And then come to find out, when they pick up Beekman he had a strap on him looked like a trace off a six-horse harness.

Mr. Ziegler — I reckon the preacher give them that for to beat time to the singing.

Mr. Moon — That was to scare him.

Mr. Hagar — Yeah?

Mr. Moon — Anyway, so I hear tell. That's what them Ku Klux said.

Mr. Hagar — Them Ku Klux sure can tell it their own way.

Mr. Wemple — Wait a minute, wait a minute. . . . Moon, how come you heared all this what the Ku Klux said?

Mr. Moon — They was just talking around.

Mr. Wemple — I ain't asking you was they talking around. I ask you what the hell you was doing around them?

Mr. Moon *makes no reply. There is a general stir.*

Mr. Funk — What the hell? . . .

Mr. Wemple — Come on, Moon. Why don't you say something?

Mr. Petry — Why, what's the matter, Mr. Wemple?

Mr. Wemple — Why that simple-looking nut, *he's in the Ku Klux!*

Several — What!

Mr. Wemple — Look at him, the lying look he's got on his face! Hell, no wonder he acted like the police was after him! No, he couldn't git it straight about the singing, 'cause they done filled him up with so much talk he don't know is he going or coming! No, he ain't afraid of no Ku Klux, 'cause he's got a nightgown hisself already.

Mr. Ziegler — But how about them questions?

Mr. Wemple — I'm coming to that. Hey you, why ain't you said something about this when they ask you them questions? When they ask you was you in the Ku Klux, how come you said you wasn't?

Mr. Moon — Lemme alone! Lemme alone!

Mr. Wemple — Quit that crying or I'll bust you one in the jaw. Now answer me what I just now ask you.

Mr. Petry — Let me talk to him, Mr. Wemple. Now Mr. Moon, when them lawyers ask you was you in the Ku Klux, what made you answer no?

Mr. Moon — I tried to tell them how it was, but they wouldn't let me say nothing. . . . That there man, he kept a-saying, "Answer yes or no." . . . I tried to explain it to them, but they wouldn't never give me no chance.

Mr. Wemple — Chance? What the hell! Couldn't you say yes?

Mr. Moon — They ain't tooken me in yet. I ain't never had the money. They won't take me in lessen I give them the ten dollars.

Mr. Wemple — Well, I'll be damned!

Mr. Petry — I *never* hear tell of nothing like this in all my life. Why Mr. Moon, don't you know that was perjury?

Mr. Moon — I tried to tell them, but they wouldn't lemme say nothing.

Mr. Petry — Don't you know that when you take oath before the judge to tell the truth you got to tell the truth else it's against the law? Ain't nobody ever told you that before?

Mr. Moon — Lemme alone! Lemme alone! *There ensues an ominous silence, punctuated occasionally by* Mr. Moon's *sobbing.*

Mr. Bassett — So now, every word what's been said in here, the Ku Klux knows it five minutes after we get out.

Mr. Ziegler — This sure is bad.

Mr. Hagar — Moon, effen a juryman tells what he heared in the jury room, they put him in jail for five year.

Mr. Lee — Ten year.

Mr. Dyer — And the penitentiary, not the jail.

Mr. Hagar — In the penitentiary for ten year. And he don't hardly ever come out. 'Cause before the time comes for him to git out, something generally always happens to him.

Mr. Moon — Lemme alone! Lemme alone!

Mr. Funk — Aw hell, what's the use of talking to him? 'Cause that dumb coot, even if you could scare him deef, dumb and blind, why he'd blab it all around anyhow and never know he done it.

Mr. Bassett — That's the hell of it. And never know he done it.

Mr. Wemple — What do you think about this, Mr. Petry? Do you think we better report this fellow to the judge?

Mr. Petry — I'm just a-thinking. I'm just a-thinking.

Mr. Wemple — Well, while we're figuring on that, I reckon we better git up a verdict. This here look like second degree to me.

Mr. Funk — First degree, I say.

Mr. Reddick
Mr. Dyer
Mr. Ziegler } First degree, I say. Me too. This here is murder.
Mr. Gail
Mr. Hagar
Mr. Bassett

Mr. Wemple — Well, I was thinking about first degree myself. 'Cause a Klansman, it stands to reason, he's as good as anybody else.

Mr. Lee — He is that. When a man gits killt, something had ought to be done about it and that goes for a Klansman same as anybody else.

Mr. Hagar — Everybody alike, I say.

Mr. Bassett — And another thing, men, what we hadn't ought to forget, Ku Klux is a fine order, when you come right down to it.

Mr. Funk — I know a fellow what he's a kind of a travelling agent for the Red Men. He got something to do with the insurance, I think it is, and believe me he's got it down pat about every kind of a order they is going. And he says to me one time, he says, "Funk," he says, "you can put it right down if they'd run it right the Ku Klux is the best order what they is going. They ain't none of them," he says, "what's got the charter and the constitution and all like of that what the Ku Klux has. Now you'll hear a lot of talk, " he says to me, "and I ain't saying the Ku Klux ain't made mistakes and is going to make a whole hell of a lot more of them. But when you come right down to what you call citizenship and all like of that, don't let nobody tell you the Ku Klux ain't there."

Mr. Dyer — Why ain't no better order in the world than the Ku Klux — if they run it right.

Mr. Reddick — That's it. If they run it right.

Mr. Lee — I swear, it makes me sick to see how they run a fine order in the ground the way they do around here.

Mr. Pennell — Well men, I tell you. It's easy enough for us to set here and bellyache like we're doing about how they run it. But just jump in and try to run it oncet. Just try to run it oncet.

Mr. Funk — And specially a order what's trying to pull off something big, like the Ku Klux is. It's just like this fellow says to me, the one I was just now telling you about. "Funk," he says to me, "there's one thing they can't take away from the Ku Klux. It ain't no steamboat-picnic order. No sir. When the Ku Klux holds a picnic, they don't sell no roundtrip excursion tickets. That they don't."

Mr. Bassett — And another thing: That there singing. You ask me, I say that was a pretty doggone nice way to invite a fellow to church. I hope to git invited that way oncet. I'm here to say I do.

Mr. Lee — And this here dirty whelp ain't got no more appreciation than to sock it to them with a pump-gun. Six shots, men. Think of that. Them poor guys didn't have no more chance than a snowball in Hell.

Mr. Hagar — Yep. Ku Klux is all right. It sure is.

Mr. Wemple — You hear that, don't you, Moon?

Mr. Moon — Lemme alone. I ain't heared nothing.

Mr. Wemple — Listen at that! Listen at that! I swear, people that dumb, I don't see how they git put on a jury.

Mr. Lee — Why hell, Wemple, that's *why* they git put on a jury. Them lawyers figure the less sense they got the more lies they believe.

Mr. Wemple — Now listen at me, Moon. 'Cause if you don't git this straight you're libel to git Ku Kluxed before you ever git outen this room. Now first off, *effen* you git it straight, we ain't going to tell the judge what you done. Then maybe you won't have to go to jail.

Mr. Moon — Oh thank you. Thank you, Mr. Wemple.

Mr. Wemple — But that ain't all of it. When you go out of here, if you got to do any talking about what you heared in here, we want you to tell what you heared and not no damn lies like some of them does.

Mr. Moon — I won't say ary word, Mr. Wemple. I hope my die I won't.

Mr. Wemple — Well you might. Now you heared these gentlemen say, didn't you, that the Ku Klux is a fine order, one of the finest orders in the United States?

Mr. Moon — I sure did, Mr. Wemple. Ku Klux is a fine order. Yes, Mr. Wemple, I heared them say that. All of them.

Mr. Wemple — Now —

Mr. Hagar — Wait a minute Wemple. . . . You got that all straight, Moon?

Mr. Moon — Yep. Ku Klux is a fine order.

Mr. Hagar — Then, Wemple, if he done learned that, why look's like to me like he ain't going to learn no more. Not today. Just better let him hang on to that and call it a day.

Mr. Wemple — I expect you're right at that. Now, Moon, just to show you what a fine order we think the Ku Klux is, we're all going to chip in a dollar so you can git took in. Ain't we men?

All — We sure are.

There is a brisk digging into pockets. Mr. Wemple *collects the money and hands it over to* Mr. Moon.

Mr. Wemple — There you are, Moon. Ten dollars for to git took in the Ku Klux and a dollar to git yourself a pint of corn.

Mr. Moon — Thank you, Mr. Wemple. Thank you everybody. Thank you. Thank you.

Mr. Gail — Well, I reckon that's all

there is to it. Look to me like we're done.

Mr. Petry — This ain't no first-degree, men. This here is manslaughter. Fact of the matter, it might be self-defense, 'cepting I always say when a man gits killt, why the one that done it had ought to be found guilty of something. There's too many people getting killt lately.

Mr. Wemple — Well, Mr. Petry, that's all right with me. If it's all right with the rest of them. . . .

There is a moment of mumbling and nodding, which betokens assent.

Mr. Gail — Then it's manslaughter.

He pokes his head out of the door, gives a signal to a bailiff, and in a moment they are filing back to the courtroom.

Mr. Wemple — And that's something else I want to bring to your attention, Moon, old man. Up to the last minute, they was all for giving him first degree. . . .

All — And fact of the matter, I always did say the Ku Klux was all right, if they'd run it right. . . . Why sure, Ku Klux is a fine order. . . . You bet . . . Citizenship. . . . Patriotism. . . . All like of that. . . .

LETTER TO SAINT PETER

By Elma Dean

Let them in, Peter, they are very tired;
Give them the couches where the angels sleep.
Let them wake whole again to new dawns fired
With sun not war. And may their peace be deep.
Remember where the broken bodies lie . . .
And give them things they like. Let them make noise.
God knows how young they were to have to die!
Give swing bands, not gold harps, to these our boys.
Let them love, Peter, — they have had no time —
Girls sweet as meadow wind, with flowing hair . . .
They should have trees and bird song, hills to climb —
The taste of summer in a ripened pear.
Tell them how they are missed. Say not to fear;
It's going to be all right with us down here.

(November, 1942)

CONVENTION

By Theodore Dreiser

THIS story was told to me once by a very able newspaper cartoonist, and since it makes rather clear the powerfully repressive and often transforming force of convention, I set it down as something in the nature of an American social document. As he told it, it went something like this:

At one time I was a staff artist on the principal paper of one of the mid-western cities, a city on a river. It was, and remains to this hour, a typical American city. No change. It had a population then of between four and five hundred thousand. It had its clubs and churches and its conventional goings-on. It was an excellent and prosperous manufacturing city; nothing more.

On the staff with me at this time was a reporter whom I had known a little, but never intimately. I don't know whether I ought to bother to describe him or not — physically, I mean. His physique is unimportant to this story. But I think it would be interesting and even important to take him apart mentally and look at him, if one could — sort out the various components of his intellectual machinery, and so find out exactly how his intellectual processes proceeded. However, I can't do that; I have not the skill. Barring certain very superficial characteristics which I will mention, he was then and remains now a psychological mystery to me. He was what I would describe as superficially clever, a good writer of a good, practical, matter-of-fact story. He appeared to be well liked by those who were above him officially, and he could write Sunday feature stories of a sort, no one of which, as I saw it, ever contained a moving touch of color or a breath of real poetry. Some humor he had. He was efficient. He had a nose for news. He dressed quite well and he was not ill-looking — tall, thin, wiry, almost leathery. He had a quick, facile smile, a genial word-flow for all who knew him. He was the kind of man who was on practical and friendly terms with many men connected with the commercial organizations and clubs about town, from whom he extracted news bits from time to time. By the directing chiefs of the paper he was considered useful.

Well, this man and I were occasionally

THEODORE DREISER'S *place in the realm of the American novel and the short story is secure*. Sister Carrie, Jennie Gerhardt, An American Tragedy *and* Twelve Men, *to mention only four of his major works, are solid additions to American literature. Of his short stories, the one reprinted here is one of his finest*. (December, 1925)

sent out on the same assignment, he to write the story, I to make sketches — usually some Sunday feature story. Occasionally we would talk about whatever was before us — newspaper work, politics, the particular story in hand — but never enthusiastically or warmly about anything. He lacked what I thought was the poetic point of view. And yet, as I say, we were friendly enough. I took him about as any newspaper man takes another of the same staff who is in good standing.

Along in the spring or summer of the second year that I was on the paper the Sunday editor, to whom I was beholden in part for my salary, called me into his room and said that he had decided that Wallace Steele and myself were to do a feature story about the "love-boats" which plied Saturday and Sunday afternoons and every evening up and down the river for a distance of thirty-five miles or more. This distance, weather permitting, gave an opportunity to six or seven hundred couples on hot nights to escape the dry, sweltering heat of the city — and it was hot there in the summer — and to enjoy the breezes and dance, sometimes by the light of Chinese lanterns, sometimes by the light of the full moon. It was delightful. Many thousands took advantage of the opportunity.

It was delicious to me, then in the prime of youth and ambition, to sit on the hurricane or "spoon" deck, as our Sunday editor called it, and study not only the hundreds of boys and girls, but also the older men and women, who came principally to make love, though secondarily to enjoy the river and the air, to brood over the picturesque grouping of the trees, bushes, distant cabins and bluffs which rose steeply from the river, to watch the great cloud of smoke that trailed back over us, to see the two halves of the immense steel walking beam chuff-chuffing up and down, and to listen to the drive of the water-wheel behind. This was in the days before the automobile, and any such pleasant means of getting away from the city was valued much more than it is now.

II

But to return to this Sunday editor and his orders. I was to make sketches of spooning couples, or at least of two or three small distinctive groups with a touch of romance in them. Steele was to tell how the love-making went on. This, being an innocent method of amusement and relief from the humdrum, was looked upon with suspicion if not actual disfavor by the wiseacres of the paper, as well as by the conservatives of the city, as a phase of loose if not immoral life. True conservatives would not so indulge themselves. The real object of the Sunday editor was to get something into his paper that would have a little kick to it. We were, without exaggerating the matter in any way, to shock the conservatives by a little picture of life and love, which, however innocent, was none-the-less taboo in that city. The story was to suggest, as I understood it, loose living, low ideals and the like. These outings did not have the lockstep of business or religion in them.

Well, to proceed. No sooner had the order been given than Steele came to me to talk it over. He liked the idea very much. It was a good Sunday subject. Those boats were full of eager spooning couples. He knew it. Beside, it was hot — very — in the city just at that time, and the opportunity for an outing appealed to him. We were to go on the boat that left the wharf at the foot of Beach street at eight o'clock that evening. He had been told to write anything from fifteen hundred to two thousand words. If I made three good sketches, that would make almost a three-fourths page special. He would make his story as lively and colorful as he could. He was not a little flattered, I am sure, by having been called to interpret such a gay, risqué scene.

It was about one-thirty when we had been called in. About four o'clock he came to me again. We had, as I had assumed, tentatively agreed to meet at the wharf entrance and do the thing together. By now, however, he had another plan. Perhaps I should say here that up to that moment I only vaguely knew that he had a wife and child and that he lived with them somewhere in the southwestern section of the city, whether in his own home or a rooming-house, I did not know. Come to think of it, just before this I believe I had heard him remark to others that his wife was out of the city. At any rate, he now said that since his wife was out of the city and as the woman of whom they rented their rooms was a lonely, and a poor, person who seldom got out anywhere, he had decided to bring her along for the outing. I needn't wait for him. He would see me on the boat, or we could discuss the story later.

I agreed to this and was prepared to think nothing of it except for one thing. His manner of telling me had something about it, or there was some mood or thought in connection with it in his own mind, which reached me telepathically, and caused me to think that he was taking advantage of his wife's absence to go out somewhere with someone else. And yet, at that, I could not see why I thought about it. The thing had no real interest for me. And I had not the least proof and wanted none. As I say, I was not really interested. I did not know his wife at all. I did not care for him or her. I did not care whether he flirted with someone else or not. Still, this silly, critical thought passed through my mind, put into it by him, I am sure, because he was thinking — at least, might have been thinking — that I might regard it as strange that he should appear anywhere with another woman than his wife. Apart from this, and before this, seeing him buzzing about here and there, and once talking to a girl on a street corner near the *Mail* office, I had only the vague notion that, married or not, he was a young man who was not averse to slipping away for an hour or two with some girl, provided no one else knew it, especially his wife.

At any rate, seven o'clock coming, I had my dinner at a little restaurant near the office and went to the boat. It was a hot night, but clear and certain to bring a lovely full moon, and I was glad to be going. At the same time, I was not a little lonely and out of sorts with myself because I had no girl and was wishing that I had, — wishing that some lovely girl was hanging on my arm and that now we two could go down to the boat together and sit on the spoon deck and look at the moon, or that we could dance on the cabin deck below, where were all the lights and musicians. My hope, if not my convinced expectation, was that somewhere on this boat I, too, should find someone who would be interested in me — I, too, should be able to sit about with the others and laugh and make love. But I didn't. The thought was futile. I was not a ladies' man, and few if any girls ever looked at me. Beside, women and girls usually came accompanied on a trip like this. I went alone, and I returned alone.

III

Brooding in this fashion, I went aboard along with the earliest of the arrivals, and, going to the cabin deck, sat down and watched the others approach. It was one of my opportunities to single out interesting groups for my pen. And there were many. They came, so blithe, so very merry, all of them, in pairs or groups of four or six or eight or ten, boys and girls of the tenements and the slums — a few older couples among them, — but all smiling and chatting, the last ones hurrying excitedly to make the boat, and each boy with his girl, as I was keen to note, and each girl with her beau. I singled out this group and that, making a few idle notes on my pad, just suggestions of faces, hats, gestures, swings of the body. There was a strong light over the gangway, and I could sketch there. It was interesting, but, being alone, I was not very happy about it.

In the midst of these, along with the latter half of the crowd, came Steele and his lonely landlady, to whom, as he said, this proffer on his part was a kindness. Because of what he had said I was expecting a woman who would be somewhat of a frump — at least thirty-five or forty years old and not very attractive. But to my surprise, as they came up the long gangplank, I saw a woman who could not have been more than twenty-seven or eight — and pretty, very. She had on a wide, floppy lacy hat of black or dark blue, but for contrast a pale, cream-colored, flouncy dress. And she was graceful and plump and agreeable in every way.

The bounder! I thought. To think that he should be able to interest so charming a girl, and in the absence of his wife! And I could get none! He had gone home and changed to a better suit, straw hat, cane and all, whereas I — I — dub! — had come as I was. No wonder no really interesting girl would look at me. Fool! But I remained in position studying the entering throng until the last couple was on. I heard the cries of "Heave off, there!" "Careful!" "Hurry with that gangplank!" Soon we were in midstream. The jouncy, tinny music had begun long before, and the couples, scores and scores of them, were already dancing on the cabin deck, while I was left to hang about the bar or saunter through the crowd, looking for types when I didn't want to be anywhere but close beside some girl on the spoon deck, who would hang on my arm, laugh into my eyes, and jest and dance with me.

Because of what he had said, I did not expect Steele to come near me, and he didn't. In sauntering about the two decks looking for arresting scenes I did not see him. Because I wanted at least one or two spoon deck scenes, I finally fixed on a couple that was half-hidden in the shadow back of the pilot-house. They had crumpled themselves up forward of an air-vent and not far from the two smoke-stacks and under the walking-beam, which rose and fell above them. The full moon was just above the eastern horizon, offering a circular background for them, and I thought they made a romantic picture outlined against it. I could not see their faces — just their outlines. Her head was upon his shoulder. His face was turned, and so concealed, and inclined toward hers. Her hat had been taken off and was held over her knee by one hand. I stepped back a little toward a companionway, where was a light, in order to outline my impression. When I returned, they were sitting up. It was Steele and his rooming-house proprietress! It struck me as odd that of all the couple and group scenes that I had noted, the most romantic should have been that provided by Steele and this woman. His wife would be interested in his solicitude for her loneliness and her lack of opportunities to get out into the open air, I was sure. Yet, I was not envious then — just curious and a little amused.

Well, that was the end of that. The sketches were made, and the story published. Because he and this girl had provided my best scene I disguised it a little, making it not seem exactly back of the pilot-house, since otherwise he might recognize it. He was, for once, fascinated by the color and romance of the occasion, and did a better story than I thought he could. It dwelt on the beauty of the river, the loveliness of the moon, the dancing. I thought it was very good for him, and I thought I knew the reason why.

And then one day, about a month or six weeks later, being in the city room, I encountered the wife of Steele and their little son, a child of about five years. She had stopped in about three or four in the afternoon, being downtown shopping, I presume. After seeing him with the young woman on the steamer, I was, I confess, not a little shocked. This woman was so pinched, so homely, so faded — veritably a rail of a woman, everything and anything that a woman, whether wife, daughter, mother or sweetheart, as I saw it then, should not be. As a matter of fact, I was too wrought up about love and youth and marriage and happiness at that time to rightly judge of the married. At any rate, after having seen that other woman on that deck with Steele, I was offended by this one.

She seemed to me, after the other, too narrow, too methodical, too commonplace, too humdrum. She was a woman whose pulchritudinous favors, whatever they may have been, must have been lost at the altar. In heaven's name, I thought to myself, how could a man like this come to marry such a woman? He isn't so very good-looking himself, perhaps, but still . . . No wonder he wanted to take his rooming-house landlady for an outing! I would, too. I could understand it now. In fact, as little as I cared for Steele, I felt sorry that a man of his years and of his still restless proclivities should be burdened with such a wife. And not only that, but there was their child, looking not unlike him but more like her, one of those hostages to fortune by reason of which it is never easy to free oneself from the error of a mistaken marriage. His plight, as I saw it, was indeed unfortunate.

Well, I was introduced by him as the man who worked on some of his stories with him. I noticed that the woman had a thin, almost a falsetto voice. She eyed me, as I thought, unintelligently, yet genially enough. I was invited to come out to their place some Sunday and take dinner. Because of his rooming-house story I was beginning to wonder whether he had been lying to me, when she went on to explain that they had been boarding up to a few weeks ago, but had now taken a cottage for themselves and could have their friends. I promised. Yes, yes. But I never went, — not to dinner, anyhow.

IV

Then two more months passed. By now it was late fall, with winter near. The current news, as I saw it, was decidedly humdrum. There was no local news to speak of. I scarcely glanced at the papers from day to day, no more than to see whether some particular illustration I had done was in and satisfactory or not. But then, of a sudden, came something which was genuine news. Steele's wife was laid low by a box of poisoned candy sent her through the mails, some of which she had eaten!

Just how the news of this first reached the papers I have almost forgotten now, but my recollection is that there was another newspaper man and his wife — a small editor or reporter on another paper — who lived in the same vicinity, and that it was to this newspaper man's wife that Mrs. Steele, after having called her in, confided that she believed she had been poisoned, and by a woman whose name she now gave as Mrs. Marie Davis, and with whom, as she then announced, her husband had long been intimate — the lady of the Steamer *Ira Ramsdell*. She had recognized the handwriting on the package from some letters written to her husband, but only after she had eaten of the candy and felt the pains — not before. Her condition was serious. She was, it appeared, about to die. In this predicament she had added, so it was said, that she had long been neglected by her husband for this other woman, but that she had suffered in silence rather than bring disgrace upon him, herself and their child. Now this cruel blow!

Forthwith a thrill of horror and sympathy passed over the city. It seemed too sad. At the same time a cry went up to find the other woman — arrest her, of course — see if she had really done it. There followed the official detention, if not legal arrest, of Mrs. Davis on suspicion of being the poisoner. Although the charge was not as yet proved, she was at once thrown into jail, and there held to await the death or recovery of Mrs. Steele, and the proof or disproof of the charge that the candy had been sent by her. And cameras in hand, reporters and artists were packed off to the jail to hear her side of the story.

As I had at once suspected on hearing

the news, she proved to be none other than the lady of the *Ira Ramsdell*, and as charming as I had at first assumed her to be. I, being one of those sent to sketch her, was among the first to hear her story. She denied, and very vehemently, that she had sent any poisoned candy to anyone. She had never dreamed of any such thing. But she did not deny, which at the time appeared to me to be incriminating, that she had been and was then in love with Steele. In fact, and this point interested me as much then as afterwards, she declared that this was an exceptional passion — her love for him, his love for her — and no mere passing and vulgar intimacy. A high and beautiful thing — a sacred love, the one really true and beautiful thing that had ever come to her — or him — in all their lives. And he would say so, too. For before meeting her, Wallace Steele had been very unhappy — oh, very. And her own marriage had been a failure.

Wallace, as she now familiarly called him, had confessed to her that this new, if secret love, meant everything to him. His wife did not interest him. He had married her at a time when he did not know what he was doing, and before he had come to be what he was. But this new love had resolved all their woes into loveliness — complete happiness. They had resolved to cling only to each other for life. There was no sin in what they had done because they loved. Of course, Wallace had sought to induce Mrs. Steele to divorce him, but she would not; otherwise they would have been married before this. But as Mrs. Steele would not give him up, both had been compelled to make the best of it. But to poison her — that was wild! A love so beautiful and true as theirs did not need a marriage ceremony to sanctify it. So she raved. My own impression at the time was that she was a romantic woman who was really very greatly in love.

Now as to Steele. Having listened to this blazoning of her passion by herself, the interviewers naturally hurried to Steele to see what he would have to say. In contrast to her and her grand declaration, they found a man, as every one agreed, who was shaken to the very marrow of his bones by these untoward events. He was, it appeared, a fit inhabitant of the environment that nourished him. He was in love, perhaps, with this woman, but still, as anyone could see, he was not so much in love that, if this present business was going to cost him his place in his commonplace, conventional world, he would not be able to surrender her. He was horrified by the revelation of his own treachery. Up to this hour, no doubt, he had been slipping about, hoping not to be caught, and most certainly not wishing to be cast out for sin. Regardless of the woman, he did not wish to be cast out now. On the contrary, as it soon appeared, he had been doing his best in the past to pacify his wife and hold her to silence while he slaked his thirst for romance in this other way. He did not want his wife, but he did not want trouble, either. And now that his sin was out he shivered.

In short, as he confided to one of the men who went to interview him, and who agreed to respect his confidence to that extent, he was not nearly so much in love with Mrs. Davis as she thought he was — poor thing! He had been infatuated for only a little while. She was pretty, of course, and naturally she thought she loved him — but he never expected anything like this to happen. Great cripes! They had met at a river bathing-beach the year before. He had been smitten — well, you know. — He had never got along well with his wife, but there was the little boy to consider. He had not intended any harm to anyone; far from it. And he certainly couldn't turn on his wife now. The public wouldn't stand for it. But he could scarcely be expected to turn on Mrs. Davis, either, could he, now that she was in jail, and suspected of sending poisoned candy to his wife? The public wouldn't stand for that, either.

It was terrible! Pathetic! He certainly would not have thought that Marie would go to the length of sending his wife poison, and he didn't really believe that she had. Still — and there may have been some actual doubt of her in that "still," or so the reporting newspaper men thought. At any rate, as he saw it now, he would have to stick to his wife until she was out of danger. Public opinion compelled it. The general impression of the newspaper men was that he was a coward. As one of them said of his courage, "Gee, it's oozing out of his hair!"

Nevertheless, he did go to see Mrs. Davis several times. But apart from a reported sobbing demonstration of affection on her part, I never learned what passed between them. He would not talk and she had been cautioned not to. Also, there were various interviews with his wife, who had not died, and now that the storm was on, admitted that she had intercepted letters between her husband and Mrs. Davis from time to time. The handwriting on the candy wrapper the day she received it so resembled the handwriting of Mrs. Davis that after she had eaten of it and the symptoms of poisoning had set in — not before —, she had begun to suspect that the candy must have emanated from Mrs. Davis.

V

In the meantime Mrs. Davis, despite the wife's sad story, was the major attraction in the newspapers. She was young, she was beautiful, she had made, or at least attempted to make, a blood sacrifice on the altar of love. What more could a daily newspaper want? She was a heroine, even in this very moral, conservative, conventional and religious city. The rank and file were agog — even sympathetic. (How would the moralists explain that, would you say?) In consequence of their interest, she was descended upon by a corps of those women newspaper writers who, even in that day, were known as sob-sisters, and whose business it was to psychologize and psychiatrize the suspect, — to dig out, if they could, not only every vestige of her drama, but all her hidden and secret motives.

As I read the newspapers at the time, they revealed that she was, and she was not, a neurotic, a psychotic, who showed traces of being a shrewd, evasive and designing woman, and who did not. Also she was a soft, unsophisticated, passionate and deeply-illusioned girl, and she was not. She was guilty, of course — maybe not — but very likely she was, and she must tell how, why, in what mood, etc. Also, it appeared that she had sent the poison deliberately, coldly, murderously. Her eyes and hands, also the shape of her nose and ears, showed it. Again, these very things proved she could not have done it. Had she been driven to it by stress of passionate emotion? Was she responsible? Of course she was! Who is not responsible for his deeds? A great, overwhelming, destroying love passion, indeed! Rot! She could help it. She could not help it. Could she help it? So it went.

Parallel with all this, of course, we were treated to various examinations of the Steele family. What sort of people were they, anyhow? It was said of Steele now that he was an average, fairly capable newspaper man of no very startling ability, but of no particular vices — one who had for some years been a serious and faithful employé of this paper. Mrs. Steele, on the other hand, was a good woman, but by no means prepossessing. She was without romance, imagination, charm. One could see by looking at her, and then looking at so winsome and enticing a woman as Mrs. Davis, why Steele had strayed. It was the old eternal triangle — the woman who was not interesting, the woman who was interesting, and the man interested by the more interesting woman. There was no solving it, but it was all very sad. One could not help sympathizing with Mrs. Steele, the wronged woman; and again one could not help sympathizing with Mrs. Davis, the beautiful, passionate, helpless beauty.

In the meantime, the District Attorney's office having taken the case in hand, there were various developments in that quarter. It was necessary to find out, of course, where the candy had been purchased, how it had been drugged, with what it had been drugged, where the drug had been purchased. Chemists, detectives and handwriting experts were all set to work. It was no trouble to determine that the drug was arsenic, yet where this arsenic was purchased was not so easy to discover. It was some time before it was found where it had been procured. Dissimilarly, it was comparatively easy to prove where the candy had come from. It had been sent in the original box of a well-known candy firm. Yet just who had purchased it was not quite so easy to establish. The candy company could not remember, and Mrs. Davis, although admitting that the handwriting did resemble hers, denied ever having addressed the box or purchased any candy from the firm in question. She was quite willing to go there and be identified, but no clerk in the candy-store was able to identify her. There were one or two clerks who felt sure that there had been a woman there at some time or other who had looked like her, but they were not positive. However, there was one girl who had worked in the store during the week in which the candy had been purchased, and who was not there any longer. This was a new girl who had been tried out for that week only and had since disappeared. Her name was known, of course, and the District Attorney began looking for her.

There were some whispers to the effect

that not only Mrs. Davis but Steele himself might have been concerned in the plot, or Steele alone, since apparently he had been anxious to get rid of his wife. Why not? He might have imitated the handwriting of Mrs. Davis or created an accidental likeness to it. Also, there were dissenting souls, even in the office of the paper on which I worked, who thought that maybe Mrs. Steele had sent the candy to herself in order to injure the other woman. Why not? It was possible. Women were like that. There had been similar cases, had there not? Argument! Contention! "She might have wanted to die and be revenged on the other woman at the same time, might she not?" observed the railroad editor. "Oh, hell! What bunk!" called another. "No woman would kill herself to make a place for a rival. That's crazy." "Well," said a third, "she might have miscalculated the power of her own dope. Who knows? She may not have intended to take as much as she did." "Oh, Christ," called a fourth from somewhere, "just listen to the Sherlock Holmes Association! Lay off, will you?"

A week or more went by, and then the missing girl who had worked in the candy-store was found. She had left the city the following week and gone to Denver. Being shown the pictures of Mrs. Davis, Mrs. Steele and some others and asked whether on any given day she had sold any of them a two-pound box of candy, she seemed to recall no one of them save possibly Mrs. Steele. But she could not be sure from the photograph. She would have to see the woman. In consequence, and without any word to the newspapers who had been leading the case up to then, this girl was returned to the city. Here, in the District Attorney's office, she was confronted by a number of women gathered for the occasion, among whom was placed Mrs. Davis. But on looking them all over she failed to identify any one of them. Then Mrs. Steele, who was by then up and around, was sent for. She came, along with a representative of the office. On sight, as she entered the door, and although there were other women in the room at the time, this girl exclaimed: "There she is! That's the woman! Yes, that's the very woman!" She was positive.

VI

As is customary in such cases, and despite the sympathy that had been extended to her, she was turned over to the police, who soon extracted the truth from her. She broke down and wept hysterically.

It was she who had purchased the candy. Her life was going to pieces. She had wanted to die, so she said now. She had addressed the wrapper about the candy, as some of the wiseacres of our paper had contended, only she had first made a tracing on the paper from Mrs. Davis' handwriting, on an envelope addressed to her husband, and had then copied that. She had put not arsenic, but rat poison, bought some time before, into the candy, and in order to indict Mrs. Davis, she had put a little in each piece, about as much as would kill a rat, so that it would seem as though the entire box had been poisoned by her. She had got the idea from a case she had read about years before in a newspaper. She hated Mrs. Davis for stealing her husband. She had followed them.

When she had eaten one of the pieces of candy she had thought, as she now insisted, that she was taking enough to make an end of it all. But before taking it she had made sure that Mrs. Dalrymple, the wife of the newspaper man whom she first called to her aid, was at home in order that she might call or send her little boy. Her purpose in doing this was to give Mrs. Dalrymple the belief that it was Mrs. Davis who had sent the poison. When she was gone, Mrs. Davis would be punished, her husband would not be able to have her, and she herself would be out of her misery.

Result: the prompt discharge of Mrs. Davis, but no charge against Mrs. Steele. According to the District Attorney and the newspapers who most truly reflected local sentiment, she had suffered enough. And, as the state of public feeling then was, the District Attorney would not have dared to punish her. Her broken confession so reacted on the public mind that now, and for all time, it was for Mrs. Steele, just as a little while before it was rather for Mrs. Davis. For, you see, it was now proved that it was Mrs. Steele and not Mrs. Davis who had been wrought up to the point where she had been ready and willing — had actually tried — to make a blood sacrifice of herself and another woman on the altar of love. In either case it was the blood sacrifice that lay at the bottom of the public's mood, and caused it to turn sympathetically to that one who had been most willing to murder in the cause of love.

But don't think this story is quite ended. Far from it. There is something else here, and a very interesting something to which I wish to call your attention. I have said that the newspapers turned favorably to Mrs. Steele. They did. So did the sob-sisters, those true barometers of public moods. Eulogies were now heaped upon Mrs. Steele, her devotion, her voiceless, unbearable woe, her intended sacrifice of herself. She was now the darling of these journalistic pseudo-analysts.

As for Mrs. Davis — not a word of sympathy, let alone praise or understanding for her thereafter. Almost unmentioned, if you will believe it, she was, and at once, allowed to slip back into the limbo of the unheralded, the subsequently-to-be-unknown. From then on it was almost as though she had never been. For a few weeks she retired to the home in which she had lived; then she disappeared entirely.

But now as to Steele. Here was the third peculiar phase of the case. Subsequent to the exculpation of Mrs. Davis and her noiseless retirement from the scene, what would you say his attitude would have been, or should have been? Where would he go? What do? What attitude would he assume? One of renewed devotion to his wife? One of renewed devotion to Mrs. Davis? One of disillusion or indifference in regard to all things? It puzzled me, and I was a rank outsider with no least concern, except, of course, our general concern in all such things, so vital to all of us in our sex and social lives. Not only was it a puzzle to me; it was also a puzzle to others, especially the editors and city editors and managing editors who had been following the wavering course of things with uncertain thoughts and I may say uncertain policy. They had been, as you may guess, as prepared to hang Steele as not, assuming that he had been identified with Mrs. Davis in a plot to do away with his wife. On the other hand, now that that shadow was removed and it was seen to be a more or less simple case of varietism on his part, resulting in marital unhappiness for his wife and a desire on her part to die, they were prepared to look upon him and this result with a more kindly eye. After all, she was not dead. Mrs. Davis had been punished. And say what you will, looking at Mrs. Steele as she was, and at Mrs. Davis as she was — well — with a certain amount of material if not spiritual provocation — what would you?

Indeed, the gabble about the newspaper offices was all to the above effect. What, if anything, finally asked some of the city editors and managing editors, was to be done about Steele? Now that everything had blown over, what of him? Go on hounding him forever? Nonsense! It was scarcely fair, and anyhow, no longer profitable or worth while. Now that the storm was passing, might not something be done for him? After all, he had been a fairly respectable newspaper man and in good standing. Why not take him back? And if not that, how was he to be viewed in the future by his friends? Was he to be let alone, dropped, forgotten, or what? Was he going to stay here in G———, and fight it out, or leave? And if he was going to leave or stay, with whom was he going to leave or stay?

VII

The thing to do, it was finally decided among several of those on our paper and several on other papers who had known him more or less intimately, was to go to Steele himself, and ask him, not for publicity but just between ourselves, what was to be done, what he proposed to do, whether there was anything now that the local newspapers could say or do which would help him in any way? Did he want to be restored to a staff position? Was he going to stick by his wife? What, if anything, and with no malicious intent, should they say about Mrs. Davis? In a more or less secret and brotherly or professional spirit they were going to put it up to him, doing whatever they could in accordance with what he might wish.

Accordingly, two of the local newsmen whom he quite honestly respected visited him and placed the above several propositions before him. They found him, as I was told afterwards, seated upon the front porch of the very small and commonplace house in which after the dismissal of the charge against his wife, he and she had been dwelling, reading a paper. Seated with him was Mrs. Steele, thinner and more querulous and anæmic and unattractive than ever before. And upon the lot outside was their little son. Upon their arrival, they hailed Steele for a private word, and Mrs. Steele arose and went into the house. She looked, said one of these men, as though she expected more trouble. Steele, on his part was all smiles and genial tenderings of hospitality. He was hoping for the best, of course, and he was anxious to do away with any new source of trouble. He even rubbed his hands, and licked his lips. "Come right in, boys. Come on up on the porch. Wait a minute and I'll bring out a couple of chairs." He hastened away but quickly returned, determined, as they thought, to make as good an impression as possible.

After he had heard what they had come for, — most tactfully and artfully put, of course — he was all smiles, eager, apparently, to be well thought of once more. To their inquiry as to whether he proposed to remain or not, he replied: "Yes, for the present." He had not much choice. He had not saved enough money in recent days to permit him to do much of anything else, and his wife's illness and other things had used up about all he had. "And now, just between ourselves, Steele," asked one of the two men who knew him better than the other, "what about Mrs. Davis and your wife? Just where do you stand in regard to them? Are you going to stick to your wife or are you going with the other woman eventually? No trouble for you, you understand — no more publicity. But the fellows in the papers are in a little bit of a quandary in regard to this. They don't intend to publish anything more — nothing disparaging. They only want to get your slant on the thing so that if anything more does come up they can fix it so that it won't be offensive to you, you see."

"Yes, I see," replied Steele cheerfully and without much reflection. "But so far as that Davis woman is concerned, though, you can forget her. I'm through with her. She was never much to me, anyhow, just a common ———." Here he used the good old English word for prostitute. As for his wife, he was going to stick by her, of course. She was a good woman. She loved him. There was his little boy. He was through with all that varietistic stuff. There was nothing to it. A man couldn't get away with it — and so on.

The two men, according to their account of it afterward, winced not a little, for, as they said, they had thought from all that had gone before that there had surely been much more than common prostitution between Steele and the woman. How could all this have been in the face of Mrs. Steele's great jealousy, Mrs. Davis's passionate declaration about pure, spiritual and undying love? Imagine it! After a few more words the men left, convinced that Steele was no longer interested in Mrs. Davis, but was interested in his wife — "yet," as one of them afterward expressed it, "with a sense of something unpleasant about it all." Just why had he changed so quickly? That was the question. Why the gratuitous insult to Mrs. Davis? Why, after the previous acknowledgment of an affection of sorts at least for her, was he now willing to write himself down a cad in that open and offensive way? For a cad he plainly was. This was at once and generally agreed upon. Mrs. Davis could not be as shabby as he had made her out. That finally fixed Steele's position in G——— as a bounder. He was never taken back on any local staff.

For myself, however, I could not quite fathom it. The thing haunted me. What was it that moved him — public opinion, fear of the loss of the petty social approval which had once been his, sorrow for his wife — what one special thing that Mrs. Davis might or might not have done? For certainly, as things turned out, she had been guilty of nothing except loving him — illegally, of course, but loving him. My mind involuntarily flashed back to the two curled abaft the pilot-house in the moonlight. And now this! And then there was dancing and laughter and love.

VIII

But even this is not the end, however ready you may be to cease listening. There is an *envoi* that I must add. This was seven years later. By then I had removed to New York and established myself as a cartoonist. From others I had learned that Steele also had come to New York and was now connected with one of the local papers — copy reading, I think. At any rate, I met him — one Sunday. It was near the entrance of the Bronx Zoo, at closing time. He was there with his wife and a second little son that had come to him since he had left G ———. The first one — a boy of ten by then, I presume, — was not present. All this I learned in a brief conversation.

But his wife! I can never forget her. She was so worn, so faded, so impossible. And this other boy by her — a son who had followed after their reunion! My God! I thought, how may not fear or convention slay one emotionally! And to cap it all, he was not so much apologetic as — I will not say defiant — but ingratiating and volubly explanatory about his safe and sane retreat from gayety and freedom, and, if you will, immorality. For he knew, of course, that I recalled the other case — all its troublesome and peculiar details.

"My wife! My wife!" he exclaimed quickly, since I did not appear to recognize her at first, and with a rather grandiose gesture of the hand, as who should say, "I am proud of my wife, as you see. I am still married to her and rightly so. I am not the same person you knew in G ———."

"Oh, yes," I replied covering them all with a single glance. "I remember your wife very well. And your boy."

"Oh, no, not that boy," he hastened to explain. "That was Harry. This is another little boy — Francis." And then, as though to reëstablish his ancient social prestige with me, he proceeded to add: "We're living over on Staten Island now — just at the north end, near the ferry, you know. You must come down some time. It's a pleasant ride. We'll both be so glad to see you. Won't we, Estelle?"

"Yes, certainly," said Mrs. Steele.

I hastened away as quickly as possible. The contrast was too much; that damned memory of mine, illegitimate as it may seem to be, was too much. I could not help thinking of the *Ira Ramsdell* and of how much I had envied him the dances, the love, the music, the moonlight.

"By God!" I exclaimed as I walked away. "By God!"

And that is exactly how I feel now about all such miscarriages of love and delight — cold and sad.

AMERICANA

ARKANSAS

FROM THE St. Louis *Post-Dispatch:*

Questioned in Police Court as to whether he had been born in this country, J. W. McCluskey, 4201A Manchester Avenue, a defendant in a peace disturbance case, responded, "No, sir, I was born in Arkansas."
(April, 1926)

CALIFORNIA

FROM the San Francisco *Chronicle:*

Daylight saving time . . . is blasphemy. . . . There is nothing said in the Bible about putting clocks ahead in the summer. . . .
MRS. E. T. WILSON
(October, 1925)

DISTRICT OF COLUMBIA

DISPATCH from Washington to the eminent Pittsburgh *Press:*

Senator Heflin startled disciples of Darwin by pointing out that not a single monkey, gorilla or chimpanzee in zoölogical gardens in hundreds of years has produced an offspring that developed into a human being. He claimed his citation was absolute proof that the theory of evolution is fallacious.
(January, 1928)

GEORGIA

DIVERTISSEMENT of Southern belles, as revealed by the Savannah *News:*

A chewing gum party will be given at high noon at Nunnally's.
(October, 1925)

WANT AD in the Atlanta *Journal:*

WANTED — At once, a sick stenographer who is willing to work 3 hours each day for her good board and bed at the most beautiful and healthy summer resort in the world. We are not interested in your present occupation nor your previous condition of servitude. You must come highly recommended and of excellent character and know your onions. Even long dresses will not bar you, nor the color of your eyes or hair. Even false teeth are permissible. No flapper will be considered. My wife don't like it. I had one once, never again. Write Patterson's Boat House, Lakemont, Ga., on Lake Rabun.

"THE DIMPLE IN GEORGIA'S CHEEK"
(November, 1929)

INCIDENT in the life of W. B. Townsend, editor of the Dahlonega *Nugget:*

Recently we bought us a new cheap shirt but found the trade very unsatisfactory, because when it was washed the garment drew up so we had to tie the collar as close together as possible with a string, and we could not meet any company with the proper politeness because when making a bow the tail of our shirt flew up out over our pants behind. So we sent it to the chicken house, hoping that there is enough cloth in it for a hen's nest. We trust none of the ladies will get hold of a dress made

---

AMERICANA *was one of the most hilarious and original departments in* THE AMERICAN MERCURY *and the repository of much of the country's rich native humor. Nothing like it had ever before appeared in a quality magazine. Future historians will find the department a valuable source for an insight into some aspects of American life in the twenties and thirties.*

of cloth that will draw up like our shirt did. (June, 1930)

The passion for service in Emanuel county, as revealed by two political cards in the same column of the Swainsboro *Forest Blade*:

FOR TREASURER

I am a candidate for treasurer for Emanuel county, subject to the recently ordered primary. I want the office because it's fairly good pay with little work, but if elected I will do that little as it should be done. I solicit the support of all parties.
Edd. C. Brown.

I am a candidate for treasurer of Emanuel county, subject to a Democratic white primary. I am old and unable to work for a living is why I want the office. I earnestly solicit the support of all voters, and promise, if elected, to merit your confidence.
A. J. Rich.
(September, 1927)

Political announcement in the eminent Augusta *Chronicle*:

Vote for
JOHN B. CHAVOUS, JR.
for
CITY COUNCIL
5th Ward
I know I'm not much
but why vote for less?
(June, 1929)

ILLINOIS

The Rev. Dr. John T. Braber Smith, of the World Service Commission of the Methodist Episcopal Church, with headquarters in Chicago, as reported by the Sioux City, Ia., *Journal*:

The Bible continues to be the only real textbook on advertising. (June, 1928)

IOWA

New champion discovered in Des Moines:

Gene Mathews can spit farther than any other member of the Junior Chamber of Commerce. He won the standing broad spit at the picnic held by the organization at Grand View Park. (October, 1925)

KANSAS

The Altoona *Tribune* makes an announcement to its readers:

Ten cents straight will be charged for all obituary notices to all business men who do not advertise while living. Delinquent subscribers will be charged fifteen cents per line for an obituary notice. Advertisers and cash subscribers will receive as good a send-off as we are capable of writing, without any charge whatever. Better send in your subscription, as the hog cholera is abroad in the land. (January, 1928)

Sermon — subject at the Baptist Church of Cherryvale:
CAN A BOBBED HAIRED WOMAN GO TO HEAVEN? (June, 1930)

KENTUCKY

Announcement of a servant of the people of Laurel county, in the London *Sentinel-Echo*:

To the Voters of Laurel County:
I am a candidate for the office of jailer of Laurel county, subject to the action of the Republican primary.

If elected your jailer I will not let any turnkey among the prisoners with a pistol or the keys to the outside door, and if elected I will spend enough money to make a doctor out of my son, Caleb McFadden, and I will buy all the stuff I can use from the man who needs the money. I will doctor the people free of charge. I am the only man in Laurel county that can cure all kinds of cancers and some other diseases.

You help me and I will help you, it costs you nothing but a cross mark to help me, but it costs me money to help you. The poor man's friend,
BUD MCFADDEN.
(June, 1929)

LOUISIANA

MORAL dictum of the Rev. H. J. McCool, pastor of the Istrouma Baptist Church, in the up-and-coming town of Baton Rouge:

> I am not against bathing. I believe that we should at least take a bath once a month. But . . . I am coming to believe that mixed bathing is one of our future problems. . . . I doubt seriously if we can retain virtuous thoughts when the whole community is in bathing together.
> (October, 1925)

NEW YORK

OFFICIAL pronouncement of the Hon. Richard C. Ellsworth, secretary of St. Lawrence University, as reported by the enterprising *Plaindealer* of Canton:

> President Coolidge is as nearly . . . a superman as any man can well be.
> (October, 1925)

THE Rt. Rev. William T. Manning, S.T.D., D.D., as reported in the Manhattan press:

> Football is one of the highest forms of spiritual exercise.
> (April, 1926)

A READER of the celebrated Schenectady *Union-Star* protests against an injustice done him by that paper:

> I noticed you printed George W. Herath as being fined $1,000 and 45 days in jail for selling intoxicating liquors at my place of business, 111 Washington avenue. The $1,000 fine was true but the 45 days was not. It is hard enough to keep one's character clean in my business without being misquoted in the newspapers. So please instruct your editor to check articles more carefully.
> *Very truly yours,*
> GEORGE W. HERATH.
(July, 1930)

OHIO

HISTORICAL pronunciamento by the Hon. Brooks Fletcher, editorial writer on the *Tribune*, published at Marion, late home of the lamented Dr. Harding:

> Jesus was the first Chautauqua orator.
> (October, 1925)

OREGON

DEFENSE of an immortal, as set forth in the *Lariat*, published at Portland:

> Close up the churches and schools, burn up every volume of Shakespeare with its forceful and faultless English, but let Eddie Guest write on and on; let his songs that bring smiles, then tears, be sung in every household, and our nation will not go wrong.
> AGNES JUST REID
(October, 1925)

PENNSYLVANIA

DR. JOHN HOWARD DICKASON, addressing the Uniontown Kiwanis Club, as reported by the *Morning Herald* of the same great town:

> Baseball will be taught in Heaven.
> (June, 1929)

ADVICE to the lovelorn in a recent calendar of the Sacred Heart Church, of Pittsburgh:

> IF YOUR GENTLEMAN FRIEND IS NOT INCLUDED IN THE LIST OF CONTRIBUTING MEMBERS OF THE PARISH, MABEL, "GIVE HIM THE GATE," FOR HE IS A FOUR-

FLUSHER, AND IF HE CHEATS GOD, HE WILL CHEAT YOU!
(October, 1925)

NORTH CAROLINA

Advice to aspiring Methodist clergymen, given by Bishop Collins Denny:

If you would keep your sex before the public, grow hair upon your upper lip. Women now cut their hair and wear men's clothes, but they cannot grow a mustache. That is your badge of masculinity.
(April, 1926)

SOUTH DAKOTA

Contribution to the science of international peace, credited to Coach Liem, of the Huron College football team:

If every high school and college in France, Germany, Russia and England had a football team, the world would never have another war. (April, 1926)

TENNESSEE

The technique of necking as described by a reader of the Etowah *Enterprise:*

In the interest of common decency I want to register a protest against such conduct as I am going to attempt to describe, which occurred on the Athens-Etowah pike in open day. . . . There was a car parked directly in front of my door with five occupants. . . . I noticed the back of a man bent over something beside him, and a woman's hand on his neck. . . . The five of them . . . talked, laughed, played tricks on each other, pinched each other, snatched caps, and ate. . . . Suddenly without any cause that I could see, the young woman in the front seat fell bodily on the young man, grabbed him around the neck in a vice-like grip and jammed her face into his Adam's apple. In the course of ten or fifteen minutes she repeated the onslaught half a dozen times or more, with variations. Sometimes she would clutch him frantically and pull his head down on her chest and hold him close. Once she enveloped him in her embrace and batted her face into his jugular vein; another variation was butting her head into his breastbone while she gripped him in her arms. . . . To all of these manipulations he submitted in a truly sheep-like manner. . . .
Nannie Chestnutt.
(October, 1925)

TEXAS

News item from the town of Holland:

Because he spent his last sixty-five cents for a copy of Shakespeare, a charge of juvenile delinquency was filed in court against Johnny Meggs, of Holland, and he was yesterday sentenced to one to three years in the State Training School for Boys at Gatesville.

Contribution to moral science by the Rev. A. B. Reynolds, reported in the *Christian Courier*, published at Dallas:

Nine out of every ten men I talked to confessed to me that a man can not get into the compromising positions that must be indulged in to dance the modern dance and go through the movements that must be gone through in the modern dance and at the same time be thinking about his next Sunday-school lesson. It can't be done. . . . (April, 1926)

Justice in this great Commonwealth:

Graves et al. v. State, 29 S. W. (2nd) 379 (Court of Criminal Appeals of Texas).
Opinion by Martin, J.: "Offense, the unlawful manufacture of intoxicating liquor; penalty, five years in the penitentiary. . . . The judgment is affirmed."
Ross v. State, 29 S. W. (2nd) 381 (Court of Criminal Appeals of Texas).
Opinion by Christian, J.: "The offense is murder; the punishment, confinement in the penitentiary for four years. . . . The judgment is affirmed." (December, 1930)

TWO POEMS

By JOHN MCCLURE

I

The Grey Goosander

As he was recalling great Alexander
   And all the glory of kingly crowns,
Gay Thomas saw the grey goosander
   Circling over the eildon downs.

This fowl was old when young Tiberius
   Pranced in green purple over Rome:
This bird was venerable and serious
   Before the sibyls fetched Julius home.

And Thomas pitied the grey goosander,
   The lone bird flapping its wistful wings,
But more he pitied great Alexander,
   And much he pitied all kingly things.
                (*November, 1925*)

II

Address to the Merchants

Pig's feet and clabber,
   These are sturdy cheer.
I have joined your circle, sirs.
   Match me pennies here.

Once I ate air only, masters,
   And shouldered no load.
Oh, I lived a great way from the world,
   But have traveled the road.
                (*November, 1925*)

CRAZY SUNDAY

By F. Scott Fitzgerald

IT WAS Sunday — not a day, but rather a gap between two other days. Behind, for all of them, lay sets and sequences, the struggles of rival ingenuities in the conference rooms, the interminable waits under the crane that swung the microphone, the hundred miles a day by automobiles to and fro across Hollywood county, the ceaseless compromise, the clash and strain of many personalities fighting for their lives. And now Sunday, with individual life starting up again, with a glow kindling in eyes that had been glazed with monotony the afternoon before. Slowly as the hours waned they came awake like *Puppenfeen* in a toy shop: an intense colloquy in a corner, lovers disappearing to kiss in a hall. And the feeling of "Hurry, it's not too late, but for God's sake hurry before the blessed forty hours of leisure are over."

Joel Coles was writing continuity. He was twenty-eight and not yet broken by Hollywood. He had had what were considered nice assignments since his arrival six months before and he submitted his scenes and sequences with enthusiasm. He referred to himself modestly as a hack but really did not think of it that way.

His mother had been a successful actress; Joel had spent his childhood between London and New York trying to separate the real from the unreal, or at least to keep one guess ahead. He was a handsome man with the pleasant cow-brown eyes that in 1913 had gazed out at Broadway audiences from his mother's face.

When the invitation came it made him sure that he was getting somewhere. Ordinarily he did not go out on Sundays but stayed sober and took work home with him. Recently they had given him a Eugene O'Neill play destined for a very important lady indeed. Everything he had done so far had pleased Miles Calman, and Miles Calman was the only director on the lot who refused to work under a supervisor and was responsible to the money men alone. Everything was clicking into place in Joel's career. ("This is Mr. Calman's secretary. Will you come to tea from four to six Sunday — he lives in Beverly Hills, number ———".)

Joel was flattered. It would be a party out of the top-drawer. It was a tribute to himself as a young man of promise. The Marion Davies crowd, the high-hats, the big currency numbers, perhaps even

---

F. SCOTT FITZGERALD, *who died in 1940, was the author of* This Side of Paradise *and* The Great Gatsby. *He reached as great heights in the field of the short story as in the novel.* "Crazy Sunday" *has been reprinted many times in anthologies.* (October, 1932)

Dietrich and Garbo and the Marquise, people who were not seen everywhere, would probably be at Calman's.

"I won't take anything to drink," he assured himself. Calman was audibly tired of rummies, and thought it a pity the industry could not get along without them.

Joel agreed that writers drank too much — he did himself, but he wouldn't this afternoon. He wished Miles would be within hearing when the cocktails were passed to hear his succinct, unobtrusive, No, thank you.

Miles Calman's house was built for great emotional moments — there was an air of listening, as if the far silences of its vistas hid an audience, but this afternoon it was thronged, as though people had been bidden rather than asked. Joel noted with pride that only two other writers from the studio were in the crowd, an ennobled limey and, somewhat to his surprise, Nat Keogh, who had evoked Calman's impatient comment on drunks.

Stella Calman (Stella Walker, of course) did not move on to her other guests after she spoke to Joel. She lingered — she looked at him with the sort of beautiful look that demands some sort of acknowledgment and Joel drew quickly on the dramatic adequacy inherited from his mother:

"Well, you look about sixteen! Where's your kiddy car?"

She was visibly pleased; she lingered. He felt that he should say something more, something confident and easy — he had first met her when she was struggling for bits in New York. At the moment a tray slid up and Stella put a cocktail glass into his hand.

"Everybody's afraid, aren't they?" he said, looking at it absently. "Everybody watches for everybody else's blunders, or tries to make sure they're with people that'll do them credit. Of course that's not true in your house," he covered himself hastily. "I just meant generally in Hollywood."

Stella agreed. She presented several people to Joel as if he were very important. Reassuring himself that Miles was at the other side of the room, Joel drank the cocktail.

"So you have a baby?" he said. "That's the time to look out. After a pretty woman has had her first child, she's very vulnerable, because she wants to be reassured about her own charm. She's got to have some new man's unqualified devotion to prove to herself she hasn't lost anything."

"I never get anybody's unqualified devotion," Stella said rather resentfully.

"They're afraid of your husband."

"You think that's it?" She wrinkled her brow over the idea; then the conversation was interrupted at the exact moment Joel would have chosen.

Her attentions had given him confidence. Not for him to join safe groups, to slink to refuge under the wings of such acquaintances as he saw about the room. He walked to the window and looked out toward the Pacific, colorless under its sluggish sunset. It was good here — the American Riviera and all that, if there were ever time to enjoy it. The handsome, well-dressed people in the room, the lovely girls, and the — well, the lovely girls. You couldn't have everything.

He saw Stella's fresh boyish face, with the tired eyelid that always drooped a little over one eye, moving about among her guests and he wanted to sit with her and talk a long time as if she were a girl instead of a name; he followed her to see if she paid anyone as much attention as she had paid him. He took another cocktail — not because he needed confidence but because she had given him so much of it. Then he sat down beside the director's mother.

"Your son's gotten to be a legend, Mrs. Calman — Oracle and a Man of Destiny and all that. Personally, I'm against him but I'm in a minority. What do you think of him? Are you impressed? Are you surprised how far he's gone?"

"No, I'm not surprised," she said calmly. "We always expected a lot from Miles."

"Well now, that's unusual," remarked Joel. "I always think all mothers are like Napoleon's mother. My mother didn't want me to have anything to do with the entertainment business. She wanted me to go to West Point and be safe."

"We always had every confidence in Miles." . . .

He stood by the built-in bar of the dining room with the good-humored, heavy-drinking, highly-paid Nat Keogh.

"— I made a hundred grand during the year and lost forty grand gambling, so now I've hired a manager."

"You mean an agent," suggested Joel.

"No, I've got that too. I mean a manager. I make over everything to my wife and then he and my wife get together and hand me out the money. I pay him five thousand a year for this."

"You mean your agent."

"No, I mean my manager, and I'm not the only one — a lot of other irresponsible people have him."

"Well, if you're irresponsible why are you responsible enough to hire a manager?"

"I'm just irresponsible about gambling. Look here —"

A singer performed; Joel and Nat went forward with the others to listen.

II

The singing reached Joel vaguely; he felt happy and friendly toward all the people gathered there, people of bravery and industry, superior to a *bourgeoisie* that outdid them in ignorance and loose living, risen to a position of the highest prominence in a nation that for a decade had wanted only to be entertained. He liked them — he loved them. Great waves of good feeling flowed through him.

As the singer finished his number and there was a drift toward the hostess to say good-bye, Joel had an idea. He would give them "Building It Up," his own composition. It was his only parlor trick, it had amused several parties and it might please Stella Walker. Possessed by the hunch, his blood throbbing with the scarlet corpuscles of exhibitionism, he sought her.

"Of course," she cried. "Please! Do you need anything?"

"Someone has to be the secretary that I'm supposed to be dictating to."

"I'll be her."

As the word spread the guests in the

hall, already putting on their coats to leave, drifted back and Joel faced the eyes of many strangers. He had a dim foreboding, realizing that the man who had just performed was a famous radio entertainer. Then someone said "Sh!" and he was alone with Stella, the center of a sinister Indian-like half-circle. Stella smiled up at him expectantly — he began.

His burlesque was based upon the cultural limitations of Mr. Dave Silverstein, an independent producer; Silverstein was presumed to be dictating a letter outlining a treatment of a story he had bought.

"— a story of divorce, the younger generators and the Foreign Legion," he heard his voice saying, with the intonations of Mr. Silverstein. "But we got to build it up, see?"

A sharp pang of doubt struck through him. The faces surrounding him in the gently molded light were intent and curious, but there was no ghost of a smile anywhere; directly in front the Great Lover of the screen glared at him with an eye as keen as the eye of a potato. Only Stella Walker looked up at him with a radiant, never faltering smile.

"If we make him a Menjoy type, then we get a sort of Michael Arlen only with a Honolulu atmosphere."

Still not a ripple in front, but in the rear a rustling, a perceptible shift toward the left, toward the front door.

"— then she says she feels this sex appil for him and he burns out and says 'Oh go on destroy yourself' "—

At some point he heard Nat Keogh snicker and here and there were a few encouraging faces, but as he finished he had the sickening realization that he had made a fool of himself in view of an important section of the picture world, upon whose favor depended his career.

For a moment he existed in the midst of a confused silence, broken by a general trek for the door. He felt the undercurrent of derision that rolled through the gossip; then — all this was in the space of ten seconds — the Great Lover, his eye hard and empty as the eye of a needle, shouted "Boo! Boo!" voicing in an overtone what he felt was the mood of the crowd. It was the resentment of the professional toward the amateur, of the community toward the stranger, the thumbs-down of the clan.

Only Stella Walker was still standing near and thanking him as if he had been an unparalleled success, as if it hadn't occurred to her that anyone hadn't liked it. As Nat Keogh helped him into his overcoat, a great wave of self-disgust swept over him and he swung desperately to his rule of never betraying an inferior emotion until he no longer felt it.

"I was a flop," he said lightly, to Stella. "Never mind, it's a good number when appreciated. Thanks for your coöperation."

The smile did not leave her face — he bowed rather drunkenly and Nat drew him toward the door . . .

The arrival of his breakfast awakened him into a broken and ruined world. Yesterday he was himself, a point of fire against an industry, today he felt that he was pitted under an enormous disadvantage, against those faces, against individual contempt and collective sneer. Worse than that, to Miles Calman he was becoming one of those rummies, stripped of dignity, whom Calman regretted he was compelled to use. To Stella Walker, on whom he had forced a martyrdom to preserve the courtesy of her house — her opinion he did not dare to guess. His gastric juices ceased to flow and he set his poached eggs back on the telephone table. He wrote:

Dear Miles —
You can imagine my profound self-disgust. I confess to a taint of exhibitionism, but at six o'clock in the afternoon, in broad daylight! Good God! My apologies to your wife.
Yours ever,
JOEL COLES.

Joel emerged from his office on the lot only to slink like a malefactor to the tobacco store. So suspicious was his manner that one of the studio police asked to see his admission card. He had decided to eat lunch outside when Nat Keogh, confident and cheerful, overtook him.

"What do you mean you're in permanent retirement? What if that Three Piece Suit did boo you?

"Why listen," he continued, drawing Joel into the studio restaurant. "The night of one of his premiers at Grauman's, Joe Squires kicked his tail while he was bowing to the crowd. The ham said Joe'd hear from him later but when Joe called him up at eight o'clock next day and said, 'I thought I was going to hear from you,' he hung up the phone."

The preposterous story cheered Joel, and he found a gloomy consolation in staring at the group at the next table, the sad, lovely Siamese twins, the mean dwarfs, the proud giant from the circus picture. But looking beyond at the yellow-stained faces of pretty women, their eyes all melancholy and startling with mascara, their ball gowns garish in full day, he saw a group who had been at Calman's and winced.

"Never again," he exclaimed aloud, "absolutely my last social appearance in Hollywood!"

The following morning a telegram was waiting for him at his office:

You were one of the most agreeable people at our party. Expect you at my sister June's buffet supper next Sunday.
STELLA WALKER COLEMAN.

The blood rushed fast through his veins for a feverish minute. Incredulously he read the telegram over.

"Well, that's the sweetest thing I ever heard of in my life!"

III

Crazy Sunday again. Joel slept until eleven, then he read a newspaper to catch up with the past week. He lunched in his room on trout, avocado salad and a pint of California wine. Dressing for the tea, he selected a pin-check suit, a blue shirt, a burnt orange tie. There were dark circles of fatigue under his eyes. In his second-hand car he drove to the Riviera apartments. As he was introducing himself to Stella's sister, Miles and Stella arrived in riding clothes — they had been quarelling fiercely most of the afternoon on all the dirt roads back of Beverly Hills.

Miles Calman, tall, nervous, with a desperate humor and the unhappiest eyes Joel ever saw, was an artist from the top of his curiously shaped head to his niggerish feet. Upon these last he stood firmly — he had never made a cheap picture though he had sometimes paid heavily for the luxury of making experimental flops. In spite of his excellent company, one could not be with him long without realizing that he was not a well man.

From the moment of their entrance Joel's day bound itself up inextricably with theirs. As he joined the group around them Stella turned away from it with an impatient little tongue click — and Miles Calman said to the man who happened to be next to him:

"Go easy on Eva Goebel. There's hell to pay about her at home." Miles turned to Joel, "I'm sorry I missed you at the office yesterday. I spent the afternoon at the analyst's."

"You being psychoanalyzed?"

"I have been for months. First I went for claustrophobia, now I'm trying to get my whole life cleared up. They say it'll take over a year."

"There's nothing the matter with your life," Joel assured him.

"Oh, no? Well, Stella seems to think so. Ask anybody — they can all tell you about it," he said bitterly.

A girl perched herself on the arm of Miles' chair; Joel crossed to Stella, who stood disconsolately by the fire.

"Thank you for your telegram," he said. "It was darn sweet. I can't imagine anybody as good looking as you are being so good-humored."

She was a little lovelier than he had ever seen her and perhaps the unstinted admiration in his eyes prompted her to unload on him — it did not take long, for she was obviously at the emotional bursting point.

"— and Miles has been carrying on this thing for *two years*, and I never knew. Why, she was one of my best friends, always in the house. Finally when people began to come to me, Miles had to admit it."

She sat down vehemently on the arm of Joel's chair. Her riding breeches were the color of the chair and Joel saw that the mass of her hair was made up of some strands of red gold and some of pale gold, so that it could not be dyed, and that she had on no make-up. She was that good looking —

Still quivering with the shock of her discovery, Stella found unbearable the spectacle of a new girl hovering over Miles; she led Joel into a bedroom, and seated at either end of a big bed they went on talking. People on their way to the washroom glanced in and made wisecracks, but Stella, emptying out her story, paid no attention. After a while Miles stuck his head in the door and said, "There's no use trying to explain something to Joel in half an hour that I don't understand myself and the psychoanalyst says will take a whole year to understand."

She talked on as if Miles were not there. She loved Miles, she said — under considerable difficulties she had always been faithful to him.

"The psychoanalyst told Miles that he had a mother complex. In his first marriage he transferred his mother complex to his wife, you see — and then his sex turned to me. But when we married the thing repeated itself — he transferred his mother complex to me and all his libido turned toward this other woman."

Joel knew that this probably wasn't gibberish — yet it sounded like gibberish. He knew Eva Goebel; she was a motherly person, older and probably wiser than Stella, who was a golden child.

Miles now suggested impatiently that Joel come back with them since Stella had so much to say, so they drove out to the mansion in Beverly Hills. Under the high ceilings the situation seemed more dignified and tragic. It was an eerie bright night with the dark very clear outside of all the windows and Stella all rose-gold raging and crying around the room. Joel did not quite believe in picture actresses' grief. They have other preoccupations — they are beautiful rose-gold figures blown full of life by writers and directors, and after hours they sit around and talk in whispers and giggled innuendoes, and the ends of many adventures flow through them.

Sometimes he pretended to listen and instead thought how well she was got up — sleek breeches with a matched set of legs in them, an Italian-colored sweater with a little high neck, and a short brown chamois coat. He couldn't decide whether she was an imitation of an English lady or an English lady was an imitation of her. She hovered somewhere between the realest of realities and the most blatant of impersonations.

"Miles is so jealous of me that he questions everything I do," she cried scornfully. "When I was in New York I wrote him that I'd been to the theatre with Eddie Baker. Miles was so jealous he phoned me ten times in one day."

"I was wild," Miles snuffled sharply, a habit he had in times of stress. "The analyst couldn't get any results for a week."

Stella shook her head despairingly. "Did you expect me just to sit in the hotel for three weeks?"

"I don't expect anything. I admit that I'm jealous. I try not to be. I worked on that with Dr. Bridgebane, but it didn't do any good. I was jealous of Joel this afternoon when you sat on the arm of his chair."

"You were?" She started up. "You *were!* Wasn't there somebody on the arm of your chair? And did you speak to me for two hours?"

"You were telling your troubles to Joel in the bedroom."

"When I think that that woman" — she seemed to believe that to omit Eva Goebel's name would be to lessen her reality — "used to come here —"

"All right — all right," said Miles wearily. "I've admitted everything and I feel as bad about it as you do." Turning to Joel he began talking about pictures, while Stella moved restlessly along the far walls, her hands in her breeches pockets.

"They've treated Miles terribly," she said, coming suddenly back into the conversation as if they'd never discussed her personal affairs. "Dear, tell him about old Beltzer trying to change your picture."

As she stood hovering protectively over Miles, her eyes flashing with indignation in his behalf, Joel realized that he was in love with her. Stifled with excitement he got up to say good-night.

With Monday the week resumed its workaday rhythm, in sharp contrast to the theoretical discussions, the gossip and scandal of Sunday; there was the endless detail of script revision — "Instead of a lousy dissolve, we can leave her voice on the sound track and cut to a medium shot of the taxi from Bell's angle or we can simply pull the camera back to include the station, hold it a minute and then pam to the row of taxis" — by Monday afternoon Joel had again forgotten that people whose business was to provide entertainment were ever privileged to be entertained. In the evening he phoned Miles' house. He asked for Miles but Stella came to the phone.

"Do things seem better?"

"Not particularly. What are you doing next Saturday evening?"

"Nothing."

"The Perrys are giving a dinner and theatre party and Miles won't be here — he's flying to South Bend to see the Notre Dame-California game, I thought you might go with me in his place."

After a long moment Joel said, "Why — surely. If there's a conference I can't make dinner but I can get to the theatre."

"Then I'll say we can come."

Joel walked to his office. In view of the strained relations of the Calmans, would Miles be pleased, or did she intend that Miles shouldn't know of it? That would be out of the question — if Miles didn't mention it Joel would. But it was an hour or more before he could get down to work again.

Wednesday there was a four-hour wrangle in a conference room crowded with planets and nebulae of cigarette smoke. Three men and a woman paced the carpet in turn, suggesting or condemning, speaking sharply or persuasively, confidently or despairingly. At the end Joel lingered to have a talk with Miles.

The man was tired — not with the exaltation of fatigue but life-tired, with his lids sagging and his beard prominent over the blue shadows near his mouth.

"I hear you're flying to the Notre Dame game."

Miles looked beyond him and shook his head.

"I've given up the idea."

"Why?"

"On account of you." Still he did not look at Joel.

"What the hell, Miles?"

"That's why I've given it up." He broke into a perfunctory laugh at himself. "I can't tell what Stella might do just out of spite — she's invited you to take her to the Perry's, hasn't she? I wouldn't enjoy the game."

The fine instinct that moved swiftly and confidently on the set, muddled so weakly and helplessly through his personal life.

"Look, Miles," Joel said frowning. "I've never made any passes *whatsoever* at Stella. If you're really seriously cancelling your trip on account of me, I won't go to the Perry's with her. I won't see her. You can trust me absolutely."

Miles looked at him, carefully now.

"Maybe." He shrugged his shoulders. "Anyhow there'd just be somebody else. I wouldn't have any fun."

"You don't seem to have much confidence in Stella. She told me she'd always been true to you."

"Maybe she has." In the last few minutes several more muscles had sagged around Miles' mouth, "But how can I ask anything of her after what's happened? How can I expect her —" He broke off and his face grew harder as he said, "I'll tell you one thing, right or wrong and no matter what I've done, if I ever had anything on her I'd divorce her. I can't have my pride hurt — that would be the last straw."

His tone annoyed Joel, but he said:

"Hasn't she calmed down about the Eva Goebel thing?"

"No." Miles snuffled pessimistically. "I can't get over it either."

"I thought it was finished."

"I'm trying not to see Eva again, but you know it isn't easy just to drop something like that — it isn't some girl I kissed last night in a taxi! The psychoanalyst says —"

"I know," Joel interrupted. "Stella told me." This was depressing. "Well, as far as I'm concerned if you go to the game I won't see Stella. And I'm sure Stella has nothing on her conscience about anybody."

"Maybe not," Miles repeated listlessly. "Anyhow I'll stay and take her to the party. Say," he said suddenly, "I wish you'd come too. I've got to have somebody sympathetic to talk to. That's the trouble — I've influenced Stella in everything. Especially I've influenced her so that she likes all the men I like — it's very difficult."

"It must be," Joel agreed.

IV

Joel could not get to the dinner. Self-conscious in his silk hat against the unemployment, he waited for the others in front of the Hollywood Theatre and watched the evening parade: obscure replicas of bright, particular picture stars, spavined men in polo coats, a stomping dervish with the beard and staff of an apostle, a pair of chic Filipinos in collegiate clothes, reminder that this corner of the Republic opened to the seven seas, a long fantastic carnival of young shouts which proved to be a fraternity initiation. The line split to pass two smart limousines that stopped at the curb.

There she was, in a dress like ice-water, made in a thousand pale blue pieces, with icicles trickling at the throat. He started forward.

"So you like my dress?"

"Where's Miles?"

"He flew to the game after all. He left yesterday morning — at least I think —" She broke off. "I just got a telegram from South Bend saying that he's starting back. I forgot — you know all these people?"

The party of eight moved into the theatre.

Miles had gone after all and Joel wondered if he should have come. But during the performance, with Stella a profile under the pure grain of light hair, he thought no more about Miles. Once he turned and looked at her and she looked back at him, smiling and meeting his eyes for as long as he wanted. Between the acts they smoked in the lobby and she whispered:

"They're all going to the opening of Jack Johnson's night club — I don't want to go, do you?"

"Do we have to?"

"I suppose not." She hesitated. "I'd like to talk to you. I suppose we could go to our house — if I were only sure —"

Again she hesitated and Joel asked: "Sure of what?"

"Sure that — oh, I'm haywire I know, but how can I be sure Miles went to the game?"

"You mean you think he's with Eva Goebel?"

"No, not so much that — but supposing he was here watching everything I do. You know Miles does odd things sometimes. Once he wanted a man with a long beard to drink tea with him and he sent down to the casting agency for one, and drank tea with him all afternoon."

"That's different. He sent you a wire from South Bend — that proves he's at the game."

After the play they said good night to the others at the curb and were answered by looks of amusement. They slid off along the golden garish thoroughfare through the crowd that had gathered around Stella.

"You see he could arrange the telegrams," Stella said, "very easily."

That was true. And with the idea that perhaps her uneasiness was justified, Joel grew angry: if Miles had trained a camera on them he felt no obligations toward Miles. Aloud he said:

"That's nonsense."

There were Christmas trees already in the shop windows and the full moon over the boulevard was only a prop, as scenic as the giant boudoir lamps of the corners. On into the dark foliage of Beverly Hills that flamed as eucalyptus by day, Joel saw only the flash of a white face under his own, the arc of her shoulder. She pulled away suddenly and looked up at him.

"Your eyes are like your mother's," she said. "I used to have a scrap book full of pictures of her."

"Your eyes are like your own and not a bit like any other eyes," he answered.

Something made Joel look out into the grounds as they went into the house, as if Miles were lurking in the shrubbery. A telegram waited on the hall table. She read aloud:

      Chicago
Home tomorrow night. Thinking of you. Love.
        MILES

"You see," she said, throwing the slip back on the table, "he could easily have faked that." She asked the butler for drinks and sandwiches and ran upstairs, while Joel walked into the empty reception rooms. Strolling about he wandered to the piano where he had stood in disgrace two Sundays before.

"Then we could put over," he said aloud, "a story of divorce, the younger generators and the Foreign Legion."

His thoughts jumped to another telegram.

"*You were one of the most agreeable people at our party* ——"

An idea occurred to him. If Stella's telegram had been purely a gesture of courtesy then it was likely that Miles had inspired it, for it was Miles who had invited him. Probably Miles had said:

"Send him a wire — he's miserable — he thinks he's queered himself."

It fitted in with "I've influenced Stella in everything. Especially I've influenced her so that she likes all the men I like." A woman would do a thing like that because she felt sympathetic — only a man would do it because he felt responsible.

When Stella came back into the room he took both her hands.

"I have a strange feeling that I'm a sort of pawn in a spite game you're playing against Miles," he said.

"Help yourself to a drink."

"And the odd thing is that I'm in love with you anyhow."

The telephone rang and she freed herself to answer it.

"Another wire from Miles," she announced. "He dropped it, or it says he dropped it, from the airplane at Kansas City."

"I suppose he asked to be remembered to me."

"No, he just said he loved me. I believe he does. He's so very weak."

"Come sit beside me," Joel urged her.

It was early. And it was still a few minutes short of midnight a half hour later, when Joel walked to the cold hearth, and said tersely:

"Meaning that you haven't any curiosity about me?"

"Not at all. You attract me a lot and you know it. The point is that I suppose I really do love Miles."

"Obviously."

"And tonight I feel uneasy about everything."

He wasn't angry — he was even faintly relieved that a possible entanglement was avoided. Still as he looked at her, the warmth and softness of her body thawing her cold blue costume, he knew she was one of the things he would always regret.

"I've got to go," he said. "I'll phone a taxi."

"Nonsense — there's a chauffeur on duty."

He winced at her readiness to have him go, and seeing this she kissed him lightly and said, "You're sweet, Joel." Then suddenly three things happened: he took down his drink at a gulp, the phone rang loud through the house and a clock in the hall struck twelve in triumphant trumpet notes.

Nine — ten — eleven — twelve —

V

It was Sunday again. Joel realized that he had come to the theatre this evening with the work of the week still hanging about him like cerements. He had made love to Stella as he might attack some matter to be cleaned up hurriedly before the day's end. But this was Sunday — the lovely, lazy perspective of the next twenty-four hours unrolled before him — every minute was something to be approached with lulling indirection, every moment held the germ of innumerable possibilities. Nothing was impossible — everything was just beginning. He poured himself another drink.

With a sharp moan, Stella slipped forward inertly by the telephone. Joel picked her up and laid her on the sofa. He squirted soda-water on a handkerchief and slapped it over her face. The telephone mouthpiece was still grinding and he put it to his ear.

"— the plane fell just this side of Kansas City. The body of Miles Calman has been identified and ——"

He hung up the receiver.

"Lie still," he said, stalling, as Stella opened her eyes.

"Oh, what's happened?" she whispered. "Call them back. Oh, what's happened?"

"I'll call them right away. What's your doctor's name?"

"Did they say Miles was dead?"

"Lie quiet — is there a servant still up?"

"Hold me — I'm frightened."

He put his arm around her.

"I want the name of your doctor," he said sternly. "It may be a mistake but I want someone here."

"It's Doctor — Oh, God, is Miles dead?"

Joel ran upstairs and searched through strange medicine cabinets for spirits of ammonia. When he came down Stella cried:

"He isn't dead — I know he isn't. This is part of his scheme. He's torturing me. I know he's alive. I can feel he's alive."

"I want to get hold of some close friend of yours Stella. You can't stay here alone tonight."

"Oh, no," she cried, "I can't see anybody. You stay. I haven't got any friend." She got up, tears streaming down her face. "Oh, Miles is my only friend. He's not dead — he can't be dead. I'm going there right away and see. Get a train. You'll have to come with me."

"You can't. There's nothing to do tonight. I want you to tell me the name of some woman I can call: Lois? Joan? Carmel? Isn't there somebody?"

Stella stared at him blindly.

"Eva Goebel was my best friend," she said.

Joel thought of Miles, his sad and desperate face in the office two days before. In the awful silence of his death all was clear about him. He was the only American-born director with both an interesting temperament and an artistic conscience. Meshed in an industry, he had paid with his ruined nerves for having no resilience, no healthy cynicism, no refuge — only a pitiful and precarious escape.

There was a sound at the outer door — it opened suddenly, and there were footsteps in the hall.

"Miles!" Stella screamed. "Is it you, Miles? Oh, it's Miles."

A telegraph boy appeared in the doorway.

"I couldn't find the bell. I heard you talking inside."

The telegram was a duplicate of the one that had been phoned. While Stella read it over and over, as though it were a black lie, Joel telephoned. It was still early and he had difficulty getting anyone; when finally he succeeded in finding some friends he made Stella take a stiff drink.

"You'll stay here, Joel," she whispered, as though she were half asleep. "You won't go away. Miles liked you — he said you —" She shivered violently, "Oh, my God, you don't know how alone I feel." Her eyes closed, "Put your arms around me. Miles had a suit like that." She started bolt upright. "Think of what he must have felt. He was afraid of almost everything, anyhow."

She shook her head dazedly. Suddenly she seized Joel's face and held it close to hers.

"You won't go. You like me — you love me, don't you? Don't call up anybody. Tomorrow's time enough. You stay here with me tonight."

He stared at her, at first incredulously, and then with shocked understanding. In her dark groping Stella was trying to keep Miles alive by sustaining a situation in which he had figured — as if Miles' mind could not die so long as the possibilities that had worried him still existed. It was a tortured effort to stave off the realization that he was dead.

Resolutely Joel went to the phone and called a doctor.

"Don't, oh, don't call anybody!" Stella cried. "Come back here and put your arms around me."

"Is Doctor Bales in?"

"Joel," Stella cried, "I thought I could count on you, Miles liked you. He was jealous of you — Joel, come here."

And then — if he betrayed Miles she would be keeping him alive — for if he were really dead how could he be betrayed?

"— has just had a very severe shock. Can you come at once, and get hold of a nurse?"

"Joel!"

Now the doorbell and the telephone began to ring intermittently, and automobiles were stopping in front of the door.

"But you're not going," Stella begged him. "You're going to stay, aren't you?"

"No," he answered. "But I'll be back if you need me."

Standing on the steps of the house which now hummed and palpitated with the life that flutters around death like protective leaves, he began to sob a little in his throat.

"Everything he touched he did something magical to," he thought. "He even brought that little gamin alive and made her a sort of masterpiece."

And then:

"What a hell of a hole he leaves in this damn wilderness — already!"

And then with a certain bitterness, "Oh, yes, I'll be back — I'll be back!"

THE REVOLT OF THE GHOSTS

By Eugene Lyons

The catastrophe did not make itself felt at once. It seemed, rather, a creeping paralysis that crippled first one organ of the body social, then another. Strange silences began to blot out the chatter of the radio stations. A leprosy of blank space broke out in newspapers and magazines. The most garrulous of our statesmen, politicians, patriots and viewers-with-alarm were suddenly struck speechless. Mysterious hiatuses developed in every department of national affairs.

And soon all life seemed disjointed and inarticulate. The public reaction to the encroaching paralysis was also queer. In the initial days of the revolt people were more curious than depressed. You might hear someone remark casually:

"Funny, ain't it, Dr. Blah's sermons stopped in the papers?"

"That so? And my favorite news commentator, you know, that guy Bill Hall, didn't show up on the air this week."

"I'll be doggoned if it don't begin to look like an epidemic," a third might add. "Only one of the five speakers at our monthly symposium on war and peace showed up on Wednesday!"

But slowly the puzzlement turned to bewilderment, then to a species of panic. Often enough we had heard of the impending "collapse of civilization." That sort of talk was fashionable. But people had discounted the phrase for the threadbare cliché that it was. Now, suddenly, it seemed a macabre reality. Civilization did seem groggy, fever-eyed and more than a little delirious. Its accustomed voice of unction had turned to an idiot stutter, or worse — oppressive silence.

Then the whole country, the whole world, began to understand what had happened. The ghosts had revolted!

From dank cellars and dizzy penthouses, inglorious holes and palatial studies, the denizens of ghostland poured into the open, blinking eyes unaccustomed to light, shrieking their protests in voices unused to anything above a whisper.

The ghosts had revolted! By hundreds and by thousands they ripped their shrouds of anonymity. They shed their humility. They kicked their typewriters into corners and rushed madly into the streets, from ghosts of highest rank even unto the lowliest ghost to a ghost's ghost. The galley slaves of intellect. The under-

EUGENE LYONS, *editor of this magazine from 1939 to 1944, has written and lectured extensively on international affairs. For six years (1928–34) he was stationed in Moscow as United Press correspondent. His books include* Moscow Carrousel, Assignment in Utopia, The Red Decade, Life and Death of Sacco and Vanzetti. *(November, 1940)*

world of creative expression. The hobgoblins of thought and speech. The artificers of ready-made and custom-made sentiments. The skilled taxidermists of lifelike statesmen. The carvers of figureheads. The ventriloquists of patriotism, eloquence, high ideals, mock emotions. The whole universe of shadows, echoes and essences suddenly bodied forth in angry men and women, protesting, demanding and defying.

It took time before the full horror of the defiance was grasped by the people. Everyday illusions and delusions went pop! pop! pop! Inflated reputations began to explode. Stuffed shirts caved in. The ghosts were throwing the ancient burdens off their meek, rounded backs, and the clatter of falling dignities and crumbling fame was like thunder through the land.

II

The mass meeting of insurgent ghosts at Madison Square Garden is vivid in my memory despite the years that have passed. Banners, floats, speeches and excitement, the awareness of similar gatherings in every center of the nation — and permeating it all, the feeling of an entire civilization teetering on the brink.

As I entered the hall, a shrill voice was sprinkling words through clusters of loud-speakers overhead and the close-packed ghosts were stirred to applause by his haranguing. The speaker was a diminutive, bald-headed, spectacled man in baggy clothes, his physical insignificance underlined by the floodlights in which he seemed to swim. His words sounded to me like wild insanities, though in the following months such statements and claims became commonplace and generally accepted.

"The public," the little man was shouting, "our dear beloved public, thought they were voting for Thomas T. Tinhorn last November when they elected him President of the United States. It's about time they knew the truth. We're finished with hypocrisy, hokum and legerdemain! I proclaim it here before the sovereign voters of our great country who are listening in on the radio. I proclaim it before you, my embattled fellow-ghosts. I proclaim it before the world and before history!

"It was not Thomas T. Tinhorn the voters chose as President. It was me, me, me — Lucius Z. Pinwinkle they elected! Those were *my* speeches the President recited, *my* sentiments, *my* slogans. By every right Lucius Z. Pinwinkle and his staff of subcontractor ghosts" — he motioned and eight men and women took a bow — "should be chief executive of the United States."

While applause rolled through the great hall, I looked around and soon began to distinguish some of the banners and delegations. Nearby was a group whom I mistook at first glance for a galaxy of motion picture stars, but their banners set me right. I learned that they were merely Doubles and Stand-Ins for Movie Stars, Local 348 of the Ghosts' Alliance. Inscribed in huge white letters on red bunting over their heads was the legend: "We take the chances — they take the checks!"

An entire section of the vast gathering place was given over to the Celebrated Names or First Person Singular Division. Among my yellowed notes of that bizarre meeting I still have the words I copied from a large chart, in the shape of a phonograph record, set up behind the section: *By X . . . Himself! His Own Story! By the Heavyweight Champion! How I Did It! From the Death Cell! By America's Sweetheart! By the Quintuplets Themselves!* Over, under and to either side of this list of exclamations one lone word was repeated in giant letters: "YEAH?"

The central portion of the Garden, of course, was given over to the speech writers, since they were the most numerous — the proletariat of ghostdom, as it were. From the placards I judged that they were deployed on both sides of the center aisle in accordance with their specialties: after-dinner persiflage, political harangues, Rotarian routines, canned lectures, sermons by the yard, debates to measure, addresses of acceptance, funeral orations, memorial grandiloquence, captain-of-industry prophecy, stuffed-shirt noises, legislator and statesman stuff, speeches from remnants and left-overs — in short, the artisans of oratory grouped according to their particular jobs.

Another speaker had by now succeeded Mr. Pinwinkle at the microphone. Immersed in the white light, he seemed frightened and spoke nervously. As he proceeded, however, mounting indignation erased his fears and he achieved a measure of real eloquence.

"Like all of you, fellow workers," I remember him saying, "I have written scores and hundreds of speeches for all occasions and many of them have been used over and over again for years. But this is the first time that I have delivered a speech myself. I have spoken through the mouths of governors and ward heelers, evangelists and bank presidents, big-time businessmen and national heroes, lady philanthropists and women's club secretaries. At last, at last, I speak with my own mouth!"

A sort of elation haloed his head at these words. A burst of applause and shouts of "Attaboy!" gave him a chance to wipe the perspiration under his chin.

"You will understand, I am sure, if I find myself a little tongue-tied and excited. Year after year I have listened to myself in voices ranging from tinny soprano to rumbling basso. It is like a blessed release, oh my fellow-ghosts, to hear my own voice!

"The distress of the audiences," he continued, "is as nothing compared to the torments you and I have suffered when our addresses were delivered. How often have I squirmed in my seat while my favorite sentences were being mangled by an orator who didn't begin to understand what he was talking about. How often have I just barely saved myself from apoplexy by digging my nails into my palms when the speaker skipped entire lines of mine, even entire pages, while neither he nor his listeners were aware of it. I have bitten my lips to blood as college presidents mispronounced my choicest words and scattered their emphasis in precisely the wrong places, despite the fact that I had underlined the proper places. Only you and I know what it means to have our speeches misinterpreted. We are like composers who must hear their works played by a tyro.

"I know you are with me in the basic demand that speakers be expected to understand every word, every figure of speech in his oration!" Vociferous approval from the embattled ghosts. "We demand that penalties be fixed for speakers who repeatedly take the wrong manuscript along and make the wrong oration!" More noisy approval. "We demand that credit for the ghost writer be given by chairmen and on printed programs for all speeches!"

The next address — an earnest, emotional outburst — was delivered by the well-known operator of a gag factory. He spoke feelingly for his brethren of the jokesmiths' guild, in their endless travail of humor, wringing new laughs from the most sapless material for radio comedians and screen clowns.

"Day after day and year after year," he exclaimed, "we must feed the public's appetite for laughs. The whole human race has become for us just a glum spectator daring us to find his funny bone. We wear down our minds, we fight and steal and go ga-ga to find ever more puns, more wisecracks, more insane exaggerations. But who gets the credit for our efforts and our sacrifices? Who gets the cash for our sad and exacting labor? Some radio or movie star or columnist who couldn't invent a gag or a joke to save his life! Is that fair play? Is it democracy?"

From the Gagsters in the galleries came cries: "No, a thousand times no!"

Other spokesmen at the mass meeting detailed the complaints of secretaries and public relations counsel who write the business reports signed by corporation heads; of the ghosts in fiction mills; of the autobiographers of well-heeled nonentities; of the composers of New Year's messages for public men and women; of the denizens of ghost sweatshops; of all those who write and compose and prophesy and exhort under other people's signatures. The impassioned speech of a delegate of the True Story Stooges, in particular, sticks in my mind.

"The chairman," he said, "introduced me as Lemuel G. Smith. But before you stands a man with more aliases than a Russian revolutionist ever had. Before you stands a reformed streetwalker many times over, an international crook who saw the evil of his ways, a high school girl whose fate it is to be dragged through slimy temptations by designing men at least once a month, a parson untrue to his holy trust, a murderer who tells all before he pays with his life.

"On every newsstand in the land I have bared my careers as a spy, a whore, a gigolo, a two-timing mamma, a dope fiend, a confidence man. I have been a kept woman for the confession pulps so often that I am ashamed to look my wife and kids in the face. I have been a kleptomaniac and a forger and a society dame gone wrong so repeatedly that I shrink from contact with decent folk. At this very moment my orgiastic past, illustrated realistically too, is for sale in the lobby. I cringed as I passed it. I have been confessing sins for a salary so long that the mere sight of a personal pronoun gives me the heebie-jeebies. The unexpected rattle of a door or window sends me scampering for cover and I run at the sight of a policeman. "But why say more? You all know how I feel. I hate to go off this platform, it is so good to appear in public in my true colors as a hard-working and respectable citizen without an illustrated orgy to his credit — in my own name, as Lemuel G. Smith. Be it ever so humble there is no name like your own."

From Madison Square Garden the ghosts marched in a body to City Hall under banners demanding more credit and more cash. The city fathers, haggard and unkempt as a result of the ordeal, greeted them from the steps of the building, greeted them with despairing gestures and said not a word: their ghosts, too, had revolted.

III

All of this is history now, and only a few of us eyewitnesses are still alive. I, for one, despair of the attempt to convey to a new generation the psychological terror of those months. One must have lived through the ominous era of the Revolt of the Ghosts to appreciate the overtones of horror as the machinery of everyday life stalled and the foundations of civilization began to wobble. It is a matter of record that three-quarters of all the current magazines suspended publication for lack of material during the revolt. The Congressional Record shrank to a mere shadow of its obese self. The lecture business collapsed. The radio networks, the vaudeville stage, journalism, the mighty flood of words, sentiments, tunes, jokes and advice sank to a mere trickle. The tabloid papers just lay down and died.

When, at last, the revolt was ended and the ghosts were back at their jobs, and the wheels of civilized existence began to turn once more, we found ourselves, it seemed, in a new world — fresher, more straightforward, less pretentious. The elaborate make-believe had been shattered forever and the terrible constrictions of routine hypocrisy were relaxed. The role of the ghosts had been a clandestine, dishonest, inhibiting force. Now it was in the open, recognized and respected and remunerated, without the need for bluff and sleight-of-hand.

Thus it has remained ever since. The employment of ghosts has become not merely respectable but well-nigh obligatory. A man worth his salt today has his ghost as naturally and publicly as he has his secretary. A statesman or big businessman nowadays will no more admit writing his own speeches or reports than doing his own laundry. We all remember the scandal evoked by the rumor that Senator Jippy writes his own speeches and articles. It aroused organized labor and cost him the nomination for the Presidency. The line "Words by So-and-So" is now on every program or announcement of speeches, and the notation "Ghosted by So-and-So" appears on every article, interview, statement or other public expression. In fact, many of the more successful ghosts now hire celebrated names to sign their stuff, paying them the small percentage permitted by the Ghosts' Alliance Code.

It is not saying too much, surely, to credit the Revolt of the Ghosts with purging our modern civilization.

(Ghosted by the Eveready Editorial Corp.)

MYSELF UPON THE EARTH

By William Saroyan

A BEGINNING is always difficult, for it is no simple matter to choose from language the one bright word which shall live forever; and every articulation of the solitary man is but a single word. Every poem, story, novel and essay, just as every dream is a word from that language we have not yet translated, that vast unspoken wisdom of night, that grammarless, lawless vocabulary of eternity. The earth, our mother, is vast. Let us remember this. And with the earth all things are vast, the skyscraper and the blade of grass. The eye will magnify if the mind and soul will command. And the mind may destroy time, brother of death, and brother, let us remember, of life as well. Vastest of all is the ego, the germ of humanity, from which is born God and the universe, heaven and hell, the earth, the face of man, my face and your face; our eyes. For myself, I say with piety, rejoice.

I am a young man in an old city. It is morning and I am in a small room. I am standing over a bundle of yellow writing paper, the only kind I can afford, the kind that sells at the rate of 170 sheets for ten cents. All this paper is bare of language, clean and perfect, and I am a young writer about to begin my work. It is Monday . . . September 25, 1933 . . . how glorious it is to be alive, to be still living. (I am a very old young man; I have walked along many streets, through cities, through many days and many nights. And now I have come home to myself. Over me, on the wall of this small, disordered room, is the photograph of my dead father, and I have come up from the earth with his face and his eyes and I am writing in English what he would have written in our native language. And we are the same man, one dead and one alive.)

Furiously I am smoking a cigarette, for the moment is one of great importance to me, and therefore of great importance to everyone. I am about to place language, my language, upon a clean sheet of paper, and I am trembling. It is so much of a responsibility to be a user of words. I do not want to say the wrong thing. I do not want to be clever. I am horribly afraid of this. I have never been clever in life, and now that I have come to a labor even more magnificent than living itself I do not want to utter a single false word. For months I have been telling myself, "You must be humble. Above all things,

---

WILLIAM SAROYAN *got his first hearing on a large scale in this magazine. His career since then as a short story writer, novelist and playwright is well-known. "Myself Upon the Earth" belongs among his most effective writings.* (October, 1934)

you must be humble." I am determined not to lose my character.

I am a story-teller, and I have but a single story, myself. I want to tell this simple story in my own way, forgetting the rules of rhetoric, the tricks of composition. I have something to say and I do not wish to speak like Balzac. I am not an artist; I do not believe in civilization. I am not at all enthusiastic about progress. When a great bridge is built I do not cheer, and when airplanes cross the Atlantic I do not think, "What a marvelous age this is!"

II

I am not interested in the destiny of nations, and history bores me. What do they mean by history, those who write it and believe in it? How has it happened that man, that humble and lovable creature, has been exploited for the purpose of monstrous documents? How has it happened that his solitude has been destroyed, his godliness herded into a hideous riot of murder and destruction? And I do not believe in commerce. I regard all machinery as junk, the adding-machine, the automobile, the railway engine, the airplane, yes, and the bicycle. I do not believe in transportation, in going places with the body, and I would like to know where anyone has ever gone. Have you ever left yourself? Is any journey so vast and interesting as the journey of the mind through life? Is the end of any journey so beautiful as death?

I am interested only in man. Life I love, and before death I am humble. I cannot fear death because it is purely physical. Is it not true that today both I and my father are living, and that in my flesh is assembled all the past of man? But I despise violence and I hate bitterly those who perpetrate and practise it. The injury of a living man's small finger I regard as infinitely more disastrous and ghastly than his natural death. And when multitudes of men are hurt to death in wars I am driven to a grief which borders on insanity. I become impotent with rage. My only weapon is language, and while I know it is stronger than machine-guns, I despair because I cannot single-handed annihilate the notion of destruction which propagandists awaken in men. I myself, however, am a propagandist, and in this story I am trying to restore man to his natural dignity and gentleness. I want to restore man to himself. I want to send him from the mob to his own body and mind. I want to lift him from the nightmare of history to the calm dream of his own soul, the true chronicle of his kind. I want him to be himself. It is proper only to herd cattle. When the spirit of a single man is taken from him and he is made a member of a mob, the body of God suffers a ghastly pain, and therefore the act is a blasphemy.

I am opposed to mediocrity. If a man is an honest idiot, I can love him, but I cannot love a dishonest genius. All my life I have laughed at rules and mocked traditions, styles and mannerisms. How can a rule be applied to such a wonderful invention as man? Every life is a contradiction, a new truth, a new miracle, and even frauds are interesting. I am not a philosopher and I do not believe in philosophies; the word itself I look upon with suspicion. I believe in the right of man to contradict himself. For instance, did I not say that I look upon machinery as junk, and yet do I not worship the typewriter? Is it not the dearest possession I own?

And now I am coming to the little story I set out to tell. It is about myself and my typewriter, and it is really a trivial story. You can turn to any of the national five-cent magazines and find much more artful stories, stories of love and passion and despair and ecstasy, stories about men called Elmer Fowler, Wilfred Diggens, and women called Florence Farwell, Agatha Hume, and so on.

If you turn to these magazines, you will find any number of perfect stories, full of plot, atmosphere, mood, style, character, and all those other things a good story is supposed to have, just as good mayonnaise is supposed to have so much pure olive oil, so much cream, and so much whipping. (Please do not imagine that I have forgotten myself and am trying to be clever. I am not laughing at these stories. I am not laughing at the people who read them. These works of prose and the men and women and children who read them constitute one of the most touching documents of our time, just as the motion pictures of Hollywood and those who spend the greatest portion of their secret lives watching them constitute one of the finest sources of raw material for the honest novelist. Invariably, let me explain, when I visit the theatre [and it is rarely that I have the price of admission], I am profoundly moved by the flood of emotion which surges from the crowd, and newsreels have always brought hot tears from my eyes. I cannot see floods, tornadoes, fires, wars and the faces of politicians without weeping. Even the tribulations of Mickey Mouse make my heart bleed, for I know that he, artificial as he may be, is actually a symbol of man.)

Therefore, do not misunderstand me. I am not a satirist. There is actually nothing to satirize, and everything fraudulent contains its own mockery. I wish to point out merely that I am a poor writer, an unpublished story-teller, and it will be nothing short of a miracle or a mistake if this story ever appears in print. Yet I go on writing as if all the periodicals in the country were clamoring for my work, offering me vast sums of money for anything I might choose to write. I sit in my room smoking one cigarette after another, writing this story of mine, which I know will never be able to meet the stiff competition of my more artful and talented contemporaries. Is it not strange? And why should I, an unpublished story-teller, be so attached to my typewriter? What earthly good is it to me? And what satisfaction do I get from writing stories I know will never be published?

Well, this is the story. Still, I do not want anyone to suppose that I am complaining. I do not want you to feel that I am a hero of some sort, or, on the other hand, that I am a sentimental fool. I am actually neither of these things. I have no objection to the *Saturday Evening Post*, and I do not believe the editor of *Scribner's* is an idiot because he will not publish my tales. I know precisely what every magazine in the country wants. I know the sort of material *Secret Stories* is seeking, and the sort THE AMERICAN MERCURY prefers, and the sort preferred by the literary journals like the *Saturday Review of Literature*. I read all magazines and I know what sort of stuff sells. Still, I am unpublished and poor. Is it that I cannot write the sort of stuff for which money is paid? I assure you that it is not. I can write any sort of story you can think of. If Edgar Rice Burroughs were to die this morning, I could go on writing about Tarzan and the Apes. Or if I felt inclined, I could write like John Dos Passos or William Faulkner or James Joyce.

But I have said that I want to preserve my identity. Well, I mean it. If in doing this it is essential for me to remain unpublished, I am satisfied. I do not believe in fame. It is a form of fraudulence, and any famous man will tell you so. Any honest man, at any rate. How can one living man possibly be greater than another? And what difference does it make if one man writes great novels which are printed and another writes great novels which are not? What has the printing of novels to do with their greatness? What has money or the lack of it to do with the character of a man?

But I will confess that you've got to be proud and religious to be the sort of writer I am. You've got to have an astounding amount of strength. And it takes years and years to become this sort of writer, sometimes centuries. I wouldn't advise any young man with a talent for words to try to write the way I do. I would suggest that he study Theodore Dreiser or Sinclair Lewis. I would suggest even that, rather than attempt my method, he follow in the footsteps of O. Henry or the contributors of the *Woman's Home Companion*. Because, briefly, I am not a writer at all. I have been laughing at the rules of writing ever since I started to write, ten, maybe fifteen, years ago. I am simply a young man. I write because for me there is nothing more civilized or decent to do.

III

Do you know that I do not believe there is such a thing as a poem-form, a story-form or a novel-form? I believe there is man only. The rest is trickery. I am trying to carry over into this story of mine the man that I am. And as much of my earth as I am able. I want more than anything else to be honest and fearless in my own way. Do you think I could not, if I chose, omit the remark I made about Dos Passos and Faulkner and Joyce, a remark which is both ridiculous and dangerous? Why, if someone were to say to me, "All right, you say you can write like Faulkner, well, then, let's see you do it." If someone were to say this to me, I would be positively stumped and I would have to admit timidly that I couldn't do the trick. Nevertheless, I make the statement and let it stand. And what is more, no one can prove that I am cracked; I could make the finest alienist in Vienna appear to be a raving maniac to his own disciples, or if I did not prefer this course, I could act as dull and stupid and sane as a Judge of the United States Supreme Court. Didn't I say that in my flesh is gathered all the past of man? And surely there have been dolts in that past.

I do not know, but there may be a law of some sort against this kind of writing. It may be a misdemeanor. I hope so. It is impossible for me to smash a fly which has tickled my nose, or to step on an ant, or to hurt the feelings of any man, idiot or genius, but I cannot resist the temptation to mock any law which is designed to hamper the spirit of man. It is essential for me to stick pins in pompous balloons. I love to make small explosions with the inflated bags of moralists, cowards, and wise men. Listen and you will hear such a small explosion in this paragraph.

All this rambling may seem pointless and a waste of time, but it is not. There is absolutely no haste — I can walk the hundred yard dash in a full day — and anyone who prefers may toss this story aside and take up something in the *Cosmopolitan*. I am not asking anyone to stand by. I am not promising golden apples to all who are patient. I am sitting in my room, living my life, tapping my typewriter. I am sitting in the presence of my young father, who has been gone from the earth so many years. Every two or three minutes I look up into his melancholy face to see how he is taking it all. It is like looking into a mirror, for I see myself. I am almost as old as he was when the photograph was taken and I am wearing the same moustache he wore at the time. I worship this man. All my life I have worshipped him. When both of us lived on the earth I was too young to exchange one word with him, consciously, but ever since I have come to consciousness and articulation we have had many long silent conversations. I say to him, "Ah, you melancholy Armenian, you; how marvelous your life has been!" And he replies gently, "Be humble, my son. Seek God."

IV

My father was a writer too. He too was an unpublished writer. I have all his great manuscripts, his great poems and stories, written in our native language, which I cannot read. Two or three times each year I bring out all my father's papers and stare for hours at his contribution to the literature of the world. Like myself, I am pleased to say, he was desperately poor; poverty trailed him like a hound, as the expression is. Most of his poems and stories were written upon wrapping paper which he folded into small books. Only his journal is in English and it is full of lamentations. In New York, according to this journal, my father had only two moods; sad and very sad. About thirty years ago he was alone in that city, and he was trying to earn enough money to pay for the passage of his wife and three children to the new world. He was a janitor. Why should I try to withhold this fact? There is nothing shameful about a great man being a janitor in America. In the old country he was a man of great honor, a professor, and he was called Agha, which means approximately lord. Unfortunately, he was also a revolutionist, as all good Armenians are. He wanted the handful of people of his old race to be free. He wanted them to enjoy liberty, and so he was placed in jail every now and then. Finally, it got so bad that if he did not leave the old country, he would kill and be killed. He knew English, he had read Shakespeare and Swift in English, so he came to this country. And they made a janitor of him.

After a number of years of hard work his family joined him in New York. In California, according to my father's journal, matters for a while were slightly better for him; he mentioned a strong sun and magnificent bunches of grapes. So he tried farming. At first he worked for other farmers, then he made a down payment on a small farm of his own. But he was a rotten farmer. He was a man of books, a professor; he loved good clothes. He loved leisure and comfort, and like myself he hated machinery.

My father's vineyard was about eleven miles east of the nearest town, and all the farmers nearby were in the habit of going to town once or twice a week on bicycles, which were the vogue at that time and a trifle faster than a horse and buggy. One hot afternoon in August a tall individual in very fine clothes was seen moving forward in long leisurely strides over a hot and dusty country road. It was my father. My people told me this story about the man, so that I might understand what a fool he was and not be like him. Someone saw my father. It was a neighbor farmer who was returning from the city on a bicycle. This man was amazed.

"Agha," he said, "where are you going?"

"To town," my father said.

"But, Agha," said the farmer, "you cannot do this thing. It is eleven miles to town and you look . . . People will laugh at you in such clothes."

"Let them laugh," my father said. "These are my clothes. They fit me."

"Yes, yes, of course they fit you," said the farmer, "but such clothes do not seem right out here in this dust and heat. Everyone wears overalls out here, Agha."

"Nonsense," said my father. He went on walking. The farmer followed my father, whom he now regarded as slightly insane.

"At least," he said, "if you insist on wearing those clothes, at least you will not humiliate yourself by *walking* to town. You will at least accept the use of my bicycle."

This farmer was a close friend of my father's family, and he had great respect for my father. He meant well, but my father was dumbfounded. He stared at the man with horror and disgust.

"What?" he shouted. "You ask me to mount one of those crazy contraptions? You ask me to tangle myself in that ungodly piece of junk?" (The Armenian equivalent of junk is a good deal more violent and horrible.) "Man was not made for such absurd inventions. Man was not placed on earth to tangle himself in junk. He was placed here to stand erect and to walk with his feet." And away he went.

Ah, you can be sure that I worship this man. And now, alone in this room, thinking of these things, tapping out this story, I want to show that I and my father are the same man.

I shall come soon to the matter of the typewriter, but there is no hurry. I am a story-teller, not an aviator. I am not carrying myself across the Atlantic in the cockpit of an airplane which moves at the rate of two hundred and fifty miles per hour.

It is Monday of this year, 1933, and I am trying to gather as much of eternity into this story as possible. When next this story is read I may be with my father in the earth we both love and I may have sons alive on the surface of this old earth, young fellows whom I shall ask to be humble as my father has asked me to be humble.

In a moment a century may have elapsed, and I am doing what I can to keep this moment solid and alive.

Musicians have been known to weep at the loss of a musical instrument, or at its injury. To a great violinist his violin is a part of his identity. I am a young man with a dark mind, and a dark way in general, a sullen and serious way. The earth is mine, but not the world. If I am taken away from language, if I am placed in the street, as one more living entity, I become nothing, not even a shadow. I have less honor than the grocer's clerk, less dignity than the doorman at the St. Francis Hotel, less identity than the driver of a taxi-cab.

And for the past six months I have been separated from my writing, and I have been nothing, or I have been walking about unalive, some indistinct shadow in a nightmare of the universe. It is simply that without conscious articulation, without words, without language, I do not exist as myself. I have no meaning, and I might just as well be dead and nameless. It is blasphemous for any living man to live in such a manner. It is an outrage to God. It means that we have got nowhere after all these years.

It is for this reason, now that I have my typewriter again, and have beside me a bundle of clean writing paper, and am sitting in my room, full of tobacco smoke, with my father's photograph watching over me — it is for this reason that I feel I have just been resurrected from the dead. I love and worship life, living senses, functioning minds. I love consciousness. I love precision. And life is to be created by every man who has the breath of God within him; and every man is to create his own consciousness, and his own precision, for these things do not exist of themselves. Only confusion and error and ugliness exist of themselves. I have said that I am deeply religious. I am. I believe that I live, and you've got to be religious to believe so miraculous a thing. And I am grateful and I am humble. I do live, so let the years repeat themselves eternally, for I am sitting in my room, stating in words the truth of my being, squeezing the fact from meaninglessness and imprecision.

And the living of this moment can never be effaced. It is beyond time.

I despise commerce. I am a young man with no money. There are times when a young man can use a small sum of money to good advantage, there are times when money to him, because of what it can purchase, is the most important thing of his life. I despise commerce, but I admit that I have some respect for money. It is, after all, pretty important, and it was the lack of it, year after year, that finally killed my father. It wasn't right for a man so poor to wear the sort of clothes he knew he deserved; so my father died. I would like to have enough money to enable me to live simply and to write my life. Years ago, when I labored in behalf of industry and progress and so on, I purchased a small portable typewriter, brand new, for sixty-five dollars. (And what an enormous lot of money that is, if you are poor.) At first this machine was strange to me and I was annoyed by the racket it made when it was in use; late at night this racket was unbearably distressing. It resembled more than anything else silence which has been magnified a thousand times, if such a thing could be.

But after a year or two I began to feel a genuine attachment for the machine, and loved it as a good pianist, who respects music, loves his piano. I never troubled to clean the machine and no matter how persistently I pounded upon it, the machine did not weaken and start to fall to pieces. I had great respect for it.

V

And then, in a fit of despondency, I placed this small machine in its case and carried it to the city. I left it in the establishment of a money-lender, and walked through the city with fifteen dollars in my pocket. I was sick of being poor.

I went first to a bootblack and had my shoes polished. When a bootblack is shining my shoes I place him in the chair and I descend and polish his shoes. It is an experience in humility.

Then I went to a theatre. I sat among people to see myself in patterns of Hollywood. I sat and dreamed, looking into the faces of beautiful women. Then I went to a restaurant and sat at a table and ordered all the different kinds of food I ever thought I would like to eat. I ate two dollars' worth of food. The waiter thought I was out of my head, but I told him everything was going along first rate. I tipped the waiter. Then I went out into the city again and began walking along the dark streets, the streets where the women are. I was tired of being poor. I put my typewriter in hock and I began to spend the money. No one, not even the greatest writer, can go on being poor hour after hour, year after year. There is such a thing as saying to hell with art. That's what I said.

After a week I became sober. After a month I became very sober and I began to want my typewriter again. I began to want to put words on paper again. To make another beginning. To say something and see if it was the right thing. But I had no money. Day after day I had this longing for my typewriter.

This is the whole story. I don't suppose this ending is very artful, but it is the ending just the same. The point is this: day after day I longed for my typewriter.

This morning I got it back. It is before me now and I am tapping at it, and this is what I have written.

ALTAR BOY

By John Fante

ONE time I served Mass with Allie Saler, and Allie had the right side to serve. I mean he had to give the priest wine and ring the bells and move the missal and pretty near all the important things that altar boys do. All of us guys on the altar boys used to like serving on the right side on account of it was so important. It is a lot more important than the left side server. He hardly ever does anything. All he does is genuflect and hold the paten at Holy Communion.

We got to the sacristy about ten minutes before Mass started, and when it came time to figure out who got the right side, I said I did, and he said he did. We started in saying dirty things back and forth, and Father Andrew came in.

He said: "Here, here, what is going on here?"

We told him.

He said: "Oh, that is nothing. I will settle it by having Allie take it this morning."

I just hated that look on Allie's face. It was just like he had it all figured out with Father Andrew that I was going to get the left, and Father looked straight at Allie, just like I was not there, and it was just like saying: "I like you better than him, and your father owns the drug-store, and his father never does come to church, so that is why you get the right."

It says in the Catechism that to think evil things is the same as doing them, so right away I knew I was sinning to beat the band while I was standing there, and I knew my sins were awful ones, maybe mortal sins, because I was standing there wishing Father Andrew was a man instead of a priest, and more my size, so I could knock the hell out of him, and get even. I was not wishing any such thing as that on Allie because it was a waste of wishes. I knew I would lay into him good and hard after Mass. He knew it too. I could tell, all right.

But it was all settled that he got the right side, so we started to get things ready for Mass. Father put on his vestments. Allie lit the candles and I got the wine and water ready.

The wine was not real wine at all. My father has swell red stuff in his cellar, but this was blackish red grape juice, kind of bitter, and just as thick as ink. The guys used to swipe a mouthful every once in a while and pretend they were stewed, but I did not because it did not taste so good, and my father says you can down a whole barrel of it without it fazing you. Father Andrew likes his wine plain, without mix-

---

JOHN FANTE, *one of the most promising younger writers, first achieved a nation-wide audience in this magazine. His books include* Dago Red *and* Ask the Dust. *(August, 1932)*

ing it with water, and about an inch of it for every Mass. I mean the wine would be an inch deep in the pitcher.

While I was fixing the wine, all of a sudden I got a hunch on how to get even. It did not make much difference then about another sin, the sin of getting even, because I had already committed a mortal sin when I wished evil to a priest. One mortal sin is just as bad as twenty. I mean if you commit one, you go to Hell just as quick as if you had twenty against you. It says so in the Catechism. I knew there was a bottle of red ink in the supply drawer, so I went there and got it. Nobody was looking, and I poured it into the wine bottle, about one-fifth, then I filled the rest with grape juice.

Mass started, and while I was kneeling at the altar I got to thinking about what I did. Father Andrew was moving softly back and forth on the altar, saying prayers in Latin, with his eyes shut, and I could see how holy he looked. The organ was playing sad, sacred music. Then it came to me all at once what I did. I committed a horrid sin because the ink I put in the bottle would be consecrated and changed into the body and blood of our Lord. I felt terrible to think that Jesus had been crucified for my sins, and there I was, kneeling at this sacrifice without even feeling ashamed.

Gosh, I was scared to death, I did not know what to do next. I could see how ungrateful I was to our Lord. I could see Him up in Heaven, with blood oozing out of His feet, and crying tears of blood for what I did. I kept saying over and over: "Sweet Jesus, forgive me! Sweet Jesus, forgive me! Sweet Jesus, forgive me!" I knew I deserved to burn forever for my sin, but I kept on begging our Lord for forgiveness anyhow, because it says in the Catechism that true contrition is sufficient for salvation, and I wanted to prove how really sad I was for my sin.

At the Consecration Allie gave Father the wine, and he gobbled it up without so much as blinking, so I guess he did not catch on. But all this time, there I was kneeling on the green carpet that covers the altar steps, and praying to beat the band for our Lord to forgive me. I prayed for all I was worth, trying to feel perfect contrition. Perfect contrition is just as good as confession if you can't go to confession. If you get a tough grip on yourself, hold yourself real stiff, and think nothing but sorrow, sorrow, sorrow, pretty soon you do have real sorrow, and that is what I was wanting.

After Mass I made another Act of Contrition and said some Hail Marys to boot. Then I went into the sacristy, and Father Andrew smiled at me, because he likes to see holy guys, and when he smiled, his teeth were red like he had been eating cherries. I did not laugh or anything when I saw his red teeth. I was really scared, and if I did not know it was ink I would have swore it was our Lord's blood. Miracles like that happen every now and then.

Father patted my shoulder, and I went around to the other side of the church and took off my cassock and surplice. Allie Saler was gone already. I hurried and ran outside and saw him a block away. The snow was starting to melt, getting ready for Spring, and Allie went along kicking up slush.

I ran up to him, put my hand on his chest and my right leg back of his knees, and pushed him, jiujitsu fashion. The trick worked swell. Allie sat down in the wettest, muddiest slush. That is how I got even with him. Nobody knew about the red ink except Father Joseph. I told him in confession. For penance, he made me promise not to do it again, and I did, and to say five Our Fathers and five Hail Marys. So all in all, I got off pretty easy.

II

On the first of May, because May is the month of our Mother, and by that I mean the Blessed Virgin, everybody in the altar boys had to line up two at a time in a great big long line and go to the Blessed Virgin's altar in the church to say the rosary. We went in with our partners and knelt down in the aisle, and Harold Maguire, who was president of the altar boys, began to say the rosary out loud. I mean like this. Here is what he said, "Hail Mary, full of grace, the Lord is with thee, blessed art thou among women and blessed is the fruit of thy womb, Jesus." He stopped there, and the rest of us guys took it up, only we prayed like this: "Holy Mary, mother of God, pray for us sinners now and at the hour of our death. Amen."

Worms Kelley was my partner. Worms hated Maguire like the dickens, and so did everybody else, but Worms hated him most because Maguire was a snitch baby, and he had a suck with the nuns. What I mean by suck is that when Maguire wanted something off the nuns, like going to the washroom every few minutes, he got to go, and nobody else did, except maybe two or three girls with sucks, too. I did not like Maguire to look at. He was sissified, with thick eye-glasses made out of black celluloid. His hands were little bitty things. He used to stay on the steps at noon with his "Bible Stories," so Sister Prefect could see him. He carried his lunch in a blue bucket, and the sandwiches were wrapped in the white tissue paper that you buy, instead of good old bread wrapper. His dessert every day was a big apple, or cake or pie or something like that. His mother came for him after school in a Studebaker. She was very tall, and looked like she had strong muscles. She was president of the Ladies' Altar Society, and when she came after Harold she would lean out of the car door and talk awful courteous to Sister Marie, who was upstairs looking out the window, keeping an eye on us guys so we would not break ranks. Mrs. Maguire used to lick Harold with a piece of garden hose, two feet long.

Harold got going good on the rosary and everything was all right when all of a sudden Worms started to make noises with his mouth. Sister Cecilia was in the first pew. She did not look up right away, but every one of the guys except Harold kept turning around, looking straight at Worms and me because we were kneeling close together. We were all snickering to beat the band, so Worms got nervier and nervier. He made noises louder and louder. Sister Cecilia moved a little, like she was itching all over, so Worms stopped the noises. I was glad because Worms was my partner, and I might get the blame.

We got to the Fifth Joyful Mystery, that is the last part of the rosary, when for no good reason, Worms made a noise that was the funniest yet. You could hear it echo away up behind the organ-pipes. All of us except Maguire sat back on our heels and just busted out laughing. Maguire turned around to Sister like he was asking for help. It was awful. I wanted to stop laughing because it is a grievous sin to be disrespectful in church, but I could not, I just could not. I laughed and laughed, and so did Worms, and so did everybody else.

Sister Cecilia was redder than a beet. She put up her hand for silence, the way Mussolini does in *Pathé News*.

She said: "No one leaves this church until I find the pig who did that."

Nobody said anything. We were just as quiet as can be.

"Very well," she said. "You'll stay until I find out."

We had to kneel up straight and it got pretty tough on the knees. Away back in the vestibule you could hear a clock ticking. After a half hour the ticking sounded like heavy rocks hitting a slate roof. The guys started to look at Worms as if to tell him to go ahead and admit it, but the longer he kept still the worse it got, until finally he did not dare to talk. Then old Maguire turned around and saw all the guys looking at us, and after a minute he got up and went to where Sister was. He was snitching, that is what he was doing. It was as plain as day.

We started to hiss: "Snitch baby! Snitch baby! Snitch baby!" And Maguire was sure in for a walloping from us guys.

Sister looked straight at me and Worms, and said: "Will you please follow me into the sacristy?"

I nearly keeled over. I held my breath and blinked my eyes and wondered what the heck. The only thing to do was to take it on the cheek for Worms. The guys whispered: "That's the boy!" and that was pretty good to hear, but it did not help much. I knew I was in for it. I gave Maguire a dirty look when I went by, and I bet he knew I was going to ruin him when I got him alone, because I sure was. Sister Cecilia was ready for me.

I was holding a rosary, fooling with it, standing in front of Sister Cecilia, waiting for her to do what she was going to do.

"Put the rosary away," she said. I did.

She rolled up her black sleeves, sort of got her distance, made a moaning sound, and with all her might she let me have one smack on the cheek. The sting was something fierce and I started crying a little, but not much. The guys must have heard the smack, because it sounded just like when a cottonwood cracks and falls. I felt awful cheap. My cheek was very hot. I rubbed it. Sister Cecilia was crying too, and I thought she was sure nuts, because I was getting hit, not her. But I felt sorry for her and I did not know why, either.

She said: "Go back and kneel down, you little heathen. I'll see you later."

The guys saw my face, which was very red. It made me feel very cheap. I gave Maguire another dirty look. He was going to get it. The guys would get him tomorrow. Me and the guys would. We could not get him after rosary because his mother would be there in her Studebaker to take the sissy home.

All the guys went home, and of course I had to go to our room, and of course I had to write "I must not be disrespectful in church" five hundred times. I did not get through until seven o'clock. After the sun went behind the peaks, and there was no light except the street lamps, I turned on the lights in the room. All by myself, I was scared and lonesome. When I got through, I put the papers on Sister's desk and went home.

My old man was waiting when I got there. I should say he was waiting. He knew all about it. Sister Cecilia had snitched, just like Maguire. My father made a run for me as soon as I got in the house. What he did to me was more than what Sister did to me, but I did not cry or anything. I took it like a real guy. The reason is, I knew he was my father, and he would stop hitting before he hurt me too serious. He kept saying he was going to kill me, but he is my father, and he does not scare me with that stuff.

Next day at school the altar boys got out at noon so we could go up to the foothills to pick flowers for the Blessed Virgin's altar. The main reason I pray to the Blessed Virgin is because we get out of a lot of school on account of her. We started out in a bunch, two at a time, and had to walk clear through town, with Sister Cecilia leading us like we were a bunch of convicts or something. Like we were dangerous. I do not like it at all. The Protestants stop every time to look at us as if we are freaks. And the Sisters look funny with their funny dresses.

We walked clear through town to the edge of the foothills. They were full of yellow anemones and wild daisies and violets. Anemones and daisies are easy to pick. Violets smell swell, but they are the nuts to pick. It takes a whole bushel to make a bouquet.

We broke ranks and my partner Worms showed me a brand new package of Camels. Worms smoked all the time. He even inhaled. Sister Cecilia went looking for flowers, and me and Worms sneaked behind some sagebrush and crawled on our hands and knees into a gulch that used to be a creek. We lit up and took it easy.

Pretty soon we finished our snipes and crawled out of the gulch. We saw the guys scattered all over the hills. They were very far away from us. Some of them were in bunches, some were alone, carrying armloads of flowers. We could barely see who they were, they were so far off. We could see Sister Cecilia in black and white. She was walking cross-wise from us, and taking it easy. The day was awfully pretty and calm. There was not a cloud or a breeze, and it was warm. Me and Worms wanted to go fishing.

All at once, who should walk into us from behind the sagebrush? No one else but Harold Maguire. He was carrying flowers in his cap. He was so surprised he was scared to death. We were surprised too, but we were not scared. We were just surprised.

This was our chance to get even, and we knew it, and so did he. It was just like our Lord had planned it out for him to meet us. But I do not know if our Lord had planned it out for us to get even, because that is a grievous sin. I do not think our Lord had anything to do with that. I guess that was the Devil.

"Let's ding-bump him," Worms said.
"Let's," I said.

It takes two to ding-bump a man. You get him on his back, and one of you grab his arms, and the other his legs, and you lift him up and down as hard as you can, so that his seat bumps the ground.

Harold was so scared he did not fight back. We told him to get on his back, and he did it. We told him to take off his specs, and he did it. We told him we would teach him not to snitch, and he said he would not any more. He started to cry. That made me want to hurry up.

After we bumped him the first time, he yelled as loud as he could. The guys and Sister heard him, because they came running from everywhere. It is too bad the guys were not closer. They would of got a big kick out of it. Sister Cecilia was nearly running. She was almost half a mile away.

I saw a cactus plant with short thorns, not even half an inch long. "Let's sit him in that, and then beat it," I said.

We did it. We sat him in the cactus and ran away.

They nearly kicked us out of school for what we did. I mean the nuns.

We had to apologize to them and to Father Andrew and to the whole school. We got lickings at home and in school. We had to stay every night until five for a month. We did not get to go to the altar boy banquet.

But we did not care a bit. We got even. You can ask any of the guys about Harold Maguire now. They will tell you he used to be a snitch baby, but he is not one now. He is a swell guy now.

III

Bill Shafer is the worst altar boy in the bunch. He swipes stuff, and he chews gum before Communion. I do not see how he does it. I do not think his mother cares because I saw him eat meat on Friday. It was a sandwich. His mother makes his lunch. If she cared, she would make him eat fish. Bill says it is not his sin if he eats meat. It is her sin. She put it in. Bill has four Sunday suits. He wears them to school a lot. His mother is sure keen looking. If my mother was as keen looking as she is, I would sure feel good. I do not mean my mother is not good looking. I mean Bill's mother is sure good looking.

Bill showed me how to swipe agates at the ten-cent store. You open your waist, and then you lean away over the counter. When the girl is not looking, you roll the miggs into your waist. It is a good way. It works every time. I do not think Bill told his in confession, but I told Father Andrew mine.

Father Andrew said I had to return the miggs or pay for them. He sure was sore. He almost hollered at me. Bill won all my miggs, so I will have to pay for them with money sometime. I will do it when I get bigger. I bet Bill never does pay for his.

One time I was walking home from school with Bill. He had a dime, so we went to Drake's to get Eskimo pies.

When we were in there, he said: "Hey, do you want a fountain-pen?"

I said: "Sure."

He said: "Wait a minute."

He said to Mr. Drake: "Hey Mr. Drake, can I use your 'phone?"

Mr. Drake said: "Sure."

So Bill went to the 'phone in back. At first I wondered what the heck. Then I knew he was going to swipe a pen for me. I did not snitch though, I am not a snitch baby. I did not watch, because Old Man Drake might catch on. He was piling Eskimo pies, and I looked at his bald head. His neck was real little. I started to think maybe somebody would come into the store. Maybe somebody would, then we would get caught and get sent to Golden. The big reform school is in Golden. Sister says there is not a Catholic boy in there. There never has been. If we were caught, we would be the first Catholics. I did not want to get caught. I thought I better pray that we would not get caught.

I looked at old Drake's bald head and prayed to myself. In my head, I mean.

I said: "Hail Mary, please do not let anybody come in. Please do not let anybody come in."

The Blessed Virgin heard my prayer, because just then Bill came back.

When we got outside, he said: "Hey, come on. Run like hell." Hell is not swearing. Hell is on every page of the Catechism. You can say it.

We did not stop until we got to the Twelfth Street bridge. We crawled under it.

Bill said: "Hey, that was sure easy as pie."

I said: "Gee Bill, you sure swipe stuff." He did not say anything. We knew he committed a mortal sin, but we did not say anything.

He opened his waist and showed me. I thought he swiped one, but he swiped fifteen. They were in a box made out of velvet. They were pens that cost a whole lot. One of them had a ticket. It said: $18. I got scared to death.

Bill said: "Hey, which one do you want?"

I did not want Bill to think I was chicken or scared or yellow.

I said: "Oh, I will take this one." I took the cheapest. It was $5.

He took the $18 one and said: "Hey, what will we do with the rest?"

I said: "I do not know."

He said: "Well, here goes." He threw them into the water. It was a sandy bottom. You could see the pens.

I wanted to run. I am not goofy, and a fountain-pen does not scare me, but I wanted to run away. I did not want to go to confession, because the last time I confessed stealing miggs, and Father Andrew got sore. I mean he talked real loud. If I told him I swiped a $5 pen, I bet he would yell. The holy people outside would hear him.

Bill said: "Hey, we better beat it. Let me go first. You wait five minutes."

He crawled away and left me all alone with the pens.

The pens did not scare me or anything, but I was scared about something. I got some rocks and mud and covered up the pens. It made the water muddy looking. There was a long streak of muddy water. It made me feel like a thief. But Bill did it. All of a sudden I felt like running. I crawled out and started in. I ran and ran. I forgot where I was going until I got right in front of Drake's. I nearly keeled over when I saw where I was. I was winded, but I started in again. I ran all the harder. Pretty soon I was right in front of the church. The church and school are right next to each other. I thought it was funny as heck to be there again, because it was pretty near five o'clock, and a school is a punk place to be at five. I thought how come, and so I started for home.

I got a block away, and then I thought I better go back and say an Act of Contrition. Then I saw I was in a heck of a fix, because it says in the Catechism that an Act of Contrition is good only if confession cannot be had, and there I was only a block away from the priest's house. The priest would hear my confession if I asked him. I thought I better go ahead and have it over with. Father Andrew would sure be sore.

Then I got a swell idea. I would ask for Father Joseph. He did not know about the miggs, so he would not be hard on me. It was sure a good idea, because now I could go to confession, and the fountain-pens would not scare me. I mean I would not be scared. Fountain-pens are nothing. It is nuts to be scared of them. I went back to the church. I ran all the way.

I asked the maid for Father Joseph, and he came down. Father Joseph has a great big belly and a double chin. He likes me. He says I am a keen pitcher. He knows a pitcher on the St. Louis Browns. He says I am the born image of this pitcher. I like Father Joseph very, very much.

I said: "Father, I want to go to confession."

He said: "Why not? So does everybody."

We went into church, and Father got in the confessional.

I told him what I did. I did not snitch on Bill. I just said I was in bad company a little while ago, and I swiped a fountain-pen. I am not a snitch baby.

Father said I had to return the pen or what it was worth or he would not forgive me. I said I would. He gave me absolution. I went out to the altar and said my penance, which was five Our Fathers and five Hail Marys in honor of the Blessed Virgin. Father Joseph is sure a keen guy. He did not make me feel cheap at all. He hardly said anything.

I got outside and started for home. I felt just grand. I started whistling hymns like I always do after confession. I had it all figured out about the $5 pen. I would keep it. I would tell my mother I found it. It was a lie, but a lie is only a venial sin. You do not go to Hell if you have a venial sin on your soul. You go to Purgatory. Then you go to Heaven. Some day I will pay old Drake for it. I will do it when I get bigger. I bet Bill Shafer never pays for his.

IV

Bill Shafer used to chew gum before Communion. He sure thought he was tough. He sure thought he was smart. When you go to Communion you cannot eat or drink anything that is food or drink after midnight. You must fast. Bill used to come around to us guys before Communion and pop gum in our ears. He sure thought he was smart.

Sister caught him doing it, and she made him spit it out. It sure was keen, the way she told him to spit. He spit, and all of us guys laughed right out loud. We were in church too, only we were in the vestibule. Bill sure thought he was tough. We did not laugh like it was real funny. We laughed different, so Bill would sort of feel cheap.

We laughed like this: "He he he he."

Bill said: "Hey, Sister, how come? Gum is not food or drink."

Sister said: "Gum has sugar in it."

We sure got a big kick out of it. Bill sure thought he was smart. He sure felt cheap.

The next day he did it again before Communion. I mean he popped his gum. He sure thought he was tough.

One of the guys snitched on him. I know who it was, but I am not going to snitch on him just because he snitched on Bill. I am not a snitch baby.

Sister pretty near ran to where Bill was standing. He was standing there popping. She got a hold of his hair and jerked him around and said: "Spit it out! Spit it out!"

Bill said: "Hey, Sister! No sugar in this gum. This is old gum. I been saving it."

Sister said: "Say, young man, I have had enough of this. You must not dare go to Holy Communion this morning. The very idea! Young man, I want you to see Father Andrew right after Mass."

In the afternoon, in Catechism class, Sister sat right up in front of Bill and told him right out, right in front of us guys. She said what she thought of a boy who chewed gum before Communion. Gosh, she sure sailed in! Old Bill was sure sore. Sister said a guy who will do that must come from a funny house. I guess Sister is right, because I saw Bill's mother chew gum a lot. She *is* sure keen looking. I mean Bill's mother. Not sister. Sister is goofy looking.

Then Sister told us a whole gob of stories about smart guys like Bill. She told us how they tried to be smart aleck with our Lord, and how He fixed them. He sure got even good and proper.

Sister said there was once another smart aleck like Bill who used to go to Communion every day. He went so many times that he got used to it, and pretty soon he started to be disrespectful. One morning he thought he would do something. Oh yes, he thought he was smart. He would to do something real swell. He was going to take the Sacred Host out of his mouth after he received it, and then take it home. So he went to Communion.

He did what he said he was going to do. When he came back from the altar, he put the Sacred Host in a dirty handkerchief. It was awful. I can hardly think about a guy who would do any such thing. But our Lord sure fixed him good and proper.

When this rotten guy got home, he took out his handkerchief, and for gosh sakes, was he scared? His handkerchief was all bloody. Our Lord's blood was all in it.

When the guy saw this, he fell on his knees and asked God to forgive him, for God's sake. Then he got up and went away and became a priest. He was so holy they made him a bishop. He is one now. He is back East some place.

Old Bill kept saying: "Bull! bull! bull!" He sure thought he was smart. He took out his handkerchief and played like he was looking for blood. He sure thought he was a wise guy.

After school, Bill said to me and Allie

Saler: "Hey, I bet she made up that story about the bishop."

Allie said: "I bet she did not."

Bill said: "Hey, what you want to bet I can do it without getting my handkerchief all bloody?"

I said: "I bet you $1,000,000."

Bill said: "Shake!"

We shook. I did not mean a real $1,000,000. I only have $2 in my bank.

The next morning after Mass, Bill ran after me and Allie. We were going home to breakfast. We go to Communion every morning in May.

He said: "Hey, you guys, come on! I want to show you."

We went to the washroom in the basement. There were some fourth-grade punks standing around.

Bill said: "Hey, you kids, beat it."

We went into a washroom and locked the door. Bill took out his handkerchief. There was a Sacred Host in it. It was wrinkled and melty. You could see he took it out of his mouth.

I said: "Oh, my God!"

Allie made the sign of the cross. I thought it was a good thing to do, so I did too. Bill, he just laughed.

He said: "Hey, where is the blood?"

There was not a drop on it.

Allie said: "Come on, Tom, I have to go."

Bill said: "Hey, where is the blood?"

I said: "Bill, God will sure get even with you for this."

Bill said: "Hey, if you guys ever snitch, I sure will get even with you."

We said we would not snitch.

When we got outside the washroom, we heard the water running. I bet Bill threw the Host in. That is a sacrilege, and a big one, I bet. Bill will get his. Our Lord will punish him. He sure thinks he is tough. He sure thinks he is smart.

V

My favorite saint is Saint John. He is the one I was named after. Saint Joseph used to be my favorite, but since writing letters to him never has done much good, I have changed back to Saint John, and Saint Joseph is not like he used to be. It is a funny thing to think, but every time I pray to Saint Joseph I think about Joe Kraut. I mean every time I pray to him and I am not in front of his statue, which is supposed to look like him, I think about Joe Kraut, and Joe Kraut is not so swell to think about. Joe is only eleven, and he has three or four whiskers on his chin already, and he has a squashy chin, and he is fat. I guess maybe that is why Saint Joseph is so hard to pray to, on account of I think of Joe Kraut, and that is not such a keen thought. But I like Joe Kraut. He always has a nickel or so, so we go to the bakery after school and buy day-old pies.

In a way, I think Saint Joseph played me kind of dirty, after all the letters I sent to him. We write to him every year on his feast day. I mean all the guys and girls have to write down on a little note what they want most, and they also write how many prayers they will say to get it, and then Sister Agnes gets all the notes together in a bunch and she burns them, with the stove-lid off, so Saint Joseph will read them in the smoke. Anyhow, that is what Sister says, but I do not think much of it any more, or maybe Saint Joseph never read my notes, or if he did, he does not like me very much.

His feast day comes once every year, and on that day, for three straight times I asked for a bicycle. I asked for one of those swell Ranger bikes, brown frame, nickel-plated spokes and vacuum-cup tires. I never did get what I wanted.

After I did not get my bike the first two times, I went to Sister Agnes and asked her how come. She said, well, seeing as how a Saint only knows what is good for us, maybe he felt like a bike would do me hurt. I might get run over and get killed. And that is the reason he did not send any. She also said maybe I asked for too much, but a Saint is a Saint, and a bike is not too much for him to get for me, and besides, I would not get run over, because I can ride a bike better than anybody. After he reads your note, Saint Joseph goes to God and tells Him what is what, and God cannot refuse very well, because Saint Joseph was the foster father of the Infant Jesus when He was down here.

The other guys did not ask for as much as I did, I guess, but still most of them got what they wanted. Reinhardt asked for a new football, and sure enough next day his father brought him home a keen Spaulding. I think I know how that came off, though. I think Sister Agnes read his note to Saint Joseph, and then she telephoned to Reinhardt's dad, who got the football right in his store, because he owns a clothing store and sells Spaulding stuff right in it.

Right after this last time I wrote to Saint Joseph, I went to Sister Agnes and said: "Sister, this makes the third time I'm asking Saint Joseph for a bike."

I told her this because I kind of had a hunch she would telephone my old man, and then I would maybe get the bike. All the time, I also kept saying over and over in my head to Saint Joseph, I mean I was praying, like this: "O Saint Joseph, dear, sweet Saint Joseph, if you do not send the bike I will not pray to you again." When I prayed like that, I thought the bike would come for sure, because if Saint Joseph found out I would quit praying to him if he did not send the bike, then he would send it. He would not want me to quit him.

I wrote to him that I wanted this bike to be on our front porch when I woke up next morning. I thought it would be keen to wake up and find it there. I also thought if Sister telephoned the old man, he would have time to get the bike on the porch by next morning.

I went to bed real early that night, about eight or half after, and I prayed to Saint Joseph until I went to sleep. I also said my night prayers. I wanted to make sure I said enough prayers.

The next morning I piled out and ran to the porch. There was a bike there, all right. But it was not what I wanted. It was the second-hand one that used to be in Benson's window all the time. It was full of fly specks. The paint was chipped off. It had crazy, old-fashioned handlebars. I fixed it up anyway, and put on new paint, but I was awfully disappointed, because I wanted a new Ranger.

My mother cried when I told her how bad I felt. But she cries about everything about God. She said the bike got ruined on the way down from Heaven. She must think I am dumb as heck.

AESTHETE: MODEL 1924

By Ernest Boyd

HE is a child of this Twentieth Century, for the Yellow Nineties had flickered out in the delirium of the Spanish-American War when his first gurgles rejoiced the ears of his expectant parents. If Musset were more than a name to him, a hazy recollection of French literature courses, he might adapt a line from the author of "La Confession d'un Enfant du Siècle" and declare: I came too soon into a world too old. But no such doubts trouble his spirit, for he believes that this century is his because he was born with it. He does not care who makes its laws, so long as he makes its literature. To this important task he has consecrated at least three whole years of his conscious — or rather self-conscious — existence, and nothing, as yet, has happened to shake his faith in his star. In fact, he finds the business rather easier than he had anticipated when, in the twilight sleep of the class-room, vague reports reached him of Milton's infinitesimal fee for *Paradise Lost*, of Chatterton's death, of the harassed lives of Shelley and Keats, of the eternal struggle of the artist against the indifference of his age and the foul bludgeonings of fate.

The Aesthete's lot has been a happier one. His thirtieth birthday is still on the horizon, his literary baggage is small, or non-existent — but he is already famous; at least, so it seems to him when he gazes upon his own reflection in the eyes of his friends, and fingers aggressively the luxurious pages of the magazine of which he is Editor-in-Chief, Editor, Managing Editor, Associate Editor, Contributing Editor, Bibliographical Editor, or Source Material Editor. His relationship to the press must always be editorial, and to meet the changed conditions of the cosmos, a changed conception of the functions of an editor provides him with a vast selection of titles from which to choose. The essential fact is that he has an accredited mouthpiece, a letter-head conferring authority, a secure place from which to bestride the narrow world in which he is already a colossus. Thus he is saved from those sordid encounters with

ERNEST BOYD *has written, edited and translated nearly two dozen books. He is a specialist in English, French and German literature, and is the editor and translator of the Collected Novels and Short Stories of Guy de Maupassant, in eighteen volumes. "Aesthete" was written at a time when dilettantism was rife in the country, and it portrayed a typical character of the movement so truthfully and skilfully that it caused violent discussion in the literary world — one conscience-stricken editor of a national magazine threatened to maul Boyd on sight —, and after twenty years it is still mentioned in some circles with guilty trepidation.* (January, 1924)

the harsh facts of literary commerce which his predecessors accepted as part of the discipline of life: Meredith reading manuscripts for Chapman & Hall, Gissing toiling in New Grub Street, Anatole France writing prefaces for Lemerre's classics, Dreiser polishing dime novels for Street & Smith.

It is natural that he should thus be overpowered by a mere sense of his own identity, for there is nothing, alas, in his actual achievements, past or present, to warrant his speaking prematurely with the voice of authority. That he does so unchallenged is a proof to him that he himself is his own excuse for being. In a very special sense he accepts the Cartesian formula: I think, therefore I am. When he went to Harvard — or was it Princeton or Yale? — in the early years of the Woodrovian epoch, he was just one of so many mute and inglorious Babbitts preparing to qualify as regular fellows. If some brachycephalic shadow lay across the Nordic blondness of his social pretensions, then, of course, the pilgrimage assumed something of the character of a great adventure into the Promised Land, the penetration to an Anglo-Saxon Lhasa. His immediate concern, in any case, was to resemble as closely as possible every man about him, to acquire at once the marks of what is known as the education of a gentleman, to wit, complete and absolute conformity to conventions, the suppression of even the faintest stirrings of eccentric personality. To this day he feels a little embarrassed when he calls on his father in Wall Street, carrying a walking-stick and wearing a light tweed suit, but he trusts that even the dooropener's scorn will be softened by the knowledge that here is an artist, whose personality must be untrammeled.

Those who knew the Aesthete during the period of his initiation will recall how he walked along the banks of his Yankee Isis, or lolled behind the bushes, discussing Life; how he stood at the Leif Ericson monument and became aware of the passage of time; — *Eheu fugaces, labuntur anni,* he now would say, especially if he were writing a notice of the Music Box Review; how he went to the cemetery to contemplate the graves of William and Henry James, and noted in himself the incipient thrill of Harvard pride and acquired New Englandism. But these gentle pursuits did not mean so much to him at first as the more red-blooded diversions of week-ends in Boston, and such other fleshy sins as that decayed city might with impunity offer. More refined were the evening parties on the northern side of the town where, in a background of red plush curtains and chairs but recently robbed of their prudish antimacassars, whispers of romantic love might be heard from well-behaved young women, whose highest destiny, before lapsing legally into the arms of a professor, was to be remembered when, at a later stage, a sonnet evolved from a brain beginning to teem creatively. For the rest, football games and lectures, the former seriously, the latter intermittently, maintained in him the consciousness of the true purpose of a university education.

From the excellent Professors Copeland and Kittredge he distractedly and reluctantly acquired a knowledge of the elements of English composition and of the more virtuous facts of English literature. He read, that is to say, fragments of the classical authors and dutifully absorbed the opinions of academic commentators upon them. American literature was revealed to him as a pale and obedient provincial cousin, whose past contained occasional indiscretions, such as Poe and Whitman, about whom the less said the better. Latin and French were filtered through the same kind of sieve, but without so many precautions, for in neither case was it possible for the aspirant after knowledge to decipher easily the kind of author to whom the urge of adolescence would naturally drive him. The Loeb classics left the un-Christian passages in the original, while the estimable Bohn unkindly took refuge in Italian, the language of a "lust-ridden country", as Anthony Comstock points out in that charming book of his, *Traps for the Young*. However, he still possesses enough Latin to be able to introduce into his written discourse appropriate tags from the Dictionary of Classical Quotations, though his quantities, I regret to say, are very weak. I have heard him stress the wrong syllable when speaking of Ouspensky's *Tertium Organum*, although he will emend a corrupt passage in Petronius, and professes to have read all the obscurer authors in Gourmont's *Latin Mystique*.

There came finally a subtle change in his outlook, from which one must date the actual birth of the Aesthete as such — *der Aesthetiker an sich*, so to speak. I suspect it was after one of those parties in the red plush drawing-rooms, when he returned to his rooms with what seemed like the authentic beginnings of a sonnet in his ears. From that moment he had a decided list in the direction of what he called "creative work". While the stadium shook with the hoarse shouts of the rabble at football games he might be observed going off with a companion to indulge in the subtle delights of intellectual conversation. His new friends were those whom he had at first dismissed as negligible owning to their avowed intention of not being he-men. The pulsation of new life within him prompted him to turn a more sympathetic eye upon this hitherto despised set, and they, in their turn, welcomed a new recruit, for the herd instinct is powerful even amongst the intellectual. Under this new guidance he came into contact with ideas undreamt of in the simple philosophy of the classroom.

Strange names were bandied about, curious magazines, unwelcomed by the college library, were read, and he was only too glad to discover that all the literary past of which he was ignorant or strangely misinformed counted as nothing in the eyes of his newly emancipated friends. From the pages of the *Masses* he gathered that the Social Revolution was imminent, that Brieux was a dramatist of ideas; in the *Little Review* he was first to learn the enchantment of distance as he sat bemused by its specimens of French and pseudo-French literature. Thus the ballast of which he had to get rid in order to float in the rarefied atmosphere of Advanced Thought was quite negligible. He had merely to exchange one set of inaccurate ideas for another.

II

It was at this precise moment in his career that the Wilsonian storming of Valhalla began. With the call to arms tingling in his blood, the Aesthete laid aside the adornments of life for the stern realities of a military training camp. Ancestral voices murmured in his ears, transmitted by instruments of dubious dolichocephalism, it is true, but perhaps all the more effective on that account, for Deep calls unto Deep. I will not dwell upon the raptures of that martial period, for he himself has left us his retrospective and disillusioned record of it, which makes it impossible to recapture the original emotion. He was apparently not capable of the strain of ingesting the official facts about the great moral crusade. It was government contract material and proved to be as shoddy and unreliable as anything supplied by the dollar-a-year men to the War Department. By the time the uniformed Aesthete got to France he was a prey to grave misgivings, and as his subsequent prose and verse show, he was one of C. E. Montague's Disenchanted — he who had been a Fiery Particle. He bitterly regretted the collegiate patriotism responsible for his devotion to the lofty rhetoric of the *New Republic*. By luck or cunning, however, he succeeded in getting out of the actual trenches, and there, in the hectic backwash of war, he cultivated the tender seeds just beginning to germinate. He edited his first paper, the *Doughboys' Dreadnought*, or under the auspices of the propaganda and vaudeville department made his first contribution to literature, "Young America and Yugo-Slavia". Simultaneously with this plunge into arms and letters, he made his first venture into the refinements of sex, thereby extending his French vocabulary and gaining that deep insight into the intimate life of France which is still his proudest possession.

When militarism was finally overthrown, democracy made safe, and a permanent peace established by the victorious and united Allies, he was ready to stay on a little longer in Paris, and to participate in the joys of La Rotonde and Les Deux Magots. There for a brief spell he breathed the same air as the Dadaists, met Picasso and Philippe Soupault, and allowed Ezra Pound to convince him that the French nation was aware of the existence of Jean Cocteau, Paul Morand, Jean Giraudoux and Louis Aragon. From those who had nothing to say on the subject when Marcel Proust published *Du Côté de Chez Swann* in 1914 he now learned what a great author the man was, and formed those friendships which caused him eventually to join in a tribute to Proust by a group of English admirers who would have stoned Oscar Wilde had they been old enough to do so when it was the right thing to do.

The time was now ripe for his repatriation, and so, with the same critical equipment in French as in English, but with a still imperfect control of the language as a complication, the now complete Aesthete returned to New York, and descended upon Greenwich Village. His poems of disenchantment were in the press, his war novel was nearly finished, and it was not long before he appeared as

Editor-in-Chief, Editor, Managing Editor, Associate Editor, Contributing Editor, Assistant Editor, Bibliographical Editor or Source Material Editor of one of the little reviews making no compromise with the public (or any other) taste. Both his prose and verse were remarkable chiefly for typographical and syntactical eccentricities, and a high pressure of unidiomatic, misprinted French to the square inch. His further contributions (if any) to the art of prose narrative have consisted of a breathless phallic symbolism — a sex obsession which sees the curves of a woman's body in every object not actually flat, including, I need hardly say, the Earth, our great Mother.

But it is essentially as an appraiser of the arts, as editor and critic, that the young Aesthete demands attention. He writes a competent book review and awakes to find himself famous. The next number of the magazine contains a study of his aesthetic, preferably by the author whose work he has favorably reviewed. By the end of the year a publisher announces a biographical and critical study of our young friend, and his fame is secured. He can now discourse with impunity about anything, and he avails himself of the opportunity. He has evolved an ingenious style, florid, pedantic, technical, full of phrases so incomprehensible or so rhetorical that they almost persuade the reader that they must have a meaning. But the skeptical soon discover that this is an adjustable and protean vocabulary, that by a process of reshuffling the same phrases will serve for an artistic appreciation of Charlie Chaplin, an essay on Marcel Proust, or an article on Erik Satie. His other expedient is an arid and inconceivable learning, picked up at second hand. Let him discuss *The Waste Land* and his erudition will rival the ponderous fatuity of T. S. Eliot himself. He will point out on Ptolemy's map the exact scene, quote the more obscure hymns of Hesiod, cite an appropriate passage from Strabo's geography, and conclude with a cryptic remark from the Fourth Ennead of Plotinus. Yet, one somehow suspects that even the parasangs of the first chapter of Xenophon's Anabasis would strain his Greek to the breaking-point.

Nevertheless, information is the one thing the Aesthete dreads. To be in the possession of solid knowledge and well-digested facts, to have definite standards, background and experience, is to place oneself outside the pale of true aestheticism. While foreign literature is his constant preoccupation, the Aesthete has no desire to make it known. What he wants to do is to lead a cult, to communicate a mystic faith in his idols, rather than to make them available for general appreciation. Articles on the subject are an important feature of his magazines, but they consist, as a rule, of esoteric witticisms and allusive gossip about fourth-rate people whom the writer happens to have met in a café. He will sweep aside the finest writers in French as lumber, launch into ecstasies over some Dadaist, and head the article with a French phrase which is grammatically incorrect, and entirely superfluous, since it expresses no idea that could not be correctly rendered in English. If one protest that the very title of a book which is a masterpiece of style has been mistranslated, that the first page has several gross errors, the Aesthete will blandly point out that in paragraph two there are four abstract nouns each with a different termination. It is useless to show him that there are no equivalent nouns in the text. Finally, one gives up arguing, for one remembers that Rimbaud once wrote a poem about the color of the vowels. Literary history must repeat itself.

The almost Swedenborgian mysticism of the Aesthete is implied in all his comments, for he is usually inarticulate and incomprehensible. He will ingenuously describe himself as being "with no more warning than our great imagination in the presence of a masterpiece". One reads on to discover the basis for this enthusiasm, but at the outset one is halted by naïve admonition that it "isn't even important to know that I am right in my judgment. The significant and to me overwhelming thing was that the work was a masterpiece and altogether contemporary". In other words, this work, which the writer says "I shall make no effort to describe", may or may not be a masterpiece, nevertheless it is one . . . presumably because it is "altogether contemporary". It is on this point of view that the solemn service of the Younger Aestheticism depends. If a piece of sculpture is distorted and hideous, if the battered remains of a wrecked taxi are labeled "La Ville tentaculaire", the correct attitude is one of delight. One should "make no effort to describe" what is visible, but clutch at the "altogether contemporaneous" element, indicating a masterpiece. In music one must not seek in the cacophonies of the current idols the gross, bourgeois emotion which one receives from Brahms and Beethoven. The Aesthete holds that a cliché, in French for preference, will dispose of any genius. One should make play with *le côté Puccini* and *le faux bon*.

The pastime is an amusing one, for it involves no more serious opposition than is to be found in the equally limited arsenal of the Philistines. What could be easier than to caper in front of the outraged mandarins waving volumes of eccentrically printed French poetry and conspuing the gods of the bourgeoisie? It is like mocking a blind man, who hears the insults but cannot see the gestures. The Aesthete tries to monopolize the field of contemporary foreign art and he is accustomed to respectful submission or the abuse and indifference of sheer ignorance. When he needs a more responsive victim he turns his attention to the arts adored by the crowd, the "lively arts," Mr. Seldes calls them, as if the Fifth Symphony were depressing. The esoteric reviews publish "stills" of Goldwyn pictures and discover strange beauties in follow-up letters and street-car advertisements. The knees of Ann Pennington, the clowning of Charlie Chaplin, the humors of Joe Cook and Fannie Brice must now be bathed in the vapors of aesthetic mysticism. But here there is a difference. The performances of the "lively" artist are familiar to every one above the age of ten; most of us have enjoyed them without feeling compelled to explain ourselves. A reference to Gaby Deslys finds its place as naturally in the works of Haverlock Ellis as one to *Der Untergang des Abendlandes*. But the Aesthete takes his lively arts uneasily. He is determined to demonstrate that he is just as other men. It is evidently not only in foreigners that one encounters that "certain condescension" of which the late Mr. Lowell complained.

III

In the last analysis the Aesthete may be diagnosed as the literary counterpart of the traditional American tourist in Paris. He is glamored by the gaudy spectacle of the most provincial of all great cities. French is the tube through which he is fed, and he has not yet discovered how feeble the nourishment is. When he turns to other countries, Germany, for instance, he betrays himself by an incongruous and belated enthusiasm for the novelties of the eighties and nineties. The contemporaries of Thomas Mann, Schnitzler and Hauptmann elsewhere are beneath his notice. Spain and Italy come onto his horizon only when Paris becomes aware of their existence. In a few years, however, his younger brother will go up to Cambridge, in his turn, and then we shall be enlightened concerning the significant form of Kasimir Edschmid and Carl Sternheim. One cannot be "altogether contemporary" all the time.

The signs, indeed, already point that way, for I notice that Hugo Stinnes is mentioned as a modern Marco Polo, and the American realtor is praised as a reincarnation of the creative will of Leonardo da Vinci. This new-found delight in publicity experts, election slogans, billboards and machinery may result in a pilgrimage across the Rhine where, in the dissolution of so many fine things, an aesthetic of Philistinism has emerged. The tone of democratic yearning which has begun to permeate German literature, recalling the dreams of Radical England in the days of Lord Morley's youth, may facilitate the understanding between two great democracies. But the fatal attraction of French, not to mention the difficulty of German, is a serious obstacle to any new orientation of the younger Aestheticism, and Paris, as usual, can provide what its customers demand. Thus the cult of the movies, with its profound meditations on "Motion Picture Dynamics", and all the vague echoes of Elie Faure's theory of "cineplastics", involves a condemnation of "The Cabinet of Dr. Caligari", a tactless Teuton effort to put some genuine fantasy into the cinema. Instead of that the faithful are called upon by a French expert to admire the films of William S. Hart and Jack Pickford, and some one carefully translates the poetic rhapsodies inspired in him by the contemplation of their masterpieces.

"Two souls", in the words of the German bard, "dwell in the breast" of the Aesthete, and his allegiance is torn between the salesmanager's desk, where, it appears, the Renaissance artist of to-day is to be found, and the esoteric editorial chair where experiments are made with stories which "discard the old binding of plot and narrative", the substitute being "the structural framework which appeals to us over and above the message of the line".

Thus it becomes possible simultaneously to compare Gertrude Stein with

Milton and to chant the glories of the machine age in America. This dualism, obviously, foreshadows the ultimate disintegration of the type, although for the moment the process is ingeniously disguised by such devices as the printing of prose bearing all the outward marks of super-modern eccentricity but made up cunningly of a pattern woven from phrases culled from billboards and the advertising pages of the magazines; by reproducing the weirdest pictures together with business-like photographs of cash-registers and telephones.

Here the Aesthete departs from the traditions of the species at his peril. Hitherto his technique has been perfect, for it has been his practice to confine his enthusiasm to works of art that are either as obscure or as inessential, or both, as his own critical comment. Now his incantations lose their potency when applied to matters within the experience and comprehension of the plain people, and not one cubit is added to the stature of William S. Hart, so far as his devotees are concerned, by the knowledge that his name is pronounced with aesthetic reverence on the Left Bank of the Seine.

The process of change is at work, for the transitional youth is already in at least one editorial chair, frowning upon the frivolities of the Jazz Age, calling for brighter and better books, his dreams haunted by fears of Sodom and Gomorrah. The Aesthete, meanwhile, is retiring with an intellectual *Katzenjammer*, which produces in some cases a violent and unnatural nausea, a revulsion against the wild delights of his former debauches. In others the result is a return to the cosy hearth of the American family; his head aches a little but his hand is steady. He is refreshed by a journalistic bromo seltzer. There is pep in the swing of his fist upon the typewriter as he sits down to a regular and well-paid job, convincing others, as his employer has convinced him, that he really knows what the public wants.

AT BREAKFAST

By Grace Stone Coates

"Where were you, last night?"

"I was in bed . . . sleeping
 Beside you . . .
 Of course!"

"And I was leaping
 Broomsticks, and burying Jesus,
 And patting Godiva's horse!"

(*September, 1927*)

AMERICAN MARRIAGE

By Mary Austin

The Way of a Woman

"Of a woman, even his own woman child," said Running Thunder, the White River Ute, "who can know except by knowing? My daughter had been in my house until her breasts were grown, and she was all my thought to me. So I married her to Taiwi, of the Uncompágres, somewhat older, as should be for a maid so tender, but a sound man and well furnished. There was also a matter of a horse and a gun which I had from him, which for the sake of my daughter he forgave me. Should not a man do according to his thought in his own house? But from the first that she heard of the marriage, my daughter kicked like a steer. Even my wife lifted her voice against me and shamed me before the Uncompágre.

"It was not true as my wife said, that I did not love my daughter. It was the wisdom of my ancients speaking in me, desiring that she should be esteemed and that her children should shine with plenty. But I thought the Uncompágre more of a man than he proved. It is often in my mind that the food that they give to our sons in Government Board School, being soft and without savor from lying in tin cans, takes something of the man from them, for in my time and my father's, if a man made a woman to know him, he could also make her follow at his back. But even after she had come under his blanket my daughter kicked against the Uncompágre, her husband. She threw the furnishings about the house that he built for her, and when he came in from tending his horses, he found her beside a cold hearth with her head wrapped in her blanket. Twice she ran away home from him, and twice I drove her back, as was my duty. 'By the soul of your grandmother!' said I to the Uncompágre, 'get her with child'; for it is known that a woman who will not soften by the giving of her body will be altogether gentled by giving the breast.

"Mind you, I could find nothing wrong with the marriage; for my son-in-law neither drank nor gambled, and even while my daughter lay grieving in my house she had around her a fine shawl of his buying. There she sat with her head against the wall and her hands

---

MARY AUSTIN, *who died in 1934, was one of the country's leading authorities on Western and Indian life. She wrote many novels and plays, the best known of which are* The American Rhythm *and* The Arrow Maker. *Her charming sketches of Indian life are among her most enduring works.* (September, 1925)

twisting in her lap, whose laughter had been like the sound of young rain. It was in my mind several times that the Uncompágre should have beaten her. Said I; 'Have you become altogether white?' What did he then, but reproach me for having brought her up without so much as a taste of the stick? But what *could* I do with my wife about to deafen me with complaints? In the end I was persuaded to ask the Council for a judgment of divorce, which they gave on my showing that the girl, having tried him, would no wise have the Uncompágre for a husband.

"Had I peace then in my house? For a handful of days merely. Like a sick crow my daughter sat by the fire; like a sick dog she snapped at me. Also she grew thin, and my wife was of the opinion that the Uncompágre had worked a spell upon her. Three bags of corn I paid to a medicine man of the White River Utes to lift the spell, though nothing came of it. Then I began to study the ways of the Uncompágre. It was in my mind that if my daughter died, or was likely to die, I should surely kill him. I found that he had shut up the house where my daughter had lived, with the furnishings inside it, and spent much time in the mountains with his horses. All this I told my wife, who never left off blaming me.

"At branding time, my daughter being still in a black sickness, Hadatsée the roper told me that the Uncompágre was married again, or about to be, Hadatsée having seen a woman at his camp as he passed it that morning. 'Rejoice now,' I said to my daughter, 'for when the bridegroom has a bride in his house, he will have no time for spell-making.' Said my daughter, 'Is she truly in the house he made for me?' and all that night I could hear the spell working in her to lift and leave her, as she lay on her bed, shaking and twisting. But the next morning, as I worked at the branding pen, my wife came running. Such was the force of the spell that my daughter had vanished out of my house completely!

"Until dark we went inquiring at the houses of our friends, but nobody had seen her. That night my wife wept in her blanket and I cleaned my gun and oiled it. Outside, the medicine drums were thumping, for when there is black medicine abroad who knows where it will strike? For between my wife and the wives of my friends this thing was much talked about the village. As soon as it was light we went up, and our friends with us, toward the house of the Uncompágre. Also we woke some of the principal men of the Uncompágres to be witnesses that what was done was done according to custom. The house stood dark against the sun, and a thin curl of smoke went up from it. As we stood, not too close — for who knew what wizardry went on inside it? — the door of the house opened and my daughter came out. Strong she looked and well, and all her ornaments upon her. 'Come away,' I cried, 'come away, daughter of mine, from that worker of evil spells, while I give him a taste of the medicine that he has made!', and I shook my rifle. Then said my daughter, and the whole of my village and the principal men of the Uncompágres heard her, 'Go away, you old fool,' she said, 'with your talk about spells and strange women! That was only his sister, come to shake the moths out of my blankets. Go home, you and your friends,' said she, 'and don't you ever come here again making trouble between me and my husband!'

"*Ehya!* Women . . . women!" said Running Thunder . . . "It was not until my grandson was born that she forgave me!"

II
Papago Wedding

There was a Papago woman out of Panták who had a marriage paper from a white man after she had borne him five children, and the man himself was in love with another woman. This Shuler was the first to raise cotton for selling in the Gila Valley — but the Pimas and Papagoes had raised it long before that — and the girl went with him willingly. As to the writing of marriage, it was not then understood that the white man is not master of his heart, but is mastered by it, so that if it is not fixed in writing it becomes unstable like water and is puddled in the lowest place. The Sisters at San Xavier del Bac had taught her to clean and cook. Shuler called her Susie, which was nearest to her Papago name, and was fond of the children. He sent them to school as they came along, and had carpets in the house.

In all things Susie was a good wife to him, though she had no writing of marriage and she never wore a hat. This was a mistake which she learned from the sisters. They, being holy women, had no notion of the *brujeria* which is worked in the heart of the white man by a hat. Into the presence of their God also, without that which passes for a hat, they do not go. Even after her children were old enough to notice it, Susie went about the country with a handkerchief tied over her hair, which was long and smooth on either side of her face, like the shut wings of a raven.

By the time Susie's children were as tall as their mother, there were many white ranchers in the Gila country, with their white wives, who are like Papago women in this, that if they see a man upstanding and prosperous, they think only that he might make some woman happy, and if they have a cousin or a friend, that she should be the woman. Also the white ones think it so shameful for a man to take a woman to his house without a writing, that they have no scruple to take him away from her. At Rinconada there was a woman with large breasts, surpassing well looking, and with many hats. She had no husband, and was new to the country, and when Shuler drove her about to look at it, she wore each time a different hat.

This the Papagoes observed, and, not having visited Susie when she was happy with her man, they went now in numbers, and by this Susie understood that it was in their hearts that she might have need of them. For it was well known that the white woman had told Shuler that it was a shame for him to have his children going about with a Papago woman who had only a handkerchief to cover her head. She said it was keeping Shuler back from being the principal man among the cotton growers of Gila Valley, to have in his house a woman who would come there without a writing. And when the other white women heard that she had said that, they said the same thing. Shuler said, "My God, this is the truth, I know it," and the woman said that she would go to Susie and tell her that she ought to go back to her own people and not be a shame to her children and Shuler. There was a man from Panták on the road, who saw them go, and turned in his tracks and went back, in case Susie should need him, for the Papagoes, when it is their kin against whom there is *brujeria* made, have in-knowing hearts. Susie sat in the best room with the woman and was polite. "If you want Shuler," she said, "you can have him, but I stay with my children." The white woman grew red in the face and went out to Shuler in the field where he was pretending to look after something, and they went away together.

After that Shuler would not go to the ranch except of necessity. He went around talking to his white friends. "My God," he kept saying, "what can I do, with my children in the hands of that Papago?" Then he sent a lawyer to Susie to say that if she would go away and not shame his children with a mother who had no marriage writing and no hat, he would give her money, so much every month. But the children all came in the room and stood by her, and Susie said, "What I want with money when I got my children and this good ranch?" Then Shuler said, "My God!" again, and "What can I do?"

The lawyer said he could tell the Judge that Susie was not a proper person to have care of his children, and the Judge would take them away from Susie and give them to Shuler. But when the day came for Susie to come into court, it was seen that though she had a handkerchief on her hair, her dress was good, and the fringe of her shawl was long and fine. All the five children came also, with new clothes, well looking. "My God!" said Shuler, "I must get those kids away from that Papago and into the hands of a white woman." But the white people who had come to see the children taken away saw that although the five looked like Shuler, they had their mouths shut like Papagoes; so they waited to see how things turned out.

Shuler's lawyer makes a long speech about how Shuler loves his children, and how sorry he is in his heart to see them growing up like Papagoes, and water is coming out of Shuler's eyes. Then the Judge asks Susie if she has anything to say why her children shall not be taken away.

"You want to take thees children away and giff them to Shuler?" Susie asks him. "What for you giff them to Shuler?" says Susie, and the white people are listening. She says, "Shuler's not the father of them. Thees children all got different fathers," says Susie. "Shuler —"

Then she makes a sign with her hand. I tell you if a woman makes that sign to a Papago he could laugh himself dead but he would not laugh off that. Some of the white people who have been in the country a long time know that sign and they begin to laugh.

Shuler's lawyer jumps up. . . . "Your Honor, I object —"

The Judge waves his hand. "I warn

you the court cannot go behind the testimony of the mother in such a case. . . ."

By this time everybody is laughing, so that they do not hear what the lawyer says. Shuler is trying to get out of the side door, and the Judge is shaking hands with Susie.

"You tell Shuler," she says, "if he wants people to think hees the father of thees children he better giff me a writing. Then maybe I think so myself."

"I *will*," said the Judge, and maybe two, three days after that he takes Shuler out to the ranch and makes the marriage writing. Then all the children come around Susie and say, "Now mother, you will have to wear a hat." Susie, she says, "Go, children, and ask your father." But it is not known to the Papagoes what happened after that.

III
The Man Who Lied About a Woman

Everybody knew that the girl who passed for the daughter of Tizessína was neither her daughter nor a Jicarilla Apache. Tizessína, being childless, had bought her squalling from a Navajo whose wife had died in giving birth, and loved her inordinately. She was called Tall Flower after the hundred-belled white yucca, and carried herself always with the consciousness of superior blood. None of the Jicarilla youths, it seemed, was good enough for her. When Tizessína, who was as anxious as any real mother to see the girl well settled, asked her what she wanted, "I shall know when I see it," said Tall Flower, and continued to give the young men who walked with her the squashes. For she was the sort that every man desired, and herself desired nothing. She laughed and went her way, and whatever she did Tizessína approved.

Nevertheless, she was disappointed when the girl hunched her shoulder to Nataldin, who besides being the richest young man of the Apaches was much sought after and would require careful handling. "But, my mother," laughed Tall Flower, "I shall handle him not at all."

This being her way with him, Nataldin, who was used to having marriageable girls go to a great deal of trouble on his account, was hurt in his self-esteem. To keep the other young men from finding out that with the daughter of Tizessína he had to take all the trouble himself, he took the manner when he walked with her of a lover who is already successful. He stuck a flower in his hat and swung his blanket from his shoulder until Tizessína herself began to nod and wink when the other women hinted.

Then suddenly Tall Flower went off over night with her mother and two or three other women to Taos Pueblo to gather wild plums for drying. She went without letting Nataldin know, and when the young men of Jicarilla found this out, they laughed and presented him with a large ripe squash. Nothing like this having happened to the young man before, he stiffened his lip and swung his shoulder. "And if I did not get the young woman," he said, "I got as much as I wanted of her."

No one liked to ask him what he meant by this, for to the others the girl had been as straight and as aloof as her name flower, and to take away a maiden's honor is a serious matter among the Jicarilla Apaches. But Nataldin, for the very reason that he had had not so much from Tall Flower as the touching of her littlest finger, salved his pride with looks and shrugs and by changing the subject when her name was mentioned. The truth was that he was afraid to talk of her, not for fear he might tell more than was seemly, but for fear somebody might find out what he had lately discovered, that if he did not have the daughter of Tizessína to be his wife, his life would be as a wild gourd, smooth without, but within a mouthful of bitter ashes.

The girl and her mother went not only to Taos Pueblo where the plum branches are bent over with bright fruit, but to Taos town, where a white man persuaded Tall Flower to be painted among the plum branches. Then they gathered *osha* in the hills toward Yellow Earth, where Tizessína, who was Government School taught, stayed for a month to cook for a camp of Government surveyors. In the month of the Cold Touching Mildly they came to Jicarilla again.

Nataldin, who found Tall Flower more to be desired than ever, was in two minds how he should punish her, but unfortunately what was in his mind turned out to be so much less than what was in his heart that he ended by thinking only how he could persuade her to be his wife. Tizessína, he saw, was wholly on his side, but some strange fear of her daughter kept her silent. Nataldin would catch her looking at him as though she wished him to know something that she feared to tell. At other times Tizessína looked at Nataldin from behind a fold of her blanket as a wild thing watches a hunter from the rocks, while Tall Flower looked over and beyond them both. There was a dream in her eyes, and now and then it flowered around her mouth.

Presently there began to be other looks: matrons watching Tall Flower out of the tails of their eyes, young girls walking in the twilight with their arms about one another, looking the other way as she passed; young men looking slyly at Nataldin, with laughs and nudges. Nataldin, who was sick to think that another had possessed her, where he had got the squash, denied nothing. If he remembered the punishment that is due to a man who lies about a woman, he reflected that a woman who has given herself to one lover cannot deny that she has given herself to two. But in fact he reflected very little. He was a man jabbing at an aching tooth in the hope of driving out one pain with another.

It had been midsummer when Tizessína had taken her daughter to gather plums, and in the month of Snow Water, Tall Flower being far gone with child, the two women talked together in their house. "I have heard," said Tizessína, "that Nataldin tells it about camp that he is the father of your child."

"Since how long?" said Tall Flower.

"Since before we had come to Taos town," said the mother, and repeated all she had heard.

"Then he has twice lied," said the girl.

"He is the richest man in Jicarilla, as well as a liar," said Tizessína, "and you will not get a husband very easily after this. I shall bring it to Council."

"What he does to another, that to him also," said the girl, which is a saying of the Apaches. "By all means take it to Council. But I shall not appear."

When Nataldin saw the *algucil* coming to call him before the Council he was half glad, for now his tooth was about to come out. But he was sick when he saw that the girl was not there; only Tizessína, who stood up and said, "O my fathers! You know that my daughter is with child, and this one says that he is the father of it. This is established by many witnesses. Therefore, if he is the father, let him take my daughter to his house. But if he has lied, then let him be punished as is the custom for a man who has lied about a woman."

Said the Council: "Have you lied?" and Nataldin saw that he was between the bow and the bowstring.

"Only Tall Flower knows if I have lied," he said, "and she does not appear against me. But I am willing to take her to my house, and the child also."

"So let it be," said the Council; and the young man's tooth was stopped, waiting to see whether it would come out or not. But Tall Flower, when the judgment was reported to her, made conditions. "I will come to his house and cook for him and mend," she said, "but until after the child is born I will not come to his bed," and Nataldin, to whom nothing mattered except that now Tall Flower should be his wife, consented. Although he was tormented at times by the thought of that other who had had all his desire of her where Nataldin himself had got the squash, the young man salved his torment by thinking that, now the girl was his wife, nobody would be able to say that he had not also been her lover. He thought that when he told the daughter of Tizessína that he had lied to save her shame, she would never shame him by telling that he had lied. What nobody knows, nobody doubts; which is also a saying of the Jicarilla Apaches. Therefore when he walked abroad with his young wife, Nataldin carried himself as a man who has done all that can be expected of him.

As for Tizessína, she walked like the mother-in-law of the richest young man in Jicarilla, and Tall Flower walked between them, dreaming.

In due time, as he worked in his field Nataldin saw Tizessína and the neighbor women hurrying to his house, after which he worked scarcely at all, but leaned upon his hoe until the sun was a bowshot from its going down, and listened to the shaking of his own heart. As he came up the trail to his house at last, he saw his wife lying under the ramada, and beside her Tizessína with something wrapped in a blanket. "Let me see my son," he said, and wondered why the neighbor women rose and hurried away with their blankets over their faces, for with the first born there should be compliments and present giving. But when Tizessína turned back the blanket and showed him the child's face, he knew that after all he should not escape the punishment of a man who has lied about a woman. For the child was white!

CHINA BOY

By Idwal Jones

I FIRST beheld Pon Look twelve years ago, and even then he was the oldest human creature in Fiddle Creek township. It was on top of Confidence Hill one August day, when the pines were withering in the terrific heat and the road was a foot deep in white dust. Pon Look came over the brow of the hill, from below.

He waddled like a crab, leaning on a staff, and extreme age had bent his body at a right angle to his stunted legs. His physiognomy was fearsome, like a Chinese actor's in print. His head was sunk forward, so that his ears were in line with his shoulders, and the protuberant chin was adorned with sparse, silvery hairs. For all he had the aspect of a crippled galley-slave, he progressed smartly, slewing that head continually from side to side with a strange grace. He seemed to be propelling himself through the heat waves with that sculling movement. He had something alive, which he held in check with a rope. It was a large, feline animal, with a bobbed tail and a funny wicker hat fitting over its head, like a muzzle. At intervals this beast leaped into the air, and, uttering frantic cries, tore furiously at the muzzle with its forefeet. It had eyes as glittering as topazes. It was a superb catamount. Pon Look no more minded its antics than if they were the antics of a mosquito.

I offered Pon Look a cigar. His face wreathed instantly with smiles, and he took it shyly. Laughter wrinkles creased his smooth high forehead.

"You are taking your pet out for a breath of air?"

"Pet?" he queried. Meanwhile the catamount was whirring insanely in the dust, at taut rope, with the velocity of a squirrel in a cage. "Pet? — oh, no — I jus' catch heem now in the canyon."

"What are you going to do with him?"

Pon Look gave a fierce yank at the rope. "Oh — I tame him first. Then in two weeks, if he not fliendly, I kill him."

Heaven only knows how Pon Look, dried-up like a cricket, captured these monsters. Certain it was that he was wise in the arcana of nature, and cunning in the manipulation of willow forks, ropes, knots and all the little tricks of leverage. Once a month, at least, he rattled down the steep road in his buckboard, with a wildcat, a cougar or a brown bear in the crate behind. These beasts he sold to mer-

---

IDWAL JONES *has been a dramatic critic in San Francisco, a foreign correspondent, editorial writer and author of many short stories and of novels, the latest of which are* Black Bayou *and* The Vineyard. *(January, 1927)*

chants in the Chinatown of San Francisco, who liked them because they drew crowds before the shops.

Though he sold his spoils for a bagful of money, he invariably came back to Fiddle Creek without a dime. He had his little failings. Fan-tan, bottles of *ng-ka-py*, dinners of pickled goose for his old cronies, bouts with the poppy, and nights of amorous dalliance — that was how the money went.

As a sort of watchman, he tyrannized over a domain of three square miles, covered with chaparral, snake-infested and repellent in summer, and no more desirable in the rainy season. It had once been called Summerfield's Place. Some bank held it in lien, or it was held in mortmain. It is of no consequence. On top of this hill Pon Look lived alone.

When he was born, I never learned, nor could he himself guess. Even his beginnings were as shrouded in mystery as his end. But I am probably not wrong in setting Pon Look's age at this meeting as about eighty-five.

He began his career at the age of ten, as stable boy to La Penelli. A few old prints, a casual note in a diary written by an Argonaut who had applauded her exploits — that is all one can find concerning La Penelli. This person was a gymnast who performed in John Rowe's Olympic Circus in Kearny street in 1850. This was the first outdoor entertainment in San Francisco. One Sampson was its star, clown, harlequin and chariot driver. But what the pioneers most applauded was the lady act, wherein the ravishing Penelli turned somersaults on the back of a galloping white horse. This being the only female exhibition in the city, Rowe made considerable money, until the equestrienne got drunk, and the secret was out. It was Sampson, who had disguised himself with a white wig and an ingenious system of padding. The Olympic habitués were furious, and there was talk of lynching the proprietor. To make things worse for Rowe, one Foley set up a rival circus a block away, and exhibited freaks — the best being Iron Jaws, who could bite through six pieces of pioneer pie at one time. This feat he performed daily until some disgruntled patron inserted a tin pie plate in the strata and wrecked his maxillary leverage.

II

The circus business declining, Sampson withdrew with his horse and China boy, and took to loafing in the Boomerang Saloon, the rendezvous of British gentlemen. Here roast beef, Yorkshire pudding and pale India ale were procurable. Once a week, a genuine Stilton cheese, venerable with age, double-creamed and mouldy, was roasted on the spit. The *Times* and *Galignani's Messenger* were on file. Sampson drank and ate well, became fat, pop-eyed and garrulous, and ran up an enormous bill. Pon Look worked it out by serving as a porter.

The spoken drama was looking up; Sampson went in for Shakespearean rôles, and set off with a barnstorming troupe into the foothills. Pon Look drove the coach, with scenery and costumes lashed behind, all over a dozen counties. Twenty months later, after an altercation with the rest of the company, Sampson absconded with the funds, and started back for England. Pon Look, who went back to the city, spent weeks in futile search for his master, but Sampson had gone to the bottom of the sea in the ill-fated *Brother Jonathan*.

The youth mooned in the alleys of Chinatown, half dead with grief, and smitten with a nostalgia for the hills. He apprenticed himself to a Cantonese cobbler who kept a booth near the plaza, and worked with such diligence that he mastered the craft in eight months, and made for himself covertly a pair of fine high boots. They were wrought of Chili ox-hide, oak-tanned and embroidered with dragons. He burnt a hundred candle-ends stitching on that pair of boots. They had to be good, for he had a hard road ahead of him.

Without saying good-bye to a soul, Pon Look tramped back into the hills, going by the devious Mariposa route into the region of the Southern Mines. He wore a coolie hat, flat-crowned, and a dolman, like an actor. At some of the camps the miners were kind and gave him bread; at other camps he was stoned, and bloody-eyed gaunt dogs were turned loose on him.

One day he heard loud singing by the side of the road, and there on a rock sat a venerable old man with a snowy beard. He held an open book, and his aspect was so benign that Pon Look paused in reverence.

"Well, well, John — stop and rest a while," said the old man, holding out both hands in greeting. His head was bare, he carried a heavy staff, and his feet were swathed in burlap. "Come and have a cup of tea."

Pon Look was touched. The aged one built a fire of pine cones, and brewed tea, which he shared with the boy from one pannikin. Between draughts he roared scraps of hymns. Pon Look was taking another swallow of tea, when his skull was struck with such violence that he fell senseless. It was night before he awoke. The beautiful old man was gone, and so were Pon Look's fine boots.

He shunned the road after that, and made his own path through the woods and over the hillsides. He would have thrown away his dolman to ensure himself against further attack, but the pockets were handy to carry bread and rice in. Toward nightfall, as he was about to cross a road, sounds of lamentation fell upon his ears. He concealed himself behind a clump of juniper. A man came riding on an agile gray pony. He wore a Mexican sombrero, with a horse-hair strap under his prow of a nose. His teeth were protruding, like a rat's; his wizened face was pockmarked; his eyes were a dead black, and humorous. To the pommel of his saddle was attached a long rope wound in bights about the necks of eight Chinese who tripped and stumbled behind. Pon Look trembled at the sight. What would be their fate? Later he could guess, for he learned that the rat-toothed man was the bandit Murietta, a merry and bloody personage.

Clearly, he had to be discreet above all else. For days and nights he kept off the trails, never ventured across country until he had first surveyed the land from a height. The second week he fell in with a party of fifteen Cantonese, foot-sore and staggering under the weight of their loaded baying-poles. These, too, groaned and whined, being under the command of a harsh giant, a hairy Manchurian who set the pace, for he was unencumbered and had long legs. This captain had been a dealer in jargoon, moonstones and beryls in Foo-Chow, and was on his mad way to explore the upper reaches of the Tuolumne in search of like things. He permitted Pon Look to tote a heavy sack of millet in recompense for company and safe convoy.

This was the party that made the great strike of Summerfield Flat. That night they had encamped in a narrow valley littered with boulders and gravel, a strip of land so barren that it sustained merely chamiso bush and a few lodge-pole pines. In digging for a fire-pit, a shovel turned up a strip of blackened metal. It was gold. Forthwith, with yells and sweating, everybody plied tools, and the Flat was discovered to be paved with shards and shields of gold, an inch thick, flattened by glacier action, and under no more than two feet of ground. By dawn, when they had dug and piled up tons of gold, a great and appalling discouragement came over them. Even the jargoon merchant was filled with inquietude. What was so plentiful must necessarily be valueless. All hurried away from that spot of disillusionment.

The big Manchu and his party in time returned, loudly cursing the day they had set forth, for luck was against them. They found the Flat throbbing with tumult and life. It was plowed deep, swarming with men like maggots in a honeycomb. Over six million dollars' worth of gold was being taken out. The Cantonese, screaming like magpies, beat their captain with staves, and he crawled away, out of his wits with chagrin.

It was then that Pon Look got a glimpse of the truth that was to abide with him to the end of his days: adventure and travel are the futile expedients of the foolish to escape from themselves. His companions scattered, he stayed on.

III

Across from the Flat was a narrow pass in a long mountain of black, igneous rock. The mountain was in a semi-circle, and encompassed many square miles of the only green land in the countryside. It was moist from hidden springs, and the virgin soil, overlaid with the humus of centuries, was phenomenal in its richness. Old Man Summerfield owned it. He was a hardscrabble Vermont farmer who lived in a good house with his haggard wife. He waylaid cattle from the ox-trains, and decoyed them into the enclosure. They bred calves, and he grew passably rich. He dwelt in antipathy with his neighbors, who at night frequently took pot-shots at him. It was on the domains of this ogre that Pon Look trespassed. The owner came riding out with a rifle.

"What do you want here, you yellow limb? Get off my place!"

"A job," responded Pon Look.

After some reflection, the farmer manoeuvred Pon Look, as if he were a stray ox, and drove him to the cow-house.

"Live there," he snarled. "You'll find some sacks to sleep on."

Pon Look entered upon his duties, and became known as Summerfield's China

Boy. There were twenty-five head of cattle, and it was his function to ride about on horseback and keep a wary eye on them, and if they showed symptoms of bursting, to dismount and stab them in the belly with a trochar. Because of the succulence of the grass they would overeat and suffer from bloat.

He acquired a sympathy with these animals, and in his solicitude would keep them moving incessantly, and try to retain them where the grass was somewhat less luxuriant. One night a handsome black bull escaped through the pass and vanished. Probably it got carved into steaks by unscrupulous neighbors. Old Man Summerfield frothed through his beard. He raged at Pon Look.

"What am I paying you board for, hey? To lose cattle for me? If that happens again—you get kicked out!"

The boy was aghast. There was every likelihood that it would happen again. It was then that he conceived the idea of building a wall around the ranch. It was a felicitous idea. Along one side of the low cliff was a talus of lava boulders; material right to hand. The stuff was in every size, from pebbles the biggness of a fist to rocks the size of a huge hog, and all rounded by æons of time. The most of them resembled footballs, and were known locally as nigger-heads.

He built a stone-boat, trained a cadgy old ox to haul it, and began to close the pass. He built a wall six feet high, and three and a half wide, with a wooden gate in the middle. The quarry was a quarter mile distant, and his tools were a crowbar and an end of plank. The job was finished after a year of back-breaking toil and the cost of Pon Look's right toe. Old Man Summerfield was so proud of this entrance that he spent hours sitting on the gate so people could see him as they drove by.

"It's all in handling the ma-terial," he would say. "You got to know how to lay them boulders and lock 'em so they won't roll off like balloons. The's nothing like a good gate to keep the cattle in."

"A better gate 'ud be one that kept other folks' cattle out," some neighbor would remark, after Old Man Summerfield had left.

The China Boy's task was only just started. He now began to haul boulders to close in the southern and open arc of the circle.

Progress was slow. The stone-boat ox would cough, then die very soon, and Pon Look had to train another one; or the vehicle would wear out, and he had to build another. Old Man Summerfield's wife, who had kept within the house and was wont to shout loud at night, gave up the ghost, so the master went to San Francisco to do some wooing, and being, as he said, "a particular man to please," it was three months before he returned with her successor. The boy did the work of two men in the meanwhile, but had to suspend work on the wall.

The new mistress was a fat shrew of a body, with a clacking tongue, and much displeased Pon Look by her interference. She made him beat carpets, trudge about the country to buy laying hens, and dig a garden. He submitted to it all, and arose an hour earlier, making a return trip with the stone-boat before sun-up. On one occasion, as he was passing by the house, she called to him to come in and wash the dishes. He said no. Whereupon she rushed at him with a broom and smote him violently as he stood in the yard. Pon Look took the blows without a murmur, and remained like a statue, with hands folded, while his mistress, still plying the broom, waxed hysterical.

There was no budging Pon Look. She spun round to beat at his face. It was serene, but pallid. The lips bespoke an obstinate resolve, but the eyes gleamed mistily at her with pity and forgiveness. Mrs. Summerfield's arms dropped, then she clutched at her throat, and staring at him walked backward into the house.

IV

When Pon Look returned to the cowhouse that night, he found on his table a hot raisin pie. On the window-sill the next morning, Mrs. Summerfield found the pie plate, scrubbed with the sand so bright that it reflected the sun like a mirror, and upon it a handful of the white daisies that grew nowhere except near the bog a mile distant. Pon Look had dined that night, as usual, on rice and beef. The mystified hens, before going to roost, had filled their craws with pastry and raisins.

Thenceforward, Mrs. Summerfield treated Pon Look with a respect that was a compound of both affection and fear. On no pretext could he be induced to enter her house. She did not know what to make of him, so she left him alone. She ran the domestic establishment, but Pon Look, since the old man spent all day and half the night in the camp saloon, saw to the running of the ranch, the sale of the cattle and, of course, the construction of the wall.

"You don't have ter build that wall entire of rocks, China Boy," she said one evening, when the indomitable mason, scrubbed, and in his fresh alpaca coat, stood surveying in the dusk the lengthening boundary of the ranch. "Wire's just as good, and fence-stakes is cheaper than they was."

Pon Look gave a smile so expansive that his eyes disappeared in the creases. "Make 'um all stone, Mis' Sommyfeel' — begin 'um stone, and finish 'um stone, allee same niggy haid."

She plucked timorously at her alpaca apron. "Oh, well, it's you're doing it, not us."

Yet she took pride in the fabulous immensity of the task. The editor of the county-town paper drove over one day and watched China Boy wrestling with the boulders. The next week he published a page story on the Summerfield's stone wall. It was a monument to Mr. Summerfield's enterprise and vision, he said; a testimony to the will, the perseverance and crag-like virtues that made New England great, etc. He dragged in quotations from the Latin poets. This story attracted a surprising lot of attention. Old Man Summerfield bought several copies, and wore them to rags in making a boozy tour of all the saloons in the county. People came to see, and amongst them were women who owned family coaches. Mrs. Summerfield made social contacts in this way, and finally joined the Ladies' Aid Society, and bought a bombazine dress and a landaulette so she could ride over to the meetings. Her period of ostracism was over.

CHINA BOY

The year 1879 was memorable in the annals of the family. Pon Look had completed the southern wall after the unremitting labors of twenty-seven years. Death enfolded Mrs. Summerfield that autumn, while she was pruning a rosebush in her garden. Pon Look worked by lantern-light in the barn and built an enormous hexagonal coffin to house her frail body. It was so heavy that eight men buckled under the weight as they carried it to the hearse. Old Man Summerfield bought a new silk hat for the occasion, and was very proud of it. The minister held a service in the parlor, with no less than six families in attendance; and all throughout the widower nursed the hat on his knees, in full view of the admiring assemblage. Pon Look participated by looking in through the open window. He did not attend the funeral at the Odd Fellows' Cemetery, for there was much to do.

He trudged all over the ground with a tape-measure, and made mental calculations. He returned very late, and sat on the veranda to smoke a pipe in the moonlight. The old lady had latterly been quiet, and his thoughts were tinged with regret that she had gone. He was gratified that the master had taken things sensibly. A wind arose, and because it was cool, and he was afraid of the moon shining on his temples and making him mad, he got up to retire to the cow-shed. Between the lower bars of the gate something white caught his eye. He thought it one of the fluffy pompons that had been blown thither from the garden where the old lady had planted a clump of Holy Thistles. He drew nearer, picked up wonderingly a new silk hat, and found that the object was Old Man Summerfield's snowy head. Whiskey and grief had done for him.

There was some wearisome business with the coroner. Pon Look wanted to attend the funeral, but could not, for some excitable men detained him for a week in a stone room with bars at the window. He was released with palliative back-slappings and a handful of cigars after the inquest. He had been put to a great inconvenience, for the rains were now on, coming down like firm and slanting spears without let-up for days and days. He had to slosh around in the bog to lay a timber road across which to sled his rock. The Summerfield heir, an elderly nephew, took over the place a month afterwards. He was a city man, with a waxed moustache and a square-cut derby. He drank somewhat, and was inclined to be companionable. China Boy avoided him, looking rigidly ahead every time they passed.

"How much longer that job, John?" he asked one day.

"No can say."

"Well, then, how long did it take to build all that wall?"

"Oh — thirty — thirty-five year."

"Good God!" murmured the heir.

He sat under the trees dismally, like a strange bird. Then he panned for gold in various corners of the ranch, and did other foolish things. He would sit hunched on the sacred gate, mope about whistling with a dirge-like note, or keep to the house and drink. He was a lonely and wistful interloper. All his actions lowered himself in China Boy's esteem, and he knew it. China Boy strutted about with aloof and cold arrogance, and the heir's morale ebbed. Finally he accosted the mason and came to an understanding. China Boy was to keep an eye on the place, market the stock and keep a percentage for himself. Then he packed up his things in a wicker suit-case, and went away forever.

The Chinaman had the place to himself now, and sold off most of the heifers so they wouldn't breed and rob him of time he could apply to building. The wall progressed handsomely. He had stretched barbed wire across the northerly side of the farm until the work should be finished. When that was done the place would be a paradise for cattle. They could cram themselves with lush grass in one part of the ranch, then chew the cud in the cropped field adjoining. That would be the end of the bloat. China Boy worked incessantly, visited by no one except the banker who came along every quarter to represent the routed heir. In time the wall got itself done. It undulated for miles over uneven ground, but plumb, as straight as a furrow, without a single bend. The job had taken China Boy forty years to complete. By this time he was doubled with age, his pigtail white and his hands rock-hard and stumpy.

V

It was in August when China Boy went up to ring the nose of the little black bull that he saw the ground was parched. Down he went on his knees in the middle of the field and pulled up a handful of soil. It was as dry as ashes. The cattle came around with their tongues, leathery and swollen, hanging out. Palsied with terror, China Boy arose, and shading his myopic eyes, turned round and round like a weather cock, and stared for a glimpse of green. The entire ranch was as brown as a brick. Drouth had laid waste to the ground as if with torches.

He saddled a pony and galloped, pigtail a-flying, to the bank. The banker, when he heard the plaint, grumbled:

"I knew there was a hoodoo on the damned place. It's cooking hot, but I'll come down and see."

Together they rode back. The banker drew up in the buggy before a new mine in the field adjoining the Summerfield ranch. Here was a tall gallows-hoist, with sheaves whirring, a mill from which poundings emanated, and an engine house with a high stack. The ditch alongside the road was filled with a roaring flood of water.

"Yea-ah," he grunted, pointing at the ditch with his whip. "That's what I expected. The shaft has tapped the springs underlying the Summerfield flat. Might as well sell off the cattle, the place will be as dry as a volcano from now on." Then he scratched his head. "I'll have to send down some goats, Angora goats. Mebbe they'll pay off the taxes. Guess we can cut down some timber, too. I'll have a look at it."

China Boy got out and walked in a daze to the grove. The banker followed afoot, then paused when his guide appeared at the door of his cabin with a musket in his hands.

"Cattle can go," China Boy informed him, "but these trees they stay up, I watch 'um."

And up they stayed. The story got

about, for the banker, who had been taken by the handsomeness of the grove, told it on himself. "An arbor-maniac, that's what he is. He made that wall business a life-long job, so he could live right there among those trees. Poor old chap, I'll have him pensioned off."

The banker kept his word, but China Boy drove a hard bargain. His terms for being superannuated were the weekly dole of five pounds of corn flour, a piece of bacon, six cartridges and a quart of whiskey, all to be delivered at his cabin.

Thereafter China Boy lived in the grove. Two hundred trees! Lordly sugar pines, gold traced with black, like Porto-Venere marble. Five sequoias, so colossal that only after staring at them for twenty minutes did their size dawn upon you, and then with a finality that took you in the pit of the stomach like a blow. Wine-stemmed manzanitas, gnarled chaparral. The rest were all redwoods, with high fluted columns; and through their branches interlaced overhead the sunlight streamed in lines and cast disks of silver upon the dark trunks and the ochre ground twinkling with ants. It was something like the inside of a church.

There was a wood for you! Visitors came rarely. Bearded blanket-stiffs, homeless men, tarried for a night on their way to the Middle Fork of the Stanislaus. An occasional prospector, reverent among trees, stayed sometimes two days. China Boy was their invisible host. He peered at them through the foliage, as if he were a bird, but never spoke to them, unless he perceived their shoes needed cobbling and he felt sure they could pay for the job, nothing less than a dollar, for even a philosopher must live. Aloof, and wrapped in an old army overcoat, he sometimes watched them all night, being afraid they would be careless with their pipes.

His house, hidden away in the trees, was rather a nice one, of a single large room, very high, and built of brick. Decades before, he had come across an abandoned express office, and had carried it thither, piecemeal, a bushel of brick at a time, and set it up exactly as it was before, even to the legend board above the doorway: "Wells-Fargo Express."

It was a forest lover's house, with blackberry bushes climbing into the window, hedgehogs and gray squirrels sunning themselves on the step, and pine cones dropping like cannon-balls on the roof. It held a cot, a stove, a shoe-last, and a library that consisted of a wisdom-banner that hung on the wall. If he found you, after years of acquaintance, worthy enough, he would translate the wiggly ideographs thus: "It is shame to be ignorant at sixty, for time flies like a mountain stream."

Here in this tree sanctuary that was of hoary age long before the Sung dynasty had started, China Boy had gone to school. He listened to the wind wrestling with the tree tops, to the language of the birds, the cries of the coyotes and owls, and other sounds that made the air articulate and vibrant. He loved to sit in the middle of his grove at night, still and pensive amid the falling leaves, like a rheumy-eyed hamadryad.

At intervals he straggled afoot to Sonora, with shirt-tail out and the sun warded off by an umbrella: quite the gentleman of leisure. But these excursions bored him finally, and he desisted, except when he had to call at the bank to complain about the quality of the whiskey. He had an educated palate. He wouldn't let the grocer's boy depart until he had first sampled the liquor ration.

Two years ago he trapped a pair of fine wildcats, and carted them off to town, and tarried over-long. Some campers came to the grove and were careless with their fire. China Boy's woods made a gorgeous blaze, singing and burning for ten hours, with the gray squirrels plumping down roasted, and the philosopher's house turning to a black lump.

The story made five lines in the county paper. The forest ranger said afterwards that he had seen the Old-Man-Mad-About-Trees pull up to the ruins in his buckboard, look on a few minutes, then drive away.

The banker was dubious. "Must have checked out through old age in the city," he said, "else he would have come up to the bank. He drove an awful hard bargain over that whiskey. He had me paying eleven dollars a bottle for the stuff I used to get for him at two before Prohibition. If anybody's ahead of the game, it's me."

THESE DARK HILLS

By Jesse Stuart

As oaks that root deep in Kentucky earth
And these eternal juts of rock that stand,
I stand with these dark hills that gave me birth
With plow and hoe and slopes of sedge-grass land.
Flesh in my body and blood in my veins
Are of the substance that has made the oaks;
This earth my living flesh, and it remains
Strong to endure more than the blackjack strokes.
This is the land where I can live and sing,
Where I can drink the rain and taste the sun;
Where I can work or not do anything
But listen to winds blow and waters run.
These hills are closer to me than my skin,
My roof could be the sky, my bed the rocks;
My only music the night blowing wind,
The pouring rivers and the barking fox.

(June, 1939)

WE ROB A BANK

By Ernest Booth

IT was midnight when Dan and I left Red and Johnny in the latter's apartment. Dan was about thirty-eight, conservatively dressed, and carried himself with an erect, military stride. A prison term had taught him, among other things, to avoid any mannerisms that might betray him. . . . Red, an enormous, taciturn Irishman, possessed, despite his comparative youth, an unusual ability to control people. I had known him to bring to a complete halt the actions of fifteen people scattered over the floor of a bank, and to do it with a single, harsh command. . . . Johnny was small in stature, hesitant in action when not engaged in a robbery, and recently addicted to the use of morphine. His light blue eyes under pale brows gave him an apologetic appearance; frequently he had been mistaken for an eighteen-year-old boy. Johnny, Red, and I were all about twenty-five.

Dan and I gained the street, and buttoned our coats against the chill, damp San Francisco fog. We boarded a streetcar and rode on separate seats to the ferry building. Keeping him in sight, I followed him on to the boat and to the deck reserved for smokers. As the boat throbbed and churned its way over the water I reflected on the lay-out of a robbery that would startle the entire Pacific Coast.

Dan and I had met by common agreement, discussed the plan, and decided that its main feature would be that we would capture the first employé as he entered the bank in the morning. Then we would take charge of the others as they came, and when the cashier arrived we would force him to open the vault. Thus we would be in possession of the place and have the vault cleaned out an hour or more before the bank would, ordinarily, open its doors to the public. Johnny and Red were to join us early in the morning at a certain street corner with an automobile they had stolen. I was going to spend the night with Dan and his girl in their apartment.

But really there had not been much actual planning, I realized. It seemed childish to scheme and talk. We knew

---

ERNEST BOOTH, *who has since been released, was serving a life sentence in Folsom Prison, Represa, Calif., for the robbery he describes so graphically and with such profound psychological insight in this article. He was twenty-eight years old at the time, and had already been a professional robber and burglar for twelve years. His article was but one of many by prisoners, which appeared in this magazine.* (September, 1927)

what to do: there was a bank on the other side of the bay which we could rob of perhaps a hundred thousand dollars: would we rob it together? That was the extent of our reasoning. Nothing of right or wrong entered into our calculations. Any aversion I might have entertained, in the dim, remote past, to such proceedings had been sublimated and found its outlet in past justifications of similar actions.

A robbery that would startle the whole Coast — had I thought it that? No; I was wrong. There had been a time when it would have made a sensation, but not now. Should a murder occur during its consummation, it might live in public interest for a week. Otherwise, it would be only a one-day flash. The public would read of it idly. One man might remark to another that bandits stole fifty thousand dollars yesterday, but he would employ the same tone as that in which he mentioned a severe rainstorm — then sigh and think of the instalments due on his radio. Others would merely glance over the headlines, mentally commenting, "Another robbery," — and then turn to the comic strips.

But to me, running over the details and possibilities, it was all very real and very important. Vividly real. So concentrated on it was I, indeed, that when a man walked in front of me I started, imagining that the thoughts of tomorrow were showing on my face. I looked about at the passengers scattered over the boat. None of them was paying me any attention.

But I tossed and turned on the davenport all that night. I executed the robbery a score of times — always with variations. I was standing near the entrance, watching the first clerk approach. Straining to move, I felt a terrifying, encroaching paralysis. Rooted to the sidewalk, I could not budge. . . . Then, waking in the semi-darkness, I would shiver off the nightmare.

II

Dan, dressed, called me at six-thirty in the morning. It was unnecessary to awaken me. He sat near while I pulled on my clothes. Mae appeared for a brief moment, holding a wrapper about her as she passed through the room to the kitchenette.

"Hell of a note!" she tossed over her shoulder, "this gettin' me up in the middle of the night. . . . But it's worth it, I guess."

"I don't like this having someone else know my business," I whispered to Dan, and nodded toward the kitchen.

He grinned. "If half the guys on our racket were as close-mouthed as Mae, there'd be less use for jails. Of course, it's a cinch she knows you're a hook, or you wouldn't be with me. What's the odds? It'll be all right. Anyway, she's going to drive the Ford coupé to meet us for a switch of machines after we work."

This last, coming as it did on the tail of my restless night, dragged in another uneasiness. A girl participating in a robbery to which I was a party was a new consideration. But I knew it was becoming prevalent in the fraternity, so rather than risk being classified as old-fashioned I said nothing more about it.

After breakfast we left the apartment, and with Mae driving, arrived at Sixteenth and Lindol streets about seven-thirty. The bank was ten or twelve blocks distant. The corner was deserted; Johnny and Red had not arrived. Restlessly, we drove a few blocks toward the heart of town; returning, we found the corner yet unoccupied.

Dan looked at his watch. "Christ almighty! Twenty to eight now!" Angrily he pushed his foot against the rifles and shotgun on the floor. Crowded together in the small compartment we were uncomfortable, and Mae snarled at him to "take it easy!" He turned his head to look back at the cross streets, and his movement pressed my revolver into my ribs. "Sit still!" I growled. My developing nervousness was irritating me. "Looking around that way will mark us," I said.

"Don't be telling me what to do!" His voice was bitter, acrid. His eyes were puffy, and the lids heavy for want of sleep. Realizing suddenly that he, too, was under the same strain and pressure, I remained silent. Again he twisted about. "What ails those guys? Here it is time to be getting down to the spot, and —"

It occurred to me that they might have gone to the bank to look it over before coming to the appointed corner. When I communicated this thought to Dan, he directed Mae to "make it snappy and get down there." It was as though we — she and I — were to blame for the non-appearance of Johnny and Red. He remonstrated with Mae, and she evinced her exasperation by jerking the wheel for an abrupt turn and jamming the throttle.

I took a last look at the corner. "There's a Cad parking there now. It may be Johnny," I offered. My words went unheeded. The three of us were possessed by an ugly mood. I was disgusted. Not with the thought of the robbery, but with the way it was going.

Mae speeded the car up between crossings, and once in Seventh street guided the wheels in the street-car tracks as she drove past the bank. It was in the middle of the block.

"See," said Dan, as we approached it, "the curtains are up and no one can see in from the street. Ain't it a gift?" He smiled with his eyes for a fleeting instant, then the look of anxiety returned. We scanned the street but saw none who even resembled Johnny or Red. Several Cadillacs passed, but they were not carrying the men we sought. I was trying to watch both sides of the street simultaneously, and for the moment I failed to notice the look Dan was giving me. I turned suddenly to meet a glare of scorn and disgust. He showed me the face of his watch — it was ten minutes to eight o'clock.

"A *fine* pair of suckers they are!" His words were mordant. "If I had another heap here I'd go up against it this way — just the two of us. . . . What say? Shall we give it a whirl? Maybe we can clout a heap and get back in time. Dash up by the high-school on Twelfth street, Mae! We might connect there. . . . It's getting late — hurry up! Step on it! Step on it! Christ, this is business!"

"Business?" said Mae, with heavy sarcasm, "business — sure it is! You're like a couple of brats going out for the first time — no organization — nothing!"

I have never had much difficulty in stealing an automobile. Usually the high-priced, closed cars are left unlocked and are easy to steal. The smaller cars receive more careful attention, probably because they represent more to their owners. Near the school was an assortment of Fords and Dodges, and a sprinkling of Buicks, Hudsons, and Studebakers. But there were people entering or leaving the cars, for this was a favorite place for business employés to park. So there was too much chance of detection — and there were chains, or wheel-spikes, on most of the cars.

"Nothing here," I said. "Follow that car. Perhaps it will park — the driver seems to be hunting a place now." I indicated an expensive, eight-cylinder machine.

The driver pushed it through the traffic past the City Hall. Dan and I had our handkerchiefs out, and were industriously wiping our noses for the time it took to travel the block. The danger of recognition was great here, and I shivered, visualizing the slaughter which would result if some officer saw us and decided to investigate our machine. Dan was cursing heatedly through his handkerchief.

"Get out of here — let the machine go to hell: Get off this street. I'm getting crazy to let myself be bummin' around like this. What the hell did you want to come up here for, Mae? You know I'm hot, here in town — and we're right in front of the police station."

The accomplished Mae realized the seriousness of our position, and refrained from comment. Deftly she extricated the car from a threatening box in traffic, and turned toward Sixteenth street at the first chance. I breathed easier then. That the robbery was not to be done that morning was evident, and by unvoiced consent we rode several blocks in silence. Approaching Lindol street I saw Johnny and a girl seated in a car, looking anxiously about the street. We drew alongside them.

"Where you been?" demanded Dan.

"Right here." Johnny was hollow-eyed. "I left over there about four o'clock and drove around the bay and up here as soon as possible. It ain't too late now. Let's get started. Where's Red?"

Dan's face was livid. Leaning across me, he said in a hoarse whisper, "Red! He was supposed to come with you! Hell, yes — of course it's too late! And we can't stop here. You, Billie," addressing the girl with Johnny, "get in here with Mae. Come on, Ernie, we'll change over so we can talk." The transfer was made. "Tail us about half a block behind," Dan instructed Mae, and we drove off.

There followed a general discussion of all our faults. Johnny and Dan stormed at each other. Occasionally I cut in, attempting to stem the useless upbraiding. I was soundly cursed, and retaliated.

Then Dan turned to where I was seated and said, "There's another jug I know of — out on San Pablo avenue — smaller, only a branch. Want to take a gander at it? We're here now — we might as well get something. God damn that red head! Why in hell didn't he show up?"

The question was purely academic: neither of us offered an immediate answer. But I awoke with renewed interest. Dan had discarded his anger.

"Suits me," I replied at length. "How about you, John?" It was a compromise, this taking a smaller place, but I needed the money, and with Johnny's affirmative nod the car started out the avenue.

III

The branch bank occupied a corner. Large plate-glass windows gave an almost unobstructed view of its interior from the street. A bad feature: a traffic officer was located in the middle of the cross streets a scant fifty feet away. There were lights within, and several clerks moving about. But it was not yet nine o'clock, so the doors were not open to the public. I left the machine and waited until the girls came up. I gave them instructions, and they parked about half a block further up the avenue. Sauntering casually to the entrance, I paused a moment to survey the counters and open vault. Its shiny steel mouth yawned wide. I watched a clerk come out with a large, locked tray which he took to his cage and opened. Busily engaged in sorting bills into their respective sections of an open drawer, he paid no attention to me. Affecting an indifferent attitude I turned my back to the bank, and lit a cigarette, puffed on it for a minute or so, and then turned about again and saw another clerk engaged upon a similar task.

My heart was beating rapidly, and I was having difficulty inhaling the smoke from my cigarette. The roof of my mouth was suddenly hot and dry. My eyes watered, and my throat tingled. A man and woman standing nearby — apparently waiting for a car — looked at me; hastily I applied a handkerchief to my face, and coughed. I was trying to forestall their seeing my face, later to recall it after they had read of the robbery. I turned from them and continued down the street.

At a drugstore on the next corner I drank a soft drink, and took a grip on myself. I was feeling an approaching loneliness. With Dan and Johnny I had fine confidence, but standing by myself, at that instant I knew the sensation of being alone in a crowd. There was considerable bustle and activity on the corner. Several streetcars passed. I returned to the bank, secure in the belief that the couple I had observed would be gone.

I paused to glance over the furnishings of the bank once more. A man brushed against me, and instinctively my left arm contracted on the revolver slung up under it. He excused himself, and as he looked into my face his eyes seemed to open a trifle with surprise. At once I felt a shock at having betrayed my thoughts! Although I tried to restrain myself, I peered over my shoulder after he had taken several steps, and was alarmed when he, too, turned to look directly at me. Little incidents: the couple, this man; but they were magnified out of all proportion. I walked to the other window of the bank and stood between an elderly woman and a man reading a paper. From time to time the man glanced up at passing cars. The old lady was indifferently clad, and fidgeted about. I ventured a side glance at her, and discovered that she was covertly watching me. She stirred, and I noticed that a pompon on her breast trembled. The nervous movement transferred itself, and I leaned hard against the glass to repress a quick shiver. She spoke to me — some question about the time. I started, then made an elaborate movement to extract my watch. . . . She thanked me, it seemed, in a queer manner.

I essayed a yawn to cover my growing confusion, but it died at birth as I looked to the middle of the street. The traffic officer, with one hand raised, was obviously staring at me. I was but one of a group of several, and it is highly improbable that he was aware of my existence, but at that moment I stood alone, naked.

Pivoting on my heel, I walked swiftly down the avenue. Two blocks away, I joined Dan and Johnny at the car. "How's she look?" queried Dan.

"All right, far as I can see." I gave the answer expected, but I wanted to say I thought we would be crazy to go any further with it. Something restrained me; for in the brief interval of my walk some of my confidence had returned. It was as though I, a solitary Assassin, returned to the citadel of Hassan and a fanatical devotion flowed out and inspired me.

"Stick with Johnny a moment — I'll take a flash myself." Dan left us. Johnny was leaning back in the seat, but there was a strained attempt to counterfeit ease in his attitude. I recognized it and felt easier in my own mind. The cheer of misery, I guess.

The motor was running, quietly, smoothly, with the gear-shift-lever enmeshed; he held the clutch out with one foot, ready for an instantaneous start. Johnny observed my interest in the arrangement and forced a grin. "Have to be set to go any second in a hot heap. Can't tell who might show up. These cruising-bulls in cars sneak up on you if you give them half a chance. It wasn't so bad when they was all in uniform, but they dress like business men now, an' you got to watch."

I lit another cigarette and began to watch each passing machine, imagining that the next one would be filled with cruising-bulls. None came, however, and I was glad when Dan returned.

"It's all right," he said after he had entered the machine, and we were out in the noises of the traffic. "That counter ends at the avenue window, and there's a small swinging gate there. You [to me] can step over it easy. That will bring all the clerks at the money-drawers in line with you. Cover them with your rod and hold it close to you, so it can't be seen from the street. Just motion 'em back — give 'em their orders, and don't worry about 'em doing anything. Just keep 'em away from the alarms. If they hit one and start the big buzzer over the door going, there'll be a lot of battle for us. So be sure an' keep 'em away. Clean the drawers as you come to each cage. Just throw the dough onto the counter and then brush it all off into the bag in one sweep. That'll be best, 'cause if you try to put in each grab as you get it you're sure to be there most of the morning."

I listened attentively. Socrates expounding to his pupils in the Forum had never a more fascinated hearer.

"You take the other end, Johnny. Come in at that other door, and vault through the second paying window. Kick the big fat geezer there in the face if you have to — but he'll take his orders same as anyone else. Just one flash of the rod, and then come over and swamp him. Surprise 'em. That's the stuff that builds fortunes — surprise. We're in, and over, and on 'em before they get a chance to squawk."

"How much do you think she'll go for?" Johnny was ahead of Dan in his planning.

"Can't tell. There's a big spike on the vault. Them iron gates are hell — but we might catch it open. It oughta give up twenty — maybe thirty grand." Dan reflected a moment before adding, "but it'll be summer dough, anyway. I wanta get away from this coast."

"You want me to go in first and wait for you — is that right?" I asked. "I take that big bag and wait at one of the check-writing counters until you and Johnny are in?"

"Bag — hell!" Dan snorted. "That's the worst rank in the world nowadays. If you started into a jug with a leather that size you'd get shot before you got to the counter. There's a couple of canvas sacks back in the car with the broads. Jesus Christ! I forgot about them. Turn this heap around, and we'll office them to follow us again. We gotta get the long rods from that car."

Dan jerked his head to the girls as we passed, and Mae steered out from the curb and followed us. We drove out toward the foothills, and in a thinly-built-up district the transfer of weapons was effected. The girls were instructed to go to a certain corner about fifteen blocks from the bank, to wait for us. It was a few minutes past ten o'clock when we parted.

A hundred yards from the bank, Johnny slowed down. Some last minute details. "Just walk down there and stall a minute," Dan said. "I'll get out right after you and follow. Soon's you get the heap parked, Johnny, — come right in. Then we're all set. I'll watch the doors from the inside. As long as no one gets out on us, we're all right. I'll keep the customers in. But make it snappy. Speed! That's the main idea. This is a fast clout. You ain't got more than a minute after you start, and you got to make every second count. If only that bull don't rank us!"

"If he does — it's just too bad for him," said Johnny.

The canvas sack — a two-foot-square affair — made a slight bulge. It made me appear like a woman enceinte.

The noise of the traffic; the harsh growl of a machine getting under way; the form of a scantily-clad girl as she minced by me, her thighs showing full against her dress at each step; a child tugging at a long chain attached to a bulldog; the acrid smell of burned gasoline; hurrying figures in bright or dark colors; a shaft of sunlight slashing across the sidewalk just at the bank entrance; — all these intermingled, and I felt as though I were a stranger from another planet. They seemed, to my heightened imagination at that time, foreign, utterly apart. They bore no relation to me or my errand.

Before entering the bank I recalled the precautions I had intended to take toward lessening the chance of later identification. An infinitesimal instant I hesitated, but I had drifted so far that retreat was impossible. The force of my present position stilled my fears, and I crossed the Rubicon.

IV

The floor seemed suddenly softened, as though I were treading on a billowy substance. I endeavored to make my feet take a normal stride, and they mocked me by lifting themselves as though inflated. With an effort I gained the side counter. With a temporary gratitude, like that of a saved sinner, I placed my hand firmly on the cold glass top. I had not yet ventured a glance at the cages or clients of the bank. I had been fully occupied in reaching this haven.

A stout woman at my elbow was scratching a pen across a check. She raised large, fishy eyes to me, and for a fleeting second I caught my own reflection in them. Sharply outlined by the strong light from the window at my back, I saw my head and shoulders in silhouette. Suspicion written plainly on her face, she dropped her eyes to the task before her, and edged slightly away from me. I reached for a blank check, and pretended to write, watching from the tail of my eye for Johnny or Dan. The small swinging gate through which I was soon to pass was but a step from where I stood.

The band of my hat grew suddenly tight. It seemed to restrict the flow of blood, congesting it at my temples. I raised a hand to touch my cheekbone, and my fingers came away as though burned by the contact. I tried to swallow, and my tongue clove to my palate. I coughed nervously, and the woman beside me started as though I had stabbed her with a pin. My cheeks felt hot, and I knew they were livid. . . . The constriction about my forehead increased. All this occurred in less than sixty seconds. The check before me was hopelessly blotched — ink stained my fingertips. I crumpled it.

Then, fearing that some of the writing might be decipherable, I shoved the paper into my pocket.

The woman turned to the paying cage nearest me. The teller looked past her in my direction, and I clinched my teeth to strangle another cough.

"Stand fast everybody! Don't move!" Sharp and ominous the command cut through my consciousness. They were in the bank — and I had missed them! I scanned the row of startled clerks, to see Johnny behind the counter. Dan was near the main door, a vicious black gun in his hand. I took a step and almost fell. My foot had gone to sleep while I had stood at the counter! Limping to the swinging door, I entered. Again that sensation of walking on billows of fluff. "Stand back!" I ordered the teller who was about to cash the fat woman's check. I caught a quick, alarmed look from him as he stepped back from the counter. The woman peered intently through the wicket, then slid from my sight. "Lay down — don't touch anything," I said in what I intended to be a harsh voice.

Two other clerks, and one woman employée, further along the counter, acted as though operated by a mechanism. They were prone on the tiles before I had extracted half the contents of the small compartments of the first drawer. Nervousness — the suspense — left me. A soothing calm followed. It seemed logical and natural to be lifting currency from a drawer. That this was the peak of a bank robbery never entered my mind. I was simply transferring bills from one position to another while a dozen people stood across the counter from me. I didn't actually look at them, but the impression I got was of a group on a motion-picture screen, suddenly frozen into unusual and awkward poses.

Through this, I was propelled by a will greater than my own. There was nothing of conscious volition in my actions, and I knew a curious division of myself. It seemed that I stood at one side and watched, dispassionately, while a chap who resembled a business-college student engaged himself in a practical study of banking. It was all impersonal, as if I witnessed it enacted upon a stage. I was an observing spectator — but with no greatly-absorbing interest. The action was flat, commonplace; there was nothing dramatic about it. It seemed to me that everyone connected with it was unnecessarily serious and concerned. They appeared to attach an importance to it beyond its worth. There came to me for one brief moment a hint of perverse amusement: if they — those grotesquely-frozen figures — could have known the turmoil raging within me a few seconds ago!

My gun was still in its holster. In my haste to get started, I had neglected to draw it out. But it was not needed. The clerks had seen the other two. The manner in which Johnny displayed his gave it a commanding personality. With both hands free I soon had one drawer emptied, and moved rapidly to the next. There the bills were stacked higher, and the jumble of yellow and green currency piled up steadily into a long, uneven mound on the polished black wood of the counter. Working with all the possible speed and precision I could command at the moment, I heard Dan growl, "Don't move or I'll blow your guts out! Do as you're told — you'll be all right."

Then I was aware that we had been working in a silence almost heavy. It seemed to press down on me. The noises from the street came as from another world. One of the men on the floor stirred. Johnny flashed a glance and covered him with his gun. I had my sack out now, and was stuffing bills into it in a glorious fan of color. Johnny held his sack in his left hand, and was sweeping the money from the counter with his gun and right hand.

From the door came Dan's cadenced voice. "Make it snappy. Make it snappy. No rank yet. Everything's going fine. Don't miss anything." Then suddenly he snarled "Come on in!" and I saw him capture a citizen who had started to enter the bank, and, seeing the situation, had attempted to escape. "Come in, you —!" Dan was almost touching him when the man obeyed. "Stand over there and be quiet!"

"All set, Bill," I called to Dan. I was finished, and started for the end of the counter.

"She's still quiet," said Dan tersely, endeavoring to keep an eye on the center of the cross-streets and watch both doors at the same time. "Try that chip. See if it's sloughed. Make it snappy! Christ! there goes that bastard!" A man had dashed out the door furtherest from Dan. "Out! Out!" Dan cried. It was an unnecessary order. I leaped to the counter and eased out through the wicket. Narrowly I avoided stepping on the face of the fat woman who had dropped from my sight. She lay in a faint near the baseboard.

At the door I slung the sack under my coat and pulled my gun out, ready for action. A squat, duck-like man with a red, bulging neck was entering. I poked the steel barrel into his belly and he stepped aside. His mouth dropped open.

"Take it on the natural," came from Dan. He was still covering the people in the bank. "Don't run, and rank yourself — the fuzz don't know what's doin' yet."

Crossing the sidewalk, I was surprised to find Johnny at the wheel of our car. He had made more speed than I had thought possible. On the floor in the rear of the car his bag lay gaping, money spilled from it. I flung down my bag beside it and looked for the traffic officer. He was still directing traffic. A gathering circle of people were about a prostrate man near the other door of the bank. Some idea of the rapidity with which all this occurred is shown in this incident: the man had left the bank, crossed to the curb and stumbled, yet before he could regain his feet we had left the counter and were in the machine.

With a jerk the car lunged forward. Dan was standing on the running-board. We passed within ten feet of the policeman. Our guns were ready, but he paid us no heed. The dash to the next intersection was made in a few seconds. "We're ranked," Dan said, and bent to lift a rifle in preparation for the chase that was forming.

I looked back and saw a bluecoat on the side of a car coming rapidly after us. Johnny steered through a stream of cross-traffic just then, and I lost sight of the pursuing car for the interval of half a block's travel. Then it shot out of the current and raced along over the intervening distance. Our car was picking up, and from the excited actions on the part of those in the machines we passed I could sense the narrow escapes from clashes that Johnny was guiding us through.

The machine following us seemed to gain slightly on us in the third block, and then—without a word of warning—Johnny skidded our car, which was then traveling nearly fifty miles an hour. For several yards we broadsided to the corner. He pressed down on the throttle, the reserve power picked us out of the skid, and he made a perfect turn down a side street. Then he raced the car until we seemed to be flying.

A swift thrill and exhilaration entered my blood. I wanted to cry out with some insane frenzy that flowed through me. A fragment of Shelley came to my mind, — "The joy, the gladness, the boundless, bursting, overflowing madness, — the vaporous exaltation not to be confined. . . . " It coursed from my head to my feet, and I knew a tingling that purged me of all the restraints the morning's preparation had imposed. The following car could not make the sharp turn, and I did not see it again. Still driving with reckless speed, Johnny brought us to where the girls awaited us.

We changed cars. Dan and I crammed the spilled money back into the sacks, and with the guns held under our coats we all crowded into the coupé.

Once in the apartment, the money was dumped on the bed, and Dan, Johnny, and I began sorting it into bills of the same denomination. The burned money — bills that had been defaced or pasted together — was thrown upon the floor. The girls got those bills. Later, they would pass them one at a time. The danger of marked money was too great for a known thief to hazard carrying it about.

Soon we had it counted into three piles. There it was on the white spread. We had divided it evenly. For an instant a revulsion swept over me: the sight of the money seemed vulgar! I was not entertaining any aversion to accepting my portion, but as it lay there heaped up, it seemed to have lost some of its dignity: it didn't represent anything. At least, nothing of the value which I felt I had, somewhere, inadvertently lost. I was descending from the heights of a transcendental emotional orgy — and I was becoming a philosopher! . . . Some latent germ of a youthfully-implanted Puritanism struggled to the surface, bleared my vision, and made the jumbled currency appear immoral. I wiped the traitorous bacilli from my eyes, strangled it, and called up visions of voluptuous delights.

"Take any bunch that suits you," Dan said. Johnny scooped together one pile. I took another, and straightened it out into a package that I could wrap with paper and carry under my arm. "Nineteen grand — eight hundred," Dan announced. "That makes — let me see — well, it's over six and a half each. Not so bad."

V

Two years later, Dan and I walked wearily from the rock-quarry to the upper yard of the prison. He had arrived the preceding day; I had been there six months. He was directly in front of me as we climbed the long stairs in line with several hundred other convicts. The heat from the granite slabs arose and scorched our faces. The large and grotesquely-shaped "mule breakfasts" covering our heads gave no protection from the forge heat welling up about us as we ascended the inferno of those stairs. The usual order was reversed: Dante descended — we climbed — into Hell. For within the close, hot, narrow confinement of our vermin-infested cell the temperature was several degrees hotter than in the yards. This because the massive stone block absorbed and held the terrific rays of the sun. The interior of the whitewashed cell was as a steam-room of a Turkish bath.

Dispiritedly, we stripped to our waists, discarded shoes, and dropped on our respective bunks — listless and too exhausted to even wash our faces or wet our lips with the tepid water from a bucket near the black, narrow door.

Dan gasped, "Get hotter'n this?"

"I guess so. Summer's just starting."

"Christ," Dan breathed — it was almost a supplication. "Red's lucky — missin' this."

"Uh, huh," I agreed.

"Yeah," continued Dan, "he's better dead."

"Dead!" I sat up and faced him. "How —? I didn't know that!"

"You should've — aw, I forgot you don't get the scandal sheets. He tried to take Johnny from the bulls while they was bringing him back from bein' sentenced for killing that flatfoot. In the battle he got slugged — twice. He died last week — look at what he's missin'."

"I knew Johnny was up here in the condemned cells, but that's news about Red —." I stopped as an insane cry shattered the sultry stillness of the corridor.

Our eyes met. Again and again the cry shuddered through the air. It rose into a frenzied screaming. We stared deeply into each other's eyes, unable to avert our gaze; held fascinated by the significance of those piercing screams: a soul in anguish, protesting against the enroaching and inevitable doom.

"That's Johnny," Dan said, a note of awe in his voice. "It's got him — he's blowed his top."

Two months later I called at the hospital to complain of recurrent pain in my lungs. The doctor looked sharply at me, listened through a stethoscope he held to my chest.

"How long are you doing?" he asked.

"Life."

"Murder?"

"No. Robbery and prior conviction."

"Well," — he paused and seemed to be considering some problem, "well, — you've got T. B. I'll have you transferred to the other prison, where the climate is less severe. But —" he busied himself with the next patient.

That BUT!

In the open-air court atop the hospital building of the other prison, I was seated in a canvas steamer-chair with a book lying open before me. A small, dwarfed thief, whom I have known for years, hobbled up to me — a visit pass in one hand. Looking cautiously about, he whispered,

"Say, Dan an' another guy beat the joint up above, yesterday."

The next evening, at count-time, the guard passed down by the row of beds and paused at the foot of mine. Removing a cigar from his lips, he looked at me.

"They got your pal Dan," he said.

"*No!*" I almost shouted it.

"Yes," he said, "found him stiff about twenty miles from the prison — died of exposure."

He flicked the ash from his cigar and continued on down the ward.

THE VICTOR

By Freer Stalnaker

All at once, it seemed, he heard the dog's barking clamorous beyond the marsh. Excited, fierce, scarcely muffled by the green bush. At the same moment he realized he had heard the dog before: it had been baying for hours, an insistent savage voice that until just now he had pushed out of his mind, hoping it would stop and go away.

He went to the well-porch. The barking grew swifter, swelled to an hysteric note, broke to a snarl and growling that came muffled out of some recess. Dirt or stone hidden. Down in the ground, maybe, or in the stone piles. There was a yelp, a sound of struggle. It stopped. The dog lifted a plaintive whine cut short by a baffled cry, then out in the open again, it settled down to a long baying. The rage was gone. Its voice was loud, informative, pregnant with all the anxiety and excitement of its brute breast. This might go on for hours, the man thought. He left the porch and made his way along a path that led across the marsh into the wood.

He located the sound in the V of a huge outcropping of rocks on a little hillside. They caught sight of each other at the same time, the man and the dog. She was a large Collie-mongrel bitch, tawny in the leaf-filtered sun of the late afternoon, her dugs heavy with milk. From some neighboring farmhouse, he supposed, or the squatters on the mountain. At sight of him the bitch wagged her tail once, plunged into a hidden angle of the cliff and backed out with a look that plainly invited assistance.

He stepped forward. Under the overhanging rock, he managed to see black earth and small roots dug out raw from around a group of large boulders. The openings between were worn slick with the dirt and saliva of hours of struggle. As he hesitated, the dog again plunged in and again backed away. He understood that, excited and furious as she was, she was overjoyed to have called this unknown man to her, that she expected aid and approval for her effort. "Good dog," he said, and worked in closer.

In one opening he saw a patch of grisly gray fur; in another, the head of a woodchuck larger than any he had ever seen. Its size and the glittering of its black eyes made it formidable. His appearance gave the animal a start. It whistled weirdly, a kind of eerie chortle so ill-fitted to its appearance that he almost believed the sound came from some other source. It

FREER STALNAKER, *one of the more promising younger short story writers, was first presented to a national audience in this magazine.* (November, 1941)

drew back its head and clicked its large rodent teeth. He feinted with his hand. It leaped shortly. Its teeth snapped on emptiness. The bitch lunged past him. The woodchuck clipped a cry of pain from her. She growled, crouched back a foot or so and barked hysterically.

"Here, here," he said, pushing her aside. "Easy. Quiet down. We'll see about this."

He studied the animal's position. It was backed under three large stones, much too heavy to lift, but so balanced he believed he could roll them outwards. Other stones, some huge and heavy, piled steeply to the outcropping above him. But these three, so far as he could judge in the shadow of the recess, seemed free of the rest. If he did roll them back, the woodchuck would be exposed and could fight it out with the dog. The bitch would probably be able to kill it. If not, he could either assist with a club or else give the woodchuck a sporting chance to get away. For a moment he considered: if he did roll the stones away his own interference would be limited to the removal of an accidental barrier which stood between the two brutes. The result, either death or escape, would be the blind work of nature.

But, the thought struck him, if he really wanted nature to have sway, he could leave everything just as he had found it. Definitely he didn't want to do this. For one thing, he didn't wish to be further annoyed by the dog's barking. And she would stay there, he supposed, as long as she could see the woodchuck. For another — well, he felt a vague excitement, whether by contagion from the dog or, directly, he didn't know. That wild smell — it was sweetish and irritant, almost sickening. Suddenly he saw the solution. He'd capture the woodchuck alive. Not for any reason, particularly — just because he wanted to. Maybe he could keep it on a chain.

Weathered limbs lay scattered about. The man caught up several forked ones and tried their strength. They snapped easily in his hands. He then took his pocket knife and began to cut off a sturdy forked bush. At this, the bitch closed in on the woodchuck again. Its snapping kept her at a distance. In her excitement, she began to dig up the ground with her paws.

"Here, here," the man called. "Just a minute now. Take it easy. Easy, I say."

But the man began to disobey his own advice to the dog. The bush was of tough wood, a young hickory. He had selected it for its toughness, but that same quality made it harder to procure. The knife-blade was dull. Instead of a clean cut, it shredded the wood and slipped along the grain.

He took the bush in both hands and tried to break it off with main force. The only result was to twist and bend it at the point where he had cut. In this state it was even more difficult to cut and it couldn't be broken at all. Finally he gave up and tried a bush of another kind. The same thing happened again. The blade was decidedly too dull.

He stopped a moment and found his clothes heavy with sweat. The bush held the air stifling and still. His temples pounded, his hands stung from their rough contact with bush and knife. The bitch's frantic barking brought his eyes back to the woodchuck. It had left the first opening and through the other he saw it trying to crawl further into the rocks.

The man dashed forward and pushed the dog out of the way. He snatched up one of the dead sticks. Using the stick as a lever, he managed to force the woodchuck back into the opening under the main rock. The animal bit at the wood two or three times, but without much force: it understood, evidently, that wood was only wood, that he was its real enemy. Its black eyes gleamed fixedly at him.

Once, with a quick motion, it grabbed his stick, forced it down and tried to bite his hand. Its forefeet were like little hands, with delicate long black fingers each ending in a rounded nail. Once or twice it shivered, once or twice he heard it take a deep breath, always, without the slightest relaxation, it held itself in readiness.

"I'm not going to hurt you. But you don't know that," he said aloud. To himself he thought, Christ, what courage! For all it knows it's fighting for its life against overwhelming odds, but it doesn't give an inch. It hasn't even whistled since that first time.

His hands kept busy building a barricade of sticks across the one opening. He thought: they're solitary except when they're breeding, this one is grisly. They're sly then, the old ones. They sit for hours in the sun. They eat plants. That smell has something of plants in it. Woodchuck, whistlepig, groundhog. Maybe he's lived here twenty years, in the stone fences and the maple woods and the growing-up meadows. He sleeps in the ground when the mountains are white and silent. . . .

The dog's leap brought him alert. The woodchuck had turned to face the other opening. Hastily he began to barricade that one, too. Again it was necessary to edge the animal back a few inches. He put a stout club against the woodchuck's nose and pushed. The woodchuck pushed back.

It exerted so much pressure with its almost hairless nose, that he had to use all the strength of his left arm to move it. Again and again, the animal stretched towards him and clicked its teeth.

"No good, that," he said. His voice sounded throaty, labored. He inserted another stick. As he did so, he saw it move too late. He half jerked it out of its hole with all its weight on the teeth in his thumb. The pain shot up his arm and with it, a hot anger. "Damn! God damn!" He jabbed it full in the face with a stick, leaped up, grabbed a heavy club. He'd roll the stone back and beat the life out of it, mangle it, drive all his own hurt into its lifeless body.

Realization of his own absurdity stopped him. He looked himself over as calmly as he could. Dark blood pulsed from his thumb. His gray flannels were already spattered with it. A nasty bite, his nail cut through, the flesh torn underneath.

He'd probably lose the nail. "Damn!" His thumb ached with each throb of blood. He laid the club carefully to one side. He'd get it now, he would, and no odds. No odds at all.

II

On his way to find the dog, he'd noticed a dump heap where his hosts wheeled iron and other sundry refuse. He scrambled from the shadow of the huge stone-pile towards it. The dog, no longer held in check, renewed its close battle. He didn't bother to call it off. He felt too grim. The air, the stillness of the wood seemed to throb with his own heartbeats. The enraged barking of the bitch at once relieved and kindled some relentless purpose within him, some dark compulsion he had never felt before.

As he approached the dump, a lone brown bird startled from a bush, leaving a stir of green leaves. He heard the soft flurry of its wings, saw it rocket into the near meadow where reddish evening took it. It could go. Then, by contrast, he saw something of his own cruelty, for so at first had he felt about the woodchuck. At first he had wondered at the dog's savage persistence. Now he understood the dog. Now he himself as ardently desired to confine it in some small cage. Yes, precisely, both to punish it for the throbbing in his arm and to redeem himself in his own estimation. The recognition of his savagery, of his sorry sweated and blood smeared plight, made him more savage and stubborn still. That's what he felt. If that was cruelty, well and good. He went about his task, obstinate even to the warning of his own mind.

The dump was strewn with bottles, tin cans, old tires, hoops, an ice cream freezer, with almost every object usable in a country house, all in a state of confusion. Finally he found what he sought, a small metal barrel of the sort that is used for roofing compounds. One end was open. The elements had seen to its cleansing. That would serve admirably. Next he sought and found a galvanized lid which fitted over the end of the barrel. Then, as he was leaving, a kind of after-thought, he picked up a pick handle still shiny from recent use. With these, and not without some trouble — for the barrel kept getting caught by scraggly branches — he trudged back to the rocks.

The bitch, who seemed to have felt herself deserted, dove recklessly into the hole. Her eagerness threatened to displace his barricade. "Out," he said. "Stay back." He poked her so roughly with the pick handle that she yelped in leaping away. The yelp angered him. "Well, stay back then." And he threw down the barrel so she had to jump to avoid being struck by it.

With exasperation, not so much at the bitch as at himself, and yet at her, too, because he began to feel she was part of the savagery which had taken hold of him, he grabbed the stone next to the one where the woodchuck crouched. It was heavier than he had thought. Nevertheless, by bracing one foot against the rocks at the side, he managed to roll it free of its settled couch in the earth. Into the space where the rock had been, he placed the barrel, kicking it, bending it down until it fitted snugly against the grating of sticks.

He turned to the stone at the far side. But that one wouldn't give. He jerked it. His foot slipped and he brought up against it, a blow that almost knocked the breath out of him. Also he caught his injured thumb in a twirk of pain that shivered all along his arm and side. The bitch added to his confusion by hurling herself in with claws that caught and tore welts in his side. He jerked up the pick handle and gave her a belt that resounded hollowly on her ribs and sent her scrambling backwards with howls of surprise and fright.

"That'll teach you better," he said. And, in a burst, "Stay back, damn you! Stay back!"

The bitch whined. The man squatted motionless. In the silence beyond him — for he, himself, was a loudness of pain and throb — he heard tinklings of a bell from far over the hills, drowsy, musical and mournful in the declining day. The sound caught in the cobweb of his senses, but he let it struggle and die without heed. Both remaining stones, he now saw, were wedged under those above his head. But only a little. He'd have to be careful. He must not disturb those heavy upper stones.

He inserted the pick handle behind the rock and pried out. The stone resisted at first; then, with a delicate scratching, moved clear. The man breathed a deep breath of relief. He braced himself as he had before and toppled the stone backwards out of his way. All that remained now was the one stone which imprisoned the woodchuck, barricaded at either end, the barrel close up against it. If he could get the animal into the barrel, he'd slip the lid over the end of it and his work would be complete. He could rest then.

But getting the woodchuck to move from its place under the rock was no easy matter. When he pulled out the sticks, the animal leaned forward and smelled of the metal barrel. It shrank back again. Its teeth chattered. But it refused to move. Indeed, if possible, it stared up at him with eyes more defiant and more menacing than ever. He tried waiting. His patience couldn't stand much of that. Rocks cut into his knees, mosquitoes whined around his head, the wood began to grow dusky and, back of it all, an overwhelming exasperation mounted in him. He wasn't used to such effort. His aching body and his curbed impulses alike cried out for an end.

He remembered the space under the rock was so small that the woodchuck had had difficulty in turning around. Watching to see the animal didn't whirl, he reached around the rock with his right hand, removed a few sticks and pushed against it from behind. Under his fingertips he felt the coarse hair, felt the animal's muscles tighten in spasms of fear. He himself trembled all over now. He shoved, squeezed hard, and yelled: "Get in there, damn you, get in!" The eerie whistle came again. He felt the muscles rigid under the loose hide. Still it didn't move. He pinched it, sunk his nails into its hide, twisted, gouged, shoved. The sweetish, irritant smell grew stronger. Its eyes became two luminous points behind which its body grew shadowy in the dusk.

"You! Christ!" And he rammed the pick handle cruelly. A sound needled every nerve in his body. The woodchuck was biting a ridge of the rock. It was grinding its teeth into the rock. A shout of rage and overstrained nerves welled hoarse from the man's mouth. He took the pick handle in both hands — jabbed, twisted, jerked against the rock. A blind muscular rage to destroy goaded him now.

The bitch sprang in, a tawny arc. He swung awkwardly at her, but she, wary of him now, ducked away from the blow with a long howl. He snatched up something and flung at her and her howl wavered behind him. He jabbed again. He strained against the rock with all his strength. Something gave, something grated, snapped. There was a slumbrous rumble overhead. The stones above, loosened at last, lurched towards him in great dark shapes. He tried to spring back. He slipped. His injured hand struck downwards. The woodchuck, a spectral gray, leaped upward and away as the overhanging rocks struck darkly down. They caught him on all fours. One smashed against his head. . . .

Several hours later the belling of the bitch, mournful and timbrous in the dark, brought a searching party from the house. Their lights wavered through the mist fuming from the marsh. The bitch bayed until their steps and voices were loud upon her, until she was caught in the furthest gleams of their lights. They saw her slink away. They found the man, his blood dark on the rocks. In the first alarm at finding him, it appeared to his friends that he had died in a struggle with some great adversary.

A LEAF-TREADER

By Robert Frost

I HAVE been treading on leaves all day until I am autumn-tired.
God knows all the color and form of leaves I have trodden on and mired.
Perhaps I have put forth too much strength and been too fierce from fear.
I have safely trodden under foot the leaves of another year.

All summer long they were overhead more lifted up than I;
To come to their final place in earth they had to pass me by.
All summer long I thought I heard them threatening under their breath;
And when they came it seemed with a will to carry me with them to death.

They spoke to the fugitive in my heart as if it were leaves to leaf.
They tapped at my eyelids and touched my lips with an invitation to grief.
But it was no reason I had to go because they had to go.
Now up, my knee, to keep on top of another year of snow.

(*October, 1935*)

THE LUMBERJACKS GO SISSY

By Stewart H. Holbrook

WHEN my father's father ran a logging camp in northern New England sixty years ago, it was commonly said of loggers that they slept in trees and would eat baled hay if you sprinkled whisky on it. Up in Maine, New Hampshire, and Quebec, I knew fellows who put on red woolen drawers and double-breasted undershirts in September, then they hit for the camps, and never took them off until the snow melted in May and it was time to go down-river on the drive. These same lads slept sixteen to the bunk, one hundred to the room. Ordinarily they didn't shave all winter long, although the camp dandies might on a dull Sunday run a whetstone over a single-bitted ax, slap some yellow soap into their whiskers, and there and then shave in the manner of the great Paul Bunyan himself. But such effeminate doings were regarded with suspicion by most of the jacks. Black Bill Fuller, an eminent camp foreman of First Connecticut Lake, held shaving in the winter to be pretty nigh as debilitating as the carrying of a handkerchief.

All tobacco in camp, both smoking and chewing, came in one-pound plugs; and if you weren't man enough to pack sixteen ounces around with you, you took your ax and whacked off a hunk large enough to last until evening. They were mighty chewers of plug, those old shanty-boys, and no punk considered himself a man until he could spit fifteen feet into a head-wind and hit a sapling fair in the crotch. The smoking tobacco, when inhaled, commonly came out the ears. Work was done in snow to the arm pits. Noon lunch was eaten in the woods, and consisted of frozen biscuits, beans, and a lye mixture that went by the name of tea. A moderately good axman could fell a spruce so as to drive a stake into the ground; and a chip from his scarf flew out with enough force to fell a yearling bull in his tracks.

But it was when the winter's work was over and the jacks headed for town that the outside world learned of the prodigious lustiness and all-round he-ness of the loggers. It made no difference whether they were Bangor Tigers from Maine or Saginaw Cats from Michigan. Such a-whoring and a-drinking and

---

STEWART H. HOLBROOK *is an authority on the more manly phases of American folklore, having written many books on the subject. "The Lumberjacks Go Sissy" is a good example of this virile writing about a virile aspect of our national life.* (October 1936)

a-fighting hadn't been seen by man since the days of the Crusades. They startled the pious folk of Bangor as they pounded on pine bars and shouted for stronger liquor. They swore they'd leave no virgin along the Kennebec. And on at least one memorable occasion, a jack jumped, calked boots and all, through the only plate-glass store window in Woodsville, New Hampshire, wherein stood the waxen figure of a woman displaying a pink nightgown of crêpe de Chine.

But soon the New England spruce began to peter out; so the loggers packed their tattered turkeys and swept on through New York and Pennsylvania like forest fire. Next they paused awhile in Michigan and Wisconsin, where the tall white pine fell like wheat before their onslaught; and they turned Saginaw, Bay City, and Chippewa Falls into howling bedlams that were to keep the pulp writers in copy for years to come. The fights grew gaudier and bloodier. It was the classic era of eye-gouging, of getting an opponent down and tramping on his face with calked shoes. Once having the boots put to him, a man was marked for life with "Loggers' Smallpox". Makers of glass eyes did a rushing business in the Lake States of the 'Eighties and 'Nineties, for no fight was worthy the name unless mayhem was committed. More than one doctor owed his livelihood to worthies such as Bulldog Fournier, who claimed—and no old-timer doubted it—to have chewed off the ears of twenty-two Michigan lads who thought they were able men.

Whorehouses grew to monstrous size. They were known as stockades, and many of them harbored a hundred short-skirted gals. These women were often called *Battleaxes,* for a reason clear enough if you recall the advertising slogan of that noble brand of chewing tobacco. In brief, it was a great and hell-roaring era. But one melancholy morning the loggers, peering out from behind a million stumps, saw that Michigan and Wisconsin timber was getting thin. They sighted smokestacks just over the hump. Their ancient enemy, Civilization, was creeping in. And so they packed their turkeys again and went on to Minnesota.

At about this stage, they were joined by hordes of Swedes and Norwegians, able drinkers all, and whoremasters and fighters to a man. The squareheads introduced a new and pleasant vice, the chewing of snuff. Not sniffing — but chewing. Heretofore, you could trace the receding timber line from Maine to Michigan by the discarded tobacco tags that came on *Spearhead* and *Climax;* but from Cloquet and Duluth to the West Coast the loggers' wake was to be strewn with the round tin covers of *Copenhagen* snuff, commonly known as Scandinavian Dynamite. The boys cut the Minnesota timber on this ration and cut it in a hurry. Then they moved on.

There were no stops in North Dakota, nor was there much halting in Montana or Idaho. With a rattling of peaveys the hordes of sharp-shod men swept on down the Columbia and into Western Oregon and Washington. Here, although they didn't suspect it, they were in their last stronghold, their backs to the sea, and Civilization, with its host of farmers and

THE LUMBERJACKS GO SISSY

traders and city slickers, creeping steadily upon them. They couldn't go on, over the hump, for there wasn't any hump. And so the saga of the lumberjacks from this point onward is a sadder story, even, than the extinction of the American buffalo.

II

First thing to happen was the beefing of the big, bellowing oxen who yanked gargantuan butts over skid-roads that smoked from friction: the oxen were made into hamburger when some genius discovered that logs could be yarded with cable and a donkey engine. Thus disappeared the colorful bulls, and with them went the buckaroo or bullwhacker, their master, the god-damnedest curser that ever raised voice against Deity and the animal and vegetable kingdoms. Soon, too, logging railroads began pushing back into the timber, and the driving of rivers was forgotten. No longer was a lad proud to be known as a cat on the logs, hurling them this way and that with his sharp calks; few of today's loggers could stand upright on a rolling hemlock in the quiet of a sawmill pond. Then came the Wobblies, as Big Bill Haywood's benevolent order of the Industrial Workers of the World called themselves. The Wobs had to have a Cause at all times, and right then it happened to be "No Bindle-Stiffs. Burn the Blankets", and "Be a Man. Don't Carry a Balloon."

What these stirring slogans meant was that the loggers should give up their ancient practice of carrying their own blankets (*bindle, balloon*) from camp to camp. "We want white sheets furnished by the Boss!" howled the Wobs from five hundred soapboxes. They pulled strike after strike, with the bindle as their objective; and presently they got their white sheets and pillows. The sad part of it was that they not only got sheets and pillows, but every week the Boss presented them with a rental and laundry charge.

Next, and worst of all, came the married man. Since the time Paul Bunyan's father started the first logging camp, back in the days when loggers had tails and slept hanging from limbs, there had seldom been a woman in the logging woods. Not even a *bad* woman. True, the enterprising madams of bumboats plying the coastal waters of British Columbia and Puget Sound had often called near a camp to display their wares, but of women, either good or bad, actually living in camp, there was almost none. Who it was, I have no idea, but not so many years ago some canny timber baron figured that it might be possible to hire loggers who would stay married for more than one night at a time. It was tried and it worked beautifully. With his ball-and-chain attached to him, the logger had no need to visit the fleshpots of the towns and cities. Labor turnover was reduced, production speeded up.

Added to these things was the happy fact that God made the wives of many loggers most fruitful. They have multiplied to such good effect that for the past twenty years or so there has been a good supply of prime young loggers born, so to speak, right on the plantation. I can think of no really large camp in either Oregon or Washington that does not have a camp school and schoolmarm.

While all this was going on, the Better Roads movement penetrated the back country, and loggers took to buying cars. You'll find a garage now in most any camp, large or small. Unmarried loggers, who in older and more moral days never saw a gaslight between October and May, took to running to town on Saturday night and sleeping it off in camp on Sunday afternoon. From this point onward, it is easy to trace the disappearance of the old-time lumberjack.

Loggers began subscribing to daily papers and the concomitant correspondence courses in everything from be-a-detective to saxophone playing. One of them got drunk on a Saturday night and brought the first radio into camp, where it still bleats nightly, to the disgust of old Nestors who had rather stove-log about the time Jigger Jones loaded too high with the crosshaul and came a-fluking down Dead Diamond Hill with no sand on the road and the snub rope broken. Aye, those were the days. . . .

Meanwhile, the camp buildings went the way of the ox-teams and five-cent whisky. The newer camps are barrack-like structures, made of boards, with *windows* in them, and shingled roofs, layouts scarcely distinguishable from wartime cantonments. Once started on the white sheets, the operators went hog-wild with "improvements". Lamps and lanterns gave way to portable electric-light machines. Many of the companies even threw out the old privies, some of them truly monumental jobs, and installed toilets.

Most indicative of all, perhaps, has been the change in the tobacco habits of loggers. This is important. When I was a youth, thirty years ago, a man who came into camp smoking a cigarette was eyed coldly, allowed to eat his supper, and then sent packing down the trail. "A man who will suck on a cig'ret," Jigger Jones once told me soberly, "won't stop at nothin'." Jigger, as well as most loggers of the time, considered a cigarette-user to be a degenerate, as well as worthless as a logger. Today the lumberjack smokes as many cigarettes as a débutante.

Years ago the operators threw away the tin plates and iron forks, and now white crockery appears on the table. And with such fancy doings has come the girl flunkey, or waitress. Most of the Western camps now have young girls slinging the hash and rolling out a string of flats (*i.e.*, hot cakes), and most of them marry loggers. They settle down in camp to raise more loggers. Plenty of camp stores stock diapers these days; and rouge, lipstick, hairnets, and two-way-stretch girdles are sold openly. The rustle of a magazine is more likely to be *McCall's* than the *National Police Gazette*.

The old lumberjack is a very lonely fellow, these days, almost the last of his race. Nearly all of Paul Bunyan's Boys — now streamlined and each wrapped in cellophane — have gone over the hump.

BRIGHT EYES

By Jim Tully

We were known as road-kids in the parlance of hoboes. And nearly a hundred of us had assembled in Chicago from every State in the nation. What a gathering we were! Embryo pickpockets, bruisers, and yeggmen, and — maybe — a few future members of Rotary Clubs, we lived, like carefree scavengers, on the very fringes of society. Out of orphanages, reform schools and jails we had come, the sniveling and the stubborn, the mongrel and the thoroughbred, the weak and the never-defeated. The youngest of us was about twelve; the oldest about fifteen. A future champion pugilist was among us, and five lads who were to serve life for murder, and fourteen others who were to be detained in different penitentiaries for lesser periods of time. One became a vaudeville head-liner; another a political boss. Some were to die fighting for a nation that, with boundless generosity, had given them but hallways and box-cars to sleep in. One became a Methodist minister, later falling from grace long enough to serve a term for forgery. He was then to climb back on the chariot of God, where he remained until he died insane. We were a variegated crew.

We lived at the Newsboys' Home — a faded, red-brick building that overlooked Lake Michigan. The most popular lad in the institution was a little Italian whose real name we never knew. Young as we were, many of us had something to hide, and he was reticent. We did not question him. His eyes were large, brown, and sparkling, so we called him Bright Eyes.

Bright Eyes and I had reached the Home on the same winter day. Blue with the cold and very lonely, we became friends immediately. Our natures were different . . . I was the rebel in knee breeches, with tangled red hair and heavy jowl, who told life to go to hell. Bright Eyes was as calm as a June morning after the rains are done.

I remember one evening in the Home when we assembled to meet a very wealthy lady. We all read compositions that we had written. I read my own aloud and it was greeted with applause. I had written about General Wolfe, who

---

JIM TULLY, *who spent many of his early years on the road as a hobo, was welcomed for the fresh note he brought to American literature. On the basis of such books as* Beggars of Life, Shanty Irish, *and* Circus Parade, *chapters from which first appeared in this magazine, he has been called the Gorky of America. "Bright Eyes" is one of his most tender and most effective pieces.* (July, 1925)

was my favorite hero in those days. The grey-haired and bespectacled lady was amazed. She shook my hand and turned to the matron and said, "There's literary talent displayed here," and asked my name.

It was my first literary triumph. All of us speculated as to the outcome of her remark. I lived in the clouds for three days, waiting for her carriage to come after me.

Bright Eyes said no word while I lived through that feverish dream. Reticent, as usual, he finally called me aside and said: "You'll never hear from her, Jim. Don't kid yourself. Those people can't be bothered with the likes of you and me. Look at last Christmas. Not a soul came near this joint all day."

He was right. I never heard from Mrs. Marshall Field again.

It was bitterly cold the week following. The wind howled from the lake for seven days and seven nights. As the Home was closed from early in the morning until late in the afternoon, Bright Eyes and I were at the mercy of the cold. We were thinly clad. We had no change of outer clothing — and no under clothing at all.

At last Bright Eyes got a job in a print-shop. He had learned something of the trade somewhere. Cold as it was, I preferred the open streets, where I sold newspapers and carried luggage for travelers going from one station to another. And so several bitter weeks passed.

One evening Bright Eyes returned wearing a bandage over his left eye. Some printer's ink had got into it. The eye grew worse. A doctor was called in. Three weeks later the eye was removed.

. . . Unskilled in words of sympathy, we knew not what to say. For several days a sadness hung over the Home. A patch was devised to hide the empty red socket . . . the sadness passed . . . and save for depressing moments, Bright Eyes was seemingly happy once again.

But we called him Bright Eyes no longer. With the terseness of our world we called him Blink.

II

He never returned to the print-shop. He had lost interest in work. The months drifted by until spring. We took to the road, and our ways diverged.

But nearly all of us became hoboes, and so I would come across him now and then in the underworld of some city. He always worried for fear the loss of his eye would affect the sight of the other. It became a mania with him. Cheerful liar that I was, I told him that such a thing was impossible. I argued that one-eyed people could always see better than people with two eyes. Blink tried to believe me. He became a hopeless vagrant.

After years of wandering some of us settled in Southern California, and there I met him again. He was still worrying about blindness, and I did my usual lying. I told him about a fellow in the navy with one eye who could see further than any other man who sailed in ships. Blink listened quietly and then said:

"God, Jim, I don't want to lose my other glim. There's so much to see!"

I immediately cut in: "But hell, Blink, you like music, and you can always hear that. And you can hear engines whistlin' far off. Bein' blind ain't so damn bad."

"Don't kid me, Jim, I'm on. I'd rather be in jail for life — than blind. There ain't nothin' worse."

A Spanish girl passed in a riot of color, her lithe body alive with joy. Some red-winged blackbirds danced on the green grass of the plaza where we talked. Far away, through a rift in the Mexican tenements, we could see the mountains.

The Spanish girl returned, singing.

"That's a song about a bird with a broken wing," said Blink. "I wonder if he had just one glim too."

I believe that now and then there blossoms in the world a flower that has been a thousand years in the forming. Blink had certain qualities that could be explained in no other way. His knowledge of music was astonishing. One-eyed vagabond that he was, he knew the folk music of all the nations, and he knew grand opera too. He would go hungry to hear music; often, indeed, he would beg his way to the topmost gallery to feed his soul.

The Spanish girl's song died away. We remained tense and silent with wonder. Two heavy-footed men approached. We knew them immediately as city detectives.

"We want you as a vag," one of them said to Blink. "You've been hangin' around here long enough."

They took him to the nearest street corner and called the patrol-wagon. Before I left him I said:

"Remember, Blink, you're not guilty — and stand trial."

"All right, Red," he answered, with absolute unconcern.

I hurried away with the hope of helping him. We were not without friends in Los Angeles — though all of them had to be careful to avoid the trap of the law themselves. So when Blink faced the police judge the next morning, five of us were there to help him. He pleaded not guilty, and stood trial.

Two of our friends who went in and out of the court-room were opium smugglers. They had hurried from the Mexican border to help a friend. When the trial was over they hurried to their work again. It was a two-hour battle. The two detectives testified, but Blink's friends proved to their own satisfaction, and evidently the judge's, that he had worked within the past six months. When the testimony was in the judge gave Blink six months in jail and suspended the sentence providing Blink got a job within a week.

In three days Blink had work as a printer's devil on the Los Angeles *Times*. He worked for two months at this job. But his fear of losing his other eye returned. Long weakened, it began to cause him trouble. His little band of uninfluential friends became alarmed. They persuaded him to go to the County Hospital, where he lay upon a bed for four months and underwent as many operations. When the doctors had finished there were two empty red sockets in his head instead of one.

I had encouraged him with lies for thirteen years. Now I found it hard to lie any further. After all, very little can be said to a man with two empty red sockets in his head. The thing to do was to keep him cheerful. Yet every subject I raised seemed to be an ocular one. He would lie on the bed, his raven-black hair rolling back from his forehead, and the tears welling out of the red holes in his head like water from a spring.

He was taught the Braille system of reading, but there was no way they could bring to him the sight of sun and rain and wild free places. So a beaten creature he became, until it was decided to send him to the Institution for the Blind. An incoherent letter came to me and I hurried to the hospital.

"Can't you do something, Jim? I'd rather be dead than in a jail for the blind. I don't want to be caged up any more."

Between us it was decided to write to General Harrison Gray Otis, owner of the Los Angeles *Times*. Our request would be small. Surely the great editor would use his influence to help Blink. All he wanted was the use of a street corner downtown, where he could sell newspapers.

I worked late into the night on a letter which I felt certain would touch the old general's heart. The next morning I had it typed, signed it Frank Thomas, the name Blink went by, and sent it by special delivery.

Weeks passed but no answer came. We sent another and even more urgent letter, but it too remained unanswered. Another, registered, followed. It was also ignored.

Then I decided to gain an audience with General Otis by hook or crook and then switch the conversation to Blink's plight. But that was no easy matter. Always fighting the world, and often in fear of his life, the general was no easy man to see.

After some days of consideration it dawned upon me that his wife had written many sentimental verses for his paper. I had also written sentimental verses, so it occurred to me to send samples of them to the general, telling him that Blink had written them, and praising at the same time the verses of his wife. Accordingly, I sent them with an ambitious letter begging an interview with the great man, telling him of my youth and the hard years, and also mentioning Ohio, for I had learned from "Who's Who in America" that he was born in my native State.

I must have written the one masterpiece of my life, for in two days I was invited to call at his home, "The Bivouac." A flunky looked at my letter to assure himself, perhaps, that I was not another labor agitator bent on murder. After some deliberation he seated me in an alcove in the hallway. A weak-looking man sat near me. He also waited for the general.

III

Soon, his secretary invited me into the library to wait for the general. I looked about and saw many volumes of sentimental verse by such poets as Alice and Phoebe Cary, Henry Wadsworth Longfellow, Felicia Hemans, Ella Wheeler Wilcox, Mary Howitt and others of even lesser fame. Presently the general entered, followed by the weak-looking man who had waited with me in the hall. The general turned upon him and said brusquely:

"Well, what do you want?"

The little lamb of a man said:

"Well, general, we are organizing an indemnity fund to protect such patriotic institutions as the *Times* against the ravages of labor agitators and socialists."

The general scowled, and said, as he paced the room restlessly:

"To hell with that damned graft! They didn't give a damn for me when my building was blown to pieces and twenty-one of my men were killed. I fought a battle, I did, for liberty and the Constitution! Without me, labor would crucify all enterprise in this State."

The lamb bleated. "But, general, Earl Rogers thinks well of our plan!" (Earl Rogers was the brilliant lawyer who had helped Clarence Darrow defend the McNamara brothers, dynamiters of the *Times* Building in 1911.)

It was a fatal bleat. The general threw his hands in the air and roared:

"He's a God damned ——!"

Then, pacing up and down the floor, he delivered a long harangue on the crimes of working men. The small man would rise to go, and the general would always shout. "Sit down! Sit down!" When the gentleman managed to leave at last the general turned to me and said:

"My God! Those fellows are hard to get rid of!"

I immediately committed a great social blunder. I called him *Mister* Otis. He turned upon me quickly:

"*General*, if you please! Not that I'm vain — but young men should be taught discipline."

My hand clenched. But I thought of Blink, and was humble once again, and generaled the general all over the room. I mentioned my verses, but he preferred to rave against union labor. He stood before me, an immense man, with stooping shoulders, and heavy pouches under his eyes. His frame, once a great deal over six feet, had shriveled. He was a withered giant with a bag of skin on his bones. His eyes were close together, and all the face wrinkles converged to the corners of them. There was fanatical zeal and finality in his every utterance. Unluckily for me, the departing sheep who wanted to help the tiger fight labor — for a price — had only succeeded in putting him in an evil mood. He raved on and on. Parrying for an opening, I shot in:

"I was reading the other day, General, some verses by your distinguished wife, General, and knowing how you must have helped her, General, I have made bold to write and ask you, General, if I might not presume upon your patience, General, not for myself, General, but for a blind boy friend of mine, General, who also writes verse, General."

"Huh!" he grunted. "But would you know a piece of news if you saw it coming down the street?"

The Irish in me was still unsubdued by so mighty a presence. I replied:

"I think so, General . . . but I'm not asking for myself, General. You see, General, I have a young friend who's blind, General. He writes verses, General, and he used to work on your paper helping printers, General. One eye was fairly good when he started there, General. We ain't blamin' anybody, General. He might have lost it, anyhow, General. Though Blink claims all the towels was full of ink around the place, General."

That was unfortunate — but I was

busy generaling him, and untrained in diplomacy.

"Damn it to hell, what was wrong with the towels? Everything's one damned complaint after another, by God! What in hell do you want?"

"Well, you see, General," I shot in quickly, "Blink's blind as a bat, General, and he only wants a street corner, General."

"Only wants! Oh, hell! Only wants — They all want something!"

"But this won't cost a dime, General. The judge told Blink if he didn't work he'd send him to jail, General, and Blink wants a corner downtown where he can peddle papers, General. Why, he'll sell two *Timeses* to one *Examiner*, General. He's a white boy, General, and I've never known him to double-cross anybody."

"How long did he work for me?"

"Not long, General. His eye went gooey quick. Then it was curtains for Blink, General."

The general walked rapidly up and down the floor, withered red hands behind his back, shaggy head bent low, and long wrinkles stretching across his forehead.

"I can't do anything. There's places for blind men in this State. That's why we have government and pay taxes."

"But you see," I answered, stepping before him, no longer the humble, reformed road-kid, "you see, Blink's worse than blind. He has a head on him. I've seen him go nuts over a sunset. . . ." Seeing a scowl, my method changed for Blink's sake. "And he used to like your wife's poems, General, and he read the *Times* and believed in all you said, General. That's why he went to work for you, General. He could have started for some other paper, but he preferred to work for the *Times*, General!"

Ignoring my scramble of words he blurted out:

"We have a State Liability Act — let that take care of him. Too many blind men peddling papers on the streets now."

"But something muffed with the State Act, General. They want to railroad him to the Blind Asylum, General. And he'll croak himself before he goes, I'm sure, General. By God! *I* would! I wouldn't eat their damned bread, General, if it was smeared with honey — and Blink's been in other asylums for the poor. And so have I, General — you know what they're like."

The defiant old man, long used to the center of the stage, was ruffled by my effrontery.

"No, and I don't give a God damn," he answered.

"But, General, you have a great soul — Blink doesn't ask for a thin dime."

"It makes no difference. The State should take care of him. He'd be in the world's way outside. . . . There he'd be treated well."

"Maybe you're right, General — but I can't sell Blink the idea. I'd be a hypocrite if I tried."

"Well, that's enough. There's nothing I can do."

"Thank you, General," I said, and left the room.

I strolled into Westlake Park unmindful of decorated nature everywhere. I would have to lie to Blink — would have to tell him that the General would take his case under advisement. I'd have to say: "You know, kid, whenever those big guys do that something always happens. You'll have to be patient, though, Blink — those guys have a lot on their minds — and you may even have to take a ride to the blind joint for a while, and then some of us can sign a bond and get you out. General Otis sure'll help us. He ain't nearly the mean guy everybody makes him out. Jack London and Clarence Darrow and that gang only have their side of it, Blink. You gotta remember that Otis has his side, too. Look what a lot of them guys did to his building . . ." and, so thinking, I arrived at the County Hospital.

Blink, as usual, was stretched out on his bed. His spirits were so low that he seldom had ambition enough to grope his way about the ward. To cheer him, his underworld visitors would disguise their voices and make him guess who had come to see him.

I said no word that day as I stood near his bed. He touched the muscles of my forearm — his way of recognizing me — and said with a touch of gaiety in his voice: "That you, Jim? God! I'm glad."

"Yep, it's me, Blink, and I sure got some good news for you. Of course, it won't happen right away — but old General Debility Otis said he'd do what he could. It'll take time, though, Blink, as you know those guys are busy . . . so you'll have to be patient."

"Oh, I'll be patient, Jim. God, I'll be patient! I can't do nothin' else."

He lay back on the bed, the black tangled hair sinking into the pillow. His hand clutched mine in a feverish grasp as I looked down into his handsome face and saw, as usual, the tears gush from the holes in his head. Overcome, I leaned on his breast and sobbed, "The God damned old ———! . . . Blink, I wish to Christ I could give you eyes. . . . You could have one of mine if I could fix it so's you could!"

The hands patted my shoulders, "That's all right, Jim . . . maybe something'll happen."

"Sure thing, Blink, nobody knows. Maybe in a year some guy'll invent eyes you can see out of — they do funnier things than that."

Hope came into Blink's voice.

"I've been thinkin' about that, Jim. You know, maybe they can do that."

"Sure," I answered, "and I'll bet they'll be doin' it, too. I'll bet you they'll be takin' dead men's eyes, and fixing them in and tying up the nerves . . . so's it'll be like it was before people go blind. I was reading something about that the other day," I lied.

IV

Three months had passed since the interview with Otis. Christmas came. The time was drawing near for Blink's journey to the Hospital for the Blind. All his poverty-stricken friends insisted that he go to the institution until more suitable arrangements could be made.

During Christmas week we took up a collection of nearly seventy dollars. We took the money to him with much forced banter and the words, "We're loaning you this, Blink, till you get a good corner downtown."

Always eager for news, he inquired what word had come from General Otis. I told him that I had heard from the general's secretary the day before, and that the general was taking the matter up with the City Council. This false news appeased him somewhat, and we talked of old times until it was time for me to go. The hospital, situated as it was on a busy thoroughfare, was no easy place for a blind man to escape from. Yet Blink did escape — after the lights had been put out, the night before he was to be sent to the asylum. The city of Los Angeles was four miles away, and the path taken there by a blind man must have been a devious one.

But Blink found his way to a cheap hotel, where the landlady gave him a room with another blind man. In the center of this room was an oil-cloth covered table. She asked Blink to be as tidy as possible and place everything on it. She let her little boy lead him about the next afternoon.

He asked the lad to go to a motion picture theatre with him — "where there was music." It was a continuous show and they remained for hours. The youngster became restless, so Blink paid him a dollar to remain another hour. Then he asked to be led to a pawnshop.

When I found that Blink had escaped I inquired in his old haunts. No one knew where he had gone. I spent the afternoon looking for him, without success, but felt reassured because of the money he had.

That evening a package came by special messenger. It was wrapped about with many rubber bands. They ran in every direction. The address was written with lead pencil and was hardly legible.

Inside the package of brown paper was fifty-one dollars in paper, gold and silver, of different denominations. The bills were crunched, the silver and gold loose among the paper. The letter said:

"I thought I'd send this back to you guys so the dicks won't get it when they search the room. I won't need it any more."

It was badly scrawled and some of the lines overlapped.

I hurried to the address the messenger gave me. Blink, gentleman to the end, had placed his head on the oil-cloth covered table before he drilled a hole through it with the revolver the pawnbroker had sold him.

The next morning the *Times* carried a little story to the effect that Frank Thomas, a printer, had committed suicide in a cheap hotel.

There was no funeral for Blink and no headstone. I did not believe in such things. A young Irish burglar wanted to pray for him every night. I told him to go ahead. He was later sentenced for life as an habitual criminal. I hope it has not interfered with his praying for Blink's soul. For I believe he had one.

THE THEATRE

By George Jean Nathan

Advice to a Young Critic

The greatest weakness of the average critic is his wish to be more than a critic. He somehow believes that, however capable he may be as a critic, there is a call for him to demonstrate his talents in fields removed from criticism if he would augment and solidify his standing in his profession. We thus find critics as novelists, playwrights, producers, poets, biographers, husbands and what not, striving to support their critical position by achievements in extrinsic directions. For they imagine that they will be regarded as greater critics if they prove that they can do something apart from criticism, however dubious the quality of their performances. They shrink nervously from the charge that they are merely critics and not what are known as creative fellows. All this has led and leads to deterioration of criticism for the simple reason that criticism worth its salt is a job quite sufficient unto itself and calling upon its practitioner's fullest time and fullest resources.

The art of criticism is too often looked upon as a mere prelude and stepping-stone to a practice of one of the other arts, when it should be regarded — as, of course, it is by those who are sufficiently familiar with it in its finest flower — as an art of itself and a thing apart. The good critic has earned his right to reward by being a good critic. If he happens also to be something of a genius and succeeds as well in some other art, he deserves a double reward, of course. But, in the general run of things, he should be content to be what he is, a critic first and last, and leave to other men the jobs that they in turn should content themselves with.

II

If you have violent prejudices, do not be afraid of them. Give them a free course. Do not be disquieted because they seem to be at variance with the convictions of other critics. Few things are absolutely true in this world and you stand as good a chance of being right as the next man. Only exercise a caution never to be in-

---

GEORGE JEAN NATHAN *is one of the most influential and most widely read of American dramatic critics, as highly respected in England and on the European Continent as in the United States. He is the author of more than a score of books. He was the co-founder and for a time co-editor (with H. L. Mencken) of this magazine. "Advice to a Young Critic," a bit cut, appeared in October, 1927, and "Fragmentary Meditations," also a bit cut, appeared in September, 1928.*

dignant and always to smile. In the event that it turns out that you have been wrong — even to the extent of being idiotic — you will thus be safe, for most persons will conclude that you were just fooling and will secretly be a bit abashed for having fallen into your trap.

III

Take your work seriously, but not yourself. Fifty years hence, your work may prove to have amounted to something. Fifty years hence, on the other hand, you will have been eaten by the same indiscriminating worms who found Clement Scott and Acton Davies such appetizing delicatessen.

IV

Don't be afraid to dissent from the opinions of the critically great. Remember that Nietzsche considered Kotzebue a more talented dramatist than Schiller, that Hazlitt placed Foote and O'Keeffe among the immortals and called the latter the English Molière, that Dryden declared that Fletcher came nearer to perfection in comedy than Shakespeare, that both Lessing and Diderot considered George Lillo a model dramatist, that George Bernard Shaw thinks Brieux the greatest living dramatic writer this side of Russia, and that William Archer once actually observed (*vide The Theatrical World of* 1895, p. 271) that he venerated Mr. Augustus Thomas' *Alabama* so highly that he wished it would be published in book form so that he might go around quoting it!

V

I need not tell you, obviously enough, that morals have no place in any consideration of art. But do not make a fool of yourself when the point comes to issue, as so many critics are in the habit of doing. The latter often make themselves as ridiculous in their way as the moralists do in theirs. If the question before the house is one of authentic art, that is, if the work criticized is of genuine artistic integrity and if the question of its morality is interposed by meddling smutsers, let fly at the dolts with full artillery. But if the work criticized has no artistic justification and integrity, don't make yourself silly by defending it with the same arguments used in the former case. There is such a thing as art, and it should be held sacred and inviolate from the assaults of dirty-minded morons; but there is also such a thing as cheap smut, and it should be frankly admitted to be just that and nothing more. Certain critics, however, having established themselves in full feather as tomahawkers of all moral interference with anything, lack all discrimination when moral issues are raised and rush to the defense of Cabell and Mae West with one and the same argument. They grow as excited over the moral assault upon out-and-out dung like *Sex* as they do over the moral assault upon a first-rate piece of work like *Jurgen*. And, in so doing, they weaken their case — a case that must be kept strong at all costs and one that needs the fighting brains of all intelligent critics — and give the enemy certain points of advantage in the minds of liberal and rational men.

VI

The better and more honest critic you are, the fewer friends will eventually send flowers up to the funeral parlor. One by one they will soon or late cool and withdraw from fellowship and good will. Even one's closest friend cannot abide criticism of himself with half the fortitude and amiability of one's worst enemy. Show me a critic with a quorum of artists as his bosom comrades and I'll show you a critic who is a hypocrite and a liar.

VII

Do not confound an aphrodisiacal actress with a talented one. The majority of critics do so, and, I regret to confess it, understandably and even a bit justifiably. If an actress stimulates your libido, say so frankly and do not try to conceal the truth in a lot of rigmarole about histrionic art.

There is certainly nothing wrong with an actress who has sex appeal; indeed, it is five times more valuable to her and to a liberal portion of her art than all the stock company training this side of Cleveland and Rochester; and even if the professors object to what you write, the girl herself, I venture to say, will be tickled to death.

VIII

Pay no attention to what people say or write of you. A man in the brick-throwing business must expect occasionally to be hit by a brick.

IX

To be a critic automatically implies a certain self-sufficiency and vanity. Never mind. You will never find an artist among the diffident and submissive. Genuine artistic expression, in whatever field, calls for a forthright faith and confidence. It took more nerve and downright courage to write the *Essay on Morals* than it took to fight Waterloo.

X

Never fall into the error of believing that simply because a thing is unpopular it must have esoteric points of merit. Vastly more trash fails to win popular approval than wins it. If Rostand's *The Last Night of Don Juan* runs only a week in the American theatre, remember that John J. Hack's *One Glorious Hour* doesn't run even that long. And if *Abie's Irish Rose* runs for five years, stop and reflect that *Hamlet* will run for five thousand.

XI

Don't be afraid of being labeled a destructive critic. You will be in good company. Where would you rather be: in Hell with Swift, Voltaire and Nietzsche or in the American Academy of Arts and Letters with Richard Burton, Clayton Hamilton and Hermann Hagedorn?

XII

Since you are an American, write like an American. Do not try to become a member of the Charles Lamb's Club and ape the so-called literary manner of the English critical essayists. Express yourself in the pungent idiom of your time, your land and your people; there is no apology necessary; that idiom may produce sound literature as well as the language of the dons. Don't be afraid of slang if it will make your point better and more forcibly than literose expression. Much that was erstwhile slang has already been accepted into the dictionaries of formal English; much more will be accepted in the near future. But, on the other hand, don't make the mistake of believing that a mere imitation of Brook, Indiana, will get you any farther than an imitation of Cambridge, England.

XIII

A sound piece of criticism has never yet been spoiled by an injection of humor, let the professors yell all they want to. There is a place for apt humor in even the most serious work. If there is a place for it in *Hamlet*, why shouldn't there be a place for it in a criticism of *Hamlet*?

XIV

Don't hesitate to indulge in personalities. The common notion that there is something *infra dignitatem* about too personal criticism is just as silly as most other commonly held notions about criticism. When you are met with this personality blather, quietly refer your counsellor to such unseemly critical dealers in personalities as the Messrs. Cervantes, Voltaire and Zola or, if your counsellor has never heard of them, to Walkley and Shaw.

XV

You will be told never to sit down to write unless you have something to say beforehand. This is the veriest buncombe; pay no attention to it. Some of the best things that a man writes occur to him after he has sat himself at his desk without the vaguest preliminary notion of what he was going to write — even, indeed, when he has cursed God for ever having put a pencil in his hand. Many a writer has produced something excellent after staring blankly at his pad of paper for hours. Ideas frequently come out of one's dull pencil in time as clear water comes eventually out of a muddy tap.

Fragmentary Meditations

To DISMISS a theatrical critic as blasé is to be at one with the donkey. The best critics of the theatre have been and are blasé men. The very circumstance of being blasé implies experience and experience, in turn, implies patience only with what is worthy and complete impatience and contempt for what is not. The blasé critic is one whose emotional equipment has been so roughened by concussion with tin-pan drama that, unlike that of the still enthusiastic idiot, it responds alone to the finest form of stimulant. No critic in his first days is blasé. He is tickled by almost everything, and indiscriminately. No critic in his first days is worth a hoot. It is the critic who has a hard time keeping awake at the theatre that is the critic whose opinions are worth reading.

II

Just as even an otherwise taciturn person is seized peculiarly with an impulse to talk the moment a doctor sticks a clinical thermometer into his mouth, so is even the most linguacious critic rendered peculiarly mute when confronted by an indubitably fine piece of work. The latter, once the prefatory hallelujahs are done with, leaves so little for him to say; the artist has said that say so much better than he can say it in his rôle of mere liaison echo. This is why we find critics, even the very best of them, driven to the resort of praising a work in terms of detraction of certain other more or less related work. The counterpoint of detraction gives them the necessary ground to dig their heels into; it vouchsafes them an articulateness that would otherwise be difficult.

III

There has never been an actor, however bad, who didn't succeed in giving a good performance in the rôle of a butler, a policeman, or a Chinaman. Nor has there ever been an actor who didn't seem completely convincing in a telephone scene. If I could figure out the reason, I'd write an essay on the subject.

IV

It is the custom to disparage drama because it deals generally with platitudes. Disparagement might be meted out on the same score, and with equal justice, to most of the world's greatest novels.

V

Modern drama is chiefly concerned with feeling the old emotions in a new way.

VI

Symbolism is the child of poetic courage and intellectual cowardice.

VII

In the minds of most critics there are two niches wherein linger the memories of two groups of plays: in one, the memories of the undeniably great and, in the other, the memories of the deniably great but nonetheless immensely enchanting. I am not at all sure, indeed, that these less august plays do not often perfume the recollection more pungently than some of the established classics. Who, by way of example, can ever quite forget Fulda's *Friends of Our Youth*, or Brieux's *Les Hennetons*, or Rostand's *Last Night of Don Juan*, or Meyer-Förster's *Old Heidelberg*, or Shaw's *Caesar and Cleopatra*, or Barrie's *The Legend of Leonora*, or de Caillavet's, de Flers' and Aréne's *The King*, or Dunsany's *Laughter of the Gods*, *The Gods of the Mountain* and *A Good Bargain*, or Birmingham's *General John Regan*, or Jerome K. Jerome's *The Great Gamble* (at least the beginning and the end), or Henry Arthur Jones' *Joseph Entangled* and *The Case of Rebellious Susan*, or Lennox Robinson's *Patriots* and *The White-Headed Boy*, or Schnitzler's *Christmas Presents*, or Chesterton's *Magic*, or Molnar's *The Swan* and *The Glass Slipper*, or Bahr's *The Master*, or Schönherr's *Children's*

Tragedy, or Hubert Henry Davies' *A Single Man*, or a number of other such plays still regarded with some skepticism by the tonier professors?

VIII

Acting is the easiest of the professions associated with the arts. Consider how many more proficient actors there are than even dancers.

IX

The best type of revue, the kind put on at the Marigny in Paris by Jacques-Charles before the war, is simply a dramatization of destructive criticism embellished with some constructive samples of femininity and a few good tunes.

X

The action of the Actors' Equity Association in curtailing the activities of English actors in America indicates once again and clearly that the organization's last consideration is the best interests of the drama. That there is personal justification for the action, no one will deny, as the English had previously curtailed the activities of American actors in England and as the doctrine of *quid pro quo* always has something in its favor. But that, justification or no justification, the decision will sooner or later serve as a boomerang so far as the members of the American actors' union are concerned is fairly certain.

The English actor, on the whole, is a better actor than the American and there are many plays to which his presence in the cast is invaluable. Played by American actors, these plays are absurdly botched and duly fail. In time, therefore, with the barring of English actors, we shall have more and more plays of the sort manhandled, more and more plays acted by inappropriate casts, more and more failures, and less and less theatrical prosperity in certain directions. The members of the local actors' union are protecting their jobs only for the moment. In a few years there will be fewer and fewer jobs open to them, English actors or no English actors.

XI

There is too much supercilious critical talk of plot at the expense of character. The great dramatists have always gone in lavishly for plot.

XII

Clear diction in the theatre is all very well, but it may be carried too far. The critics have much to answer for in this regard. They have harped upon perfect enunciation so insistently that they have scared the poor actors to death. The result is often a comical distortion of dramatic values, with actors playing gutter bums reading their lines with the painstaking purity of professors of English and with others playing hayseeds laboriously manœuvering their wads of chewing tobacco out of the way of the King's tongue.

HAPPY DAYS

By Raymond Clapper

PROHIBITION gave Washington its first wallop in 1903. The wets who then flourished in Congress dropped their guard one day, and before they had recovered the ancient bar in the basement of the Capitol had been abolished and the sale of liquor stopped in the House and Senate restaurants.

For some years the white ribbon lobby had been in a great state of horror over this vending of drink in the very halls of Congress. The bar was at one end of the House restaurant, directly below the hall of the House — a long, mahogany bench running the width of the room and set in front of large mirrors against which rested neat stacks of polished glasses, decanters, stock bottles of Overholt, Old Taylor, Johnny Walker in either label, and little basketed flasks of Chianti, which last made very neat gifts for the ladies. Three hard-working bartenders ministered to the congressional trade. Nine-tenths of all Congressmen, in those far-off sinful days, were steady guzzlers. Toward noon they would wander in from their morning committee meetings, so that when the House convened at noon and the chaplain launched into his morning prayer, the quorum was usually assembled downstairs, with its feet on the brass rail.

The Senators, more dignified, did not permit an open bar in their wing of the Capitol. The trade in wines and liquors there was restricted to service with meals. There was, however, no rule against a Senatorial luncheon of one cheese sandwich and five highballs. To the Senate dining-room the elder statesmen brought their constituents when polite jobs of oiling were to be done. Liquor was sold with meals in the House restaurant also.

This iniquitous traffic was rooted out quite unexpectedly, and largely because of a fumble by the wets, in the spring of 1903. A general immigration bill was before the House. A pious Congressman from bleeding Kansas, mainly for the purpose of bringing cheers from home, proposed an amendment to prohibit the sale of intoxicants at all immigration stations. This novel proposal was resented by the chairman in charge of the bill, Shattuck of Ohio. He retaliated with an amendment authorizing the selling of beer. Landis of Indiana, the Upshaw of his

---

RAYMOND CLAPPER, *who was killed in the South Pacific in the line of duty as a correspondent, was the well-known newspaper columnist. He was one of the many newspapermen who found this magazine the only medium that would print such of their pieces as were too "hot" for their usual channels. "Happy Days" is one of the most amusing commentaries on the Prohibition issue.* (September, 1927)

day, protested that it was ridiculous and immoral to propose handing a glass of beer to each arriving immigrant.

"Then why don't you distinguish yourself by offering a resolution to stop drinking in this Capitol?" shouted the exasperated Shattuck. Landis snapped up the taunt and offered the amendment.

"If the same members of Congress who seem so eager to close the bar in the basement of the Capitol would abstain from patronizing it," declared the sarcastic Cochran of Missouri, "it would close for want of business."

But this bitter remark had no effect and the Landis amendment was adopted by 108 votes to 18, more than half of the House not voting. The absentees were downstairs in the bar.

The wets on Capitol Hill were chagrined but not alarmed. The powerful Senator Boies Penrose was then chairman of the Senate Immigration Committee, and it was expected that he would kill the amendment when it reached him, for he was the wettest wet ever heard of. But for some occult reason he let it go through. Why, nobody knows to this day. Possibly he was sensitive about the reputation that had fastened itself upon him.

"Look at Knox," he complained one day later on, referring to his fellow Senator from Pennsylvania. "He drinks three times as much as I do and goes into the Senate and never shows it. But if I take one drink my face gets red and everybody says, 'Penrose is drunk again.'"

Or possibly he had just been irritated by some petty incident like the one which occurred when a constituent came to him for a trivial favor. Penrose was unable to locate any Pennsylvania Congressman to do the necessary errand.

"Everybody seems to be off drunk," he explained to his visitor. "But I'm temporarily sober, so I'll do it myself."

Whatever was in his mind, he let the amendment come out of his committee. Other Senators, seeing that the wettest of wets accepted it, were not disposed to object. A few days later the Federal attorney for the District of Columbia served notice that the liquor stocks in the House and Senate must be disposed of by July 1 or a prosecution would follow. Thus perished the House bar.

This primeval Prohibition act was observed just about as its big brother is being observed today — in spots. The old employés on Capitol Hill say that after the bar was closed the members and their friends were served with drinks in teacups. Brock's saloon was on a nearby corner in those days, where the House Office Building now stands. A dry Congressman would send over for a quart and make away with it in the cloakroom.

"It was a lot worse than before," one old House employé told me. "When there was a bar they used to go downstairs and take a couple of drinks and behave themselves. But after the bar was closed they got to bringing liquor into the cloakrooms by the jug, and they wouldn't quit until they had killed the jug. Congressmen went around like boiled owls."

Today, as everyone knows, Prohibition is in force all over the Republic; nevertheless, it is no secret that liquor is still obtainable in the Capitol. Not long ago a waiter in the Senate restaurant dropped a pint flask on the hard floor in full view and hearing of many eminent diners. It was announced next day that the contraband belonged to him, and every suggestion that it was destined for a Senator was indignantly denied. So the waiter was discharged with loud hosannas — and quietly hired again a few days later.

During the last session of Congress one peevish Senator complained that bootleggers were so numerous, and so persistent in canvassing the Senate Office Building, that they had become a downright nuisance. Policemen on duty at the entrance to the building have been known to fall into the *faux pas* of arresting bootleggers, mistaking them for peddlers, who are not permitted in the place. On one such occasion, the trapped purveyor, eager to protect his distinguished clients, fled into the nearest Representative's office and hid his brief case before he would submit to arrest.

Congress contains numerous amphibians who have, in the historic words of the Hon. George Brennan, "dry throats and wet bellies." One was exposed not long ago, when it was testified in another member's divorce suit that he had presided over a party of dry Congressmen with a pitcher of liquor. He decided not to run for reëlection. But such catastrophes are rare. It is hardly necessary for even the most impassioned dry Congressman to pull down the blinds in Washington when he wants to wet his whistle. The Prohibition agents there all have very poor eyes. And so long as a Congressman votes right, he need have no fear of trouble from the Anti-Saloon League, which takes the high moral position that what a member of Congress does outside of business hours is nobody's — at least not its — business.

Sometimes an eminent souse sails right out into the open bearing a full cargo, as happened one afternoon when a well-known Southern Senator, a faithful supporter of Prohibition, ambled into the Senate chamber listing heavily to port, and fell asleep in the over-sized chair of Senator Penrose, who was then still alive, and who seems to turn up in every Washington liquor anecdote. Visitors in the galleries recognize Senators by means of numbered seat charts distributed by the ushers. The devoted public servant from Pennsylvania feared that he might become a victim of mistaken identity, so he announced formally to the Senate that his seat at that moment was being occupied by another Senator.

II

But after the Capitol bar was closed the tendency of Senators and Congressmen was more and more to contain themselves until the end of the day and then go downtown to drink their way along Pennsylvania Avenue from the Capitol to the White House, the historic route of inaugural parades. It was an Appian Way of Bacchus, with forty-seven bars to its mile. Probably nowhere in America were there such superb drinking facilities in equally compact form. Nor such distinguished gullets to be quenched. Nowadays a Congressman meeting another in the cloakroom boasts that he played thirty-six holes of golf yesterday; in the old days he boasted of making thirty-six bars on his way up Pennsylvania Avenue. To get as far up as Hancock's, at No. 1234, without having to call a hack was equivalent to breaking a hundred at Chevy Chase today.

Hancock's was a place of manifold and incomparable delights. Mint juleps there had thick frost on the outside of the glass — surely something to sit down to in Washington's summer heat! But the big drink was Hancock's fruit punch — a punch likened at the time to that of John L. Sullivan, for its man always went down for the count. Any time you went into Hancock's you'd find a couple of Senators with their noses deep in mint at a bare table in the back room. The old place is lost now in a row of second-hand shops, but at night, I suppose, many an illustrious ghost comes back to sniff the musty walls. In the old days the pungent breath of lager mingled with the sweet scent of corn pone and chicken à la Maryland frying in the kitchen. Hancock's Old Curiosity Shop got its name from its ancient collection of rusty pistols, faded theatre programmes, helmets of Washington's early volunteer firemen and other such things. There was a piece of blanket said to have wrapped the body of John Wilkes Booth, and beside it was what was said to have been Jeff Davis's toddy glass. The firemen's hats were in great demand on nights when the dry and distinguished boys from Capitol Hill were in a playful mood.

Shoomaker's was another favorite resort of statesmen. Shoo's, as it was usually called, was in the heart of Rum Row, just around the corner from Newspaper Row. Strangers were almost invariably disappointed when they first entered. Shoo's was known among well-informed bibuli the length of the land as Washington's most remarkable saloon, the birthplace of the celebrated concoction dedicated to Col. Joe Rickey, the favorite bar of Cabinet members, Supreme Court Justices, generals, and politicians. But it was nothing to look at. Its appeal grew only with acquaintance. There was no more disreputable looking bar in town. Dilapidated is a better word. Cobwebs hung across the dark corners. Boxes, barrels and packing cases littered the none too spacious drinking room. The place was never dusted. Cats crawled over the rubbish. A stale smell of souring malt greeted customers at the door. The dingy walls were hung with faded cartoons and yellowed newspaper clippings, most of which clung on by one corner and seemed in imminent danger of dropping off.

Shoo's scorned the free lunch that was set up in most other Washington saloons. Every afternoon, just before the four o'clock rush, a small plate of rat-trap cheese and a bowl of crackers and gingersnaps were put out. You could take it or leave it. Shoo's depended entirely on the quality of its drinks. Its gin rickey was nationally famous, of course. Its barrel liquor supported an excellent bead and was as good as could be bought. The place always had a quiet, dignified air about it; it was more like a decaying club than a dramshop. The bartenders did not wear the white jackets of their trade. Instead, they worked in well-pressed business suits and carried themselves with dignity. Gloomy Gus Noack, the chief of the staff, was suspected of being a Sunday-school superintendent on Sundays. One of his colleagues, Billy Withers, worked there throughout the sixty years the old joint was open.

Odd characters were more numerous in Shoo's than in any of the other bars of the town. One was an ex-faro dealer, a patriarchal old fellow with a long white beard. He always wore a plug hat and a Prince Albert coat. Another was a faded poet who, given a drink and a patient ear, would argue interminably that he, and not Ella Wheeler Wilcox, wrote "Laugh and the World Laughs with You." There were legends of famous men who in bygone days had enjoyed their daily libations in Shoo's quiet retreat — Grant, Sherman, Little Phil Sheridan (who was fond of brandy smashes) Rosecrans, Custer, Miles and Pope, and Senators and Congressmen without end.

The District of Columbia went dry on October 30, 1917. Shoo's held on as a near-beer stand for a few months. But its customers disappeared, and so, in March 1918, the doors were closed. There was no ceremony. A few eminent clients were allowed to carry away mementoes. The next day carpenters came in and began remodeling the place into a cheap restaurant to feed war workers.

Pre-Prohibition Washington knew many other noble bars: Sawdust Hall, where Jack Kane kept a set of boxing gloves for customers to use; Count Perreard's, where Bastille Day was celebrated each year with great damage to the premises but none to the generous heart of the kindly little Frenchman; Klotz's behind the State, War and Navy Building, an Army and Navy filling-station where you were greeted by Bartender Harry's growl, "Don't speak to me, I've got everything but a harelip"; Made's, with its back-yard pond of live bullfrogs, whose croakings were extremely annoying to Senators in their cups, Gerstenberg's, famous for its beer and sauerkraut; and many that were more noted for their food than for their liquor, such as Losekam's, Bucholtz's, and Harvey's, the home of sea food.

Across the street from the Treasury, where the National Press Club and Keith's Theatre now stand, was the Riggs House, whose genial bar was a popular first aid station for government clerks. This bar was the home of the Foolish cocktail, a Martini with a floating slice of onion. Miss Frances Willard, founder of the W.C.T.U., often stopped at the Riggs House, but was seldom, if ever, seen in the bar. But Ollie James and Gumshoe Bill Stone were there often. The bar was a fine old black walnut affair, kept cleaner than some of the other troughs of the time, with fresh towels always ready for the more refined boozers.

Then there was the Ebbitt House bar, where the racing crowd and Army and Navy officers congregated before a sumptuous free lunch every afternoon. The hot Virginia ham, served with salads and other delicatessen, often sustained indigent Washington newspapermen until payday. The Raleigh Hotel bar was a highly ethical place, where a bartender almost lost his job when he was discovered filling an Apollinaris bottle with seltzer water. It was scandalized one day when a woman shot a Senator in the adjoining lobby, an episode which the sedate Washington *Star* heralded with the headline: "At the Raleigh."

One of the favorite saloon-keepers of those glorious and departed days was Dennis Mullany, who was educated for the priesthood but preferred to keep a modest gin-house at the southwest corner of Pennsylvania Avenue and Fourteenth Street, opposite the New Willard. Mullany's equipment was meager. He drew his beer direct from the keg and had no coils. There was a very plain bar in the front room and a pine table and a few chairs in the back room. Here the Brain Trust of Newspaper Row met every afternoon, to exchange news and gossip. Sam Blythe spent many happy hours there before he took the veil and mounted the water-wagon. Bob Wynne, later Postmaster-General, James Rankin Young, once a Congressman from Pennsylvania; Major Stofer, and other famous correspondents made it their headquarters. Mullany, a well-read man, often neglected his trade to sit, with his chair turned backward, his chin hung over the back of it, arguing the tariff, free silver, or anything, no subject barred. Sunday closing being then in effect, he left his back door open, and his favorite customers enjoyed open house in the back room. Everything was free on the Sabbath.

Free drinks were also frequent at Engel's — that is, during the baseball season. The old man's son, Joe, now a scout for the Washington baseball club, was a star pitcher in those days. Every time he won a game his father would order drinks on the house. There was always a rush from the scoreboard into Engel's when Washington won. The old man would tuck back his white apron and go around exclaiming proudly, "My poy, Choe!"

III

It all passed into the shadows very quietly. On the fatal day all the serious drinkers of the town, official and private, were lined up at the bars three and four deep. It was a mournful time. Only one saloon reported any disturbance. Arrests for drunkenness were fewer than usual for a Saturday night. The Willard, Raleigh and Shoreham Hotels had closed their bars a few days before. The clubs auctioned off their supplies. When the final hour drew near, all partially empty bottles on the saloon bars were given away. Glasses were distributed to eminent clients as mementoes. The final toasts were drunk quietly.

In a house in Massachusetts Avenue a little tight-lipped man sat before his fireplace reading the evening newspaper. He was the Hon. Morris Sheppard, Senator from the State of Texas, author of the fateful act that made Washington dry.

THE SOUTH KILLS ANOTHER NEGRO

By William Bradford Huie

You never heard of Roosevelt Wilson. I never saw him more than twice. But Roosevelt Wilson continues to disturb me. Whenever I try to feel that I am an honest and self-assured supporter of the American Dream, Roosevelt Wilson perches on my shoulder, laughs sardonically, and reminds me that I am just another lousy compromiser; that once when I had my chance to strike a blow in defense of the Great Dream, I turned aside with the Pontius Pilates and whimpered: "What the hell can I do?"

To understand Roosevelt Wilson you'll have to visualize the loneliest, most insignificant human being in the world. The cipher in a social system. He never knew who his mother was. He just appeared as a nameless black brat in a cotton patch. He breathed. He grew. He chopped cotton for bread. He stole. And somebody, somewhere, labeled him Roosevelt Wilson. Think of him as a black, burr-headed creature who felt no superiority to a hound dog, and whose death would not have brought a waft of regret across any heart in America.

When I first heard of Roosevelt Wilson he was a dog being chased by other dogs. He was a scurrying black animal to be shot on sight and left naked to rot in a ditch and be picked by buzzards. He had raped a white woman in a potato patch at Bug Tussle, and bloodhounds and a posse were chasing him. It is the old familiar fabric to every Southern reporter, so I methodically ground out eight paragraphs on The Chase. And when the black quarry had been captured by a sheriff and "spirited away for safekeeping," I ground out two editorial paragraphs congratulating the sheriff for preserving Alabama's proud record of not having had a lynching in three years.

When I arrived at the county courthouse to cover the trial, there was nothing unusual about the scene. The AP reporter and I sat in a dysentery parlor across the street, drank coffee, griped about the assignment, and hoped Justice would act swiftly so we could get back to Birmingham before night.

There were two or three thousand people massed in the streets leading up to the courthouse square. A scattering of

---

WILLIAM BRADFORD HUIE *comes from Birmingham, Alabama, the locale of this article, which after three years is still the subject of heated discussion throughout the South. He is the author of two books,* Mud on the Stars, *a novel, and* The Fight For Air Power. *(November, 1941)*

sticks and shotguns. Two companies of National Guardsmen had mounted machine guns around the courthouse and an officer with a loudspeaker kept issuing warnings forbidding anyone to cross the street to the courthouse. Only those who had stood in line and obtained tickets for the two hundred seats in the courtroom were allowed to pass into the courthouse, and these — both men and women — were searched for weapons. The scene in the courtroom was usual for such trials. State police and Guardsmen, armed with sidearms and nightsticks, were stationed around the walls and in the aisles.

The jury had been selected when I seated myself at the table which the sheriff had hastened to provide for the two out-of-town reporters. We had not been expected. It was a routine trial. We would not have been sent to cover it except for a dull news week. The jurors were farmers and townsmen and I observed that they appeared more intelligent than the average Alabama jury. This was because the verdict was a foregone conclusion and thus counsel had not made the usual effort to strike the more intelligent men but had simply taken the first twelve in the venire.

I looked across at the plaintiff. She was a husky, loose-jointed farm woman, perhaps thirty, with big, red hands, big feet, and a matted mass of blonde hair which some amateur barber had chopped squarely and roughly off. She reminded me of a gangling battle-axe I had once seen in a brothel whom the Madam used only as a shock trooper to take on the heavier and more bellicose clients who came in very late and very drunk. The two great press services drily agreed that young Roosevelt had shown damn poor taste in his selection of a Queen Bee worthy of his life.

Next to the plaintiff sat her husband, a burly farmer whose cheap clothes were much too small for his bulging muscles and whose flushed face gave evidence of the great rage pent up inside him. Around the two sat an imposing array of counsel for the state. The Attorney-General himself was on hand, his hackles up, and issuing brash statements by the bucketful. Every elected prosecutor in district and county was present, with assistants and volunteers, to see that swift justice was done. Such a case provides rare political opportunity and every attorney who plans to run for office rushes into participate gratis in the prosecution and make a hell-raising speech to the jury.

You had to look at counsel for the defense to appreciate the contrast. These two lawyers had been appointed by the Court, their names drawn from a box containing a list of all practicing members of the bar. Fate had frowned on poor Roosevelt again. For he had drawn a couple of old men who had no stomach for trial procedure. They were in mortal fear the populace would get the idea that they had willingly taken Roosevelt's case and that they believed him innocent. Before the trial began, one of them rose and addressed the Court.

"Your Honor," he stammered, "to avoid any misconceptions here, my colleague and I would like you to explain publicly that we have been drafted by the Court to safeguard the constitutional rights of the defendant and that no sympathy for this defendant is implied by our actions."

This the judge did solemnly in the presence of the jury. But still the old fuddy-duddies weren't satisfied. They came over to us and requested we make clear in our stories that they were appearing only in compliance with constitutional requirement. The judge, a grayish politician of about sixty, tried nervously to rush the procedure. He wanted the trial over and the defendant safely back in state prison by nightfall.

There was a rumble in the courtroom. The big coppers and the Guardsmen hefted their nightsticks. You could feel the hackles rise and the hate charge the air. The defendant was trudging in with an escort of troopers. I gave him an unconcerned and half-amused glance and jotted down a note. Barefooted. Faded and patched pair of blue overalls and jumper. Hundred and thirty pounds. Five feet six. Burr-headed bastard. The troopers handcuffed him to a chair directly in front of us. With the trial about to start, his attorneys spoke contemptuously to him. It was the first time, apparently, that they had seen him.

"What's ya' name, boy?"

"Ruseyvelt Wilson."

"How old are ya?"

"Ah thinks ah's twenty-two."

Then they sat back and were ready. They assumed the defendant had no witnesses and that he should be pleaded not guilty so as to be certain of the death penalty.

The state called the plaintiff and recorded her story. Her husband had been off working in another county. While she was digging potatoes in one of the more remote fields, the nigger had sneaked out of the thicket and accosted her with a shotgun. He had threatened to kill her if she didn't go into the thicket and submit to him. So, with a choice between death and such a sacrifice, she had complied with his demands. After he had run off, she had heard the yells of some women looking for her, and she had rushed to them and reported the crime.

The defense cross-examined softly and sympathetically. "Not that we doubt your story, ma'am," they explained, "but just for the record." The plaintiff agreed that the nigger had laid down his gun before the rape occurred, but the judge promptly explained to the jury that she had already been intimidated with the gun and was thus in mortal fear for her life even though the gun had been cast aside. The irreverent AP cocked an eyebrow and shook his head. The plaintiff weighed a good thirty pounds more than the defendant and could obviously have smacked him silly when he laid the gun down.

Then followed a succession of witnesses who established that the defendant had run when approached by the posse, that he carried the gun, and that he had resisted arrest. Two women testified to the nervous state of the plaintiff after the crime.

II

At the noon recess I overhead a conversation between Roosevelt and his attorneys. They were telling him that there would be no need for him to take the stand, that it would be best just to submit the case when the state closed. But Roosevelt objected.

"Naw, suh, boss," he said. "De truf aint being tole heah. Ah got to git up deah an' tell de truf. Ef dey kills me, ah got to git up deah an' tell de truf."

Believe me, it was no noble motive which inspired my intervention. I only wanted to blow up a dull story. I stepped up and said: "That's right, Roosevelt. If they're not telling the truth, you get up there and tell it. They've got to listen to you." The lawyers then admitted to him that "of course, the court couldn't deny him his constitutional right to testify in his own defense," but his testimony would do no good. When they had gone, I stepped back in and gave Roosevelt some more encouragement.

"Get in there and give it to them straight, Roosevelt," I said. Then, in that burr-headed nigger's face, I saw something I didn't want to see. I must have been the first white man ever to have spoken a civil word to him. He reacted like a dog when you pat him on the head. He let down his guard and I saw that he wasn't a nameless animal but a living, breathing, feeling — even aspiring — person. He showed me all the loneliness and fear of his wretched life. The loneliness of the cotton patch and a dog howling under the moon. The loneliness and fear of the swamp with bloodhounds baying. The loneliness and fear of a jail cell and a thunderbolt exploding in your body. I shrugged and turned away quickly.

Shortly after noon the state rested and defense counsel rose to inform the Court solemnly that counsel had advised the defendant not to testify, but that he insisted on his constitutional right. The defense, therefore, was calling the defendant, Roosevelt Wilson, to the stand. If you had struck a match while that nigger was walking to the stand, the courtroom would have exploded. I have never felt such tension, such organized hate focused on one insignificant object. Troopers clutched their nightsticks and the judge unconsciously rapped for order though the room was breathlessly silent.

"Now, Roosevelt, just go ahead and tell your story," defense counsel said. "And make it short." There was no effort to guide his testimony or to help him in any way.

"Well, jedge, it wuz lak dis," he began. "Ah got up dat mawnin' an' ah borr'd Sam Winson's gun to go rabbit-huntin'. Ef Sam wuz heah he'd tell ya ah did. Ah went ovah tow'd de nawth fawty an' ah seed dis lady a-diggin' taters. Ah'd seed her atime o' two befo' an' she'd tole me she wanted a ring ah had. Ah wawked up to her an' ah show'd her de ring an' we tawked a minute. Den ah axed her de question an' she lukked aroun' an' said she wuz willin'. . . ."

The room exploded. In a split second the husband had yanked open his britches and from somewhere under or between his legs had come up with a forty-five. And he had come up shooting. The crowd rioted and the Guardsmen began laying them in the aisles with the nightsticks. Two big troopers jumped on the hate-crazed husband and wrested the gun from him. Two reporters who had been standing up, the better to hear Roosevelt's story, had done a dual jacknife under a table.

It was half an hour before order could be restored. The jury, the husband, and the defendant were removed from the courtroom, and AP and I began burning up the wires with flashes. I asked the judge if he wouldn't have to declare a mistrial. "I suppose I should," he said, "but, hell, we've got to get rid of this mess." He looked as if he were bothered by an offensive odor.

I went in to see Roosevelt, and his lawyers were upbraiding him. "We told you so. We told you not to get up there. Now you see we were right. When court goes back in session, we'll just close the case."

"Naw, suh, boss," Roosevelt objected. "Ah's jest got started good. De whole truf ain't been tole yit."

By now Roosevelt had me pulling for him. "Get back up there, Roosevelt," I told him. "Don't let 'em scare you. Tell it all."

When trial was resumed, the defense apologized profusely and explained again that they had urged the defendant not to testify. Then they moved for a mistrial. The motion was denied and Roosevelt went back to the stand, completely surrounded by troopers. In a deadly silence broken by heavy breathing, he finished the story of a mutual pine-needle affair, hastened near the end by "some women hollerin' fo' dis lady."

The cross-examination thunder began to roll. The prosecutors began jumping and yelling and shaking their fists.

"If you hadn't committed a crime," the Attorney-General bellowed, "why did you run like a scared rabbit when these men found you over there in that field?"

The reply was cool. "Ah seed a buncha men come a-runnin' at me. Dey wuz a-cussin' an' a-shootin'. So ah jest run. Dey kept a-chasin' me, so ah kept runnin'."

For an hour the state battery took turns working out on Roosevelt. They attempted to cross him in every way. But his story never changed. The woman had gone to the woods with him willingly in exchange for the ring he had given her.

During the impassioned oratory to the jury, I convinced myself that the woman — the plaintiff — had smuggled the gun into the courtroom. The husband could hardly have brought it in, for he was the most suspect of all the spectators and two deputies had searched him thoroughly. But the matron admitted her search of the woman had been perfunctory. The plaintiff had known the story the nigger might tell and she had brought the gun in to have her husband kill him before he could tell it.

The jury required four minutes to go out, organize, and bring back death. While it was out, I whispered to the judge: "Judge, I've lived around niggers all my life and if I ever heard one tell the truth, that little bastard was telling it this afternoon, wasn't he?" The judge crouched down low behind his desk, nodded his head, and grinned: "By God, he shore was, wasn't he?"

When the jury had been discharged, I spoke privately to several of the jurors. To each one I made the same statement I had made to the judge. In each case I got the same reply. "Shore he was telling the truth. But what the hell, he deserves the chair for messin' around with a white woman. Besides, if we'd turned him loose, that crowd outside would'a lynched us. We gotta live with these folks."

After the troopers had rushed Roosevelt through the crowds and away toward the penitentiary, the judge called the husband back to reprimand him for creating a disturbance, not to mention attempting to murder a man still presumed to be innocent. The husband told the judge.

"Judge, I felt like I had to kill that sonuvabitch. I intended to do it this mawnin' while he wuz a-settin' over there at the table. But ever' time I'd reach down to pull my gun, the Lawd would tell me not to do it fo' them two newspapermen wuz a-settin' right smack behind him."

"Whew!" AP had turned white around the gills. "We got something to thank the Lord for, haven't we, boy?" he said.

III

As we rode back to Birmingham that night, I kept thinking of Roosevelt Wilson in his faded overalls and bare feet, riding alone toward Death Row with a hundred and twenty Guardsmen to see him safely in the chair. I thought of Pontius Pilate. I thought of Emile Zola and the few men who have had the courage to defy the mob. I sneered. What the hell! AP pulled in toward a roadhouse. "Let's have a drink," he said.

We had several drinks. We told the waitress some stories and pinched her on the thigh. To hell with Roosevelt Wilson. Smart guys don't go around butting their heads against stone walls. Smart guys make the most of the inevitable.

Next morning, in my clean-up story, I inserted two paragraphs about Roosevelt's testimony. In polite language I hinted at its substance. I watched the managing editor when he picked up the story at the copy desk. He looked over at me, made a wry face, and jerked his nose to tell me it stank. I saw his pencil go down in an impatient gesture, and I knew those two paragraphs would never see print.

No person reading my story could have guessed on what claim Roosevelt based his plea of innocence. I suggested we use a picture of Roosevelt Wilson with the story. His face might impress somebody with his innocence. But my paper, like others in the South, had a policy against using pictures of Negroes. So we used the latest piece of Marlene Dietrich leg art instead.

I wish I could tell you that the Case of Roosevelt Wilson perched on my shoulder like a raven, and that I never rested until I had freed him from his cell and thrown him back into the faces of the Pontius Pilates. I wish I could tell you that I made a brave speech to the editor of my paper; that I flung my job in his face; and that I fought for Roosevelt's freedom with pamphlets printed on a hand press. But none of these things happened. I told the editor the filthy facts and suggested a further story, but when he said, "Hell, Bill, you're crazy," I just said, "Yeah, I guess you're right."

I told the Governor the same filthy facts. He shrugged and said: "Boy, you're crazy. What the hell can I do? You know what it would mean if I intervened in a case like this."

"Yeah, I guess you're right," I said. "But you know I've read of governors who couldn't sleep after they had let an innocent man go to his death."

He laughed. I laughed, too. The kind of laugh you laugh to keep from crying. Then — incredible as it seems — I forgot Roosevelt Wilson and it was quite by accident that I ever saw him again.

IV

Thursday night is execution night at Alabama's big Kilby Prison. Most every week the state fries some black meat and occasionally a little white meat is thrown in for good measure. There was a young cop-killer sent up from Birmingham. He was a white boy from somewhere out West. He had been in the Marines and had hit the highways. He had gone jittery during a hold-up and plugged a cop. We had played the case with a lot of sob stuff and I was sent down to Montgomery to cover his burning.

The warden was impatient. "Come on, you guys, let's get started," he said to the reporters. "We got eight black boys to burn after we finish off this yellow cop-killer."

The cop-killer was yellow all right. There were six preachers with him when they brought him in the death house — all anxious to get their names spelled right — but he went hysterical and guards had to throw him in the chair.

I had filed my story and was ready to leave the prison when I remembered I had left my coat in the corridor near the death house. I went back for it and just happened to notice the black boy who was being led toward the green door.

It was Roosevelt Wilson.

In his white prison clothes the burr-headed little bastard looked smaller and less significant than he had looked in his overalls. Friendless and alone, he was going to his death. During his weeks of waiting he had not had a single visitor nor communication from the world outside. His eyeballs were rolling in fear, but he was walking without support. I tossed down my coat and called to the warden to wait a minute.

"You're Roosevelt Wilson, aren't you?" I said. "The boy from up in Webster County." He recognized me. I was still probably the only white man who had ever spoken civilly to him. "Yassuh, boss, ah is. And yo're de newspapah genmun who wuz at mah trial, ain'tcha?"

The warden was annoyed. "Come on, Huie," he snapped. "We're in a hurry. We got three more to go and it's gettin' late." But I insisted and he reluctantly agreed to take another nigger on and get Roosevelt last. He locked us back in the cell and we had a few minutes to talk.

"Roosevelt, would you like to see a preacher before you go?" I asked him.

He said he would, so I called an attendant and sent him for a preacher. But the only preacher around now was a nigger preacher and he was in the death house. So I borrowed a greasy little Testament from an old white prisoner on the

Row. I couldn't remember a suitable passage in the New Testament, so I opened the little Bible, pretended I was reading, and recited the last five verses of the Twenty-Third Psalm. Roosevelt repeated after me.

I fumbled for something to say to that Negro boy. I wanted to say something that would give him faith and comfort and hope. Something he could understand. Finally, I said: "Roosevelt, before you go in there, I want to say this to you. You are not guilty of the crime for which this state is going to kill you. All of us who heard your story know that you are innocent. The judge knows you are innocent. The jurors know you are innocent."

"Den why is dey killin' me, boss? Fo' God, ah didn't fo'ce dat lady."

"I know you didn't. We all know you didn't. But we couldn't help it."

"Is dey killin' me jest fo' messin' aroun' wid dat lady?"

"Yes, that's one reason. And there's a bigger and more awful reason that I haven't time to explain. But what you want to do now is to buck up. Everybody has to die. It's not bad in there. You never feel it at all. So don't be afraid."

He thought for a minute. "Does ya reckon ah'll go to Hebben, boss?"

"Well, Roosevelt," I answered, "I've heard it said that the folks here on earth who are done wrong like you, and the folks who have the worst luck — they are the folks who go to Heaven, and they are the ones who get the biggest crowns and the most gold. So I think you deserve to go there and I believe you will."

"Thank, ya, boss," he said. The warden was coming, and he turned and asked: "Will ya go in wif me, boss? It won't be so bad ef ya'll go wif me."

God, I hated to go back in there. It always made me sick. But I nodded. My folks don't shake hands with Negroes, but I took Roosevelt by the hand and we walked down the corridor. An old whiteheaded Negro preacher joined us.

You would have been proud of Roosevelt in the death house. He was scared, but there were no hysterics. At the chair he turned around and said: "G'bye, boss. G'bye, parson." The attendants clapped on the hood and adjusted the electrodes and the old preacher broke into "I am the Resurrection and the Life. . . ." For a second the frail form quivered in the chair, and then the sovereign State of Alabama exploded twenty-three hundred volts of lightning.

They buried him in the prison plot for unclaimed bodies. My paper ran a story under my by-line. It was a stinking account of the execution of a yellow cop-killer. "I have found God!" he was quoted as having said to the reporter before the switch was thrown. The last paragraph of the story was inconsequential. It would have been killed by the make-up man had it run over the column. It said: "Among the eight Negroes also executed last night was Roosevelt Wilson, 22, convicted of rape in Webster County."

Perhaps in retrospect I attach too much significance to this story of Roosevelt Wilson. It is a sordid story involving only an unfortunate woman and a black maverick. Of the score of interracial rape trials I have covered, it is not typical because the innocent defendant is the exception rather than the rule. But an innocent man went to his death.

It is apparent, then, that the cases of the Roosevelt Wilsons involve more than plaintiffs and defendants. They involve the faith and the hope and the courage of a nation. Small wonder that we have such difficulty rousing the Great Soul of America for its own defense. Small wonder that we can't project our dreams through the clouds of our own cynicism and behold a vision worth dying for. We are all soul-sick in America. It is a what-the-hell sickness compounded of cynicism and disillusion.

Who knows? Perhaps some day when we have regained the American Vision for ourselves and given it to others, we may erect a monument to Adolf Hitler. And when I have atoned for my own complacency and what-the-hell, I think I'll erect a monument to a bare-footed black boy named Roosevelt Wilson.

"*Stinker!*"

(*December, 1941*)

YOUR LIFE EXPECTANCY

By Louis I. Dublin

It is one of the paradoxes of our paradoxical times that life is so cheap, yet the expectation of life increases decade by decade. Here in the United States, between 1930 and 1940, four more years were added to the length of life, so that today the average American can expect to live almost 64 years. The importance of this fact in our economic and social life is tremendous, especially when our expectancy is compared with the average of under thirty for India, forty-eight in Japan and fifty-five in Italy. It means that Americans are not wasted in infancy or childhood, but achieve a well-rounded and productive life even in moderate old age. Under peacetime conditions in our country, science and the individual in combination can combine to prolong life to an extent that at present is undefinable.

First of all, however, let us clear up a primary cause of confusion in the matter of living longer. There are two concepts involved, the first known as the life span, and the second known variously as the expectation of life or the average length of life. They are not the same thing, even though people use them interchangeably. The life span is concerned with the natural limit of human longevity. In round numbers, one hundred years has always been the limit of the individual life span. People do live longer, needless to say, but those cases are exceptions.

The average length of life is an entirely different concept. In its simplest form, it is the average number of years lived by a group of persons from their birth until the entire group is accounted for by death. The average length of life thus computed is commonly called "the expectation of life at birth." America's expectancy of sixty-four years is topped only by New Zealand and Australia. Norway, Sweden and the Netherlands once equalled the American figure for longevity, but the war has already pushed their figures below ours.

During most of history, progress toward a longer life has been slow, but the trend has not retrogressed. In ancient Rome, the expectation of life at birth was probably under twenty-five years; pestilence, famines, wars and the harsh servi-

---

LOUIS I. DUBLIN *has been statistician for the Metropolitan Life Insurance Company since 1911 and third vice-president since 1931. He has written many books and monographs on population and health problems, which are regarded as standard in their fields. His studies of life expectancy, in which he has specialized for years, are accepted as of the highest scientific authority.* (July, 1942)

tude of the masses led to a heavy mortality among children and young people. Conditions of life during the Middle Ages were presumably no better than in Rome, so it is reasonable to conclude that the average lifetime was equally short. Toward the end of the seventeenth century, according to a life-table computed by the English astronomer, Halley, for the city of Breslau, the average length was thirty-three and a half years. By 1850, in America, the average had increased to a little more than forty years.

Then came the beginning of the modern sanitary era, about one hundred years ago, and the average life expectancy began to rise rapidly. Modern medicine and public health curbed the terrible inroads of cholera, diphtheria, tuberculosis and typhoid fever, and set up systems of protection over water and milk supplies, the quality of food, and other sanitary procedures. As a result, the expectation of life in the United States by 1900 had advanced to about fifty years. The fourteen years added to the expectation of life since that date are the result of an intensive application of our knowledge of disease prevention, and a general and profound improvement in the standard of living. As a result, we are a more populous and a stronger people today.

One of the major results of our battle for a longer life is the fact that we are becoming an older people, which raises a whole new set of social problems. In the past forty years, the number in our population at ages sixty-five and over increased from three million to almost nine million. If this process continues, the population at these ages will reach twenty-two million about 1980. Along with this increase in number, and largely because of the decline in the birthrate, with a consequent diminution in the number of children among us, the proportion of persons 65 and over in our total population is mounting sharply. Figures show that in 1900 the proportion in that age group was about 4 per cent of the total; today, it is nearly 7 per cent, and by 1980, if the trend continues as expected, it will reach 14 per cent.

II

It is only natural that we should continue to seek for added years of life. What, then, can each of us do in his own behalf? Primarily, there are a few simple rules of personal hygiene which people learn in grade school and later neglect shamefully in adult life. These rules are obvious but important: Get plenty of fresh air and sunlight. Take daily exercise in moderation. Take a shower or bath frequently to keep the pores open and active. Be sure that you are getting the correct balance of foods. Wear comfortable, warm clothing in cold weather. Avoid worry, anger, hatred and envy as much as is humanly possible. These are the basic rules. Add to them an annual medical checkup, an annual dental examination, and a constant alertness to safety precautions in the home, on the job and in the street.

These are things the normal individual can do for himself. Now let us consider what extensions in our average length of life we may expect from the advancing front of science. I have, from time to time, attempted to answer the question by constructing so-called "hypothetical" life tables. In 1922, for example, at a time when the average length of life in our country was a little under fifty-eight years, I prepared a table which indicated that if official and voluntary medical and health agencies joined with the people themselves in an intensive effort to utilize the knowledge available, the average length of life for the entire nation could be raised to about sixty-five years.

Since 1922, this table has had to be revised twice because health conditions improved faster than was believed possible. I prepared a new table in 1933 and it gave an average length of life of just under seventy years. Today, scarcely a decade later, I have had to revise it again to reflect the constantly improving standards in mortality. The new life table may be again on the conservative side, but in any event it projects the average length of life to seventy-one years. The gain it shows is based entirely on reasonable assumptions of improvement in mortality.

Does this really set the limit for the future? Decidedly not. No claims of any kind were made in any of these estimates which would reflect the gains possible when the mysteries of certain important diseases are solved, as they certainly will be. At least one year would be added to the average length of life if we could solve the cancer problem and another year if we could achieve control of heart and circulatory impairments in middle life. Significant results would also follow the virtual elimination of tuberculosis and pneumonia as causes of death among people before they reach their prime. These diseases cut off many lives prematurely, whereas cancer and heart disease, although they cause more deaths, are concentrated largely in old age, when there are few years of life left to salvage. On the whole, therefore, it is possible to look optimistically toward further additions to the average lifetime, even beyond the present hypothetical limits.

But the hope for a longer life is not based alone on successful attacks against individual disease problems. There are wide possibilities in new fields which only now have been opened. This new work is so fundamental that in the long run it may create a level of human vitality so high that the average length of life will be increased well beyond the figure now attainable. Even the life span itself may be raised a little.

The new fields lie in the rapidly growing knowledge of nutrition and of gerontology — the study of the aging process. These two studies have much in common. Research indicates that a long period of poor diet hastens the degenerative changes associated with aging. What we eat certainly leaves its mark on us during our lifetimes, and indeed, may have an important influence on the length of our lives.

Nutrition laboratories have disclosed our nation's cruel dietary deficiencies, and the paradox of widespread malnutrition in the midst of huge food surpluses. Staple foods have been deprived, through ignorance, of the basic elements necessary for adequate nutrition, while we have pampered our taste with over-refined and rich foods. Moreover, in sizable areas of America, principally in the South, foods are lacking in certain essentials because the soil lacks basic chemical factors. Nor are bad diets necessarily due to poverty. The slim debutante, who stints herself on milk but overindulges in sweets, may suffer as serious nutritional deficiencies as the impoverished slum child.

From the standpoint of health and longevity, too much food can be as dangerous as too little. Fat people, for instance, succumb far more often than slim ones to the early onset of high blood pressure and its associated ailments of the the heart, kidneys and blood vessels — all common causes of disability and death after forty-five. Overweight people are the chief victims of diabetes; they suffer more frequently from diseases like gallstones; and they are generally poorer surgical risks than persons of average weight or less.

If the findings among our men called for Selective Service are any index of the nation's health condition, then we are generally below the standards which the vast physical and medical resources of this country can provide us. Our young men, called up by the first draft, should have been at the peak of their physical fitness, but 28 per cent of those examined were classified as unfit for any service at all and another 15 per cent were accepted only for limited service. Although it is impossible to determine how far poor nutrition contributed to this state of affairs, it is significant that defective teeth led the causes for rejection. It is also known that serious inadequacies in diet may lead to functional eye disturbances, nervous and mental conditions, and to diseases of the respiratory system, all of which were prominent among the causes for rejection.

While medical science has labored successfully to prolong life at the far end of the age scale, nutrition experts have been dealing with the problem of infant mortality in the first few days and weeks of life. Today, as the result of experimentation with the diets of pregnant women, it is entirely possible that proper prenatal feeding will save the lives of many thousands of infants and launch them into a healthier childhood. Infant feeding, too, is now practically an exact science. This knowledge, along with better food and control of infections, is largely responsible for the sharp decline in infant mortality to the point where it is now only a small fraction of what it was two or three decades ago. Modern pediatricians find it easy to bring a child suffering from rickets and other nutritional deficiencies up to the physical and intellectual level of normal children. In the future, such deficiencies will be very largely prevented. And today, as the child grows up, his health is watched in the baby clinic, the pre-school clinic and in the school, to supplement the care he receives at home. All these steps, which fortify the bodies of children, increase resistance to the infections and breakdowns that prepare the way for early heart and kidney impairments in adult life. The effects are already apparent: children under fifteen years of age today have a death rate 60 per cent less than children of the same ages in 1920.

The core of the tremendous contribution which the science of nutrition has made to a longer life is contained in a succinct statement made by Professor Henry Sherman, of Columbia, in which he asserts that "a generous surplus of calcium, above the level of minimal adequacy or absolute need, results in better growth and development of the young, a higher norm of adult health and vitality, and a longer lease of what we may call the prime of life — the period between the attainment of maturity and the onset of old age." This is one example of what the comparatively new science of nutrition is doing to open up new avenues for increasing the vitality of our people and thereby also increasing their average length of life. If we, as a nation, would take seriously these new discoveries of science and apply them intensively in our daily lives, there is even the possibility of an increase in the span of life at some time in the future.

III

Science may have still another approach to the problems of vitality and life extension, although this one is much more conjectural. It has to do with the studies made on malfunction of the endocrine glands. Recent investigations show that such malfunctions appear generally to increase as we grow older and, as a result, vital activities begin to suffer. Hopes have been raised that our knowledge of endocrine functions might give us a measure of control over the aging processes, but unfortunately, the field has been infested with quackery and pseudo-science so that the public has been considerably misled about the progress in this direction.

Nevertheless, there have been first-rate scientific contributions which relate the hormones to health and vigor. Step by step, therapeutic measures of an effective character are crystallizing out of the welter of research. It has long been clear that glandular deficiencies may be treated by administering the appropriate hormone, sometimes with striking results, but attention is now directed to an increasing degree on the prevention of these deficiencies.

Hormone therapy is strikingly demonstrated in the modern treatment of diabetes, a disease which usually results from a deficiency of insulin, a hormone of the pancreas. There are about six hundred thousand diabetics in this country. These diabetics, thanks largely to insulin, not only live longer but live more abundantly than pre-insulin diabetics. The gain is most impressive among diabetic children. A generation ago, most of them died within a year of the disease's onset. Today, according to the records of a leading clinic, the diabetic child of ten may expect to live another forty years. The expectation of life of diabetics aged fifty rose from eight years, in the pre-insulin period, to fourteen and a half years, all within the last decade.

In spite of this and other successes, the hormone field is so vast and intricate that our knowledge of most of it is still relatively elementary. Some discoveries have been so extraordinary as to suggest that in the future, when more knowledge of the physiological action of the hormones and of the means to manufacture or synthesize them is obtained, powerful aids will be at our command to maintain healthy and vigorous bodies. But this is still prophecy; we cannot yet, nor in the immediate future, count on these aids.

One of the problems waiting exploration is the extent of the already known chemical relationship between vitamins and hormones. Many of the glands which produce the hormones are also depositories for the vitamins. A vitamin deficiency may, therefore, play some part in producing a hormone disorder. Conversely, adequate vitamin intake promotes proper hormonal balance.

To sum up, modern science offers the promise of, first, a greater vitality and longer life through correct nutrition. Secondly, by correcting disturbances in the chemistry of our bodies which arise as we grow older, we may be able to carry the activities of our prime years well into old age. Our whole concept of the prime of life may be changed. Prevention of defects by vitamins is an accomplished fact, but it is only foreshadowed as yet in the hormonal field.

Such scientific study virtually ignores the claim of some biologists that heredity has a major part in determining the length of life. As a result of several investigations based on extensive insurance records, I can say that the influence of inheritance has clearly been of a minor order. One investigation disclosed that the average length of life for a group whose parents had both lived to be seventy-five years old was about two and one-third years greater than for a group in which both parents died before they were sixty. Heredity might have effected the present changes in longevity through complicated social mechanisms operating over many generations, but the same result has been achieved through the control of environment. For example, our gain in average length of life during the last decade — four years — is more than could be achieved in a century by a virtually impossible system of eugenic marriages.

Finally, the natural question arises: What can be done to realize the promises implied in current research? Clearly, it is the task of bringing the knowledge of these new facts to the people through intelligent and intensive use of every appropriate agency, public and private. Our health officers should expand their programs to include the promotion of correct and adequate nutrition. We must also encourage, by every means, the continued investigation of the medical and health problems which are still unsolved, such as cancer and the processes that lead to degeneration of the heart and blood vessels. As individuals interested in life prolongation, obviously we should submit ourselves to competent medical examination for routine checkup. And to further the usefulness of our medical examinations, they should include a critical review of our diets.

The stakes are truly immeasurable. We all want to enjoy as long a period of activity as possible, — and for this, science is now providing the means more generously than ever. We must use them. An average length of life for our citizens of well over seventy years, or even as much as seventy-five years, is not a mirage; it can be a fact in little more than a generation. Further developments in the field of vitamins, or of hormones, or even in some as yet unforeseen direction, would open up new possibilities — not only of adding to the average length of life, but even of stretching the present limit of the life span. Then an altogether new vista would be opened.

FOOLISH ABOUT WINDOWS

By Carl Sandburg

I was foolish about windows.
The house was an old one and the windows were small.
I asked a carpenter to come and open the walls and put in bigger windows.
"The bigger the window the more it costs," he said.
"The bigger the cheaper," I said.
So he tore off siding and plaster and laths
And put in a big window and bigger windows.
I was hungry for windows.

One neighbor said, "If you keep on you'll be able to see everything there is."
I answered, "That'll be all right, that'll be classy enough for me."
Another neighbor said, "Pretty soon your house will be all windows."
And I said, "Who would the joke be on then?"
And still another. "Those who live in glass houses gather no moss."
And I said, "Birds of a feather should not throw stones and a soft answer turneth away rats."

(*October, 1928*)